REPLOTTING MARRIAGE IN NINETEENTH-CENTURY BRITISH LITERATURE

Replotting Marriage in Nineteenth-Century British Literature

EDITED BY

Jill Galvan

AND

Elsie Michie

THE OHIO STATE UNIVERSITY PRESS | COLUMBUS

Library of Congress Cataloging-in-Publication Data
Names: Galvan, Jill Nicole, 1971– editor. | Michie, Elsie B. (Elsie Browning), 1948– editor.
Title: Replotting marriage in nineteenth-century British literature / edited by Jill Galvan and Elsie Michie.
Description: Columbus : The Ohio State University Press, [2018] | Includes bibliographical references and index.
Identifiers: LCCN 2018000399 | ISBN 9780814213681 (cloth) | ISBN 0814213685 (cloth) ISBN 9780814254745
Subjects: LCSH: Marriage in literature. | English fiction—19th century—History and criticism. | English literature—19th century—History and criticism.
Classification: LCC PR878.M36 R47 2018 | DDC 823/.8093543—dc23
LC record available at https://lccn.loc.gov/2018000399

Cover design by Lisa Force
Text design by Juliet Williams
Type set in Adobe Minion Pro

CONTENTS

INTRODUCTION

THE *MARRIAGE PLOT*: the phrase has come to ground our sense of the long nineteenth century. We teach and write about this period as one of revolutionary democratic energy, wide-scale industrial change, imperial expansion and rebellion, religious self-questioning and alternative spiritual movements, and the institutionalization and dispersion of scientific thought. But if, despite all this dynamism, anything seems to bear out the cliché that the nineteenth century was a morally and socially conservative time, it is the notion that its fiction possessed an internal drive towards blithe marital endings—that the course of true love may not always run smooth but nonetheless arrives at the goal, often with the arrival ratified by a child (or the promise of one). This theory of the hegemonic marriage plot is, moreover, inseparable from our understanding of contemporary gender. As Nancy Armstrong's *Desire and Domestic Fiction* (1987) has influentially argued, the late eighteenth- and nineteenth-century domestic novel, along with the conduct book, produced a type of woman whose social power was invisible but immense. Fiction disciplined the middle-class reader through a psychology of desire; the plot of love and its conjugal imperative invented modern genteel womanhood and its masculine complement. By the end of the century, this plot had become so calcified that it would be burlesqued as the very heart of staid Victorianness in Oscar Wilde's *The Importance of Being Earnest* (1895).

Literary scholars' most concerted investigation of the marriage plot has delved further into the cultural logic of separate spheres, uncovering patterns of resistance or uncomfortable accommodation even in fictions that seem to celebrate wedlock, or questioning the social and literary dominance of the separate-spheres paradigm itself. Critics have likewise recognized the rise of protofeminism in the late 1800s as a further pressure on cultural ideals of domesticity. Authors from Mona Caird and Sarah Grand to Grant Allen and Thomas Hardy explored the personal, sexual, and vocational constraints on women's lives when marriage is considered the cynosure of them.

While this work has no doubt deepened our understanding of nineteenth-century literature, it has also, we believe, reached a certain point of stasis. This collection attempts to scrutinize nineteenth-century marriage in fresh ways, treating it neither as a cultural bedrock in a time of vast change nor as thought-provoking only or primarily in terms of gender formations. Our aim is to widen our sense of how the period's fictions contemplated and aestheticized conjugal coupling and thus to diversify the repertoire of critical questions we bring to its representation. Essentially we ask: What has taking marriage as a literary and cultural given concealed from our view? What happens when we unseat many of our basic ideas about the domestic heart of the narratives we study? What ideas and formations become newly visible? And how can new perspectives illuminate more familiar discussions of gendered and sexual institutions, roles, and relationships? Additionally, insofar as the marital ideal still seems central to our assessment of the Victorian period—marking it off from other periods—the essays that follow are also meant to prompt a rethinking of this literary historical period and, in turn, of long-nineteenth-century studies as such.

The perspectives in this collection deepen the vein of inquiry established by several early twenty-first-century studies on literary courtship, intimacy, wedlock, and family—studies that have made exciting moves to destabilize our views of love and marriage, allowing new insights into their social, emotional, and erotic foundations. Building on the groundbreaking work of Eve Kosofsky Sedgwick on male homoeroticism in *Between Men* (1985), Sharon Marcus's *Between Women* (2007) argues for the importance of female homoeroticism vis-à-vis the marriage plot, suggesting the limitations of looking at what we would now term the heterosexual union in isolation, apart from the female bonds that contextualize and determine it. Our expectations of Victorian heterosexuality are unseated as well in the analyses of masculinity in Holly Furneaux's *Queer Dickens* (2013), which rethinks family and domesticity in examining male–male relations in a diversity of structures throughout Charles Dickens's fiction. Mary Jean Corbett's *Family Likeness* (2008) focuses on incest, viewing it not only in terms of developing concepts of heredity but also as a surprising guarantor of moral and class-appropriate endogamy: while earlier nineteenth-century law sanctioned cousin marriage (as seen in novels like Jane Austen's and Charlotte Brontë's), marriage to a dead wife's sister was prohibited, associated as it was with the uncivilized habits of the cohabiting poor. While we think of marriage as a product of desire, other factors, including social and economic ties, of course play an important role in its plotting—or, to put this another way, desire is more than a simple matter of affect or erotic orientation. It is often difficult to separate characters' feelings for one another from financial questions, as Elsie Michie argues in *The Vulgar Question of Money* (2011), which examines the heiress as a figure representing the Victorians' nervous sense of the crassness of capitalist accumulation. Talia Schaffer's *Romance's Rival* (2016), in its analysis of the marital motives of fictional women, considers priorities other than desire altogether—ones of vocational fulfillment, for example—and shows that the "familiar lover," known through kinship or communal relations, might seem as enticing a possibility as the "romantic lover."

To re-examine the marriage plot means addressing not only domesticity or the choices leading characters to marriage but also their experience of the couple within marriage, and in this area as well scholars have been gradually broadening our view. Joseph Allen Boone's *Tradition Counter Tradition* (1987) was an early work unsettling the notion that nineteenth-century fiction offers wedlock as a blissful state. As Barbara Leckie argues in *Culture and Adultery* (1999), extramarital affairs filled nineteenth-century divorce-case journalism and were approached cautiously in the English novel, helping to shape its omissions and perspectival experiments. Marlene Tromp's *The Private Rod* (2000) and Lisa Surridge's *Bleak Houses* (2005) have productively explored the classed and generic parameters of the depiction of spousal abuse. Here again, the fictionalization of unhappy marriage is inseparable from contemporary law and the newspaper; sensational journalistic or other tales, often with a focus on violence against the working-class woman, paved the way for middle-class realist representations. More recently, Kelly Hager's *Dickens and the Rise of Divorce* (2010) reveals "failed-marriage plots" that, as she observes, seem all the more telling for being written by an author we tend to regard as the Victorian "paterfamilias."[1] Hager emphasizes that miserable marriages are everywhere in Dickens's oeuvre and, in many cases, such as *Dombey and Son* (1846–48) and *Hard Times* (1854), are given considerable narrative space; these representations invite us to read his depictions of hearth and family in

1. Hager, *Dickens and the Rise of Divorce*, 23.

more critical ways, linking them to contemporary legal and other struggles for ways to escape disastrous matrimony. Maia McAleavey's *The Bigamy Plot* (2015) likewise forces us to recognize another pervasive Victorian alternative to the happy marriage tale, as well as varied trajectories and strange doublings in wedlock's plotting.

Offering sustained analysis through a variety of approaches, *Replotting Marriage in Nineteenth-Century British Literature* consolidates the gains of these past scholarly works, pointing to a new, potentially wide-ranging field of inquiry, nineteenth-century marriage studies. We seek to spark a fruitful conversation, largely by decentering longstanding narrative expectations, ones we think have thus far been too easily comprised in the term *marriage plot* itself. Consider how common yet how overgeneral and potentially obscuring this formulation is, in both its parts. Even the basic term *marriage,* while seemingly self-evident, encompasses any number of emotional, sexual, and familial situations, adding up to much more than simply the union of one man with one woman. The discrete emphasis on marriage, moreover, risks isolating it, as if it were not a social institution imbricated with any number of others. Marriage is a discursive condition that cannot be lived or imagined apart from other conditions. Accordingly, the essays here work to reintegrate tales of wedlock into diverse contexts, including contemporary conversations around crime, anthropology, education, evolutionary biology, national identity, and health and disability. These perspectives throw into relief that the communal and moral meaning of marriage is not restricted to issues of sexual virtue, or of even class consolidation. Rather, marriage distills a culture's multitudinous concepts of itself, and the marital tale, the fictionalization of those concepts at a personal and domestic level, has the potential to reorient or think through them in fascinating ways.

Additionally, to focus exclusively on the marriage *plot* oversimplifies the narrative and formal intricacies we know to be operable in nineteenth-century fiction. This use of *plot* here carries certain unstated presumptions, namely of unity and teleology: as if tales of marriage always progress in the same way, winding toward the same ending. But this usage clearly defies the multiplottedness and, as Richard Menke and others have shown, the networked, contiguous, or overlapping patterns of characters and their actions in much nineteenth-century fiction.[2] In other words, to single out any one narrative strain, separating it from the others, erases the structural complications that lend this period's literature its scope and complexity. Further, not only does the implication of a teleology—a typologically happy conclusion—elide the

2. Menke, *Telegraphic Realism.*

Victorian period's vast array of plots (whether major or sub) of unhappy marriage; it also privileges conclusion over the path towards it, dismissing that whole path as thematically and discursively subordinate. In a sense, our collection doubles down on Caroline Levine and Mario Ortiz-Robles's urging that the "narrative middle" has been sorely disregarded, specifically applying that exhortation to stories of conjugal union. Indeed, we would claim that stories of marriage constitute a particularly intransigent site of underinvestigated middle: they are most liable, in our current critical practice, to activate our tendencies to prioritize narrative culmination.[3] All this is to say that taking apart the marriage plot, as more than marriage and more than single plot, can better attune us to the meaningful narrative throughways, crossings, and disturbances a given text can hold.

I. THE FORMING AND TRANSFORMING OF THE MARRIAGE PLOT

Replotting Marriage is committed to showcasing the amazing theoretical pluralism of current approaches to the marriage plot. Its first section offers an overview of the collection's critical interventions through three essays that map out the volume's temporal and formal territories in broad strokes. Bookending the century, these first essays analyze the formation of the marriage plot in the early 1800s and its attenuation in the 1880s and 1890s. All three read novelistic structure in tandem with other models of development and change, scientific or otherwise. They establish the marriage plot as about much more than marriage and initiate some of the themes that run through the volume: the transnational or global presence of the marriage plot; the tension between the marriage plot and other narratives, specifically the Bildungsroman; the links between marriage and violence; and limitations on human agency in the marriage plot.

Ian Duncan's "The Bildungsroman, the Romantic Nation, and the Marriage Plot" provides a European frame for the rise of the marriage plot in the British novel by grounding its discussion in the philosophies of Hegel, Herder, and Schlegel and analyzing the work of J. W. Goethe and Madame de Staël.

3. Tellingly, Levine and Robles-Ortiz may themselves underestimate the potentially intricate middleness of narratives of marriage, in reaffirming Franco Moretti's suggestion that it is the "marriageable woman who stands in for the normalizing forces of socialization," the telos of the English Bildungsroman (*Narrative Middles*, 8–9). In her own essay in this volume, "Everyday Life in Anne Brontë," Amanda Claybaugh suggests that Anne Brontë's *The Tenant of Wildfell Hall* (1848) draws on stock plots of adultery and temperance reform to represent the otherwise difficultly narrated everydayness of marriage (109–27).

Suggesting that the Bildungsroman arises out of and reflects the philosophical anthropology of the late Enlightenment, Duncan argues that the hero's marriage replaces rather than completes his emergence into full humanity at the end of *Wilhelm Meister's Apprenticeship (Wilhelm Meisters Lehrjahre,* 1795–96). A synthesis of the marriage plot with the plot of education or development takes place in the Irish national tales of the early 1800s, in which the nation provides the medium of union. In British novels of that period, those of Scott and Austen, the marriage plot crystallizes as key to the novel as a genre. But Duncan also outlines the limitations of the marriage plot through an analysis of *Corinne, or Italy* (1807), which "mounts a feminist critique of the nation-state as historical horizon of totality for *Bildung*" (32). Demonstrating that woman is the sacrificial victim, who must be excluded from full participation in the category of the human for the narrative of personal development to be fulfilled, Staël also shows that when marriage closes the story, the novel form becomes less heterogeneous, less a collection of diverse artistic practices and more a clearly defined genre, whose narrative moves toward a specific end.

Elisha Cohn's "Darwin's Marriage Plots: Unplotting Courtship in Late Victorian Fiction" demonstrates that by the end of the century authors like Olive Schreiner and Mona Caird explicitly critiqued the Bildungsroman, the marriage plot, and the belief that the two could support one another. For Cohn the publication of Charles Darwin's *The Origin of Species* (1859) and *The Descent of Man* (1871) changed the nature of both choice and event in the marriage plot. The rise of evolution set individual decisions within the context of the *long durée* of biological time that rendered them relatively insignificant. Both *The Story of an African Farm* (1883) and *The Daughters of Danaus* (1894) include a New Woman plot in which a heroine expounds on the importance of choices other than marriage, positing a cultural evolution that would expand the options available to women. But while the heroines of both novels endorse the power of choice, the novels' plots elide choice, thereby resonating with "the evolutionary narrative of deep time" (37). Rather than reading fiction as affirming or opposing evolution, Cohn posits that experimentation with variations of the marriage plot enabled late nineteenth-century novelists to place themselves in conversation with scientists about models of time and development.

For Kathy Psomiades the marriage plot is as much a form of narrative theory as a novelistic structure. In "Mythic Marriage: Haggard, Frazer, Hardy, and the Anthropology of Myth" she argues that nineteenth-century novelists engage in the same work as 1860s anthropologists; both read the history of civilization as an evolution of political and sexual relations. At the end of the century, however, these theoretical possibilities were complicated by a new version of the marriage plot that derived from the anthropology of myth. That version told the story of a goddess whose partially mortal lover is killed in a cycle of sexuality, violence, and eternal return. In H. Rider Haggard's *She* (1886–87), James Frazer's *The Golden Bough* (1890), and Thomas Hardy's *Tess of the d'Urbervilles* (1891), that new mythic plot becomes "the marriage plot's other and double." In the case of Hardy's novel in particular, the two plots occupy the same novelistic space; Tess functions simultaneously as victim in the marriage plot and goddess in the mythic plot. This doubleness enables the novel to explore "the ways in which different genres make different narratives out of the same material" (75).

II. MARITAL AND OTHER LOYALTIES: CULTURAL CONTEXTS FOR THE MARRIAGE PLOT

The four essays in the middle section of *Replotting Marriage* read the marriage plot in the context of specific social institutions—schools, politics, the legal system, and the British empire—and reflect on competing possibilities for devotion and life commitment, particularly for women. Analyzing literary and cultural texts from the 1840s through the 1890s (and even, in Lauren Goodlad's case, down to 2012), these essays trace the evolution of marriage from old spousal models of "faithfulness and domination" to later ones of "companionability and discernment" (152). They point to an uneven development in which women are granted some freedoms in marriage but also pursue others outside of it, and they suggest that conservative models of marriage and gender relations are inextricable even from putatively modern or progressive contexts. The first two essays expand on the complex relationship between women's self-development and the marriage plot initially set forth by Duncan. The second two explore the connections between marriage and stories of murder and bigamy; tracking the fractures between marital loyalty and disloyalty, these essays emphasize the sensational, even violent, conflicts that arise as cultures seek to move away from traditional models of marital relations.

Kelly Hager's "Playing the *Princess*: Enacting and Resisting Marriage in the Victorian School Story" traces Alfred, Lord Tennyson's *The Princess* (1847) as a narrative about school and marriage that intertextually influences L. T. Meade's late Victorian school story, *A Sweet Girl Graduate* (1891). Both texts lay out the familiar dichotomy for women between marriage and education/career, yet they also invite us to see it as more than simple dichotomy. Employing Sharon Marcus's critical strategy of "just reading," Hager gives an account in which the courtship plot does not necessarily devalue the "interregnum of college": education and marriage are not mutually exclusive but rather represent a range of life options for women. In turn, Hager complicates critical labels of Tennyson's and Meade's texts as either in line with or against feminism, encouraging instead an attention to their agile function in Victorian debates around the "marriage question."

Lauren Goodlad's "The *Longue Durée* of the Political *Bildungsromane*: Putting George Eliot into Dialogue with Danish Television," akin to Duncan's essay, emphasizes the vexed interrelation of the Bildungsroman and the marriage plot, reaching from Victorian texts to our own fictions today. Goodlad analyzes narratives that find "male characters advancing radical politics while female counterparts wage countervailing reactions through marriage and domesticity," beginning with George Eliot's *Felix Holt* (1866), *Middlemarch* (1872), and *Daniel Deronda* (1876) and ending with two modern Danish television series: *Forbrydelsen* (2007–12), a police procedural, and *Borgen* (2010–12), a drama about a woman prime minister's challenges in both politics and marriage. Nineteenth-century versions of this double plot "turn successful courtship from a symbolic redress for class unrest into a character test for aspiring male leaders" (102) but leave women without career options in the public sphere. The modern version of the Bildungsroman and the marriage plot shows the woman to be successful in politics but unable to hold the marriage together. Despite their overtly feminist emphasis, the Danish shows are as "much about the 'disability of being women' as any Eliot novel" (122).

In "'Til Death Do Us Part: Marriage, Murder, and Confession," Tromp extends the work she did on marital abuse in *The Private Rod* by detailing the trials of four nineteenth-century women who killed their husbands. Moving outside fiction, this essay explores versions of the marriage plot that appeared in legal and popular responses to women's violence. Tromp presents two sets of paired cases: those of two poisoners, Sarah Westwood (1843) and Catherine Foster (1846), and of two women who killed their husbands with an axe and a knife, Elizabeth Martha Brown (1856) and Agnes Osbaldeston (1866). Grounding her arguments in Foucault's theories of confession, Tromp shows that in each case the woman who either refused to confess or provided a false confession received a harsher sentence and a more hostile public response than the woman who confessed. When women follow the marriage plot by painting themselves as good, devoted wives who violated conjugal loyalty only after being pushed to the breaking point, they receive more sympathy and lighter sentences. As Tromp concludes, these events took place within "a cultural milieu desperately trying to normalize gender roles in marriage and marriage itself" (144).

In "Marriage, Modernity, and the Transimperial," Sukanya Banerjee suggests that plots of bigamy highlight issues of conjugal loyalty, which she argues became a topic central to the institution's modernization in the nineteenth century. Juxtaposing a sensation novel by an English novelist, Mary Elizabeth Braddon's *Aurora Floyd* (1863), with one by an Indian novelist, Bankim Chandra Chatterjee's *Rajmohan's Wife* (1863), Banerjee proposes that sensation fiction's scandalously multiplied marriages staged a tension between, on one hand, older forms of polygamy, obedience, and dutiful devotion and, on the other hand, modern notions of monogamous, companionate wedlock. As this essay further suggests, analyzing *Aurora Floyd* and *Rajmohan's Wife* alongside one another provides a useful opportunity for reassessing our critical approach to the "orient" in literary studies generally. Whereas we often focus on the Indian as simply the Victorians' figure for the "civilizational 'other' marked by lag or stasis," adopting, instead, a transimperial view of English and Indian "sensation-marriage plots" (148)—a view attuned less to imperial hierarchy than to contemporaneous phenomena in different locales—can help us to recognize these plots' equally complex attitudes toward questions of cultural change.

III. BEYOND COUPLING: QUEER, COMMUNAL, TERTIARY

The essays in the last section of *Replotting Marriage* all provide readings of Charles Dickens; two focus specifically on *Our Mutual Friend* (1864–65). That novel functions as a benchmark for tracing the evolution of modern critical readings of the marriage plot that was initiated by Eve Sedgwick's transformational reading of *Our Mutual Friend* in her 1985 *Between Men.* The essays in the last section of *Replotting Marriage* build on and complicate the approaches of queer theorists like Sedgwick (as well as Marcus). The critics featured here do not so much seek to replace a familiar reading of the marriage plot with a new one as to recognize that that familiar narrative structure serves many different purposes—a multiplicity highlighted by our decision to include in this collection more than one reading of the same novel.

In "'Even Supposing—': Reading/Writing Outside the Marriage Plot in Dickens Fan Fiction," Holly Furneaux show how fan fiction resists the narrative closure inscribed in the marriage plot. Fan fiction typically looks at triads that end in marriage and posits narratives in which the same-sex characters bond. Through fan fiction, readers imagine alternative couplings and alternative endings that echo the logic of critics like Marcus, who has argued for the importance of relations between women, and of Furneaux, who, in *Queer*

Dickens, argued for the importance of relations between men. But the stories proposed by fan fiction go beyond the homo-/heterosexual binary, as readers posit a plurality of sexual relations that queer the form of narrative itself. For Furneaux here, these popular but also implicitly critical interventions provide what Sedgwick in her own later work famously called "reparative readings";[4] they repair the exclusions of the marriage plot by treating Dickens's novels as open-ended texts that invite readers to reconfigure familiar stories about marriage.

In "Disabling Marriage: Communities of Care in *Our Mutual Friend,*" Talia Schaffer uses disability theory to uncover a new strain of the marriage plot, one that she identifies in her book *Romance's Rival* as "familiar marriage." Familiar marriages are not centered on couples or erotic bonds; instead, they follow the patterns that Eva Kittay has described in her work on the ethics of care, in which a community forms around a disabled individual. Focusing on Jenny Wren in *Our Mutual Friend,* Schaffer, like Furneaux, theorizes beyond the couple. Starting with the triad of Jenny, Lizzie Hexam, and Eugene, she moves outward to show the role that groups of characters play in bringing about the resolution of the novel. By mounting a sustained critique of traditional romantic and erotic versions of marriage plot, Schaffer offers a reading of the nineteenth-century novel that challenges the paradigm Ian Watt established in *The Rise of the Novel.* In insisting that Victorian novels trace and value the emergence of communities of care as much as the satisfaction of personal desire, Schaffer demonstrates that the individual is not necessarily central to the ideological work the novel performs.

In "Extra Man: Dining Out Beyond the Marriage Plot in *Our Mutual Friend,*" Helena Michie uncovers the insufficiencies of the marriage plot by focusing not on dyads or triads but on the singular. Functioning as an extra man, who must be invited to complete the numbers at dinner parties, the novel's bachelor Twemlow suggests that narratives about couples or groups of various kinds depend on excluding the unpaired individual. This exclusion is underscored by Twemlow's relegation to the category of an object. He becomes, in Michie's words, "lignified" and identified with the dining room table, a cultural signifier of community and coupledom. Michie's essay returns to the question Duncan raises initially through his reading of Staël of what the marriage plot must exclude. For both Duncan and Michie, and for the authors of *Replotting Marriage* as a whole, the key question is how and whether the marriage plot can accommodate the full range of what it means to

4. Sedgwick, *Touching Feeling*; see chapter 4.

live. Exploring the limits and capacities of this story type uncovers "the novel's complicated relationship to marriage, humanity, and community" (216).

The overall movement of *Replotting Marriage* is toward reconsidering not just marriage but also the contours of narrative. Challenging the assumption that the marriage plot is primarily about linear development, individual choice, or hermetic coupling, the essays in this volume view wedlock as, rather, intricately structured and restructured by larger discursive frameworks and social institutions. Examining factors of cultural and species development, of community and empire, and of history and deep time allows us to see the marriage plot anew. It allows us to begin to ask broader questions about the ways in which wedlock both reveals and critiques the shape of fiction. As a whole, *Replotting Marriage* reads a familiar narrative as enacting a sophisticated form of thought, inviting critics to meditate from varied perspectives on a well-known tale of human experience.

PART I

THE FORMING AND TRANSFORMING OF THE MARRIAGE PLOT

CHAPTER 1

The Bildungsroman, the Romantic Nation, and the Marriage Plot

IAN DUNCAN

I

IN HIS *Lectures on Fine Art*, G. W. F. Hegel issued an influential critique of the novel as a degenerate case of "the romantic form of art." The chivalric quest for an ideal, which constituted the old (medieval) romance, has shrunk to the banal, bourgeois plot of an "apprenticeship," or "education of the individual into the realities of the present":

> Young people especially are these modern knights who must force their way through the course of the world which realizes itself instead of their ideals, and they regard it as a misfortune that there is any family, civil society, state, laws, professional business, etc., because these substantive relations of life with their barriers cruelly oppose the ideals and the infinite rights of the heart. . . . In the modern world these fights are nothing more than "apprenticeship," the education of the individual into the realities of the present, and thereby they acquire their true significance. The end of such apprenticeship consists in this, that the subject sows his wild oats, builds himself with his wishes and opinions into harmony with subsisting relationships and their rationality, enters the concatenation of the world, and acquires for himself an appropriate attitude to it . . . at last he gets his girl and some sort of position, marries her, and becomes as good a Philistine as others.[1]

1. Hegel, *Aesthetics*, 2:593.

The unnamed model of this modern romance is J. W. Goethe's *Wilhelm Meister's Apprenticeship* (*Wilhelm Meisters Lehrjahre*, 1795–96), routinely cited in the critical tradition as the prototypical Bildungsroman: the "novel of formation," of a subject's moral and sentimental development or self-cultivation (*Bildung*). Hegel's commitment to the idea of *Bildung*—he was one of its major Romantic theorists, alongside J. G. Herder, Friedrich Schiller, and Wilhelm von Humboldt—adds philosophical force to his identification of the marriage plot, the axis of the modern novel, as *Bildung*'s contradiction. Marriage solemnizes the subject's assimilation into what Hegel calls "the prose of the world," the restricting, fragmenting particularity of social roles and conventions—in short, the novelistic medium of common life.[2] To be at home in this world is to have betrayed one's authentic, poetic potential. *Bildung* or marriage: the two are incommensurate, at least for the hero of the story.

The major "new genres or sub-genres characteristic of realism," born in the "novelistic revolution" of European Romanticism,[3] develop a powerful solution to the problem diagnosed by Hegel, although not necessarily one he would have countenanced: an expansion of the prose of the world to encompass national life. Critical commentary on the Bildungsroman and subsequent declensions of the genre align the psychic formation of the protagonist with the historical formation of the modern nation-state, in what Jed Esty has called a "soul-nation allegory of emergence."[4] The mundane network of social relations and determinations, far from smothering individual *Bildung*, dilates it to the scale of a collective destiny, that of the nation, through which the hero's progress may achieve universal equivalence—the form of totality Hegel had charged the novel with abandoning. National destiny endows the contingent forms of social life with an epic necessity and grandeur.

The analogy between *Bildung* and nation-formation has a tenuous hold in *Wilhelm Meister's Apprenticeship*. It is forged more strongly in another Romantic genre, the Anglo-Irish "National Tale" pioneered by Sydney Owenson in *The Wild Irish Girl* (1806), where the link that joins them is the marriage plot. The English hero's sentimental education unfolds through his courtship of an Irish heiress; their nuptial union models the political union of nations that constitutes the modern British state, supplying its libidinal, affective, and moral content.[5] A few years later, Walter Scott's *Waverley* (1814) invests this national-allegorical marriage plot with scientific histori-

2. Ibid., 1:150.

3. Moretti, *Distant Reading*, 19–21; Jameson, *Antinomies of Realism*, 145.

4. Esty, *Unseasonable Youth*, 39–40.

5. The classic account of the Romantic national tale and the "allegory of union" is Trumpener's (*Bardic Nationalism*, 128–60). On its diffusion into the nineteenth-century British tradition, see Corbett, *Allegories of Union*.

cism and a fully developmental logic. Scott's novel overcomes the antagonism between *Bildung* and marriage by submitting both to the regulative narrative of national history. Positing the nation-state as the secular horizon of totality for *Bildung*, realized in a domestic union symbolizing—with its fixing of roles of sex and gender—the modern regime of civil society, the historical novel fulfills the epic ambition that the Bildungsroman itself, bound to an individual life-story, could not.

This essay considers the structural antagonism between *Bildung* and the marriage plot in a third novel, produced between *Wilhelm Meister's Apprenticeship* and *Waverley* and scarcely less influential than they were for nineteenth-century culture. In her popular and controversial *Corinne, or Italy* (1807), Germaine de Staël transfers the role of protagonist from the sensitive hero to the "girl"—supposedly his prize, in Hegel's summary of the modern novel. This transfer reverses the Bildungsroman's takeover of a role occupied by women in the domestic novels that dominated the fiction industry in the latter half of the eighteenth century. The young man's journey to self-cultivation was preceded by the young lady's entrance into the world—in other words, by the marriage plot. Staël, repossessing a role newly invested with the universal project of *Bildung*, indicts the marriage plot as a betrayal of her heroine's full and harmonious development. It is Hegel's critique, only now applied to a female protagonist.

Goethe sent Staël a presentation copy of *Wilhelm Meister* in 1797, after translating some of her essays for Schiller's *Die Horen*; Staël did not know German, but she may have read the 1802 French translation by the time she and Goethe met during her visit to Weimar in 1803. Intensive study of German literature and culture followed. Staël devotes a chapter to *Wilhelm Meister* in her treatise *Germany* (written 1808–10), citing it as exemplary of a distinctively German kind of "philosophical romance."[6] She criticizes Goethe's plot and protagonist for being too weak to hold the reader's interest, and praises, instead, his realization of a secondary character, the mysterious orphaned Italian girl Mignon. Mignon's premature death, barring her from the destinies of *Bildung* and marriage alike, consummates a pathos that overwhelms everything else in *Wilhelm Meister's Apprenticeship.*

Staël magnifies the figure of Mignon, the Bildungsroman's lyric sacrificial victim, into the heroine of her own philosophical romance, as though to realize a potential that Goethe's novel could not find room for.[7] In *Corinne* the

---

6. Staël, *Germany,* 2:55.

7. On *Corinne* as *roman philosophique,* see Zanone, "L'esthétique du 'tableau philosophique,'" 11. On the heroine as avatar of Mignon, see Cave, *Mignon's Afterlives,* 88, 90, 251–52; Siegel, *Haunted Museum,* 42–43.

enigmatic Italian girl has survived adolescence and grown up to inhabit her art as a fully realized, triumphantly public vocation. Reciting her rhapsodies to adoring crowds on the Roman Capitol, Corinne establishes, for the century to come, "the myth of the famous woman talking, writing, performing, to the applause of the world."[8] This embrace of a public career as bardic performance artist flouts the ideological task assumed by nineteenth-century fiction: in Nancy Armstrong's summary, the creation of "a private domain of culture that was independent of the political world and overseen by a woman," whose quiet command of "taste" proscribed any indulgence in "self-display."[9]

Transvaluing the eighteenth-century stock figure of the Female Quixote,[10] Staël inaugurated the European novel's claim on *Bildung* for a woman protagonist through the medium of art. At the same time, *Corinne* brings into focus the national theme passingly evoked in *Wilhelm Meister* and decisively developed in the Romantic national tales and historical novels. The novel's full title, *Corinne, or Italy*, announces an alignment of protagonist and nation only to scramble it, with the copula "or" implying alterity or incommensurability as well as equivalence.[11] Far from reconciling *Bildung* and marriage, the national theme sharpens the antagonism between them, with fatal consequences for the heroine. Corinne embodies a cosmopolitan and universal ideal of the "aesthetic state," in Schiller's phrase, realized in her rhapsodic art, which turns out to be at odds with the imperative of national political formation—rigorously endogamous, enforced by a gendered separation of spheres—that governs the marriage plot. The novel closes not with Corinne's achievement of her vocation within a national-allegorical union but her exclusion from both, sealed with her death.

Recent feminist criticism, rescuing *Corinne* and its author from twentieth-century condescension, has been alert to its challenge to the emergent genre typified by *Wilhelm Meister* as well as to the conventions of domestic fiction. Corinne's sampling of Mignon's famous lyric "Kennst du das Land" in her Capitoline rhapsody, writes Kari Lokke, invites us to "reread Goethe's novel from the perspective of its sacrificial victim."[12] The present essay explores not only the rereading of *Wilhelm Meister* in *Corinne* but also, through it, Staël's

8. Moers, *Literary Women*, 176.

9. Armstrong, *Desire and Domestic Fiction*, 98–100.

10. See Soare, "The Female Gothic Connoisseur."

11. "From the beginning this riddle seems open to a double solution: one a metonymic performance, Corinne in Italy; the other a metaphoric description, either Corinne or else Italy." Vallois, "Voice as Fossil," 52.

12. Lokke, *Tracing Women's Romanticism*, 4–5. Corinne translates the opening lines of Mignon's lyric, "Do you know the land where orange trees bloom?": "Connaissez-vous cette terre où les orangers fleurissent . . ."

critique of the ideological system of the novel, as it was coalescing into a set of norms for nineteenth-century practice, via a wider engagement with German Romantic theory. As well as Schiller's ideal of aesthetic education, *Corinne* realizes Friedrich Schlegel's conception of a "progressive universal poetry," a dynamic interaction of heterogeneous forms and genres modeling the infinite potential of human becoming. Before discussing *Corinne* in more detail, then, I will consider the status of *Wilhelm Meister* as prototypical Bildungsroman in relation to its contemporary critical and philosophical contexts.

Of those contexts, the one that loomed largest on the intellectual horizon was philosophical anthropology. Corinne's fate models the vexed relation of women to the global category that subsumed local projects of individual *Bildung* and national history, namely the grand universal particular "man." Late-Enlightenment philosophers from Rousseau to Kant and Herder debated the constitution of a *Bildung der Humanität,* a "formation of humanity" or progress of the human species. Hegel, refining that progress into a system, made the gender of its universal subject explicit. In Toril Moi's handy summary: "Men, but not women, can achieve self-consciousness, that is to say, can become fully individualized human beings," due to their competition and collaboration with other men in the public sphere; while women, relegated to family life, "have no understanding of the universal, that which serves the common good," and hence "remain generic creatures."[13] The biopolitical division of labor analyzed by Armstrong receives full-blown justification in *The Phenomenology of Spirit.*

Philosophical anthropology provided a scientific matrix for the ascendancy of the novel as the nineteenth-century genre of "The Human Comedy," human life viewed as a totality. Early commentary identified "the harmonious formation of the purely human" as the Bildungsroman's teleological principle, while Scott himself, in the introductory chapter to *Waverley,* claimed a universal human nature, manifest in the "passions common to men in all stages of society," as the historical novel's philosophical basis.[14] With its heroine's charismatic claim on a universal human nature through her art, undone by the collision of rival plots of *Bildung,* marriage, and national formation, *Corinne* challenges the anthropological program of nineteenth-century realism as it was being assembled. If domestic fiction established "the modern individual [as] first and foremost a woman," in Armstrong's phrase, Corinne's defiance of a regime "in which women are invited to consider themselves as women

13. Moi, "Expressivity and Silence in *Corinne,*" 156.
14. Morgenstern, "On the Nature of the Bildungsroman," 655; Scott, *Waverley,* 5.

or as human beings, but not as both at once," makes her—as Moi contends—"politically . . . the first modern woman in Western literature."[15]

II

The Bildungsroman and the historical novel exhibit a new kind of protagonist as well as a new, developmental conception of novelistic form—redeeming the aesthetic scandal of the novel's formlessness. "With the (modern) novel, literary form becomes a matter no longer of poetical forms but of the form of life," writes Rüdiger Campe: hence, "novels don't have form, they are in quest of it."[16] The youthful heroes of *Wilhelm Meister* and *Waverley* are accordingly *unformed,* susceptible and malleable, drifting with the story rather than driving it. Appropriation of the female role of protagonist, in other words, brings with it an appropriation of feminine character: soft, passive, mutable, and so on.

The new figure of man (this essay will retain period usage) comes into focus in the writings of Herder. Born without instincts, unfettered to a special task (like the bee building its cell), man's "forces of soul are distributed over the world . . . [so that] he has free space to practice in many things, and hence to improve himself constantly":[17]

> [He is] never the *whole human being*; always in development, in progression, in process of perfection. . . . We are always growing out of a childhood, however old we may be, are ever in motion, restless, unsatisfied. The essential feature of our life is never enjoyment but always progression, and we have never been human beings until we—have lived out our lives.[18]

Amplifying this developmental conception, which encompasses both individual and species, Herder draws on the new scientific hypothesis of a self-organizing force or formative drive (*Bildungstrieb*) inherent in organic matter: "Every creature seeks *to acquire form, and forms itself.*"[19] All living beings are joined in a continuous, progressive scale of historical development, culminating in humankind: "The end of our present existence is the formation of

15. Armstrong, *Desire and Domestic Fiction,* 4; Moi, "Expressivity and Silence," 157.
16. Campe, "Form and Life in the Theory of the Novel," 55.
17. Herder, "On the Origins of Language," in *Philosophical Writings,* 79.
18. Ibid., 130–31.
19. Herder, *Outlines of a Philosophy of the History of Man,* 3:5.

humanity [*Bildung der Humanität*], to which all the meaner wants of this Earth are subservient, and which they are all contrived to promote."[20]

Wilhelm Meister's Apprenticeship marks the debut in European fiction of this new anthropological subject. In contrast to the hard-shelled protagonists of earlier picaresque, Wilhelm is distinguished by his "easy adaptability" and "many-sided receptivity,"[21] an "inner dissatisfaction and mobility" that makes him the representative creature of modernity, "[sharing] in the 'formlessness' of the new epoch, in its protean elusiveness."[22] Goethe's novel is correspondingly loose, fluid, miscellaneous, hosting various genres and discourses, from lyric poetry to theatrical treatise and spiritual autobiography, as well as open, self-interrupting, unfinished—the story does not close but breaks off, with Wilhelm preparing to set out on another journey.

Critics promptly harnessed this open form to a thematic emergence of human nature. "The work that appears to us in gentle radiance as the most general and comprehensive tendency of human *Bildung* is Goethe's *Wilhelm Meister*," declared Karl Morgenstern, coining the term *Bildungsroman* in 1819: "no previous novel has to such a high degree and expansiveness attempted to represent and promote the harmonious formation of the purely human."[23] This account of the Bildungsroman's project has remained remarkably stable across two centuries of commentary, filtered through Romantic philosophical programs for the production of a complex human totality: Schiller's letters on aesthetic education, Humboldt's civic pedagogy, Hegel's world-historical evolution of Spirit. *On the Aesthetic Education of Man*, in particular, has shaped the reception of *Wilhelm Meister*, not least because of Schiller's close association with Goethe during the novel's composition.[24] The aesthetic education is meant to reintegrate the "inner unity of human nature," fragmented by the division of labor, under the aegis of Kantian reason. Early on, Schiller identifies "the *State*" as the "objective and, as it were, canonical form" of that "ideal man, the archetype of a human being," which resides within every individual.[25] The passage has informed a robust vein of commentary for which the state or nation constitutes the Bildungsroman's pragmatic horizon. Readings of *Wilhelm Meister* in this vein identify the Tower Society (*Turmgesellschaft*),

20. Ibid., 123.

21. Friedrich Schlegel, "On Goethe's *Meister*," in Bernstein, ed., *Classic and Romantic German Aesthetics*, 271.

22. Moretti, *The Way of the World*, 5.

23. Morgenstern, "On the Nature of the Bildungsroman," 655.

24. Schiller read and criticized portions of the work in progress; the *Aesthetic Education* and the first part of *Wilhelm Meister* were published in 1795. See Swales, *The German Bildungsroman*, 24–26; Kontje, *The German Bildungsroman*, 10–11.

25. Schiller, *Aesthetic Education*, 17–19. Cited parenthetically in the text hereafter.

the crypto-masonic fellowship that claims tutelary authority over Wilhelm's life-story in the last two books, with an emergent or incipient national state formation: furnishing the objective and canonical form of the hero's *Bildung*, retroactively ordering what has appeared up until now a haphazard string of episodes.[26]

Such readings exaggerate the teleological confidence of Goethe's novel as well as Schiller's treatise. As the *Aesthetic Education* proceeds, the state—the political state—gives way to the "aesthetic state," posited at first as a "middle state" (123) or "middle disposition" (141) between the state of nature and the moral state governed by reason. Later, however, the moral state recedes to the condition of a regulative or heuristic principle, while the aesthetic state accommodates an actual, empirical convergence of individual and species being via the humanizing principle of the "play-drive" (*Spieltrieb*): "Man only plays when he is in the fullest sense of the word a human being, and *he is only fully a human being when he plays*" (107). Schiller's closing paragraph distinguishes the aesthetic state from any extant political state:

> As a need, it exists in every finely attuned soul; as a realized fact, we are likely to find it, like the pure Church and the pure Republic, only in some few chosen circles, where conduct is governed . . . by the aesthetic nature we have made our own. (219)

The secret society that adopts Wilhelm towards the end of *Wilhelm Meister* might seem to exemplify such a chosen circle. Nationalism is debunked early in the novel, in Goethe's satiric treatment of the theatrical troupe's attempt to revive the national drama as a medium for "Germanness," in the absence of a German state. The Tower Society itself, a cabal of aristocrats concerned with offshoring their assets to safeguard them against the coming wave of European revolutions, resembles a private corporation more than it does an incipient national state formation.[27]

Nor is the Tower's hold over the plot authoritative. Despite an elaborate surveillance apparatus its guidance remains erratic, challenged, in the last

---

26. See, e.g., Esty, *Unseasonable Youth*, 39–40; Slaughter, *Human Rights, Inc.*, 101; and Jameson, *Antinomies of Realism*: "The plot is thus turned inside out: from a series of chance happenings it is suddenly revealed as a plan and as a deliberately providential design" (208). For Moretti the Tower represents the Hegelian idea of civil society as historical telos: *The Way of the World*, 53–54.

27. "*Wilhelm Meister's Apprenticeship* refuses to find closure in an allegory of the state," writes Boes: "Instead, Goethe's Tower Society reinvents itself as an explicitly cosmopolitan organization." *Formative Fictions*, 7.

chapters, by a chorus of dissenting voices. Wilhelm's bride-to-be Natalie disputes its educational program; its busiest agent, Jarno, disavows it as "a youthful enterprise that most initiates first took very seriously but will probably now just smile at";[28] while the frivolous couple Friedrich and Philine make fun of it. They set up their own tower, complete with a library in which they read for amusement until they get bored, in a gleeful parody of Schiller's humanizing play-drive. The end of the novel finds Wilhelm taking a bride and acknowledging a son, but still unsettled in a vocation. The book closes with his affirmation of a guiding principle of luck and serendipity, reinforcing the reader's understanding of a "contingent and variational logic of play"—unbound by a moral teleology—as the novel's "comprehensive organizing structure."[29]

Hegel's critique of modern fiction established the ironical interpretation of *Wilhelm Meister* as a surrender of romantic aspiration to the toils of everyday life. This capitulation brings into relief a formal dialectic between the poetry of inner idealism and the prose of the world—the "world of finitude and mutability, of entanglement in the relative, of the pressure of necessity," of "external influences, laws, political institutions, civil relationships," the paradigm of which, we saw, is marriage.[30] Hegel's diagnosis of the "apprenticeship" laid the foundation for Georg Lukács's *Theory of the Novel,* which contrasts the "organic" infinity of classical epic, its formal capacity to represent a totality of human life, with the novel's "bad" infinity, a constitutive formlessness that necessitates the artificial imposition of contingent forms, such as the individual life-story. "The novel overcomes its 'bad' infinity by recourse to the biographical form": archetypally in the Bildungsroman, which seeks "the reconciliation of the problematic individual, guided by his lived experience of the ideal, with concrete social reality."[31] Given the impossibility, in modern conditions, of such a reconciliation, Goethe falls back on "creative irony." The last book of *Wilhelm Meister* deploys the "fantastic apparatus" of the Tower while disclosing "its playful, arbitrary and ultimately inessential nature," deflating "the miraculous" into "a mystification without hidden meaning"—a play of mere or empty form.[32]

28. Goethe, *Wilhelm Meister,* 335. Cited parenthetically in the text hereafter.

29. Pfau, "*Bildungsspiele,*" 581, 579. See also Redfield: "Schillerian *Bildung* is negated and recuperated as the irony of luck: as the lucky chance that only fiction can reliably provide." *Phantom Formations,* 80.

30. Hegel, *Aesthetics,* 1:149–50.

31. Lukács, *Theory of the Novel,* 81, 133.

32. Ibid., 142.

III

Lukács's appeal to "creative irony" alludes to the best contemporary critic of *Wilhelm Meister's Apprenticeship*, Friedrich Schlegel,[33] whose powerful alternative to the Hegelian account of the Bildungsroman opens directly onto Staël's engagement with the form in *Corinne*. The leading Romantic theorist of the novel and of irony, Schlegel identified a tension between infinite process and formal containment as the structuring energy of the literary. "A novel is a romantic book": in his "Letter on the Novel" Schlegel exalts the novel (*der Roman*) less as a form than as a force, a metagenre breaking up, mixing, and recombining existing genres.[34] Heterogeneous, fragmentary, open-ended, a "mixture of storytelling, song, and other forms," the novel or romance is equivalent to what Schlegel elsewhere calls a "universal, progressive poetry," the literary work as medium of a recombinatory developmental energy that reconstitutes all genres and discourses in its drive toward an unrealized horizon of universality.[35] "The romantic kind of poetry is still in the state of becoming; that, in fact, is its real essence: that it should forever be becoming and never be perfected":[36] it is a creative act expressive of the new, Romantic conceptions of life and human nature. Schlegel's alignment of the novel, the medium of progressive universal poetry, with infinite emergence or becoming stands the Hegel-Lukács opposition between epic totality and novelistic "bad infinity" on its head.[37] The novel, like humanity, is always in formation, surging toward an unrealized future; it is the genre of infinity, not totality.

In their exegesis of Schlegelian aesthetics, *The Literary Absolute*, Lacoue-Labarthe and Nancy pose a key question: "From the moment that the novel, in the romantic sense, is always *more than the novel*, what happens to the novel itself, in the restricted sense?"[38] They are paraphrasing Schlegel's dialogic *Letter on the Novel*. "The Romantic [i.e., novelistic] is not so much a literary genre as an element of poetry which may be more or less dominant or recessive, but never entirely absent," declares Schlegel's spokesman, who goes on,

---

33. Schlegel hailed Goethe's novel as one of three great tendencies of the age, alongside the French Revolution and Fichte's philosophy, and wrote an appreciation, "On Goethe's *Meister*," in 1798.

34. On Schlegel's "combinatory method," see Duff, *Romanticism and the Uses of Genre*, 165–68.

35. Schlegel, "Letter about the Novel," "*Athenaeum* Fragment No. 118," in Bernstein, ed., *Classic and Romantic German Aesthetics*, 293, 249.

36. Ibid., 249.

37. On *progressive Universalpoesie* and Romantic irony, see Bode's discussion, "Absolut Jena."

38. Philippe Lacoue-Labarthe and Jean-Luc Nancy, *The Literary Absolute*, 98–99.

"I detest the novel as far as it wants to be a separate genre!"—as opposed to an emergent poetic energy, shaping all literary forms and settling in none.[39] Officially, the novel establishes itself as a "separate genre" in Great Britain in the second decade of the nineteenth century, in the works of Scott and Jane Austen, which consolidate the devices of realism, including the marriage plot and the topoi of domestic manners and national history, that will define the novel in English for the next hundred years. Schlegel's "mixture of storytelling, song, and other forms," characterizing the emergence of the novel in Romantic Germany, has increasingly marginal presence in the British tradition. In Germany, conversely, a tradition of the realist novel does not take root until much later in the nineteenth century, after the formation of a national state.

The Scottish historical novel, in contrast to the German Bildungsroman, is the flower of a strong modern state: which it makes its theme, at least to begin with. In *Waverley* the defeat of the 1745 Jacobite Rising completes the political absorption of Scotland into the United Kingdom. The plot of national formation, structured by the progressive sociological history formulated in the Scottish Enlightenment, contains the energy of *Bildung* and gives form to the novel's protagonist, or rather, it stabilizes his internal formlessness. National history gives Edward Waverley's life-story a shape, a settlement, an end.

Scott amplifies the national-allegorical union of Saxon milord and Celtic heroine pioneered by Owenson in *The Wild Irish Girl* and developed by other Anglo-Irish authors.[40] These British Romantic national tales and historical novels take as axiomatic (even as they may problematize it) the figure of the nation as the "objective and canonical form" of a human totality for its subjects.[41] Scott makes programmatic the substitution of marriage for a heroic, public orientation of *Bildung* that occurs, seemingly by accident, in *Wilhelm Meister*, by narrating the historical obsolescence of an epic conception of *Bildung* in modern life. Waverley's identification of "romance" with military adventure and dynastic struggle, at early stages of the story, turns out to be disastrously misconceived, the anachronistic relic of a superseded (absolutist) cultural politics. He learns to accept, instead, the destiny forecast by the novel's Corinne-like antiheroine, Flora Mac-Ivor: "you seek, or ought to seek in the object of your attachment, a heart whose principal delight should be in augmenting your domestic felicity, and returning your affection, even to

---

39. Bernstein, ed., *Classic and Romantic German Aesthetics*, 293.

40. Despite the schematic similarities between their heroines, it seems unlikely Staël could have read *The Wild Irish Girl* in time for it to have influenced *Corinne*, which she began in 1805 and completed in November 1806. I thank Claire Connolly and Joep Leerssen for a discussion of the relation between Staël and Owenson.

41. See Anderson's well-known analysis in *Imagined Communities*.

the height of romance."[42] What might look like a retreat into private life is enlarged to national representativeness in the eventual resolution of the marriage plot. "Domestic felicity" characterizes not just the erotic interiority of married life, and the biopolitical order of the family it must reproduce, but the greater order of civil society which is the hard-won prize of historical progress—the dialectical product of the conflict between ancient and modern regimes, rehearsed, one last time, in the 1745 rising.

IV

"As I scan the great changes in the world and the succession of ages, I never divert my attention from one prime notion: the perfectibility of the human species," wrote Staël, echoing the Marquis de Condorcet, in her introduction to *On Literature, Considered in Its Relation to Social Institutions* (1800).[43] Condorcet had included women in his vision of universal perfectibility, and he advocated their civil enfranchisement. Accordingly, the heroine of *Corinne* affirms the right of "every woman, like every man, to make a way for herself according to her nature and her talents," and to contribute to the general progress of humanity.[44] The Napoleonic Code shut down that universalist vision by reaffirming the legal subordination of women to their husbands and fathers in March 1804, a little over a year before Staël began writing *Corinne.*

Staël's novel constitutes an antithetical midpoint, a negative dialectical fulcrum, between *Wilhelm Meister* and *Waverley.* More polemically than they, *Corinne* acknowledges the claim of the nation-state and its ideological apparatus (history, domesticity, civil society) over human *Bildung,* and diagnoses its repressive force—despite Staël's reputation as the leading proponent of Romantic nationalism after Herder. At the same time, Staël charges her protagonist with a more purposeful subjective drive—a veritable *Bildungstrieb*—than is given to Goethe's hero or Scott's. Corinne personifies the Schlegelian ideal of a progressive universal poetry only to fall, to her misfortune, into the plot of a novel. Her fate dramatizes the problem we saw Schlegel bringing into view, in which national history precipitates a contradiction between the novel as an emergent force, or universal potential, and the novel as a finite,

42. Scott, *Waverley,* 143. See Duncan, *Modern Romance,* 79–92; on *Waverley* as Bildungsroman, see Millgate, *Walter Scott,* 35–57.

43. Staël, *Politics, Literature, and National Character,* 153; cf. Condorcet, *Progress of the Human Mind,* 11.

44. Staël, *Corinne,* trans. Raphael, 246–47. This edition cited parenthetically in the text hereafter. Citations in French are from Balayé's edition.

local, settled form, a genre among others—bound, in the British tradition, by the marriage plot.

In her role as a rhapsodic performance-poet (*improvvisatrice*) Corinne realizes Schlegel's "mixture of storytelling, song, and other forms." She combines them in voice and gesture, in a total artwork which is authentic for being embodied and hence transient, ever varying, flowing through her rather than fixed.[45] Her "cosmopolitan synthesis of improvisational styles"[46] embraces different forms, media, nations, and epochs. Dancing the Neapolitan tarantella, Corinne evokes Indian "temple dancing girls" (*Bayadères*) and "dancing girls of Herculaneum," recreating "the poses depicted by the ancient painters and sculptors." In a triumphant fulfillment of aesthetic education, she reconstitutes an organic, universal artwork, before the arts were subject to the division of labor, delivering her audience to a transcendent state of unity: "As she danced, Corinne made the spectators experience her own feelings, as if she had been improvising, or playing the lyre, or drawing portraits. Everything was language for her [*tout était langage pour elle*]. . . . An indefinable passionate joy, and imaginative sensitivity, stimulated [*électrisait*] all the spectators of this magical dance, transporting them into an ideal existence which was out of this world" (91).

Correspondingly fluid and heterogeneous, Staël's "romantic book" interpolates a love story with extended descriptions of Italian scenery and monuments, samples of the heroine's improvisations, her impromptu lectures on history and art, debates on politics, religion, and national character, frivolous salon *causerie,* and impassioned exchanges of letters and confessions. At first, Corinne plays the role of tutor to her lover Oswald—reversing the gendered authority of the Abelard-and-Héloïse plot established for the modern novel by Rousseau in *Julie.* As it progresses, Staël makes the love story conventionally novelistic: desire is aroused but deferred, clogged by past secrets and family histories, thwarted by duty and circumstance, frozen into an anguished domestic triangle. The love story prevails, binding the heroine, mortifying her into another Italian tomb or ruin. "My talent no longer exists . . . the source of everything is dried up" (356–57): she can only recover her art in the sacrificial staging of her own death.

This obliteration of the heroine's *Bildung* by the love story casts a cold light back on what now becomes visible as the doubled structure of *Wilhelm*

45. See Klettke, "Germaine De Staël," for an analysis of Corinne as a personification of Schlegel's combinatorial aesthetic, realized in a "choreographic" "art of the moment." On Corinne's improvisations, see also Poulet, "The Role of Improvisation in *Corinne*"; Simpson, *Literary Minstrelsy,* 51–57; Esterhammer, *Romanticism and Improvisation,* 86–91.

46. Esterhammer, *Romanticism and Improvisation,* 91.

Meister's Apprenticeship. Goethe's novel counterpoints Wilhelm's vocational plot, the theatrical mission and fellowship of the Tower, with a serial courtship plot—the prehistory of the marriage plot into which the story resolves. Mariane, Philine, the Countess, Aurelie, Therese, Natalie: the succession of women, objects of erotic interest to Wilhelm and his male companions, supplies the directional structure to his narrative that the vocational plot fails to deliver. Each of the women marks a stage in the hero's progress (colored by interesting confusions of sex and gender). Their failure to accompany him to the next stage gives the narrative its progressive form, and casts them, literally or figuratively, as sacrificial victims. The sacrificial role is reiterated on a formal level by the interpolation of the "Confessions of a Beautiful Soul" in book 6, dividing the first part, the "theatrical mission," from the last two books and the aegis of the Tower. The episode makes room for a pietistic, feminine, autobiographical mode of *Bildung* in order to distinguish it from the narrative of Wilhelm's career and, thus, exorcise it from the novel.

The erotic plot of *Wilhelm Meister* makes explicit a disciplinary logic of substitution that structures the apparent free play of the hero's *Bildung.* As the Tower Society (itself theatrical, a masquerade) replaces the theatrical mission, so Wilhelm's accession to paternity and marriage replaces his vocation at the end of the book. Where the first of these substitutions takes place diachronically, implying a dialectical succession, the second operates synchronically, nondialectically, that is, metaphorically or allegorically. The marriage plot displaces rather than subsumes the vocational plot, as the closing lines of the novel acknowledge. "You seem to me like Saul, the son of Kish, who went in search of his father's asses, and found a kingdom," Friedrich tells Wilhelm, who replies: "I don't know about kingdoms, but I do know that I found a treasure [*Glück*: fortune, happiness, luck] I never deserved. And I would not exchange it for anything in the world" (373). Luck, no plan or program, emancipates the merchant's son from his bourgeois destiny. An accidental exchange (finding a different object from the one he was seeking) yields the object that is beyond exchange—a wife. Others, instead, have paid for Wilhelm's fortune: the Countess, whose decline into pietism follows Wilhelm's impersonation of her husband; Aurelie, whose fatal inability to separate herself from her stage roles releases Wilhelm from the theatrical mission; Mariane, whose death in childbirth gives Wilhelm a son; and, above all, Mignon, whose death and apotheosis cast her as the novel's paradigmatic sacrificial victim.

In her critique of *Wilhelm Meister,* mentioned earlier, Staël finds Mignon's sublime pathos filling the void left by the attenuation of plot and hero:

> We cannot represent to ourselves without emotion the least of the feelings that agitate this young girl; there is in her I know not what of magic simplicity, that supposes abysses of thought and feeling; we think we hear the tempest moaning at the bottom of her soul, even while we are unable to fix upon a word or circumstance to account for the inexpressible uneasiness she makes us feel.[47]

Mignon's antithetical relation to the narrative that frames her affords her posthumous fate, in which she breaks free from the matrix of Goethe's novel to lead an autonomous career in the nineteenth-century imagination.[48] Singer of exquisite lyrics of Romantic longing, she embodies the spirit of poetry, which the novel must abandon in its commitment to the prose of the world. Lyric purity quarantines her outside the progressive movement of plot, until the pressure of development, somatic as well as narrative, destroys her. Stunted, feral, androgynous, tormented by illicit desire, she dies upon hearing of Wilhelm's impending betrothal, paused forever on the brink of adult sexuality and gender. Mignon's obsequies replace Wilhelm's marriage ceremony, deferred beyond the close of the novel. Her ornate funeral pageant takes place in the Hall of the Past, the setting for a synthesis of the arts configured around death and memory.

Corinne inherits Mignon's role as spectacular sacrificial victim, invested with a pathetic sublimity, as well as the *Gesamtkunstwerk* aesthetic of the Hall of the Past. She takes over the show, however, as though in fulfillment of Wilhelm's abandoned theatrical mission, as both author and manager. Rallying her talents for a last performance, she directs the multimedia spectacle of her death, composes her own eulogy, and seizes posthumous control of the family romance. "Since I must soon die, my only personal wish is that Oswald should find again in you and in his daughter some traces of my influence, and that at least he may never enjoy a feeling without recalling Corinne," she tells her rival, Lucile (404): colonizing, in effect, the sacred interior space of the domestic affections.

Strikingly, Staël codes the marriage plot as "English"—not just by making the Scottish peer Oswald choose fair, mild, English Lucile over dark, passionate, Italianate Corinne, but by making this outcome a reflex of national conditions, and setting it within the generic matrix of English domestic fiction. England (which apparently, if inconsistently, includes Scotland) is the novel's

47. Staël, *Germany*, 2:56–57.

48. In *Mignon's Afterlives* Cave traces the character's posthumous flight across nineteenth-century fiction and other artistic media.

exemplary case of a historically ascendant, unified nation-state, in which a masculine public sphere of governmental and military institutions entails a gendered division of moral as well as economic labor. In England, Corinne learns, "the strength and reality of [the] social order . . . dominates all the more in that it is based on pure, noble ideas" (269). Oswald's duty to his country, as an officer and peer, justifies his desertion of her in the name of those noble ideas, which reciprocally produce his private character (in contrast to his public gallantry) as melancholy and vacillating—he is a depressive variant of Wilhelm and Waverley.[49] In England, Corinne's father warns her, "women have no occupation but domestic duties" (245). Corinne's narrative of her upbringing discloses the stifling psychic violence of this gendered ethos of duty in English provincial life: "I felt my talent slipping away. In spite of myself, my mind was occupied by petty things [*petitesses*], for in a society lacking all interest in science, literature, pictures, and music—in which, in short, no one is interested in the imagination—it is the little things [*petits faits*], the minute criticisms, which of necessity form the subject of conversations" (250).

The English episodes of *Corinne* form a satiric rebuttal of Staël's later encomium to the British constitution in *Considerations on the French Revolution* (1818), as well as her earlier analysis of the role of women in English culture in *On Literature*. Thanks to their relegation to private life, Staël argues in *On Literature*, "nowhere so much as in England have women enjoyed the happiness brought about by the domestic affections." This is the main reason, in turn, for the pre-eminence of the English in "one genre of imaginative works: fiction without marvels, without allegory, without historical allusions, based solely upon the invention of characters and events of private life"—in other words, the domestic realist novel developed by Richardson and Burney.[50] Despite longueurs that try the patience of French readers, "English novels hold our attention by a steady succession of accurate and moral comments on life's tender emotions."[51] But it is one thing to read the prose of the world and another to dwell in it. For Corinne, the "thousand little hurts" of domestic life, "like the bonds in which the pygmies wrapped Gulliver," provoke only "boredom, impatience, and loathing" (250).

Corinne may thrive in Italy, conversely, because it is not a nation-state. She redeems the pejorative association of effeminacy and Italian decadence made by northern travelers, such as Oswald. "Men's characters have the gentleness

49. On the eclipse of Corinne's utopian enthusiasm by Oswald's "British melancholy"—a "contagious but prestigious disease that Oswald passes on to Corinne"—see Lokke, *Tracing Women's Romanticism*, 47.

50. Staël, *Politics, Literature, and National Character*, 204–5.

51. Ibid., 207.

and flexibility of women's," he complains, "in a country where there are no military careers nor free institutions" (97). For women the case is otherwise. The absence of a state opens public life to Corinne. She assumes a national role, hymning "the glory and happiness of Italy," crowned at the Capitol in the place of ancient emperors. The narrator notes her freedom from the gendered role-splitting dictated by the English system: "At one and the same time she gave the impression of a priestess of Apollo who approaches the sun-god's temple, and of a woman who is completely natural in the ordinary relationships of life" (23). That freedom entails, to Oswald's scandalized disapproval, the taking of lovers, and an indefinite postponement of marriage, at least until he comes along.

The heroine's role as "national metonymy" is complicated by the historical condition of the country.[52] Corinne's performance convokes Italy as a realization of Schiller's "aesthetic state," in which the arts have replaced an extinct political sphere. Enjoying "the last glory that is allowed to nations without military power or political independence, the glory of the arts and sciences" (99), Italy's famed hospitality to the imagination resides in its condition as a former empire. The pastness of national power, fossilized in ruins, monuments, and artworks, inspires Corinne's poetry, which she dedicates to "the dignity of humankind and the glory of the world":

> I am a poet when I admire, when I despise, when I hate, not out of personal feelings, not for my own sake, but for the dignity of humankind and the glory of the world. (46) [*la dignité de l'espèce humaine et la gloire du monde,* 85]

Although at several points she joins Oswald in deploring Italy's lack of republican virtue, Corinne issues no call for national political revival. Her coronation enacts the triumph of art over empire, whether Augustan, Napoleonic, or Britannic.[53] The good cosmopolitanism of the aesthetic state reconstitutes

52. "Le titre du roman se trouve parfaitement justifié par la fiction: Corinne, c'est l'Italie et l'Italie, c'est Corinne . . . véritable métonymie nationale." Phalèse, ed., *Corinne à la page,* 96.

53. Compare, for a contrary argument, Susan Tenenbaum: "Staël described the eclipse of politics by aesthetics as a principal cause of Italy's servitude to Napoleon" ("*Corinne*: Political Polemics," 157). Giulia Pacini argues that Italy's inchoate national condition allows Staël to showcase "the instrumental function of the arts in the construction and definition of a nation" ("Hidden Politics in Staël's *Corinne,*" 171). For Patrick Vincent, Staël's "female genius" resolves the "contradiction between Enlightenment universalism's openness and the parochialism of romantic nationalism" by making literature the medium of "an enlightened, liberal form of nationalism" (*The Romantic Poetess,* 76). Suzanne Guerlac argues that Corinne sets "literature, the imagined, and imagining, community of the nation" in opposition to (Napoleonic) militaristic and imperial ideology ("Writing the Nation," 52). In Caroline Franklin's account, sensitive to the Napoleonic context, "the tension between Romantic genius and Romantic patriotism

Italy as a universal nation where all may find themselves at home, because its political life lies in the past, not in the future. "Is Rome not now the land of tombs? . . . Perhaps one of Rome's secret charms is its reconciliation of the imagination with this long slumber" (32). Corinne's rhapsodic time, the time of an emergent humanity, is postnational and posthistorical.

My argument presses against the usual story of *Corinne*'s international reception, summarized by Susan Tenenbaum:

> In *Corinne* Staël portrayed her heroine as an agent of social redemption. Corinne's inspired odes alluding to Italy's glorious past were intended to awaken its citizens' dormant civic consciousness: her poetic images of ancient Rome and the medieval Italian republics served as metaphors of lost dignity and inspiration to national rebirth.[54]

The story is encouraged, to be sure, by Staël's other writings on national questions; but here, as with her account of English domestic life, women, and the novel in *On Literature,* we need to be wary of resorting to the author's essays and treatises for an explanation of her fiction, which develops its own internal logic. In a pre-emptive strike against British Romantic fiction's allegories of union, *Corinne* mounts a feminist critique of the nation-state as historical horizon of totality for *Bildung,* separating a cosmopolitan aesthetic ideal of the nation from its political reality. The topical deflection of that critique, from Napoleonic empire to the British instance of a unified national state founded on a gendered separation of spheres, also directs satirical energy at the ascendant English tradition of the domestic realist novel, which fixes the nation in an ethos of duty and the habitus of provincial life. *Corinne* reroutes the relation between personal and universal histories—between individual *Bildung* and the perfectibility of the species—along the fault-line of gender, driven open rather than closed by the mediating term of national history.

---

produces a fault-line separating art from politics." Staël enthrones her poetic genius in "the decentralized feminine realm of Italy where art flourished undisturbed by civic duties and rivaled religion in nourishing the Italian soul . . . as a fitting opponent to Napoleon, the colossus of public violence, who was crowned 'Rex Totius Italiae' in 1805" (*Female Romantics,* 11–13).

54. Tenenbaum, "*Corinne*: Political Polemics," 158. In a nuanced account of *Corinne*'s nationalist project. Glenda Sluga reads "the story of a nation in discursive gestation," in which the submission of female liberty to national liberty is a melancholy historical necessity ("Gender and the Nation," 243). More optimistically, Susanne Hillman describes "the exceptional women with lyres who were destined to act as the nation's unifying agents by recreating the gallants' deeds in writing. By imagining the nation these women fulfilled the supreme task of citizenship" ("Men with Muskets, Women with Lyres," 232).

V

Barred from it while alive, Corinne occupies the marriage plot after her death, turning it into a haunted site of remembrance, repression, and regret. The novel closes on a note of melancholy dubiety: "Lord Nelvil was a model of the purest and most orderly domestic life. But did he forgive himself for his past behaviour? Was he consoled by society's approval? Was he content with the common lot after what he had lost? I do not know, and, on the matter, I want neither to blame nor to absolve him" (404). Half a century later, George Eliot's Maggie Tulliver declares her wish to avenge the wronged sisterhood of "the dark unhappy ones," the antiheroines of Staël and Scott.[55] Expelled from the novel because they are (in Schlegelian terms) "more than the novel," their darkness is pitched less against the gentle blondes that replace them than against the lucky lightness of the Wilhelms and Waverleys. Their *Bildung* is deflected into a passionate intensity that, like Mignon's lyric pathos, eclipses the other characters around them.

The impact of "the myth of Corinne" on subsequent women writers has been well noted, by Ellen Moers and others.[56] It receives searching reassessment in two mid-Victorian romances of female artistic vocation, cosmopolitanism, and the aesthetic state. Elizabeth Barrett Browning's *Aurora Leigh* (1856) repairs the breach between *Bildung* and marriage for its Anglo-Italian poet-heroine, but at a high cost, since the combination still requires a sacrifice. That comes to bear on a substitute, Marian Erle, whose martyrdom allows Aurora to take her place in the marriage plot at the last minute, as though only by such drastic means can its fatality be averted.[57] Aurora must also renounce the purity of her earlier dedication to her art—in tandem, to be sure, with her spouse's renunciation of his (failed) political career. Marriage as a mystical union with the divine nature sublimates both masculine and feminine paths of *Bildung* in the poem's extraordinary final movement.

George Eliot's *Daniel Deronda* (1876) plays a more intricate set of variations on the performing heroine and the realization of female *Bildung* through art. The courtship plot of Julius Klesmer and Catherine Arrowpoint, early in the novel, redeems the conjunction of aesthetic education and marriage by making the universal artistic genius a man and the heroine who weds him in defiance of English domestic norms his pupil: restoring the Abelard-and-

55. Eliot, *The Mill on the Floss*, 332.

56. Moers, *Literary Women*, 176–210.

57. On *Corinne* and *Aurora Leigh* see ibid., 182, 205–6; Lewis, *Germaine de Staël, George Sand, and the Victorian Woman Artist*, 107–16; Kaplan, "*Aurora Leigh*"; Chapman, *Networking the Nation*, 101–5, 113–14.

Héloïse ratio of male tutor and female student capsized in *Corinne*. With the absorption of the English heiress Catherine into her husband's mixed-race cosmopolitan domain of art, their union also undoes the domestic national allegory. *Daniel Deronda* moves beyond this solution, marking it as exceptional but insufficient, to recombine the key elements of the fable. Although antiheroine Gwendolen Harleth's lack of talent thwarts her attempt to escape from a destiny of English provincial marriage into art, Italy nevertheless affords her release from a soul-destroying fate into an ambiguous penitential afterlife (an equivalent of the convent to which Scott dispatches Flora MacIvor at the end of *Waverley*).

A viable synthesis of *Bildung*, marriage, and national destiny coalesces meanwhile around the hero, Daniel Deronda. This involves the dialectical repudiation of an English national ground via a succession of Jewish plots: first, the cosmopolitan cultural ideal of the aesthetic state claimed by Klesmer, and then, reinstating the national theme, the genetic heritage and Zionist mission discovered and embraced by Daniel. Daniel's bride Mirah is a gifted musician, but she eschews a public forum for her art and is absorbed into her husband's career. Eliot's expansion of the Bildungsroman to a world-historical stage, as though in answer to Hegel's critique, decisively subordinates the marriage plot to ancillary status—a disposition reinforced by its catastrophic failure in Gwendolen's story.

A vehement protest against this solution comes from Daniel's estranged mother Leonora Halm-Eberstein, "the Alcharisi," a famous opera-singer and the most powerful avatar of Staël's heroine in *Daniel Deronda*. "Had I not a rightful claim to be something more than a mere daughter and mother?" she demands: "Whatever else was wrong, acknowledge that I had a right to be an artist, though my father's will was against it. My nature gave me a charter."[58] In Daniel's eyes, her devotion to her art has brought a double betrayal, of his paternal heritage and her maternal nature. The judgment reveals his national kinship with Oswald: Staël never endorses such a view of Corinne, who retains her "natural" womanliness even at the height of her public triumph. The Alcharisi's sacrifice of nature for art entails in turn the novel's compensatory sacrifice of her in order to achieve its resolution, sealed with her lonely, painful death. Where Corinne was able to outwit posterity, she is forced to admit defeat. The echo of her protest saddens the close of this novel too.

---

58. Eliot, *Daniel Deronda*, 664. On *Daniel Deronda* and *Corinne*, see Weliver, "George Eliot and the Prima Donna's 'Script'"; Heller, *Literary Sisterhoods*, 3–6, 37–45.

CHAPTER 2

Darwin's Marriage Plots

Unplotting Courtship in Late Victorian Fiction

ELISHA COHN

IN THOMAS HARDY'S *Jude the Obscure,* Sue Bridehead declares her intention to live with Jude freely—"As I choose." She justifies her decision by quoting from "On Liberty," declaring, "She, or he, 'who lets the world, or his own portion of it, choose his plan of life for him, has no need of any other faculty than the ape-like one of imitation.'"[1] Sue claims a robust form of choice that J. S. Mill presents as distinctively human. In his "On the Subjection of Women" (1869), Mill condemns the diluted form of choice that women exercise and rejects any evolutionary account of women's agency: "They have always hitherto been kept, as far as regards spontaneous development, in so unnatural a state, that their nature cannot but have been greatly distorted and disguised; and no one can safely pronounce that if women's nature were left to choose its direction as freely as men's . . . there would be any material difference." Biological *durée* is "always" "distorted" by culture, delegitimating the possibility that women have wielded a true "entitle[ment] to choose pursuits."[2] Late nineteenth-century revisions of the marriage plot such as Hardy's, however, brought evolutionary thinking to bear on the human act of choosing a partner.

This essay examines the fate of the marriage plot in the wake of Darwin's *The Descent of Man* (1871), considering the narrative consequences of an evo-

1. Hardy, *Jude the Obscure,* 215.
2. Mill, "On Subjection of Women," 188, 218.

lutionary framework that recasts humans'—and especially women's—capacity for choice. Typically, the key events of the marriage plot comprise the conscious choices men and women make: proposal, refusal, betrothal, and union. In a sense, these plot events enable the propagation of the species (or at least of the upper and middle classes of Victorian England). However, in novels of the 1880s and 1890s, the structure of the event, like the nature of choice, appears disrupted by evolutionary thinking. *The Origin of Species* (1859) emphasized the long timeline of near-infinite generations, diminishing the eventfulness of any individual life. *The Descent of Man* partly reinvigorated the power of individual agency through its account of sexual selection, the process by which individual animals—whether instinctively or consciously—choose their reproductive partners. Sexual selection makes "social power depend upon the ability to exercise sexual choice," Rosemary Jann explains, much as it often does in the English novel.[3] Thus *The Descent of Man* would seem likely to have provoked less troubling effects on the novel. In fiction, both male and female protagonists often exercise choice, and Nancy Armstrong and Ruth Bernard Yeazell argue that Darwin's text, like the novels of his contemporaries, dramatizes the process of selecting a mate.[4] This perspective takes Darwin's work to reiterate modes of literary narrative that confirm sexual choice. Yet marriage plots developed in the wake of *The Descent of Man* often diminish human action with reference to a long evolutionary view: rather than restore the power of (women's) choice, they disentangle plottedness from the act of choosing.[5]

Interest in the long evolutionary past had profound effects on the marriage plot: plottedness was attenuated by a diminished emphasis on choice as event; it was no longer necessarily the case that "deliberate choice leads to a satisfying conclusion."[6] Talia Schaffer's recent account of Victorian marriage complicates this story, arguing that marriage plots often valorized choices oriented toward serving the "familiar" needs of "larger social organization," which broadens the concept of choice. Familiar marriage may not require the

---

3. Jann, "Darwin and the Anthropologists," 287.

4. See ibid., esp. 302. See also Psomiades, who claims that "Victorian anthropological theory had a marriage plot," and that novels written in the wake of this theory were inflected by anthropology ("Marriage Plot," 53). The fit between Darwin's text and the Victorian marriage plot holds even if, as queer readings have stressed, *The Descent of Man* explores cases in which instinct becomes disarticulated from reproductive success (Grosz, *Becoming Undone*, 118; Kaye, *Flirt's Tragedy*, 89–90).

5. While I focus here on novels by women, I note that several of Hardy's novels—particularly *The Woodlanders*, *Tess of the d'Urbervilles*, and *Jude the Obscure*—also trouble choice through shifts of narrative scale.

6. Yeazell, *Fictions of Modesty*, 219.

exercise of absolute individual autonomy, but it captures the way individual subjects are constituted by their social networks. As if pointing at the way evolutionary thought redefines the "familiar," Schaffer figures familiar marriage choice in evolutionary terms: it "was not a fossil from a past era, but rather a descendent that underwent multiple mutations."[7] While for the novels Schaffer examines, familiar choices still constitute major plot episodes, for some late Victorian novelists, evolution's expansion of the "familial" significantly altered not only the feeling of choosing but also the rhythms of narrative event.

Narratology understands the "event" as a break from a situational norm. In the typical marriage plot, a new union disrupts the pre-existing norm of two separate families; in many novels, the chosen suitor is often an unexpected one who deviates from the "conventional marriage script"; such a marriage choice has a "high degree of eventfulness."[8] The encounter between the evolutionary narrative of deep time and the conventional, novelistic narrative of the individual life-choice prompted novelists to explore temporalities that dwarf the human scale of the event.[9] According to Gillian Beer and George Levine, *The Origin of Species* affected novels' plot structure because Darwin's evolutionary narrative stressed never-ending change over teleology, hierarchic networks of relation over bounded individuality, and expanded timescales over the single lifetime.[10] The infamously open form of the novel rendered it elastic enough to reconfigure or eliminate the conventional narrative event in the face of incremental, gradual change.

Taking up these observations, this essay turns to two experimental novels that engage with evolutionary thinking: Olive Schreiner's *The Story of an African Farm* (1883) and Mona Caird's *The Daughters of Danaus* (1894). Both novels feature conflict between narrative form and didactic, dialogic content, in which characters argue for the renovation of women's powers of choice in explicitly evolutionary terms so that women might reinvigorate "the race." Both narratives searchingly question the naturalness of marriage, but they feature protagonists who intentionally refuse—yet helplessly drift toward—mar-

7. Schaffer, *Romance's Rival*, 3.

8. Hühn, "Functions and Forms of Eventfulness," 154, 153.

9. In other words, the "affordances" of the novel form—to use Caroline Levine's term—challenged the stability of the event in the wake of evolutionary thought. For Levine, a novel is well designed to "connect[] events over time" (*Forms*, 6). This conception of narrative aligns with the concept of "plot" as narratology defines it: the causal and temporal arrangement of events, ordered by boundary-crossings. However, forms "often fail to impose their order when they run up against other forms that disrupt their logic and frustrate their organizing ends" (7).

10. For Beer, a novel's focus on the individual lifespan is "no longer an absolute but polemical," countering Darwin by making the "single generation carry the weight of signification" (*Darwin's Plots*, 223).

riage as the telos of a woman's life. Sexual selection may function as a topic of debate, but it is no longer a deep structure governing plot itself.

I. EVOLUTIONARY CHOICE

Writers working for women's rights in the second half of the nineteenth century actively attended to evolutionary thinking, often theorizing women's capacity to exercise sexual choice as a biological means of equalizing gendered behavior in the future.[11] However, evolutionary thinking also opened a troubling vista onto the insignificance of the individual life. George Levine observes that an evolutionary perspective often ironizes marital endings because endings are no longer truly conclusive. If biological change is the norm, what happens to the event, especially the connubial special event that so often secures narrative closure? The tidy marriage plot now feels falsely bounded because "the world is larger than anyone's imagination of it; connections extend out endlessly."[12] The novel's increasing capacity to capture much deeper scales of time and vaster networks of relation obscures individual endings in favor of ongoingness and embeddedness.

In *The Origin of Species,* the scale of individual existence is less meaningful than the long history of a species. Darwin explains, "The mind cannot possibly grasp the full meaning of a hundred million years; it cannot add up and perceive the full effects of many slight variations, accumulated during an almost infinite number of generations." These generations, much less those they comprise, are uncountable: "The whole history of the world, although of a length quite incomprehensible by us, will hereafter be recognised as a mere fragment of time, compared with the ages which have elapsed since the first creature, the progenitor of innumerable extinct and living descendants, was created." This perspective renders individual survival important only insofar as it contributes incrementally to speciation. While Darwin claims that "as natural selection works solely by and for the good of each being," the vastness of time diminishes the significance of any single individual life, or event in that life (birth, mating, death), along its line of hereditary progress.[13]

As one example of how an evolutionary perspective affects the nature of the plotted event, George Eliot's *The Mill on the Floss* (1860) considers the diminution of the individual life in its failed-love plot. Eliot's narrator describes a grand sweep of cultural and biological destruction:

---

11. Helsinger, Sheets, and Veeder, *The Woman Question,* 89–90.
12. Levine, *Darwin and the Novelists,* 17, 148.
13. Darwin, *Origin,* 422, 381, 360.

> These dead-tinted, hollow-eyed, angular skeletons of villages on the Rhone oppress me with the feeling that human life—very much of it—is a narrow, ugly, grovelling existence, which even calamity does not elevate, but rather tends to exhibit in all its bare vulgarity of conception; and I have a cruel conviction that the lives these ruins are the traces of were part of a gross sum of obscure vitality, that will be swept into the same oblivion with the generations of ants and beavers.[14]

The narrator turns to the "emmet-like Dodsons and Tullivers" to be swept into oblivion, an analogy that poses the novel's investment in the fate of Maggie Tulliver—an individual ill-adapted to her social environment—against the perspective that lumps individuals into "a gross sum of obscure vitality." The traits that emerged in "the crossing o' breeds"—the topic of several conversations early in the novel—do not suit her to survive, and the Tulliver line ends in an animal "oblivion" tallied in "generations." The narrator remarks, "In natural science, I have understood, there is nothing petty to the mind that has a large vision of relations, and to which every single object suggests a vast sum of conditions. It is surely the same with the observation of human life."[15] The novel situates Maggie's stalled trajectory within a biological and cultural environment, suggesting that a historical vantage shows nature's ongoing flux. Conceiving history in evolutionary terms is "cruel" insofar as the individual life no longer registers, and doing so significantly impacts how the novel's conclusion might be understood. The destructive flood in some ways appears as the outward symbol of Maggie's inward state, but the passage above implies that the flood is a nonsymbolic environmental pressure, a "happening": narratologist Marie-Laure Ryan classifies events according to their degree of intentionality, contrasting actions (human-driven) with happenings and moves with passive moves or "deliberate nonaction."[16] Happenings and passive moves predominate in Eliot's narrative. While the novel adheres to the scope of Maggie's individual life-scale, her efforts to shape her life are not granted the force of closure in the narrative. Her last few scenes find her praying for the strength to leave St. Oggs and refuse the man she loves—to make a next step in her intellectual evolution—but she is stuck in deliberate nonaction. The flood is larger than herself, disrupting the expectation that individual purposiveness drives narrative closure.

Whereas *Origin* diminishes the importance of individual actions, *Descent* re-emphasizes the role individual choices play in the trajectory of a species'

14. Eliot, *Mill on the Floss,* 282–83.
15. Ibid., 15, 283.
16. Ryan, *Possible Worlds,* 129, 132.

development. A shift in the construction of the event of "selection" occurs when Darwin turns his attention to sex.[17] The phrase "natural selection" involves a syntactic ambiguity that "sexual selection" lacks. While it might appear that nature is the agent doing the selecting, the phrase also suggests that selection occurs "naturally," without any agent behind an autotelic process. "Nature" designates the process itself. The synonym "struggle for existence" is similarly misleading insofar as "struggle" does not refer to the personal troubles of particular ants and beavers but to the accreted reproductive success of generations. Selection is a long-term event; the choices that an individual creature makes contribute to its ability to survive, but this kind of intentional act is not what Darwin means by "selection."

But it is what he means when he turns to sex: sex isn't a personified entity doing the selecting (as "nature" appeared to be), and sexual selection occurs through choices undertaken by individual animals. Darwin writes, "Sexual selection depends on the success of certain individuals over others of the same sex in relation to the propagation of the species; whilst natural selection depends on the success of both sexes, at all ages, in relation to the general conditions of life."[18] Sexual selection "depends on the will, desires, and choice, of either sex" in finding a reproductive partner, and can be understood as "add[ing] to natural selection the vagaries of individual [. . .] taste."[19] In much of the animal world, female choice, more than male, often drives sexual selection. And unlike Mill, for whom a biological account of female choice is obstructed by cultural explanations, Darwin understands culture and biology as intertwined through the accreted pathways of choice over many generations, and traces the interplay between biological traits and habits, customs, rituals, and values.[20] This is not to say that he portrays human women as robust agents of species development: his account of sexual difference makes "male agency and male control of women the engine of human progress."[21] According to Darwin, in humans (unlike most other animals) choice belonged to males: because "man is more powerful in body and mind than woman,"

---

17. According to Susan David Bernstein, "Like Victorian middle-class courtship practices, active roles are the prerogative of males, while females occupy a more passive position, with the exception of their supposed ability to 'choose the most attractive partner.'" "Designs after Nature," 69.

18. Darwin, *Descent*, 664. Frederickson observes that the concept of instinct allowed "multigenerational timeframes [to] work in tandem": beings could live without imagining the future while "being animated by a force that is [. . .] at least ambivalently oriented toward futurity." *Ploy of Instinct*, 7, 79.

19. Darwin, *Descent*, 225; Grosz, *Becoming Undone*, 131.

20. Richardson, "Against," 29.

21. Jann, "Revising," 149.

human males "gained the power of selection."[22] Many of Darwin's contemporaries understood his work to license cultural masculine domination, as shown in statements like James Crichton Browne's: "That which has been settled millions of years ago by the prehistoric protozoa, from whom we are supposed to be descended, cannot be reversed by acts of Parliament or the resolution of Women's Righters."[23] Yet, taking the long view, *Descent* itself does not subscribe to an essentialist concept of the sexes because the species everlastingly undergoes change that inflects cultural values; although the text focuses on the individual more than *Origin* did, Darwin again scales up his analysis to consider the open-ended fate of all life—a gesture that potentiates new freedoms yet also diminishes their significance.[24]

And it is this long view that troubles the capacity of *Descent* to invigorate the projects of politically minded writers. Gillian Beer proposes that fiction might "restore to the female the power of selection which, Darwin held, men had taken over."[25] Yet whether this effort succeeded depends not only on the late Victorian politics of gender but also the representation of "selection" or choice itself, and how the concept of choice reshapes literary plot. Thus, we might question whether literature takes its coordinates from scientific frameworks, or whether the literary uptake of scientific ideas might be more complex than either affirmation, or even, alternatively, criticism.

II. SCHREINER

The Story of an African Farm appears to search for a genre that could accommodate the incongruity of individual, European lives—which risk assimilation to generic social types yet must be ratified through marriage—against a deep-time backdrop of the colonial South Africa's ancient Karoo.[26] *African Farm* invokes both a *Bildung* plot and a marriage plot while suggesting that these trajectories do not or no longer complement one another. Waldo undergoes an Emersonian process of self-unfolding cut short; much of what he experiences is presented as universal through the narrator's use of the first-person

---

22. Darwin, *Descent*, 665. Richardson defends Darwin's descriptive rather than prescriptive attitude toward sex roles: "What Darwin describes is a process of *becoming*, which he sees as capable of altering." "Against," 34.

23. Browne, quoted in Shuttleworth, Dawson, and Noakes, "Women, Science and Culture," 69.

24. Grosz, *Becoming Undone*, 122.

25. Beer, *Darwin's Plots*, 203.

26. I am grateful to Aaron Rosenberg for discussions about the relation between scale and genre.

plural to describe his early efforts of perception, knowledge, work, and self-revelation. Lyndall, meanwhile, generates a New Woman plot: she grows to reject the modes of self-making available to women through marriage only to die after giving birth to a baby conceived out of wedlock. The novel almost entirely cancels any freedom either protagonist could be said to exercise. In the history of the novel, marriage has often been central to *Bildung*: it functions as, in Franco Moretti's words, a "metaphor for the social contract" and a marker of closure in the story of burgeoning autonomy, rather than as an act or condition that itself constitutes growth.[27] Jed Esty points out that "Lyndall's plot does not merely parallel but implicitly comments on Waldo's [. . .] youthful idealism."[28] This doubling is profoundly negative: Waldo's and Lyndall's fates suggest the impossibility of free self-making, yet marriage appears to be at odds with that cancelled ideal.

I build on Esty's claim that national context disorders the Bildungsroman form by attending specifically to the evolutionary valence of individual choice for Schreiner in the context of her longer career. The end of *African Farm* substantially revises the marriage plot: Waldo chooses to serve Lyndall's refusal of convention in a presumably chaste but loving lifelong commitment—what Schaffer might deem a particularly radical "vocational" familiar marriage.[29] But Schreiner presents this choice through a temporality that diminishes the characters' powers of intention. Waldo affirms Lyndall's desire to make an impact on the future of the species at the end of the novel when he writes to her without knowing she is already dead. He proposes a marriage of minds and labor: "You will work, and I will take your work for mine."[30] As Esty points out, Waldo's letter compresses the whole of what in other novels constitutes a *Bildung* plot of urban experience, alienation, and reintegration through a revelation of his place in the world; "indirect" and "retrospective," the letter closes off the possibility of development from the current events of plot. Written to reinvigorate a dead woman's future, it not only renders the possibility of individual choice as "contingent and outmoded," but compacts the scale of the individual life that previously appeared natural and coextensive with plot itself.[31] Furthermore, Schreiner refuses to portray the belated quasi-marriage that Waldo proposes as an event—it cannot be because the conditions he hopes to alter foreclose it. This episode confirms the novel's diminishment

27. Moretti, *Way of the World*, 22.

28. Esty, *Unseasonable Youth*, 82.

29. Schaffer, *Romance's Rival*, 8.

30. Schreiner, *Story of an African Farm*, 263. Hereafter abbreviated S and cited parenthetically.

31. Esty, *Unseasonable Youth*, 78.

of choice in a number of ways. Giving the most radical choice—to reframe marriage as a political commitment of souls *and* as a form of personal submission—to a man rather than a woman, Schreiner retreats from Lyndall's efforts to appropriate choice for herself. Yet what looks like Waldo's choice becomes determinism; what feels to Waldo like a difficult, active, individual effort of thought becomes a futile episode in the face of the biological constraints on the life of the species—the baby's death, Lyndall's death after childbirth, and Waldo's own incipient, overdetermined demise. The reframing of what a marriage plot might become in the union of Lyndall and Waldo is offered only to be retracted by a temporality that precludes its even being negotiated, much less coming to fruition. Meanwhile, the novel constellates less radical marriage plots as if to suggest the impossibility of dispensing with marriage as the source of narrative structure.

Throughout, courtship serves as the backdrop of the novel's critique of self-formation. Lyndall declares, "Marriage for love is the beautifulest external symbol of the union of souls; marriage without it is the uncleanest traffic that defiles the world" (*S*, 190); most of the novel's proposed marriages are the second kind: Bonaparte Blenkins's courtship of Tant' Sannie before he transfers his attraction to her niece Trana, Sannie's marriage to a meek Boer farmer, Gregory Rose's love for Em before he transfers his attraction to Lyndall, their quickly abandoned plan to marry. Much of this emphasis, especially when it comes to male desire, is darkly comic, as in Bonaparte's exaggerated promise to Sannie, "I shall lead thee, lighted by Hymen's torch, to the connubial altar" (*S*, 100), or Gregory's self-involved pining. Consistently, women make the marital decisions, from Sannie's domineering decisiveness; to Em's firmness when she withdraws from her engagement to Gregory; to Lyndall's excoriating unconventionality. These choices mark many of the novel's events: they shift networks of relation and power at the farm. Schreiner would seem to satirize male desire and transfer choice to women—if the structure of the novel did not diminish the force of event.

The issue of the agency of choice, especially for women, had a distinctively evolutionary cast for Schreiner. Her essay *Women and Labour* (1911) reconfigures the choice of whether to marry as "the choice between finding new forms of labour or sinking slowly into a condition of more or less complete and passive sex-parasitism."[32] Her biologistic term "parasitism" invokes the natural sciences, and she continues, "It is not without profound interest to note the varying phenomena of sex-parasitism as they present themselves in the animal world, both in the male and in the female form. Though among the

32. Schreiner, *Women and Labour*, 72.

greater number of species in the animal world the female form is larger and more powerful rather than the male [. . .], yet sex-parasitism appears among both sex forms."[33] In redefining choice, she argues for ongoingness rather than take current relations between men and women as permanent: "If at the present day, woman, after her long upward march side by side with man, developing with him through the countless ages, by means of the endless exercise of the faculties of mind and body, has now, at last, reached her ultimate limit of growth, and can progress no farther; that, then, here also, today, the growth of the human spirit is to be stayed."[34] Schreiner conceives women's evolution as an "endeavour toward readjustment and expansion,"[35] a process by which the social environment becomes mutually influenced by and adapted to women's widening sphere. Readjustment also has a psychological dimension—it means reconceiving the ends of a life at the scale of species: a woman's realization that "beyond the little struggle of today, lies the larger struggle of the centuries" is what "renders almost of solemn import the efforts of the individual female after physical or mental self-culture."[36] John Kucich remarks, "In Schreiner's omnipotent vision, women possess the power to either destroy or save the species."[37]

Schreiner's novel, however, obscures the potent effects of choosing through narrative strategies that compress or expand scales of time to diminish the force of human intention both in relation to marriage and in general. For instance, after considering Waldo's efforts to become an artist, the narrator shifts focus to his dog:

> The dog . . . walked off to play with a black beetle. The beetle was hard at work trying to roll home a great ball of dung it had been collecting all the morning: but Doss broke the ball, and ate the beetle's hind legs, and then bit off its head. And it was all play, and no one could tell what it had lived and worked for. A striving, and a striving, and an ending in nothing. (*S*, 107)

The passage links Waldo—intensively working, yet dreamy and impractical—to the dung-beetle, an animal used in *The Origin of Species* to illustrate the uselessness of seemingly important bodily structures.[38] Striving itself appears

33. Ibid., 72–73.

34. Ibid., 127.

35. Ibid.

36. Ibid., 127, 121.

37. Kucich, *Imperial Masochism*, 103.

38. Darwin is fascinated by the useless appendage: "the anterior tarsi, or feet, of many male dung-feeding beetles are often broken off" (*Origin*, 109). In Schreiner's passage, mutilation

as a useless appendage. Moreover, the lines of this passage reappear as the epigraph for the second book of the novel, giving them greater importance than they might otherwise have as an illustration of natural checks on industry and intention. Formally, the reuse of the passage transforms it from a metaphor presaging an event in Waldo's development into an index of useless striving. This shift from text to paratext underlines the novel's overall diminution of the force of evolution, progress, effort, and choice as structuring narrative events.

The novel opens with and often recurs to the scale of evolutionary time to mark the futility of human endeavor. Early on, young Waldo reacts with horror to the ticking of his father's watch:

> He saw before him a long stream of people, a great dark multitude, that moved in one direction; then they came to the dark edge of the world and went over. . . . He thought of how that stream had rolled on through all the long ages of the past—how the old Greeks and Romans had gone over; the countless millions of China and India, they were going over now. Since he had come to bed, how many had gone!
>
> And the watch said, "Eternity, eternity, eternity!"
>
> "Stop them! stop them!" cried the child.
>
> And all the while the watch kept ticking on; just like God's will, that never changes or alters, you may do what you please. (*S*, 37)

As Joseph Bristow observes, the image of the watch resonates with the famous opening of William Paley's *Natural Theology* (1802), which was supposed to demonstrate God's purposive design in the world. The watch is far from reassuring, for "How can life have any meaning if it is reduced to infinitesimal units of time?" or expanded across millennia?[39]

Waldo's fascination with eternity matches the narrator's own expansive pace in telling his story, particularly in the long first chapter of the second book, "Times and Seasons." The chapter theorizes a child's progress through wonder, religious fervor, and positivist satisfaction in the material world, culminating in his realization that "the life that throbs in us is a pulsation from it; too mighty for our comprehension, not too small" (*S*, 155). As Sally Ledger explains, the work of Herbert Spencer, particularly his evolutionary

---

affects the head—a much harder body part to live without. Schreiner's modification suggests darkly that the head itself (site of creativity and striving) might be useless.

39. Bristow, introduction to *The Story of an African Farm*, xiv. Waldo's capacious view is contrasted with racist uses of progressive thinking, like Tant' Sannie's view that her servants need not attend church services because "they were descended from apes, and needed no salvation." *S*, 68.

First Principles, "persuaded Schreiner that the social order reflected a deeper biological order, and that progress was a law that underpinned the whole of organic creation."[40] Although the chapter tells such a story of development, its languorous stretch has a dreamlike quality, presaging Schreiner's publication of her highly allegorical *Dreams* (1890) and resonating with a bleaker claim that repeats throughout—that development falters through sleep and dreams, nonagential states. The narrator explains, "Before us there were three courses possible—to go mad, to die, to sleep. We take the latter course; or nature takes it for us" (*S*, 144). If "nature takes" this trajectory "for us," this deterministic formulation implies the attenuation of human agency in the universal process of growth it describes. As Esty points out, Schreiner "organizes (or disorganizes) her novel according to a more random and cruel form of temporality, a naturalist clock whose uneven, unpredictable strokes cut across any sense of pure progress, whether individual or civilizational."[41] The expanded timescale of the chapter itself diminishes human choosing, even if Schreiner critiques her own turn to the *longue durée* when her narrator comments, "After struggling to see the unseeable, growing drunk with the endeavour to span the infinite, and writhing before the inscrutable mystery, it is a renovating relief to turn to some simple, feelable, weighable substance; to something which has a smell and a colour, which may be handled and turned over this way and that" (*S*, 105). The chapter's own impulses—the use of a generic self, the languor of its prose—refute a finite materialism and side with the troubling "endeavour to span the infinite."

Lyndall—anticipating Schreiner herself in *Women and Labour*—is also attentive to evolutionary time. When she talks with Waldo as they daydream together in the wagon, her musings waver between the human scale of "small things" (*S*, 216) and the longer span. At first she cautions herself, "We must not think so far; it is madness, it is a disease." But her efforts at optimism fade out as she continues her speech, as if mimicking the process of waning effort she describes:

> Men have set their mark on mankind for ever, as they thought; but time has washed it out as it has washed out mountains and continents. [. . .] And what if we *could* help mankind, and leave the traces of our work upon it to the end? Mankind is only an ephemeral blossom on the tree of time; there were others before it opened; there will be others after it has fallen. Where was man in the time of the dicynodont, and when hoary monsters wallowed

40. Ledger, *The New Woman*, 73.
41. Esty, *Unseasonable Youth*, 83.

> in the mud? Will he be found in the aeons that are to come? We are sparks, we are shadows, we are pollen, which the next wind will carry away. We are dying already; it is all a dream.

"Yes, we will work" (*S*, 217), Waldo replies placidly, but they do not move, a lack of gesture that resonates with Lyndall's evocation of extinction. Her goal of autonomy reduces again and again to anhedonic paralysis. Lyndall's emphasis on the dreamlike ephemerality of action resonates throughout the novel's remainder, particularly in the dreamy narration associated with Waldo.[42]

Lyndall, whose voice dominates in the second half of the novel, argues that women's subjectivity is not captured by progressive models of autonomous self-development, and she understands marriage as a profoundly flawed compromise of the possibility of freedom. But to read this idea as the novel's lesson depends too much on the contents of Lyndall's speeches, rather than on how her most individualistic claims are embedded within a plot that de-emphasizes autonomy.[43] *The Story of an African Farm* certainly refuses marital closure for Lyndall, but also secures it coercively for Em. Since marriage has been the conventional form of closure, by granting that closure in a secondhand, indirectly represented way to Em, a character who lacks a say in her ultimate condition, Schreiner diverges from autonomy as a governing principle of plot. The novel does not fully uphold Lyndall's desire for expanded freedom, nor does it depend on alternatives to the path Lyndall rejects, since her effort to forge a new path ends in a death that occurs before the time of its narration.

Lyndall's initial choice to go with her lover unmarried once she is already pregnant is depicted as the result of a long negotiation between the two in the primary story-time of the narrative. She will not marry him "because if once you have me you would hold me fast" (*S*, 236), suggesting her desire to retain her autonomy, and yet, as Kucich points out, she also evinces a masochistic desire to be overpowered—"You are the first man I was ever afraid of," she tells him (*S*, 238). This unexpected choice has a narratological "high degree of eventfulness" not only because she flouts the expectations of what the lover calls "the practical world," but also because of its inner contradiction, in which autonomy is secured through a seemingly painful submission. This eventfulness seems marked by the use of present tense in the first three paragraphs of

42. For Heilman, Schreiner "resorted to utopian or dream modes to conjure up the idea of an equal partnership between the sexes that would allow for individual artistic development, while at the same time denying the feasibility of such a relationship in contemporary society and their own private lives." *New Woman Strategies*, 123.

43. As Barash notes, "Lyndall's feminist rhetoric is at odds with the novel's plot." "Virile Womanhood," 272.

the chapter, previously reserved for the universal story of development narrated in "Times and Seasons." Past tense resumes once they have exchanged words, creating ambiguity as to whether their exchange about her lateness in meeting him takes place in the past tense or the present. Her deferral—"I waited till all had gone to bed" (S, 235)—seems to spark the belated quality of the narrative's past tense, which resumes after she offers this explanation. However, when he proposes marriage, she offers a crisp refusal: "I cannot marry you [. . .] because I cannot be tied" (S, 239). Lyndall's second refusal to marry him after their baby's death is narrated in more mediated form through Gregory. Lyndall writes a letter she does not send: "I cannot marry you. I will always love you for the sake of what lay by me those three hours; but there it ends. I must know and see, I cannot be bound to one whom I love as I love you. I am not afraid of the world—I will fight the world. One day—perhaps it may be far off—I shall find what I have wanted all my life; something nobler, stronger than I, before which I can kneel down"—but the letter goes unfinished because she is "so sleepy," and she plans to "write more tomorrow" (S, 279), a day of energy and readiness to take on the challenge of self-empowerment that never comes. Her negative choice, then, is ultimately irrelevant because death comes first. Her death itself is strange kind of narrative event, particularly since it is not the immediate death after childbirth that would more clearly signal a punishment for her sexual transgression. Lyndall's protracted illness highlights a disconnect between the decisive force of her own extinction and its slow, belated narrative unraveling. Lyndall refuses to believe she is dying, suggesting her ongoing desire for what she calls "power." But her adulthood (from pregnancy to death) is structured by "happenings" that occur against her will, suggesting the limited efficacy of choice and also the *belief* in its efficacy.

More conventional proposals of marriage abound in the text. Even when they are relegated to the novel's B-plots, they also feature disturbed eventfulness associated with uncertain agency. Em initially accepts Gregory Rose's love with the phrase "I will do everything you tell me" because "her idea of love was only service" (S, 180). This acceptance marks a straightforward event in the narrative, as does her reversal when she informs him "it would be better if you and I were never married" (S, 222), even if the precise reason for her decision is unclear (there are many good ones). However, her eventual, unnarrated acceptance of Gregory after all comes from a letter from the already-dead Lyndall—an unsent missive to Gregory that he finds in her desk after her death. The letter's choice—"You must marry Em" (S, 294)—that concludes the novel with an impending wedding is presented in the form of a command that was never intentionally issued. The multiple resolutions of this relationship—

as with the repetitious resolutions of Lyndall's bond with her lover—further disorganize without totally obscuring the more recognizable choice-driven events that constitute a marriage plot (where one refusal is followed by an acceptance, or one partner is substituted for another).

These profoundly flawed processes of courtship structure the novel even while Lyndall argues lucidly that marriage is an outmoded ideal. Thus both the novel's plot structures—*Bildung* and marriage—operate despite being everywhere discredited. The novel, then, not only disarticulates marriage from a progressive ideal of self-realization but also suggests a more profoundly troubled attitude toward human agency by distorting the timescale of the narrative event.

III. CAIRD

Mona Caird's essays, particularly "Marriage," which riled the British public when it appeared in the *Westminster Review* in 1888, are profoundly indebted to Mill's argument for the reinvigoration of choice as well as to Darwinian biology. Elsewhere, Caird casts contemporary marriage as slavery, arguing, "if it be in the interests of the race to deprive one half of it of all liberty of choice, to select for them their mode of existence and to prescribe for them their very sentiments."[44] With Mill, she rejects biological accounts of the past, but she breaks from his approach by using evolutionary thinking to envision a more equal future. However, her novel *The Daughters of Danaus* frames the question of women's capacity to choose whom or whether to marry as one of the relation between character and environment, an evolutionary orientation that subverts this optimism.

In the novel's opening, the Fullerton siblings discuss choice in their private debating club. The protagonist, Hadria, presents Emerson's idea that individuals form their own circumstances: Emerson writes, "But the soul contains the event that shall befall it, for the event is only the actualization of its thoughts; and what we pray to ourselves for is always granted. The event is the print of your form. It fits you like your skin. What each does is proper to him. Events are the children of his mind and body."[45] Emerson renders events the simultaneously biological and cultural manifestation of unique individuality. In Hadria's interpretation of Emerson, events function like instinct, working inevitably and unconsciously toward goals consciousness would endorse.

44. Caird, "A Defence of the 'Wild Women,'" *Morality of Marriage*, 159.

45. Quoted in Caird, *Daughters of Danaus*, 8. Hereafter abbreviated *D* and cited parenthetically in the text.

She opposes this doctrine, supporting the idea that "there is a subtle relation between character and conditions" (*D*, 10) by invoking Darwinian fitness when she complains about individuals—especially women—burdened by "parasites who are living on the moral capital of their generation." She claims, "There is nothing to prove that thousands have not been swamped by maladjustment of character to circumstance" (*D*, 12). Observing competition for resources, parasitism, and "adjustment" or adaptation, Hadria echoes the emphasis on networks of relation over individual choice. She also eliminates Emerson's term, "event," from her evaluation of his idea. In the quotation, outward events—changes of state—are immanent within the individual. But Hadria evokes lateral relations in which events are replaced by stasis, and inwardness becomes disconnected from outward actions. This perception feeds her critique of natural selection: "It is cunning, shallow, heartless women who fare best in our society; its conditions suit them. . . . *That* is the sort of 'woman's nature' that our conditions are busy selecting. . . . We live in a scientific age; the fittest survive" (*D*, 347). Suggesting the need for a force for change beyond natural selection, Hadria advocates cultural shift, affirming that "it is human *conditions*, not human nature, which constitute the difficulty" (*D*, 515), and suggesting, like Mill, that human nature cannot be evaluated biologically.

Yet Caird's own attitude toward evolution sometimes stressed the possibility of altering conditions. Her investment in evolutionary thinking appears in her essay "The Future of the Home," which observes that evolution does not preclude the human capacity to alter the behavior of the species. "Education is the sum of habits," she writes. "It is, in fact, the theory of evolution. Evolution! the word awes us." But eventually, this idea "will cease to mean for us a spirit more powerful than ourselves." A perspective oriented toward the future allows for greater trust in human agency, enabling further change: "*Belief in the power of man to choose his direction of change*:—this is the creed of the future, and it will soon come to be the distinctive mark of the essentially modern thinker."[46] By looking toward the future instead of the deep past, Caird suggests that evolution might be harnessed to changing the habits that accrete into instincts.

The evolution of women's roles constitutes a major topic of debate in this highly discursive novel; many of its pages are taken up by discussions among Hadria, her novelist-friend Miss Du Prel, and two Professors. When Du Prel and Professor Fortescue debate the social implications of natural selection, the latter (with whom Hadria sides) argues against a eugenic ideal of sacrificing the weak for the good of the race. Angelique Richardson notes that only Du

46. Caird, "The Future of the Home," *Morality of Marriage*, 115, 116.

Prel, an "ineffectual character," adheres to a strict concept of natural selection, suggesting that Caird aims to "satirize" this idea (*D*, 94).[47] Their fervent arguments structure much of the novel, centering around natural selection, maternal instincts, and the sovereignty of the will. Debate itself manifests the movement toward the social evolution Caird advocates, as when the Professor observes that their "own revolt against the brutality of Nature, was proof of some higher law in Nature, now in the course of development" (*D*, 102). The human capacity for critical reflection constitutes an underrecognized check on natural selection. Thus, Hadria can argue against the idea that women are instinctively meant to be mothers: she declares, "It gives me a keen, fierce pleasure to know that for all their training and constraining and incitement and starvation, I have *not* developed masses of treacly instinct, in which mind and will and every human faculty struggle, in vain, to move leg or wing, like some poor fly doomed to a sweet and sticky death" (*D*, 210). Hadria's own ability to reflect critically on instinct constitutes a more legitimate application of evolutionary thinking than citing women's "instinct." Thus these debates themselves—so central to the novel's conception—might be understood as constituting the narrative's primary "events" insofar as they might evolve the reader's own views.

Nonetheless, there is significant conflict between the ideas Hadria voices and evolutionary thinking at the level of the novel's subtly complex structure. As in *The Story of an African Farm,* the novel cannot be reduced to the argumentative content of discursive scenes. Caird's renderings of narrative events counter characters' most optimistic accounts of women's capacity to choose their future. Moments of sexual choice—especially choosing to engage rather than reject—are undernarrated, which implicitly makes them passive moves. Without even the explicitness that would highlight them as such, the novel reinforces the dissonance between the scope and scale of theory and the lived experience it tempers. In a cynical moment in her discussion of Emerson, Hadria imagines human life passively: "We just dance our reel in our garret, and then it is all over; and whether we do the steps as our fancy would have them, or a little otherwise, because of the uneven floor, or tired feet, or for lack of chance to earn the steps—heavens and earth, what does it matter?" (*D*, 13). The passage presages the narrative nonevent of her engagement to be married. Hadria has endured a flirtation with Hubert Temperley, who proposes at a dance while a reel is being played. The narrator reports, "The music was diabolically merry. She could fancy evil spirits tripping in swarms around her. They seemed to point at her, and wave their arms around her,

47. Richardson, "People," 188.

and from them came an influence, magnetic in its quality, that forbade her to resist. All had been pre-arranged. Nothing could avert it. She seemed to be waiting rather than acting" (*D*, 138–39). After rejecting the marriage "bond," Hadria tells Hubert "Let us go" and dances with another partner. Yet, by the end of the page, Hadria's siblings observe "that Hubert was again by Hadria's side before the evening was out. The latter looked white, and she avoided her sister's glance" (*D*, 143). The conditions of Hadria's acceptance go unnarrated here at the end of book 1, and by book 2 Hadria is miserably married, the mother of two sons. This compression of narrative time underlines how the elision of Hadria's choice resonates with her critique of agency. Similarly, Hadria's decision to leave her family and move to France to support herself goes unnarrated, whereas her return to England to care for her sick mother and sons is presented as an unavoidable occasion of self-sacrifice, a time when "her memories burnt, as corrosive acids, in her brain" (*D*, 456). The weight of the past forces her into a gendered paradigm she had rejected. This experience, which *is* narrated, leads her to doubt her freedom: "She was but an atom of the vast whole, a drop in the ocean of human life" (*D*, 457).

Though Hadria at times envisions "Images of the Past joined with visions of the Future" (*D*, 295), the narrator often gestures to the burden of evolutionary and personal history. Miss Du Prel argues, "The centuries are behind one, with all their weight of heredity and habit; the order of society adds its pressure—one's own emotional needs. Ah, no! it does not answer to pit oneself against one's race, to bid defiance to the fundamental laws of life" (*D*, 71). For Du Prel as for Darwin, it is difficult to disarticulate the concept of cultural habit from the biological force of inheritance because they mutually reinforce one another. Despite Caird's unflattering portrait of Du Prel, the novel as a whole appears to side with her by presenting the past as an ineluctable burden in representing Hadria's lengthy, bitter meditations on the determining force of biological *durée*. While dialogue produces one set of views, another emerges through free indirect discourse. Lyn Pykett observes that such meditative passages make it impossible to dismiss Caird's fiction as simply didactic: "One of the most important achievements . . . is [Caird's] sympathetic representation of the tormented and fractured female subject produced by the contradictions inherent in the ideology of the domestic, affective, feminine woman."[48] Hadria questions the agency of human beings: "After all, humanity was a puny production of the Ages. Men and women were like the struggling animalculae that her father had so often shown the boys, in a drop of magnified ditch-water; yet not quite like those microscopic insects for the stupen-

48. Pykett, "Cause of Women," 137.

dous processes of life had at last created a widening consciousness . . . which could, in some measure, get outside its own particular ditch, and the strife and struggle of it, groping upwards for larger realities" (*D*, 116). While she grants human intention a unique place in the vastness of "Ages" and imagines "struggle" occurring on an individual scale, she self-punishingly concludes that such efforts are futile in a social context that privileges stasis. She meditates, "Continue to wriggle industriously, O animalcule, in that particular ditch wherein it has pleased heaven to place thee" (*D*, 117). The passage's expansive style itself conjures the overwhelming force of the past while laying the groundwork for Hadria's acceptance of Hubert, who appears in the chapter's next section; Caird links taking the long view of the cultural marriage plot to the evaporation of choice.

When Hadria returns to England, she admits, "I believe that there are thousands and thousands of women whose lives have run on parallel lines with mine." This thought is connected with a remembered "waking-dream," underlining Hadria's sense of historical determinacy: a vision "of a vast abyss, black and silent, which had to be filled up to the top with the bodies of women, hurled down to the depths of the pit of darkness, in order that the survivors might, at last, walk over in safety" (*D*, 451). Although the passage proposes a future of survival, the bleak image of the mass grave makes clear the profound cost of evolutionary thinking by illustrating the historical scale that renders the individual life insignificant. Moreover, by suggesting that this image comes from a past reverie, Caird more deeply underlines the diminution of any woman's access to the active, present thought she usually deems necessary to achieve this future. Ledger observes of this passage that "Caird's negotiation of evolutionist discourses finally seems to defeat the powerful feminist vision of her fiction."[49] But we might instead understand the novel's oscillation between Hadria's fervor and a narrative structure that undermines her agency as suggesting a kind of ambivalence about the novel's own force as a tool for securing the desirable evolutionary future of safety, choice, and freedom. After all, Du Prel writes novels about liberated women, but adheres to a more fatalistic view for herself and for Hadria. As "meta-fiction" the novel suggests that fiction's reimagination of women's lives is not sufficient to alter social realities, as Ledger acknowledges; Richardson identifies this as a "homeopathic" model of writing, which "leads [Caird] to describe what was, rather than what ought to be, in her novels."[50] This check on what a novel can accomplish, then, implies also that a novel's narrative form, particularly its capacity to evoke temporal

---

49. Ledger, *The New Woman,* 30.
50. Ibid., 28; Richardson, "People," 206.

vastness alongside the compressed time of individual compulsion, is more complex than simply animating or critiquing a scientific theory.

IV. CONCLUSION

In these novels, regenerating women's power of choice means that they might not choose marriage at all. In *The Story of an African Farm* and *The Daughters of Danaus,* marriage appears unworkably oppressive, but those who theorize alternatives are not empowered to pursue them—an outcome that implies ambivalence toward theorization itself. Although both novelists were committed to conceiving the politics of gender through a scientific lens, their fiction cannot be understood to reinvigorate female choice in the wake of *The Descent of Man.* Choice itself appears an idealized concept for both men and women; it is often invoked but rarely demonstrated.

Their uncertainty about the possibility of choice also has a further implication, an alternative to the idea that late Victorian marriage plots could be understood as either affirming or critiquing Darwin's concept of sexual selection. Though many treatments of their work have considered their relationship to science that way, to see the relationship between literature and science as either for or against evolutionary thought is to make science the privileged discourse. This approach would flatten the aesthetic dimensions of their ambivalence toward sexual agency. Their novels' formal strategies are more complex than adherence to the scope of the individual lifetime would demand; the experimental use of multiple, conflicting timescales pulls against the female protagonists' desires for freedom. These writers' sense of the diminution of individual agency certainly reflects a mode of expansive thinking instigated by evolutionary thought and particularly the framework of natural selection. Nonetheless, they cannot therefore be said to side with natural selection at the expense of sexual selection. Rather, both Caird and Schreiner produce works that innovate formally in conversation with scientific concepts, even while their plots are not determined by them. In other words, their novels refrain from presenting a singular, scientifically valid stance at all; instead, their experimental forms present a complexly negative account of contemporary marriage.

CHAPTER 3

Mythic Marriage

Haggard, Frazer, Hardy, and the Anthropology of Myth

KATHY PSOMIADES

MARRIAGE IS CENTRAL to the nineteenth-century novel, both as subject matter and as structure. But beginning in the 1860s, a new kind of writing appeared that also took marriage as its content and structure: Victorian anthropology. At the point at which the laws that subsumed married women's economic and legal identity into their husbands' were beginning to seem like the remnants (as John Stuart Mill and legal theorist Henry Maine claimed) of a much older form of social organization, John McLennan's *Primitive Marriage* (1865) took marriage and family out of nature and into culture.[1] Patriarchy was no longer the natural order of things: there must have been a time when fathers did not exist, a universal period of matrilineage and polyandry. The old liberal story of how an original state of constant warfare gave way with the development of private property to increasingly ordered and cooperative relations was now also a story about gender and sexuality. The original violence was sexual violence; the original property was sexual property; the original forms of social organization were sexual forms of organization. From disorganized sex to stealing other people's women, through promiscuous polyandry to patriarchal tyranny to modern egalitarian monogamous marriage, social organization was the organization of sexual activity and gender relations.[2] McLennan

1. See Mill's "On the Subjection of Women" and Maine's *Ancient Law.*

2. Some writers of the Scottish Enlightenment included marriage in progressive narratives of the development of civil society. John Millar and Henry Home, Lord Kames made the status

gave a marriage plot to the story of the foundation of society and its progress towards civilization.

The 1860s and 1870s saw a rich cross-conversation between anthropology and the novel on these issues.[3] Realist novelists like Anthony Trollope and George Eliot drew upon anthropological concepts to think about economic and political agency in post–Reform Bill modernity. Anthropological theories of marriage gave novelistic marriage plots new meaning when they gave marriage a long global history and recast gender relations as variable over time and space, rather than fixed by divine authorization or a single law of nature.

By the 1880s, however, both realism and realist marriage plots were at the center of public debate about what the novel should be. In the periodical press, writers like Henry James, William Dean Howells, Andrew Lang, H. Rider Haggard, and Thomas Hardy debated genre and gender.[4] One significant strand of argument chafed against the limitations imposed on subject matter by the respectable periodicals and lending libraries, seeing the marriage plot as a restrictive control on writing about sexuality.[5] Another suggested that the problem with realism was that it was too girly: realist marriage plots require that readers spend too long a time in the narrow confines of feminine interiority (and not the fun kind) and preclude the great masculine epic and romance plots of heroic action and adventure.[6] The question of what

---

of women the measure of civilization but considered patriarchy to be natural and reported cases of matrilineage exceptional. For more on the theory of matrilineage, see Eller, *Gentlemen and Amazons.*

3. Elsie Michie (*The Vulgar Question of Money*) and Supritha Rajan (*A Tale of Two Capitalisms*) have both showed how anthropological theories of kinship and realist marriage plots bring gender and economics together to think through capitalist modernity. Sara Maurer (*The Dispossessed State*) has demonstrated how Trollope's Palliser series draws upon Mainian anthropological ideas about communal property to use marriage to think about the political relations of empire. And I ("*He Knew He Was Right*") have read Trollope's *He Knew He Was Right* in light of a language of tyranny and consent common to marriage and politics alike around 1867.

4. This debate in England begins in 1882, with an essay by William Dean Howells on Henry James and one by Robert Louis Stephenson on romance, and continues throughout the 1880s and even into the 1890s, with Walter Besant's 1884 lecture "The Art of Fiction," which set off Andrew Lang, James himself, and a series of periodical conversations among which I would include Haggard's "About Fiction" and Hardy's 1891 essay on "The Science of Fiction." For more on this debate, see Spilka, "Henry James and Walter Besant."

5. Haggard, "About Fiction." Hardy, "Candour in English Fiction."

6. Lang's "Realism and Romance," as we shall see, deals with these concerns directly, and lends itself to Elaine Showalter's claim that the turn to romance was part of "a men's literary revolution intended to reclaim the kingdom of the English novel for male writers, male readers, and men's stories." *Sexual Anarchy*, 79.

fiction ought to be like was inextricably caught up in the question of how gender and sexual relations ought to be represented.

It is in this environment that, between 1886 and 1891, a new plot emerges alongside a new genre and a new theory of genre. It is both an anthropological and a literary plot, and it emerges not out of the anthropology of marriage but out of the anthropology of myth. The outlines of the plot are simple: there is a goddess—a fertility goddess in that she is defined by her desirable body and by the connection of that body to a sexualized landscape. The goddess has a lover, at least partly mortal, less powerful than she is, subjected by his desire for her. This desire is perilous for him; it will result in him being killed, his blood being spilt, his body being returned to the earth. He will rise again, or another mortal lover will replace him. In the end, the goddess herself will be destroyed. She will wittingly or unwittingly give herself up to be sacrificed, but being immortal, she may also return, and the plot begins again. In this plot, "marriage" means the sexual union of the goddess and her mortal or part-mortal lover and the bloodshed that inevitably follows.

Unlike even the disastrous realist marriage plots, the mythic plot doesn't involve courtship, the choice of suitors, or the negotiation of a marriage market; nor does it employ the gothic tropes of masculine tyranny, mad aristocrats, and imperiled heroines. The goddess is a little like a sensation-fiction femme fatale, but the death of her lover is due to forces outside her, an agency that at best works through her, rather than the result of her own plan. The mythic plot is an old plot: it comes out of classical mythology (Venus and Adonis, Diana and Actaeon, Cybele and Attis, Isis and Osirus), and versions of it appear in poetry well before the onset of anthropology. It is the plot behind those stories about goddesses and their mortal lovers that populate the poetry of Keats ("Endymion"), Tennyson ("Tithonus"), and Swinburne ("Laus Veneris") and that appear in the anthropological era in Walter Pater's writing, often in same-sex versions (Demeter and Persephone, Apollo and Hyacinth). What makes it a marriage plot is its appearance in novels and in the context of the 1880s realism conversation in which the realist marriage plot and the problem of representing sex figure largely. The goddess plot is only one of many mythic sex plots, but it becomes at this particular juncture the marriage plot's other and double, the plot around which a new conception of art begins to formulate itself.

I focus here on three texts written between 1886 and 1901 that foreground the plot of mythic marriage—H. Rider Haggard's *She* (1886–87), James Frazer's first, two-volume version of *The Golden Bough* (1890), and Thomas Hardy's *Tess of the d'Urbervilles* (1891). Historically, critics have read the turn to myth in all three of these writers as a mode of mystification. *She*, for example, has famously been read by feminist critics Elaine Showalter and Sandra Gilbert and Susan Gubar as an expression of masculine anxiety about and aggression against late Victorian feminism and the dominance of the late Victorian literary market by women writers and readers.[7] For Laura Chrisman and Anne McClintock, the anxiety and aggression wasn't just about women but about race and imperialism. The larger-than-life nonrealist body with its magical strengths and abilities could contain a whole range of psychosexual and political projections, and its violent destruction could be triumphant in ways in which the destruction of a realist heroine could not be.[8] Similarly, the mythic references in Hardy's novel seem connected to aesthetic/erotic appeal of the heroine's body, which displaces/confuses/problematizes the material conditions of her existence as industrial laborer.[9] Caught in a conventional dynamic of heterosexual romance, Angel calls Tess by the names of goddesses, erasing her specificity by transforming her into an avatar of the eternal feminine. When Hardy has her respond "Call me Tess," he calls our attention to the problematic nature of Angel's desire and mythic imagination and has Tess request a return to the realist mode. Finally, Catherine Gallagher has read Frazer as the writer of mythic version of Thomas Malthus's *Essay on the Principles of Population*: Frazer's myth of the goddess and the rituals that myth narrativizes turn Malthus's dilemma about population and food supply into a universal given of human culture.[10] Myth, in all these readings, is a turn away not just from realism but from the real itself: it masks real sexual, racial, and class politics with imaginary universal biopolitical imperatives.

My reading here is not so much an alternative to these readings as a supplement. Myth certainly does a lot of ideological work for all three of these

7. Elaine Showalter explicitly characterizes masculine romance as a replacement for "the heterosexual romance of courtship, manners and marriage" (*Sexual Anarchy*, 79). Gilbert and Gubar see *She* as addressing "a complex of late-Victorian anxieties" (*No Man's Land*, 7).

8. Chrisman ("The Imperial Unconscious?") points out the ways in which Ayesha's power figures anxieties about the excesses of British imperial power and yet contains and defuses those anxieties. McClintock doesn't read *She* in *Imperial Leather*, but she does read *King Solomon's Mines* in light of the material realities of women's labor in South Africa.

9. Key classic feminist readings of *Tess* include Mary Jacobus, "Tess: The Making of a Pure Woman"; Kaja Silverman, "History, Figuration and Female Subjectivity in *Tess of the d'Urbervilles*"; Penny Boumelha, *Thomas Hardy and Woman*; and Ellen Rooney, "Tess and the Subject of Sexual Violence." Two more recent articles on Tess that seek to explicate formal features of Hardy's realism by reference to material historical reality are Jessica Martell, "The Dorset Dairy, the Pastoral and Thomas Hardy's *Tess of the d'Urbervilles*," and Zena Meadowsong, "Thomas Hardy and the Machine: The Mechanical Deformation of Narrative Realism in *Tess of the d'Urbervilles*."

10. See Gallagher's "*Tess of the d'Urbervilles*: Hardy's Anthropology of the Novel" and her *The Body Economic*.

writers, but it also does some important theoretical work, theoretical work in which we, as twenty-first-century readers of marriage plots, are still engaged. In the 1880s and 1890s, the myth of the goddess was intimately connected to questions about representation and interpretation. *She*, *The Golden Bough*, and *Tess of the d'Urbervilles* all directly address the question "What does it mean to represent sexual activity in narrative form?" The goddess story references not just Greek myth but myth as it is coming to be understood in anthropology in a much broader spatial and temporal context, a context that primitivizes the Greeks but also sees their stories connected up to similar stories across the globe as examples of a larger universal stage of culture. In both late Victorian anthropology and the late Victorian novel, mythic marriage marks a turn from theories about marriage as social structure to theories about marriage as genre and representation. McLennan's *Primitive Marriage* gave sexual relations a fantastic prehistory; anthropological mythic marriage gave a prehistory to the *representation* of sexual relations.

All three texts I discuss here tell the story I've outlined above: the story of the goddess and her lover, the shedding of that lover's blood, the death of the goddess herself. All three tell that story as a repetitive story that transcends historical time and geographical space. For all three, the goddess story moves between genres, gestures towards an archaic mythic space, on one hand, and a modern realist world, on the other. All three texts move back and forth between temporal and generic layers of meaning—between contemporary material places, things, and practices, and archaic magical tales; all three position a bourgeois intellectual subject in an archaic plot he must witness and interpret. For all three, Victorian anthropology of marriage and Victorian anthropology of myth come together to create a new way of thinking about realism's old double and other, "romance." The new romance is anthropological romance: the word "romance" no longer denotes the common features of narratives produced at moments in the historical past, but rather the process whereby a global, prehistoric story makes itself visible in a specific modern present. Romance becomes a form of mediation between an archaic realm of "mythic" meaning, based in human experience of natural phenomena, and a realist world of contemporary individuals and social structures. Haggard, Frazer, and Hardy all locate their difference from Victorian realism in how they represent sex. But the mythic marriage plot goes further—not only does it replace the realist marriage plot whose other it claims to be, it also announces itself as the origin of that plot and thus its explanation. The mythic marriage plot of anthropological romance makes the representation of sex central to the production of culture; it turns the marriage plot into a late, attenuated version of itself.

I. H. RIDER HAGGARD'S *SHE*: GODDESSES AND GLADSTONE BAGS

The study of myth by no means begins with Victorian anthropology: the problem of what myths mean has been addressed repeatedly since the time of the pre-Socratic philosophers. But the evolutionary anthropology of myth begins with Edward Tylor's *Primitive Culture* (1871). As introduced and practiced by Tylor, Victorian anthropology saw myth as a theory of the universe, a kind of primitive scientific explanation of how the world worked, shaped by primitive man's notion of animism, or the idea that everything has a soul. What seemed like poetic metaphor-making was really primitive man's literal understanding of how things worked: divorced from their original moment of production, his theories travel through time and come to seem like metaphors, poetry, or mystic utterances. As Herbert Spencer says, when the Orinoco say that dew is "the spittle of the stars," they aren't being poetic; they really literally mean that the stars are spitting.[11] Primitive man is a realist whose limited knowledge base gives rise to what only seems to be a fantastic theory of how the world works, but is really a kind of primitive scientific realism.[12]

Tylor's work was important to all three writers of the goddess plot and widely disseminated in the periodical press thanks to Andrew Lang, prolific writer of poetry, anthropology, and literary criticism, and friend and champion of Haggard and his work. Lang supported Tylor's theory against the philological theory of myth put forward by F. Max Müller. Müller's theory was more romantic and idealistic: behind myth was the primitive intimation of the divine through the wonder of nature, a perception of the ideal inexpressible in the insistent materiality of language. When primitive man gave his gods sky names, it was because the infinite overarching nature of the sky was something he wanted to attribute to them, but only having the language for concrete and not abstract things, he had to use the word for the most similar concrete thing. In other words, for Müller, a sky god or sun god arose because

11. Spencer, *Principles of Sociology* 1.i.102. This interpretation says more about Spencer's literal-mindedness than the thought of the Orinoco: "Observe the genesis of this belief. Dew is a clear liquid to which saliva has some resemblance. It is a liquid which, lying on leaves, etc., seems to have descended from above, as saliva descends from the mouth of one who spits. Having descended during a cloudless night, it must have come from the only things then visible above; namely, the stars. Thus the product itself, dew, and the relation between it and its supposed source, are respectively assimilated with those like them in obvious characters; and we need but recall our own common expression 'it spits with rain,' to see how natural is the interpretation" (102–3).

12. For a more detailed discussion of Tylor, Müller, Lang, and myth, see Psomiades, "Hidden Meaning."

primitive man was attempting to express the ineffable grandeur of divinity, whereas for Tylor a sky or sun god arose because primitive man was trying to explain astronomy. For Müller, primitive man was a poet/mystic whose language was inadequate to his perceptions; for Tylor, he was a scientist/theorist working with inadequate data and technology. For Müller, interpretation meant remetaphorizing what language and time had made concrete, in order to make it make sense; for Tylor, interpretation meant literalizing what modernity had come to see as metaphor.

These debates, which Lang, the dedicatee of *She* for "his learning and his works," popularized in the 1870s and '80s, foregrounded the question of interpretation, as well as the question of literal versus metaphoric reference. When Haggard begins his novel with the editor's tongue-in-cheek meditations on what Holly's story can possibly mean (Is it a gigantic allegory? A scientific speculation on what the effects of extreme longevity might be? Or just actually, really true?), he sets the story's own metaphorizations and literalizations in the context of this larger theoretical set of concerns about interpretation. By making She literally two thousand years old, a body whose mysteriousness comes from its removal from its original temporal context, he makes her not only a goddess but a literalization of what Tylor called "a survival"—a cultural feature whose temporal dissonance with the rest of the culture makes it seem mysterious and inexplicable, but which becomes logical once its temporal dissonance is exposed and the logic of the moment in which it was produced is reconstituted. And by setting that body in the double context of classical mythology and an imaginary contemporary Africa, Haggard draws upon the comparativism that put the classical past into a broader spatial and temporal context. For survivals point not only to their own particular pasts but to a universal past that constitutes a common human condition. Furthermore, Haggard self-consciously constructs his own work as having a special relationship to this past, and as mediating between mythic past and realist present.

The anthropological theory of literature implicit in Tylor's theory of myth is made explicit in Lang's 1887 essay "Realism and Romance": books like *She* are valuable because they are survivals that appeal to the savage who survives within, "the natural man within me, the survival of some blue-painted Briton or of some gipsy."[13] Lang applies Tylor's word—"survival"—both to romances and to their readers:

> The advantage of our mixed condition, civilized at top with the old barbarian under our clothes, is just this, that we can enjoy all sorts of things. . . . Do not

13. Lang, "Realism and Romance," 689.

> let us cry that, because we are "cultured," there shall be no Buffalo Bill. . . . If we will only be tolerant, we shall permit the great public also to delight in our few modern romances of adventure. They may be "savage survivals," but so is the whole of the poetic way of regarding Nature.[14]

Stories like *She* seem wild and fanciful now, but their value and meaning are revealed when we see them as temporally dissonant forms that appeal to readers who are themselves temporally dissonant subjects, containing in their bodies both personal past selves (the child) and historical past selves (the primitive). This is a theory of genre as a kind of temporal dislocation. Lang expresses this dislocation in the same way Haggard does, by the jarring juxtaposition of realist characters and events and nonrealist ones—juxtapositions that foreground the fantastic as an anomalous feature in a realist world:

> The dubitations of a Bostonian spinster may be made as interesting, by one genius, as a fight between a crocodile and a catawampus, by another genius. One may be as much excited in trying to discover whom a married American lady is really in love with, as by the search for the Fire of Immortality in the heart of Africa.[15]

Feminine interiority, connected up to realist variations on the marriage plot here (the Boston marriage plot of James's *Bostonians*, the almost-adultery plot of Francis Hodgson Burnett's *Under One Administration*) is the other to masculine adventures. Realism is the realm of girls and girly men, romance the province of masculine savages who allow for the survival of masculinity. But notice that Lang doesn't just contrast these modes, he also connects them: external literal battle (crocodile and catawampus) becomes internal figurative battle (spinster's dubitations), external quest in the metaphorical "heart" of Africa becomes internal quest in the heart of the married lady. This is a theory of genre that takes the same shape as Tylor's theory of myth: the literal becomes metaphorical, interest in conflict and discovery moves from the world of action to the world of thought. Realist marriage plots are late, cerebral, figurative versions of older, earthier plots of literal battle and quest.

The story of the goddess is not a core story for either Müller or Tylor: Müller's gods are sky gods; Tylor is more interested in how savages (presumed male) think or don't think like scientists (ditto). In order for myth to be useful to the novel, in order for the new romance to articulate its relation to realist fiction, the anthropology of myth needs to be sexualized. For Haggard and

14. Ibid., 690.
15. Ibid., 693.

Lang, writing novels and writing about novels, sexuality and gender are central to the question of genre and interpretation. We may associate Haggard primarily with King Romance today, but his capacious oeuvre is overrun with heroines whose melodramatic marriage plots are operatic in their sheer soapiness (take, for example, *Belinda,* in which all the elements of *She*—including a gigantic, beautiful, intellectual atheist who sacrifices herself for the man she loves, and a woman who conveniently burns up—are rearranged into a realist adultery plot so over-the-top that even the narrator seems bemused by it). For Haggard, in other words, the common story of myth, romance, and realism is a sex story. Or, as Haggard himself puts it in 1887, in gloriously mixed metaphors: "Sexual passion is the most powerful lever with which to stir the mind of man, for it lies at the root of all things human."[16]

She begins in a realist, if somewhat gothic, England, with a family history that is also an imperial history, and that entails the passage through time of a story of a priest of Isis who abandons his vows to marry, only to find himself caught between his wife and a magical lady whose desire for him proves deadly to him. The fantastic nature of the tale seems explicable by reference to its historical origins; the failures of successive Vinceys to replicate it would seem to prove its fictionality. When Holly and Leo finally get to Africa, they first meet not a supernatural lady but a set of imaginary savages, who immediately involve them in a primitive marriage plot. Holly's narration of the marriage customs and matrilineal social structure of the Amahagger copies and parodies the language of Victorian ethnographers, as the "marriage" between Amahagger Ustane and British Leo echoes both exotic marriage plots and the plot of imperial conquest as consensual marriage.[17] Leo's name underscores his status as representative of Britain (the Lion is featured on the Royal Arms) and goes along with his blond curls. We are in a made-up world here, but ultimately a realist one: even Ustane has a realist imagination. She does not believe that her queen is an immortal being, but rather that successive queens secretly take mortal lovers to produce the daughters that will replace them. In this reading, the legend that She is two thousand years old is both propaganda for and a metaphorical displacement of the literal truth of a two-thousand-year-old matrilineal bloodline.

The realist imagination, however, is wrong. She IS her own literal truth. And once She appears on the scene, the anthropology of myth replaces the anthropology of marriage. References to goddesses and their lovers begin to proliferate. When Holly asks to see her face, She replies, "It seems that thou

16. Haggard, "About Fiction," 176.

17. For a perceptive recent reading of *She* as a critical engagement with Victorian matriarchal theory, see Julia Reid, "'She-who-must-be-obeyed.'"

knowest the old myths of the gods of Greece. Was there not one Actaeon who perished miserably because he looked on too much beauty?"[18] She goes on to draw the parallel insistently, likening herself to Diana: "I too, oh Holly, am a virgin goddess, not to be moved of any man, save one, and it is not thou."[19] Holly, however, thinks of her as a Venus Victrix. She also resembles the goddess whom Kallikrates once served: as critics have noted, She participates in the trope of veiled Isis common in Greek prose romance and referenced by Madame Blavatsky in the recently published *Isis Unveiled.*[20] She is thus not like any one goddess but like all of them, and in being like all of them she connects all of their stories together as versions of each other's and of her own. All these stories make Leo into Kallikrates, whose name means "beautiful strength" and thus describes not his character or political significance but his body. The mythic plot erases the features of choice, consent, agency that mark the realist marriage plot: *She* doesn't reflect on the relative virtues of the decorative brainless Leo and the far smarter Holly; Leo doesn't have a choice to make between her and Ustane; even Holly can't choose whether he wants to be her rival for Leo, or her lover. The mythic plot drives the union of bodies that have been united before. The stabbing of Kallikrates is a moment of sexual violence that She wishes to revise into a happy sexual moment but that She winds up recapitulating in her own death by rosy pillar. The lever that lies at the root of all things human can, apparently, kill you.

In *She* sex is not the key to social structure but the secret of life. The fundamental joke of the novel is that the high and elevated secret of life is really the actual, literal secret of life—sex and reproduction. The body of the goddess is both a symbol and a literal body. The novel works itself around her body, taking the editor's speculations about the book itself being "a giant allegory" and providing an actually gigantic allegorical statue of a veiled goddess, Truth, to embody that idea. The statue suggests that goddesses are impersonations of abstract concepts, that their naked bodies are ideas, not flesh, that their veiling and unveiling are about knowledge and not about sex. It seems to mark a moment at which the text interprets itself—the statue should help you to see the high meaning of *She.* But then Holly undercuts that argument by connecting She to the goddess statue metonymically, rather than metaphorically: maybe She got the idea to veil herself from the statue. Maybe She's just copying the physical act of veiling for her own practical ends; maybe a veil is just, literally, a veil and not a trope at all. Similarly, this resemblance is both

18. Haggard, *She,* 154.

19. Ibid., 156.

20. For more on *She,* Isis, and Greek and Egyptian prose romance, see Vinson, "They-Who-Must-Be-Obeyed."

a joke about interpretation and a dirty joke to remind us that, veil or no veil, what we've got here is naked ladies.[21] Moving between metaphorical and literal meaning, high mythic/biblical language and low realist references, past and present, Haggard's literary practice redefines romance as the movement back and forth between these extremes. This is the romance that Northrop Frye will describe some seventy years later as "suggest[ing] implicit mythical patterns in a world more closely associated with human experience."[22] The goddess and novel heroine converge; the secret of life is both magical and sexual, both supernatural and smutty.

And indeed this takes us to Haggard's "About Fiction," where yet another statue of a naked goddess appears to pose an answer to the problem of how novelists ought to represent sex in the present day. American, British, and French fiction, Haggard argues, all have problems: American heroines have too much interiority, the French have too much sex, the British are conventional and insipid. What is needed is a new way of talking about sexual passion:

> Art in the purity of its idealized truth should resemble some perfect Grecian statue. It should be cold but naked, and looking thereon men should be led to think of naught but beauty. Here, however, we attire Art in every sort of dress, some of them suggestive enough in their own way, but for the most part in a pinafore. The difference between literary Art, as the present writer submits it ought to be, and the Naturalistic Art of France is the difference between the Venus of Milo and an obscene photograph taken from the life. It seems probable that the English-speaking people will in course of time have to choose between the two.[23]

Haggard conflates how the erotic female body is represented in art with art itself—he turns art into a version of the female body it represents. The Venus

21. For the pornographic aspect of Haggard's imagination, see Scheick, "Adolescent Pornography and Imperialism."

22. Frye, *Anatomy of Criticism*, 139–40. You might argue that romance always does this. The Quixote plots of the eighteenth century, the comic gothic fictions of the early nineteenth—they stage the encounter between the idealist or fantastic world produced by nonrealist genres and a realist world by making their heroes or heroines misread the realist world through extra-realist codes. But anthropological romance is different—it is not about the dangers of mistaking the fantastic for the real, but about the common roots of real and the fantastic in the fantastic. The fantastic, in this model, is the real of the past. I quote Frye here to point to the historical specificity of his theory of genre—he is often invoked in criticism of Haggard's work in order to define the genre of romance, but that very definition of romance comes out of the anthropological theory of myth in which Haggard participates and that he helps create.

23. Haggard, "About Fiction," 170.

de Milo is a less "realist" representation of the erotic body than the pornographic photograph—the difference in genre is also a difference in time here—the classical past/modernity. But the pinafore motif suggests that British domestic fiction is not radically other to the statue but based on the statue—covered over in time with fig leaves. What links all the representations is sex—covered or uncovered, hot or cold, idealized or real. The marriage plot and pornography are modern, debased, forms of the old mythic story.

II. JAMES FRAZER'S *THE GOLDEN BOUGH*: MYTH AND RITUAL

Like Haggard's *She*, Frazer's 1890 *Golden Bough* tells the story of the goddess and her doomed lover or lovers.[24] And like Haggard's novel, Frazer's book tells the story of the intellectual who makes sense out of the goddess's story, who searches for meaning, who discovers the "secret" that lies behind appearances. In Haggard's novel, Holly witnesses and analyzes the story of She and Kallikrates/Leo: he is part of the apparatus that allows Haggard not only to stage his version of the goddess story but also to constitute that story as an object of theoretical inquiry. Unlike the sacrificed lover, the scholar confronts the phenomena of mythic sex and death with an intellectual apparatus that explicates but does not exhaust them. And just as Holly is aware that he is compromised, that his identity as scholar is not really separable from his status as lover/victim, so Frazer himself in *The Golden Bough* is aware that his own critical methodology—of creating meaning by piling up similitudes, making causal connections between structurally similar things—is not all that different from the methodologies of magic that he claims produce ritual sacrifice.[25]

Like Holly and Leo, Frazer's narrator seeks to discover a secret connected to a goddess: Diana. Like She, Diana is connected to a particular place and landscape: her shrine at Nemi. Like She, Diana is connected to the secret of life: she is the goddess of childbirth. Like She also, she has a lover—Virbius/Hypolitus—who manages to get slain. Her rites also involve fire. Frazer's book seeks to explain a classical legend about her priests, as he wrote to his publisher, George Macmillan:

24. Monsman ("Of Diamonds and Deities"), Hilton ("Andrew Lang, Comparative Anthropology and the Classics"), and Hinz ("Rider Haggard's *She*") all read Haggard's *She* as anticipating *The Golden Bough*. Archetypal readings of *She* come out of the theoretical tradition that Victorian anthropological romance enables.

25. The reading of Frazer that seems to me to take most account of his self-consciousness about the fragmentary provisional nature of his own enterprise is Christopher Herbert's in *Victorian Relativity*, 180–226.

> According to Servius the Golden Bough grew on a certain tree in the sacred grove of Diana at Aricia, and the priesthood of the grove was held by the man who succeeded in breaking off the Golden Bough and then slaying the priest in single combat. By an application of the Comparative Method I believe that I can make it probable that the priest represented the god of the grove—Virbius—and that his slaughter was regarded as the death of the god.[26]

Like Haggard, Frazer begins with writing from the classical period, with texts that tell a fantastic and mysterious story. Like Haggard, he cannot solve the mystery of this plot with reference to classical texts and locations alone; he must go to Africa and to other "primitive" cultures with the Comparative Method, to uncover the meaning of rites that seem out of place in their own time. Famously, Frazer conceives of his work as having a plot, like a novel—he writes to Macmillan that he doesn't want a detailed table of contents, which would be "like the mistake of a novelist who should prefix a summary of the plot to his novel."[27] As John Vickery put it in *The Literary Impact of "The Golden Bough,"* the work is "less a compendium of facts than a gigantic romance of quest cast in the form of objective research."[28]

Haggard's novel sexes up Tylorian myth by literalizing the concept of survival in female form. Frazer sexes up myth by bringing to it the concerns with originary sex and violence that structured the anthropology of marriage.[29] What Frazer did, when he explained the slain priests by reference to a global network of similar myths and practices, was to turn myth into an aspect of fertility ritual.[30] In the first edition, he seems to have been more interested in the slain god/man for reasons having to do with the obvious question of what the idea of ritual fertility sacrifice does to Christianity. But the Goddess is a necessary part of the story, because it is she who makes the slaying of the god/man into an act of sexual significance. In later editions, Frazer would tie the

26. Frazer, Letter, November 1890, quoted in Fraser, *The Making of "The Golden Bough,"* 52.

27. Frazer, Letter, March 1890, quoted in ibid., 54.

28. Vickery, *The Literary Impact of "The Golden Bough,"* 128.

29. John McLennan's matrilineal theory structured the work of Frazer's mentor and inspiration, W. Robertson Smith, whose *Kinship and Marriage in Early Arabia* (1885) found evidence of pre-patriarchal matrilineal cultures in the Middle East. In "The Worship of Plants and Animals," McLennan himself had connected matrilineage to primitive totem rituals—though that connection seemed merely to consist in the ideas that totems delineated matrilineal groups, that they were expressive of matrilineal social relations.

30. Pamela Gilbert has pointed out to me that he certainly is not the first to locate the origins of religion in fertility rituals. Richard Payne Knight's *Discourse on the Worship of Priapus* (1786) is perhaps the most famous early instance of that claim, and was still being republished and read in the late nineteenth century.

existence of the goddess to matrilineal cultures, and elaborate more on how goddesses preceded gods historically.[31] Even in the first edition, however, what the Tylorian savage seeks to get at, both with his rituals and with his myths, is precisely Haggard's "secret of life."

Just as Haggard's novel moves away from the problems of social organization towards an archaic elemental body tied to natural landscape, so too does Frazer's anthropology move gender and sexual relations out of the context of primitive social relations and into mythic gendered bodies tied to nature and natural landscapes. In the process, he moves the problem of sexual violence out of the realm of sexual politics and into the realm of representation. McLennan's progressive story had paralleled progress away from violent sexual relations with progress away from other kinds of violent hierarchical social relations. The Frazerian problem is the problem of interpreting a sexualized violence that is itself a representation, a product of culture. Like Haggard, Frazer is interested in the question of the metaphoric and the literal: he imagines a Tylorian world in which primitive man seeks to control nature by manipulating what he thinks are literal causal connections between similar things—having sex in a certain way will make the crops grow, symbolically killing and resurrecting a god will ensure the return of light/life, and so forth. Of course we know these connections are perceptions of similar structure, not literal connections—human fertility is only *like* the fertility of plants, the disappearance and return of the sun is only *like* the disappearance and return of a person. But Frazer does not exempt his own perceptions of similitude as connection from the possibility that they may signal only similitude and not connection at all. "After all," he famously says as he stresses the likeness of modern and primitive science, "what we call truth is only the hypothesis which is found to work best."[32]

What Frazer adds to the Müller/Tylor problematic of literal and metaphoric meaning in myth is the idea of ritual. For Müller and Tylor, myths are about how primitive man perceives—how he perceives the divine, for Müller, and how he perceives nature, for Tylor. For Frazer, myths are not religious perception or a theory of the universe but the attempt to interpret, by narrativizing, the cultural acts of ritual. Priests do not get slain in Diana's grove to commemorate the slaying of Hypolitus/Virbius; rather the story of Diana and Hypolitus is a narrative explanation and reorganization of ritual acts, one that makes sex and violence into plot events enacted by characters. The story of Diana and Hypolitus isn't a theory about why plants grow, are harvested,

31. The third edition contains a chapter on mother kin and mother goddesses. For more on McLennan, Smith, and Frazer, see Fraser, *The Making of "The Golden Bough."*

32. Frazer, *Golden Bough,* I.212.

die off, return again; it is a narrative version of the ritual that ascribes mythic meaning to that ritual. The poetic concern with metaphoric and literal language gives way to a concern with narrative and genre. In a way, ritual and myth are two different genres circling around the same acts—in ritual the Darwinian/Malthusian acts, fucking and killing, are removed from animal instinct and become human and cultural simply by being repeated in ways that do not have anything directly to do with individual survival.[33] Culture originates when you do natural things in unnatural ways, not out of passion, not out of an immediate struggle to survive, but in ways that render natural acts symbolic. In myth, symbolic sex and violence become features in stories about the gods—they generate narrative art. In a way, then, ritual is a nonnarrative genre, a kind of lyric repetition. But in another way, ritual, like romance, bridges the mythic and the real: it generates a mythic narrative on one hand, and enacts concrete activity in the real world on the other.

Like the anthropologists of marriage and kinship, then, Frazer begins his anthropology of myth with sex and violence. For the Victorian anthropologists of kinship, culture is the organization of sex and violence in social structure, the setting up of systems that indicate who you can have sex with and who you can kill, who is part of your group and who is not, who is and is not blood. Both violence and sexual violence in this theory are part of a progressive narrative that moves from force to consent as the basis for social organization. Frazer's anthropology of myth is also about organizing sex and violence, but it is about organizing them by making them symbolic, first by simply doing them repeatedly in a different way, then by turning them into narrative. Just as Haggard's repetitions of the mythic plot work against a model of the subject as agential individual, so too does Frazer's larger structure suggest that myth and ritual have an agency of their own. The actions of the priest of the grove are not instinctive natural actions, but neither are they the actions of individual will and choice. Rather they are representational actions that gather meaning and force from a vast crowd of such actions over space and time. The concept of ritual produces a nonrealist nonindividualist version of cultural action and agency.[34]

---

33. Gallagher sees Frazerian ritual as putting the Malthusian project of regulating population in relation to food supply at the origins of culture itself. For her, ritual sex and sacrifice are all about keeping the number of humans and the amount of food in proper ratio, in a magical way, "the Malthusian obsession with fertility metamorphosed into a theory of the symbolic." *The Body Economic*, 172.

34. As Von Hendy points out, Frazer is still a rationalist about ritual—those who followed him like Emile Durkheim, and Jane Harrison and the Cambridge ritualists, took a more emotive view of ritual as expression. Von Hendy, *The Modern Construction of Myth*, 92–111.

Finally, Frazer, like Haggard, takes advantage of the eternal appeal of narrativized sex and violence, the Haggardian "lever" of sexual passion. His theoretical account turns the mythic plot of the Goddess and her lovers into the ur-plot of human cultural production. If Victorian anthropology gives culture a marriage plot, Frazer's mythic version anthropologizes the cultural production of such plots, locating the emergence of culture itself in turning sex into representation and narrative. That he does so at the end of a decade in which the problem of turning sex into representation has been thoroughly discussed and practiced by literary writers points to the close connection between literary and anthropological writing in the period. Frazer expresses, in an anthropological register, the ideas about sex and genre that circulated in the literary world.

III. THOMAS HARDY'S *TESS OF THE D'URBERVILLES*: CLARISSA AND CYBELE

Hardy's journals indicate that he began reading *The Golden Bough* in July of 1891, after the publication of the first installment of *Tess of the d'Urbervilles* in the *Graphic*, where *She* also had appeared between October 1886 and January 1887. Hardy met Edward Clodd, the president of the British folklore society, in 1890 and through him gained access to Tylorian folklore theory and to Frazer and his work. There is, of course, a substantial body of critical work on Hardy's interest in folklore, evolutionary social theory, and anthropology, and some wonderful, detailed accounts of the impact of *The Golden Bough* on *Tess*, chief among these Catherine Gallagher's "*Tess of the d'Urbervilles*: Hardy's Anthropology of the Novel" (1998), followed by chapters in more recent books by Andrew Radford (2003) and Michael Zeitler (2007).[35] All these critics have detailed how Hardy takes up the Frazerian themes: goddesses, scape-

35. In "*Tess of the d'Urbervilles*: Hardy's Anthropology of the Novel," Catherine Gallagher reads both Frazer's *Golden Bough* and Hardy's novel as participating in "sexing the archē," putting the Malthusian dilemma at the origins of cultural production. The adjustment of the ratio between population and food supply is, in Frazer, turned into the motive for fertility ritual, which seeks to control the fertility of crops and people through symbolic acts. In incorporating Frazerian ritual into the very structure of his novel, Gallagher argues, Hardy seeks to activate ritual affect through his own art. Because I'm concerned with what the move to myth does to the realist marriage plot, my emphasis is slightly different here—I'm interested in Frazer not as a theorist of ritual emotion but rather as a theorist of interpretation. Drawing on Gallagher's insights into the relationship between events and plot in the novel, I focus less on the affect that events generate than on the ways in which they allow the plot to function across a range of genres and open up the novel's consideration of how different genres make use of sex and marriage.

goats, sacrifice, May festivals, mistletoe, killing the god. Gallagher eloquently summarizes the plot points of the story of the goddess and her lover that indicate both Frazerian ritual acts and plot points in Hardy's novel—"sex in the primeval forest, murder by stabbing of the priest-husband, and the execution of the goddess herself [here she's referring to the hanging of Artemis in effigy]."[36] Reading this list of plot points transforms the experience of reading Hardy's novel: suddenly, nothing looks the same. Even the death of the horse, Prince, resonates entirely differently, in light of Frazer's association of Hypolitus/Virbius with the sacrifice of horses.[37]

The emphasis of much of the work on Hardy and Frazer is either on how Hardy makes use of Frazer, or on Hardy and Frazer as engaged in a common project, a project Gallagher wittily calls "sexing the archē."[38] Hardy does make use of Frazer, and he does independently contribute to the larger project of anthropological myth, but he also seems to have had the rather unique experience of coming across Frazer in the midst of producing a narrative that suddenly looks different because of him.[39] That is, he does not only make use of Frazer, or co-create with Frazer, but he must also, of necessity, read his own work in light of Frazer. This is not just a matter of Frazerian imagery and detail but specifically a matter of plot events. For, as Gallagher points out, the key events of the novel's melodramatic plot read in light of Frazer become ritual events. The ritual nature of these events is registered formally by what Gallagher calls "the dissociation of event from plot and of plot from narrative."[40] The bloody death of the horse, Prince, Alec and Tess's sexual encounter in the wood, and Alec's stabbing all are "barely narrated . . . they seem to exist at the vanishing point of representation."[41] This distinction between sex and murder as plot points and sex and murder as ritual events whose significance is only revealed by a theoretical apparatus outside the plot is foundational to Frazer's distinction between myth and ritual, rendering both the mythic goddess plot

36. Gallagher, "*Tess of the d'Urbervilles*," 429.

37. Zeitler connects Prince to the Frazerian scapegoat/sacrifice, and also to Alec: "Prince is sacrificed and symbolically reborn as Alec D'Urberville, who in each of his key early scenes appears aristocratically on horseback." *Representations of Culture*, 107.

38. Gallagher, "*Tess of the d'Urbervilles*," 422.

39. In *The Shaping of "Tess of the d'Urbervilles,"* J. T. Laird makes his own list of Frazerian features—though he does not identify them as such—that "either make their first appearance or receive a marked increase in attention during the later layers of the manuscript . . . the bough of mistletoe, the hunted animal, the altar victim, and the willing scapegoat" (89). These features proceed from Hardy's Frazerian reading of his own work.

40. Gallagher, "*Tess of the d'Urbervilles*," 429.

41. Ibid., 430.

and the realist heroine plots of the novel secondary narrative forms that explicate but also disguise the meaning of the events they narrate.

In Haggard's novel, anthropological romance takes the form of the joke of literalization; the mythic enters the real and the general effect is a comic one as worlds collide. But in *Tess,* there is no comic collision of opposites: when ritual triangulates the relationship between myth and realism, it opposes, but also parallels them. They haunt, distort, and change each other. Andrew Lang famously compared Tess to Richardson's Clarissa Harlowe, implying that Hardy had down-shifted the class dynamics of Richardson's seduction plot. But Tess, whose body is associated literally (as field worker) and figuratively (as sexy nature) with the land, is also numerous fertility goddesses. Cybele doesn't suddenly find herself in the midst of a Richardson novel; rather Tess's Clarissa aspect and Tess's Cybele/goddess aspect indicate two possible ways of narrativizing ritual events, two possible modes of giving narrative significance to killing and having sex. Ritual means that Hardy's anthropological romance works by holding mythic and realist plots side by side.

What I am calling the realist marriage plot of *Tess* is, like many postanthropological realist plots, also inflected by a gothic/sensation-fiction plot. On one hand, we have a classic choice-of-suitor-as-choice-of-ruler plot, one in which tyranny and consent, unjust and just rule, involuntary and voluntary association are figured through the erotic relations of the heroine. It is this plot that makes it possible for critics to see in Tess the plight of agricultural workers in an industrial era and to see in Alec's sexual exploitation of Tess the political relations of this agricultural class to a new industrial capitalist bourgeoisie bringing industrial methods and new technology into farming. Angel, intellectual and member of an older professional middle class, might provide a more egalitarian form of social organization—but he also oppresses the very class he would value and help by trying to regulate its behavior according to outmoded bourgeois forms of sexual regulation. In this plot, the problem of rape/seduction is a central way of figuring the political problem of consent and agency; the novel's purity polemic is both sexual and political. That much of the description of the effects of the modernization of farming on agricultural workers is drawn from Hardy's 1883 essay "The Dorsetshire Labourer" links this plot to the larger issue of liberal reform.[42] Written in the context of the government's promise to extend the franchise to agricultural workers, the

42. Originally published in *Longman's Magazine,* 2 (July 1883), 252–69, reprinted in *Thomas Hardy's Public Voice,* ed. Millgate. Excerpts, Millgate notes (37), appeared in Hardy's contribution to Haggard's 1902 *Rural England.*

essay circumspectly makes a case for their need for the franchise and for their competency to exercise it.[43]

This realist plot is supplemented by a gothic plot that pushes it in the direction of sensation fiction's critique of marriage as institution. Here, Tess is the heir of aristocratic blood and aristocratic taint. In this plot, Tess's experience in the wood is payback for the sins of the fathers, and Tess's murderousness is inherited aristocratic violence. If the realist present is supposed to be a place of consent and freedom, the gothic sensation plot associates tyranny and violence with aristocratic blood and aristocratic social structures. Tess's murder of Alec is connected to this plot, and like most of the sensational gothic murders of husbands by wives in sensation fiction and in post-sensation-fiction realism, it has about it some of the violence of just revolution against a tyrannical social system. Lady Audley's attempt on her first husband's life, Lucinda's murderousness towards her fiancé in *The Eustace Diamonds*, Gwendolen's plans for Grandcourt, the murderous ravings of Sarah Grand's syphilitic Evadne in *The Heavenly Twins*, are all examples of similar responses to the husband-tyrant. This is a plot that suggests that the violence that liberalism claims to have left behind is not gone as long as unjust social hierarchies remain. In realist novels this kind of violence is contained and internalized through its association with gothic madness. The gothic d'Urberville inheritance gestures towards a similar containing gesture. But these gestures of containment are necessary because realist violence always has political implications.

The mythic plot takes the same events—sex and stabbing—and gives them another meaning entirely. Tess becomes the inhuman goddess, feminine essence, visual and verbal mystery. Alec becomes the goddess's lover, more like Actaeon than Adonis, since he meets his fate at her hand. The mystery of sex in the wood is not a mystery of agency in the mythic plot but the mystery of sex with the divine. In Hardy's trope of the coarse pattern traced on feminine tissue, sex *becomes* representation, a sign to be interpreted. In the mythic plot too, violence is no longer about the overthrow of tyranny but about mythic slaying. Like the stabbing of Kallikrates, the stabbing of Alec is violence and sex together. The "scarlet blot" on the white ceiling that turns it into "a gigantic ace of hearts" is also a representation, a mark to be interpreted.[44] Real blood in the shape of a stylized heart symbol, it graphically links violence and sex. And as blood turned into a symbol or emblem, it recalls the blood of Adonis turned into an anemone. As many readers of Tess have noted, the death of the horse Prince, stabbed by "the pointed shaft of the cart" which "had entered

43. Classic readings of the class dynamics of the novel can be found in Kettle, *An Introduction to the English Novel*, and Williams, *The English Novel*.

44. Hardy, *Tess of the d'Urbervilles*, 370.

the breast of the unhappy Prince like a sword" serves as the symbolic act that prefigures both Tess's defloration and Alec's murder. In the mythic plot it also connects them, turning them into repetitions of itself and each other.[45]

It is not just that the mythic plot is outside of politics and history but that it also is a radically different plot, in which Tess and Alec play radically different roles than they do in the realist plot. Victim and Tyrant become Goddess and Doomed Mortal Lover. Tess and Alec play these radically different roles at the same time, and they can only do so by being two different kinds of characters at once. As a result, Tess, like She, has an archaic mythic body. At one and the same time a realist and mythic heroine, she occupies that body uneasily, and her unease is registered by the novel, which separates out her agential rational realist individual self from the archaic body that operates according to another logic, the body that is a burden to the agential self. The archaic body-self is present at the moments of mythic death and mythic sex: at these moments the agential self is beside the point. As in Haggard's novel, in *Tess of the d'Urbervilles* masculinity is also split between mythic lover and scholar. Like Leo, the masculine mythic body of *She,* Alec seems weirdly vacant. But unlike Leo, he finds himself with wildly different roles to play in the realist and mythic plots: his status as representative of tyranny is at odds with his status as lover/priest to the goddess.

What connects these plots is that they narrativize the same set of key events, the events that Frazer makes it possible to see as ritual events. In the realist plot, with its problematic of consent, choice, and limitations of choice by history, the sexual and sexualized violence of the novel is political violence. In the mythic plot, violence is not political; killing and fucking are events whose meaning comes not from the specificity of history but from a world outside the text, where representations of violence and sex over time and space make these events about *representing* violence and sex. The problem of reading the novel is in reading multiple genres that mean and function in different ways. When Margaret Oliphant, a writer of domestic fiction, finds that Tess's return to Alec and her killing of him is implausible, what she's really getting at is its inexplicability in a realist plot of choice, agency, and contract—the gap between realist Tess and goddess Tess.[46] When D. H. Lawrence sees Alec's

45. Ibid., 55.

46. "She would not have stabbed Mr. Alec D'Urberville, her potential husband, with the carving knife intended for the cold ham (which, besides, awakens all sorts of questions, as—why did Alec D'Urberville, a strong young man, allow himself to be stabbed? and how did it happen that the lodging-house carving knife, not usually a very sharp instrument, was capable of such a blow?), but have turned him head and shoulders out of the poorest cottage in which he had insulted her with such a proposition." Oliphant, rev. in *Blackwoods Magazine,* March 1892, reprinted in Cox, *Thomas Hardy: The Critical Heritage,* 213.

archaic erotic masculine energy as somehow akin to Tess's feminine erotic energy, he's reading Alec as Attis to Tess's Cybele, and not explicating Alec's strange blankness.[47]

Ultimately, then, the Frazerian concept of "ritual" is what makes it possible for the novel to stage generic difference, to be about genre and the ways in which different genres make different narratives out of the same material. The realist plot and its concerns are not replaced by the mythic plot—rather the two plots stand side by side, unreconciled. In the process, the novel suggests that representation also has a history. By the time we get to the end of the novel, then, we have the outlines not only of an alternative to the realist marriage plot but of a new theory of the realist marriage plot, made possible by Frazer's distinction between ritual as representation and myth as narrative. Frazer's ritual turns myth and realism into narrative modes that while they are very different and produce contrary results nevertheless have the same relationship to a set of events. These events have meaning in relation to global transhistorical networks of other such events, and the movement between different modes of narrativizing them is part of what makes up the history of representation. It is thus possible to redefine the realist marriage plot as a kind of survival of the impulse to narrativize ritual sex.[48]

In all three of the works I have discussed here, the plot of the goddess is not just a plot, not just a classical reference point, but a theorized plot: a plot that invokes a set of theories about cultural production and interpretation. One result of the production of this plot is a new articulation of romance as a genre in which myth and realism are brought into contact; another is a theoretical association of representation and violence; another is a kind of globalization of culture itself, since the goddess plot is never any more a plot of classical myth alone but one given meaning by a global network of stories and practices, occurring throughout time. All these developments help make the literary criticism that we practice today. If we identify "the marriage plot," and discuss its possible functions in the novel, it is in part because late Victorian literary and anthropological writers began to theorize sexual and gender relations as in some way constitutive of culture itself.

---

47. Lawrence, "Study of Thomas Hardy."

48. Margaret Doody actually does such a reading of the genre of the novel in a more historically specific way, tying the genre to specific historic goddess cults in the classical period and seeing it emerge first in Greek and Roman prose romance. Frazer is indirectly responsible for this reading, which seems to come out of his impact on classical scholarship through the Cambridge ritualists. See Doody, *The True Story of the Novel.*

PART II

MARITAL AND OTHER LOYALTIES

CULTURAL CONTEXTS FOR THE MARRIAGE PLOT

CHAPTER 4

Playing the *Princess*

Enacting and Resisting Marriage in the Victorian School Story

KELLY HAGER

IN THIS ESSAY, I consider what I've come to think of as Tennyson's school story, *The Princess* (1847), alongside one of L. T. Meade's most popular contributions to the genre.[1] While it might seem surprising to link the poet laureate and a popular writer of mass fiction for young girls, I'm compelled to do so not only for generic reasons but also because of the pivotal role that Tennyson's poem plays in *A Sweet Girl Graduate* (1891) and because *The Princess* was often performed at the end of the century in the kind of girls' schools and colleges depicted in Meade's novels.

I'm specifically interested in the way the marriage plot sometimes conflicts but more often intersects with and works alongside the curricular/career plot in these two narratives of female education. The critical debate over Tennyson's poem is remarkably similar to readings of Meade's novel; both often hinge on the reductive question: do they endorse marriage or education? But an attentive reading of Tennyson, Meade, and accounts of the poem's performance

1. The most famous school story is Thomas Hughes's *Tom Brown's Schooldays* (1857), and Rosemary Auchmuty points out that just as "the growth and reform of the public school system in the mid-nineteenth century" "inspired" the proliferation of the genre for boys which that novel inaugurated, "the girls' school story, like the girls' public school, emerged about 50 years after its masculine counterpart" (*A World of Girls*, 57, 58). Mavis Reimer suggests this "other tradition might be said to have begun in earnest with L. T. Meade's publication in 1886 of *A World of Girls*" ("Traditions," 218). Meade wrote a number of school stories (Reimer estimates about forty) set in boarding school, day schools, private schools, and colleges.

(in fictional and actual schools) reveals that marriage was not always viewed in opposition to education and the careers education made possible. Indeed, within *The Princess* and its enactments, we find the same range of (often contradictory) positions that characterize the arguments of, for instance, John Stuart Mill, Emily Davies, John Ruskin, and Charlotte Mary Yonge.

Marion Shaw situates *The Princess* within "a group of writings published in the middle of the century . . . which summarize the debates of the preceding years on marriage and the position of women";[2] she finds the poem to be both "the most comprehensive in its range of discussion of the women-and-marriage question" and "also the most anxious":

> on the level of its surface argument the poem carefully and not unsympathetically states women's educational demands and appears to effect a liberal compromise between those demands and the requirements of marriage and maternity. But as Kate Millett has pointed out, the poem takes fright at its own daring and turns away from the logical pursuit of its argument to plead with "urgent insecurity" the fear that if women become independent they may cease to love men and bear their children, may no longer succor and console them, no longer serve, as Virginia Woolf has expressed it, as "looking glasses."[3]

While "the feminism or anti-feminism of Tennyson's poem *The Princess* has been a matter of debate ever since the poem's first publication in 1847," as Laura Fasick so plainly puts it, its contradictions and anxieties are more fruitfully (and accurately) studied, not as evidence of the poem's protofeminism[4]

---

2. "The group of writings to which *The Princess* and *Jane Eyre* belong includes A. H. Clough's *The Bothie of Tober-na-Vuolich* (1848), Elizabeth Gaskell's *North and South* (1855), Coventry Patmore's *The Angel in the House* (1854–60), and Elizabeth Barrett's *Aurora Leigh* (1857)" (Shaw, *Tennyson*, 42). This list also highlights the suggestive fact that *The Princess* and *Jane Eyre*—both of which, Shaw reminds us, depict a "partnership between two equal if complementary individuals"—were published in the same year (41).

3. Shaw, *Tennyson*, 42–43. Other critics who give careful and suggestive readings of the gender politics of the poem and to whom I am indebted for my thinking about *The Princess* include Christopher Ricks, James Eli Adams, Dwight Culler, and Carolyn Williams.

4. The term *feminism* was not coined until 1895 (first appearing in a review of Mrs. Alfred Sidgwick's novel *The Grasshoppers* in the *Athenaeum*); accordingly, I use the term *protofeminism* to describe works written before that date. I do so to highlight the fact that twentieth- and twenty-first century understandings of feminism are not the same as nineteenth-century positions on the Woman Question. Julia Bush notes that "avowedly feminist approaches to educational history have tended to perpetuate the use of a feminist yardstick," and I'm concerned to avoid that anachronistic tendency ("'Special Strengths for Their Own Special Duties,'" 387). I'm impressed, in this regard, by Helen Bittel's careful approach to Meade's novels and her determination not to read them "as unequivocally or consistently feminist, especially by *Fin-*

or of its conservative attitude toward women, but rather as indications of the precise nature of the debate over marriage in the second half of the nineteenth century.[5] Fasick indicates as much when she suggests that "the crux of the poem may indeed be its dissatisfaction with all the alternatives that are currently available for social and individual life."[6]

A "just reading" (the phrase is Sharon Marcus's) of the poem and its place in schools and school stories reveals how influential *The Princess* became in thinking both about marriage and alternatives to marriage for New Women (and "New Girls"[7]) and how flexibly the poem was employed to illustrate the conflicting aspects of the marriage question. As I show how imbricated the debate over women's education was with the marriage plots of actual and fictional young women at the end of the century, I resist labeling Tennyson's poem protofeminist or conservative and focus instead on how *The Princess* was utilized in that debate. In exploring the way *The Princess* was plotted into Meade's 1891 school story, I also seek to reveal the role that popular fiction for young girls played in that debate. Further, reading the poem in light of its role in *A Sweet Girl Graduate* will expose what privileging the marriage of the Prince and Ida in that poem obscures about its contribution to the marriage question. Similarly, I argue, highlighting the marriages referred to (though rarely depicted) at the end of school stories treats as foreground what the genre typically presents as background. That is, while it is true that the Princess seems to agree to marry the Prince at the end of the interpolated tale,[8] the last three lines of the poem are devoted to Lilia, whose desire for "a college like a man's" in the prologue inspires the medley that follows. By the same token, while Maggie (an heiress, and the most popular girl in the school) marries at the end of *A Sweet Girl Graduate,* Priscilla, the novel's protagonist and its focus from the first sentence to the last, does not, committing instead to a course of study that will enable her (and her alone) to support her three sisters. Further, Maggie does not marry until after she graduates—and after she "takes a first class in her tripos examination."[9]

---

de-Millennium standards," even though she certainly finds that they "promote feminist social change" ("Required Reading for Revolting Daughters?" par. 32).

5. Fasick, "Angels and Ingénues."

6. Fasick, "The Reform of Women's Education," 28.

7. Sally Mitchell uses this phrase to describe "new ways of being, new modes of behavior, and new attitudes that were not yet acceptable for adult women (except in the case of the advanced few)." *The New Girl,* 3.

8. I say "seems" because the only evidence I can find that they marry is Walter's "I wish she had not yielded" in the conclusion (line 5). A crucial line in this regard ("The Prince to win her," line 220 of the prologue) was not added until the 1853 edition of the poem.

9. Meade, *A Sweet Girl Graduate,* 163. Cited parenthetically in the text hereafter.

I. A JUST READING OF *THE PRINCESS*

A Sweet Girl Graduate contains no suggestion that a woman must choose between marriage and education; the Vice Principal of St. Benet's College for Women, Miss Heath, indicates only that "we do not care that our students should think of love and courtship *while here*," a stricture that echoes Ida's "not for three years" (emphasis added).[10] Miss Heath's echo of Ida's stricture suggests that we need to look carefully at Ida's beliefs about marriage. And indeed, when we look at the poem and its representations of marriage, it becomes clear that Ida objects to it most strenuously as an institution and an arrangement foisted on her by her father: "as to precontracts, we move, my friend, / At no man's beck."[11] While she has resolved "never to wed" because she wants to devote herself "to this great work" of her college, the permanent proscription of marriage is one she applies only to herself and those who choose to teach alongside her. Further, that proscription seems to have more to do with her sense of all that needs to be done than with a belief that marriage and higher education are antithetical to each other. She makes it clear that the former will be improved by virtue of the latter, and, in fact, she links the three-year proscription for her students to a more equitable version of the institution:

> You likewise will do well,
> Ladies, in entering here, to cast and fling
> The tricks, which make us toys of men, that so,
> Some future time, if indeed so you will,
> You may with those self-styled our lords ally
> Your fortunes, justlier balanced, scale with scale. (2.47–53)[12]

10. As Fasick notes, this is "a condition remarkably similar, as the poem itself points out, to the conditions of contemporary male universities" ("Angels and Ingénues," par. 11).

11. Ricks, ed., "*The Princess*, 1847," 2.210–11. Cited parenthetically in the text hereafter.

12. Men are also thought to interfere with the work of college in Catherine Fuller's 1897 school story *Across the Campus: A Story of College Life*, as we see from the following exchange:

> "Don't you think," asked Clare, hesitatingly, "that it's better not to have men around—I mean in that way, of course—until we're out of college? Of course I don't know many men, but I've always noticed—in the case of girls who do—that they interfere dreadfully with the work."
>
> "Yes," said Christine, "I think that, as a rule, the best college girl doesn't go in for that sort of thing, any more than the best college man does."
>
> "We should do college thoroughly while we're in it," said Clare, "and then—"
>
> "Do the other thing thoroughly when we get out if, if we want to," finished Christine.

Ida's most pointed critique of the institution comes in response to the Prince's "Swallow, swallow" song, which she characterizes as "a mere love-poem," the kind of thing that "knaves" use to "play the slave to gain with tyranny" (4.108, 110, 114). Men, she insists, offer not love but "mock-love" and "mock-hymen," for they view women as "vassals to be beat" and "pretty babes to be dandled" (4.125, 126, 128, 129). She holds out for an egalitarian relationship, one in which men "rate us at our worth" as individuals with "living wills, and sphered / Whole in ourselves and owed to none" (4.127, 129–30). Shaw suggests that Ida's "feminist arguments are ones John Stuart Mill would be ready to use in another twenty years."[13] But, in fact, they're ones he articulated fifteen years before Tennyson published the first version of his poem. In his 1832 essay on marriage and divorce, Mill insists "there is no natural inequality between the sexes," that "nature has not made men and women unequal."[14] Like Ida, Mill believes that the remedy for the constructed nature of women's inequality is "that she be so educated, as not to be dependent on either her father or her husband for subsistence: a position which in nine cases out of ten, makes her either the plaything or the slave of the man who feeds her; and in the tenth case, only his humble friend."[15] The consonance between Ida's "pretty babes to be dandled" and Mill's "plaything," between her description of women as "vassals to be beat" and his "the slave of the man who feeds her" is striking, and it is just one of the ways the poem both echoes and participates in the debate over the rights and capabilities of women.

Ida's objections to the institution of marriage are, as many critics have demonstrated, remarkably consonant with the attack on the institution (and, more generally, on the doctrine of separate spheres and the status of women) mounted by Caroline Norton, the Owenists, William Thompson, Mary Wollstonecraft, Anna Jameson, and Harriet Martineau.[16] Ida's critique of marriage is one the poem endorses, too, for those that represent and uphold the patriarchal version of marriage to which Ida objects (chiefly the Prince's father, but also the opportunistic Cyril, who is surely one of the best arguments in favor of the Married Women's Property Bill that will begin to circulate in a few years) are clearly revealed to be in the wrong and behind the times. As Carol Christ points out, "The events of the poem reveal the inadequacy of the old

13. Shaw, *Tennyson*, 45.

14. Mill, "Essay on Marriage and Divorce," 73.

15. Ibid., 74.

16. John Kilham's *Tennyson and "The Princess": Reflections of an Age* is the most detailed exploration of the way in which the poem's concern with marriage "was suggested to Tennyson by contemporary theories and events" (18). Virginia Zimmerman, Karen Chase and Michael Levenson, James Eli Adams, and Dwight Culler also provide careful contextualizations of the poem's representation of marriage.

king's response. The resolution of the poem owes nothing to the king's vision of marital and sexual conquest, which in fact alienates both the Prince and the Princess, but depends upon their mutual respect and compassion."[17] Or, as James Kincaid succinctly puts it, this king puts "the common male position so bluntly it cannot be accepted."[18]

As in the contemporary debate, Ida's objections to marriage are influenced by examples of the institution's failure and by women spurred to work for reform because of their oppressive marriages. Like the relationship between Caroline Norton's failed marriage and her efforts to reform the child custody and married women's property laws, Lady Blanche's unhappy experiences as a wife—"she says / (God help her) she was wedded to a fool"—gave rise to her conviction "that with equal husbandry / The woman were an equal to the man" and compelled her to raise Ida with that conviction uppermost in her mind, an upbringing that led Ida to open her university (3.66–67, 1.129–30). Indeed, Lady Blanche claims the university was her idea—"The plan was mine. I built the nest"—and she implies that "the inscription on the gate, / LET NO MAN ENTER IN ON PAIN OF DEATH," was a direct result of her experience as a wife (4.346, 2.177–78). "That law your Highness did not make," she proclaims, when Ida sets it aside in order to nurse the wounded Prince; "'twas I. / I had been wedded wife, I knew mankind, / And blocked them out" (6.306–8). Kilham notes that many of the protofeminists whose lives and work influenced the poem were themselves "*mal-mariées,*" and that fact suggests how personal the political is for the fictional and the actual wives who worked to change the institution from one that allowed the Prince's father[19] to behave like such an alpha male into a companionate union like that shared by John Stuart and Harriet Taylor Mill.[20]

Careful attention to Ida's critique of marriage leads me, then, to agree with Shaw's assessment: the poem indicates that "the story of marriage taken merely as a social arrangement comes to represent a doomed enterprise, that sexual relations founder on the gender constructs which characterize them."[21] But, as Kilham argues, *The Princess* also "sketch[ed] out the lines of a new type of relationship," a sketch which Meade will fill out in Maggie's plot in *A Sweet Girl Graduate.* Maggie's marriage to Geoffrey Hammond, the Senior Wrangler

17. Christ, "Victorian Masculinity," 155.

18. Kincaid, *Tennyson's Major Poems,* 62.

19. He, it is worth noting, "cared not for the affection of the house" and believes that "Man is the hunter; woman is his game," "Man to command and woman to obey; / All else confusion" (1.26, 22–24, 5.147, 440–41).

20. Kilham, *Tennyson and "The Princess,"* 110.

21. Shaw, *Tennyson,* 56.

of the neighboring men's college, realizes the poem's vision of an egalitarian marriage that the poem can present only as the Prince's interpolated fantasy.[22]

II. THE PRINCESS GOES TO GIRTON

Education for women is also represented as an interpolated fantasy in *The Princess,* and a failed one at that. But that fantasy is realized just a year later with the founding of Queen's College in 1848. Queen's (and Girton and Newnham) is, in some very specific ways, in fact, the realization of Ida's interpolated vision, for a number of nineteenth-century educational reformers responded to the vision of higher education for women in the poem and used it in their plans for women's colleges. These attentive and pragmatic readers of the poem, including F. D. Maurice, Dorothea Beale, and Barbara Bodichon, found in it not only clear support for educating women but also a blueprint for a women's college. In *Higher Education for Girls in North American College Fiction 1886–1912,* Gunilla Lindgren notes the perhaps surprising fact that "the founders of Queen's College . . . thought that Tennyson had thoroughly penetrated the pros and cons of female higher education" and "turned to him for consultation when planning their own bold enterprise."[23] Alicia Percival, too, points out that "the founders of Queen's College. . . . had, indeed according to the preface of their *Jubilee Book,* talked over their plan of establishing this college with the poet—the founders themselves being such recognized authorities on education as Kingsley, Hullah, Mrs Marcet, and Mrs S. C. Hall."[24] In *Queen's College, London: Its Objects and Methods,* Maurice's 1848 pamphlet outlining his goals for the first women's college, Maurice proclaims that "we should indeed rejoice to profit in this, or any undertaking, by the deep wisdom which the author of the 'Princess' has concealed under a veil of exquisite grace and lightness; we should not wish to think less nobly than his Royal heroine does of the rights and powers of her sex; but we should be more inclined to acquiesce in the conclusions of her matured experience."[25] As Karen Chase and Michael Lev-

22. Kilham, *Tennyson and "The Princess,"* 4.

23. Lindgren, *Higher Education for Girls,* 119.

24. Percival, *The English Miss To-Day & Yesterday,* 148. John Hullah was the musical director at Queen's and a professor of vocal music at King's College, London. Mrs. (Jane) Marcet was the author of *Conversations on Chemistry, Intended More Especially for the Female Sex* (1805) and a chaperone at Queen's. Mrs. S. C. Hall (Anna Maria Fielding Hall) was a novelist and, according to the DNB, "instrumental in founding the Hospital for Consumption at Brompton, the Governesses' Institute, the Home for Decayed Gentlewomen, and the Nightingale Fund. . . . She worked for the temperance cause, for women's rights, and for the friendless and fallen" (54).

25. Maurice, *Queen's College,* 7.

enson conclude, "At this founding moment in the history of women's education Tennyson's poem is precedent and guide . . . the passage leaves no doubt that the strange poem of 1847 was seen as confirming the plans for a woman's college. Maurice, who recognized the controversy over Queen's College was inescapable, understood his 'feminist' provocation in terms of the dialectic of extremism and reformism drawn from *The Princess.*"[26]

Further, Lindgren finds that the "ideas voiced in *The Princess* recur both in contributions to the contemporary debate in America and in women's college fiction," indeed, that the poem "formed an undercurrent both in the general debate and in the college stories written" in the decade before World War I, and she goes on to mention the striking fact that "Wellesley students nicknamed their respected young president [Alice Freeman] 'The Princess.'"[27] Similarly, and perhaps even more strikingly, Barbara Bodichon, one of the co-founders of Girton, described herself as Ida on a visit to Girton in 1877.[28] The Girls Public Day School Trust, founded in 1873, took their motto from the poem ("Knowledge is now no more a fountain sealed," 2.76), Anna Julia Cooper quotes lines from the poem in "The Higher Education of Women," her 1890 talk to the American Conference of Educators, and L. M. Montgomery (the author of *Anne of Green Gables* [1908]) employs two passages from the poem as epigraphs to her 1896 essay celebrating women's access to higher education in Canada, "A Girl's Place at Dalhousie College." It probably goes without saying that it was part of the curriculum at many girls' schools.[29]

The Princess was also, as I have indicated, frequently performed in colleges in Britain and the United States around the turn of the century. Lindgren tells us that "*The Ladies' Home Journal* printed photographs of college girls . . . 'giving a burlesque adaptation'" of the poem in May 1902; Sally Mitchell discovered that the poem was "performed by Girton students during Lent term of 1891 to an audience of women from Newnham and Girton"; and Carol Dyhouse notes a performance by students at Royal Holloway College in June 1898.[30] Even more telling is Megan Norcia's recovery of Elsie Fogerty's *The Princess. By Alfred Tennyson, Adapted and Arranged for Amateur Performance*

26. Chase and Levenson, *The Spectacle of Intimacy,* 135.

27. Lindgren, *Higher Education for Girls,* 19, 118.

28. Pam Hirsch cites a letter from Bodichon to a niece in which "she imagined herself as the eponymous heroine of Tennyson's *The Princess,* describing herself as 'in the College for 3 days resting in my own Palace!'" "Barbara Leigh Smith Bodichon," 97.

29. The poem is listed as part of a recommended reading-course for girls 14 to 16 years of age in *Work and Play in Girls' Schools,* a collection of essays by teachers at the Cheltenham Ladies' College "intended to be a practical one, helpful chiefly to teachers in our large Secondary Schools," as Dorothea Beale puts it in her preface to the 1901 edition (v).

30. Dyhouse, *Students,* 118, 215n71, n6 to ch 6.

in Girls' Schools. This 1901 adaptation included "an introduction, sketches, and extensive notes," as well as "directions for costuming, casting, and blocking."[31] Fogerty published it after having staged multiple performances of the poem in girls' schools in the 1890s.[32]

III. "SWEET GIRL-GRADUATES"

The arguments of *The Princess* as I've just(ly) read them, the poem's use in the founding and shaping of schools, and its performance history in schools in the second half of the century provide crucial contexts for the role it plays in Meade's novel. These collocations, in fact, make the poem a school story that provides the perfect model for Meade's text,[33] and Meade makes it immediately and unmistakably clear that she's using the poem as a model for her novel by using a phrase from the poem as her title. Accordingly, I'll begin my analysis of the role *The Princess* plays in and for Meade's novel by focusing on the title phrase as it occurs in the poem. Tennyson puts the phrase "sweet girl-graduates" in the mouth of one of Walter's college friends, and he uses it in a flattering (but ultimately belittling) response to Lilia's desire to "build / Far off from men a college like a man's" (Prologue 134–35). "Pretty were the sight," he exclaims, "With prudes for proctors, dowagers for deans, / And sweet girl-graduates in their golden hair" (lines 141–42). Lilia calls him on his patronizing reply ("That's your light way"), but the poet here seems just as patronizing as the college boy, introducing her accurate assessment of his reply with a description of "her tiny silken-sandal'd foot," which she "petulant[ly]" "tapt" (Prologue lines 148–52).[34]

---

31. Norcia, "Performing Victorian Womanhood," 2, 3–4.

32. Fogerty, Norcia tells us, studied drama at the Paris Conservatoire "and went on to stage plays at prestigious schools in the greater London area." She also "taught dramatics at Royal Albert Hall and founded the Central School of Speech and Drama. Her roster of students includes John Gielgud and Peggy Ashcroft" (3).

33. Bittel suggests that one role the poem plays in the novel is to advance the cause of higher education for women:

> To an alert reader, this earlier poem might serve to legitimize the all-female educational community represented in the novel, naturalizing it by refuting its newness, authorizing it by association with the poet laureate. It also might multiply the levels on which the reader is invited to share Meade's fictional vision of such a community and thus—through fiction—render it an increasingly imaginable possibility for "real-life" girls. (par. 36)

34. It's this patronizing reply that causes Lilia to issue her edict of death to all male invaders, too, in response to his insistence that "If there were many Lilias in the brood, / However deep you might embower the nest, / Some boy would spy it" (lines 146–48).

Meade, however, takes Lilia's vision more seriously. Her girl graduate, nineteen-year-old Priscilla Peel, is "going out into the world": to "St. Benet's far-famed College for Women," to get an education that will enable her to support herself and her orphaned sisters (26). As she puts it, "I'm the girl who is to fight the world, and kill the dragon, and make a home for the nestlings," and St. Benet's is the ideal place for her, for it's "where young women received the advantages of University instruction to prepare them for the battle of life" (8, 5). Described not in terms of her "golden hair" but her "earnest spirit" and her "almost careworn face, thoughtful, grave, with anxious lines already deepening the seriousness of the too serious mouth," Priscilla has a "strong intellectual nature," "a great gift for acquiring knowledge," and an "active, strong, young brain" (1, 23).

Meade thus seems to be using the college boy's phrase with the tacit scare quotes it deserves, not only on the novel's cover and title page, but throughout, as the title appears at the top of every page, providing a continuous ironic counterpoint to the story of Priscilla's studies. Later in the novel, we find the phrase used in reference to Priscilla's shabby, homemade clothes ("so deliciously quaint . . . Quite the sweet girl graduate, I do declare") and in contrast to the novel's antagonist, the doll-like Rosalind Merton (63). Rosalind is also a student at St. Benet's, and she is precisely the decorative object Walter's college friends imagine when they fantasize about girl graduates. In fact, she is cast as Lady Blanche's daughter, Melissa ("A rosy blonde, and in a college gown, / That clad her like an April daffodilly") in St. Benet's production of *The Princess* (Tennyson 2.301–2, quoted in Meade 158). But, as Meta Elliot-Smith, Rosalind's friend (and rival), says to her, as she compares her appearance to Priscilla's, "You don't at all answer to the *rôle,* you naughty Rosalind!," clad as she is in "a fascinating toilet of silk and lace . . . vastly becoming to its small wearer" (63, 62). Meta is more right than she knows, for Rosalind was, the narrator tells us, "by no means one of the 'students' of the college. She attended as few lecturers as was compatible with her remaining there," and she does not remain there for long. In a most satisfying scene, she leaves the college ("never to come back") after it is discovered that she has stolen money from a classmate—money she needs to pay for clothes and jewelry she can't afford but desperately desires (155).

Rosalind does not belong at St. Benet's, it is clear, and she is reminiscent of those students who don't belong at Ida's college, those older students who

> murmur'd that their May
> Was passing: what was learning unto them?

> They wish'd to marry; they could rule a house;
> Men hated learned women. (II. 439–42)

These students are also the invention of the college boys, not a facet of Lilia's dream of education for women. More in line with Lilia's agenda for a women's college ("I would teach them all that men are taught; / We are twice as quick!") is the revelation that Priscilla can hold her own in a conversation about Homer with the Senior Wrangler of the neighboring men's college, a moment in the novel that brings to mind the fact that some women outperformed men on the tripos in actuality (Prologue, lines 136–37). Mitchell catalogs some of these triumphs, including the fact that Philippa Garrett Fawcett scored higher than the Senior Wrangler on the mathematical tripos at Cambridge in 1890, a Girton student (Agnata Ramsay) wrote "the only examination paper put into the first division of the first class in classics" in 1887, and "sixteen women in addition to Fawcett were among the top hundred in mathematics" in the class of 1890.[35] These examples—one fictional and several actual—of women's academic prowess are particularly telling in terms of the debate over education and marriage, for they not only counter the conservative belief that women were simply not as intelligent as men[36] but also contradict the stereotypical beliefs that "men hated learned women" and that educated women are unattractive.

Priscilla's conversation with Geoffrey Hammond, the Senior Wrangler, comes about when he takes pity on her at Meta's tea party, which Rosalind takes her to under false pretenses and where he then abandons her, "miserable, self-conscious, ill at ease," in a society drawing-room (63). As the narrator tells us, in a description that makes it clear that the values of town and gown are opposed to each other, "It was in vain for poor Priscilla to whisper to herself that Greek and Latin were glorious and great, and dress and fashion were things of no moment whatever. At this instant she knew all too well that dress and fashion were reigning supreme" (63). But not for long, for once Geoffrey engages her in conversation, she becomes "both eloquent and attractive, her eyes were bright, her words terse and epigrammatic. She looked so different a girl from the cowed and miserable little Prissie of an hour ago that Rosalind

---

35. Mitchell, *The New Girl*, 47.

36. The poem also counters this belief:

> Let them not fear: some said their heads were less:
> Some men's were small; not they the least of men;
> For often fineness compensated size:
> Besides, the brain was like the hand, and grew
> With using. (2.131–35)

Merton . . . felt a pang of envy" (67). The coupling of "eloquent and attractive" suggests that learning makes a girl graduate pretty, an impression underscored by the fact that when they leave Hammond "absolutely scowled down" at Rosalind but "shook hands warmly with Priscilla" (67). It's not clothes or "golden hair" that makes Priscilla pretty; it's her deep knowledge and love of the *Iliad* and the *Odyssey.*

Further supporting my conviction that Meade has in mind Lilia's vision of education for women, not that of the college boys, is the fact that the narrator cites Ida's college as the inspiration for St. Benet's: "that first college for women—that poet's vision, so amply fulfilled in the happy life at St. Benet's" (158). And it is, for the most part, a happy and deeply satisfying life for those "earnest workers" for whom "St. Benet's is really meant. It was endowed for them, and built for them," as one of Priscilla's classmates explains (29). St. Benet's turns Priscilla, for instance, into "a happy girl," for "she had found her niche in the college, her work was delightful" (76). Further, we hear throughout the novel about the alums who "have brought fame to St. Benet's . . . earning honorable livelihoods as teachers, or in other departments where cultivated women can alone take the field" and about current students "whose names were destined to be known in the world by-and-by" (132).

Mitchell finds that "college novels typically have multiple heroines, who validate plural roles for women: the scholarship girl who will teach, the rich girl devoted to social work, the beauty who will marry."[37] I've been concentrating thus far on the scholarship girl, Priscilla, who belongs at St. Benet's, and on the beauty, Rosalind, who does not (and who does not manage to find a husband while at St. Benet's, either). But Meade's novel also has a "beauty who will marry," and that beauty—Maggie Oliphant—is also rich. She has "brilliance, beauty, wealth," and she does not marry until after she graduates with a first class in the tripos. Maggie's plot has as much to do with education as it does marriage: her love of learning brings her to St. Benet's and fosters her friendship with Priscilla; her courtship plot figures prominently in the novel's production of *The Princess.*

In a scene early in the novel, we see how translating a passage from Aeschylus absorbs and fulfills Maggie: "A fine fire filled her eyes; her brow, as she pushed back her hair, showed its rather massive proportions. Now, intellect and the triumphant delight of overcoming a mental difficulty reigned supreme in her face. She read on without interruption for nearly an hour" (35). Just a few pages later, Priscilla's declaration "I love Latin and Greek better than anything else in the world" prompts Maggie to ask "What have

37. Mitchell, *The New Girl,* 60.

you read? Do tell me," questions which lead to the first of the long, intellectual conversations that characterize the friendship between heroine and protagonist (45).

There are, then, as Priscilla says to her aunt, "all sorts of girls at St. Benet's," and that multiplicity offers readers a number of possibilities, just as Tennyson's poem is used as evidence for both sides of the debate, illustrating for some critics (and for some characters in the poem) women's aptitude for higher learning ("they do all this as well as we") and thus indicating the urgent need for them to have access to an Oxbridge education, while revealing to other readers women's domestic and maternal nature (104, 2.367). Priscilla describes "some" of her classmates as "real students, earnest, devoted to their work," but she doesn't contradict her aunt's suspicion that for many at St. Benet's, college is "a little bit of learning, and a great deal of dress," for, as the narrator puts it, "girls of all kinds were living under these roofs" (104, 114). "The learned students who are going in for a tripos" are the most esteemed, but the narrator certainly approves of students like Miss Marsh ("a bright-eyed, merry looking girl, the reverse of over-studious") and Nancy Banister, Maggie's best friend, who frankly admits that "no one can accuse me of killing myself with work" (10, 29). What is more, it is made clear that the college offers a variety of paths to its diverse student body: "all the inmates of St. Benet's were trying, each after her kind, for the several prizes which the life they were leading held out to them. . . . the idle as well as the busy. Both the clever and the stupid were here, both the good and the bad" (114). That's true of Ida's college, as well, and the similarities between the two schools become especially clear in St. Benet's production of Tennyson's poem.

IV. "TELL HER TO MARRY HIM"

The performance of *The Princess* is "the great event of the term" at St. Benet's, and it is also the denouement of Meade's novel, bringing to a happy conclusion both Priscilla's plot and Maggie's. But while the novel certainly has a happy ending, that ending is neither trite nor neat. Maggie takes full advantage of the academic opportunities offered at St. Benet's and also marries, while Priscilla is well on her way to achieving the goals that will enable her to support her family. That the novel achieves these ends by means of *The Princess,* and by means of the poem's interpolated, fairy-tale-like medley, not its more realistic, nineteenth-century frame, may be surprising given the ironic use Meade makes of the college boys' vision described in that medley. When I teach this novel, students are dismayed at the way Meade's characters "play *The Princess,*" but that dismay indicates something crucial about the status of marriage at the end of the century and something I think we tend not to acknowledge about the gender politics of this cultural moment. I said at the outset of this essay that a "just reading" of the poem and its place in school stories would reveal how the poem was employed to illustrate the many aspects of the marriage question, and in the reading that follows, my goal is to do justice to what both *The Princess* and *A Sweet Girl Graduate* "make manifest on their surface" in the service of an accurate (if not always satisfying to a twenty-first-century feminist) assessment of the many strands of the debate Meade braids together as she concludes *A Sweet Girl Graduate.*[38]

St. Benet's production of *The Princess* is confined to the medley, and it seems, in fact, only to consist of sections 2 through 7. The curtain rises "on the well-known garden scene, where the Prince, Florian, and Cyril saw the maidens" of Ida's college for the first time, and the play ends with the Prince's invitation to Ida, "Lay thy sweet hands in mine and trust to me" (Meade 158, Tennyson 7.344 quoted in Meade 161). Maggie, appropriately enough, plays the Princess, and Priscilla plays the Prince. The description of the production takes up two-thirds of the penultimate chapter, most of which is dedicated to the Prince's wooing of the Princess. Indeed, this production of the poem is decidedly conservative; it emphasizes the scenery and the costumes (the "academic silks" and the maidens "clad in purest white"); the only aspect of college life recounted is the first scene the Prince and his friends witness, which consists mostly of students at their leisure: petting peacocks, singing as they "oar'd a shallop," while "others tost a ball" or "lay about the lawns" (2.433, 436, 438 quoted in Meade 158–59). The "older sorts" who "wish'd to marry" are depicted, and we only see one student studying (2.439, 441 quoted in Meade 159). It is true that when the curtain first falls on Maggie as the Princess, the audience sees on her face "all the pride . . . of indomitable purpose," and they respond enthusiastically: "'Perfect!' exclaimed the spectators"; "each individual in the little theater felt . . . that Maggie was not merely acting her part, she was living it" (159). And indeed she is, but she's living a much more romantic version of the poem: her first action in the play (both in and out of character) is to lift her head, look out into the audience, and blush. "It was evident," the narrator tells us, "that she had encountered a glance which disturbed her composure" (159).

At this point, Meade's school story—which takes place at a women's college and is exclusively concerned with girl graduates and which contains within it the dramatization of another narrative of female education—becomes almost

38. Marcus, *Between Women*, 3.

entirely a story of courtship. For the glance that disturbs Maggie's composure comes from the man she loves, and the chapter ends with the announcement of their engagement, an engagement the (unmarried) Vice Principal supports and one that Priscilla helps bring about (in other words, an engagement approved of by the novel's two most admirable, serious, and studious women). Their courtship plot has been in evidence throughout the novel, running beneath the plot of Priscilla's academic endeavors and alongside the plot that chronicles the spiteful antics of Rosalind and her friends. These three plots and these three different versions of college life are, as I suggest above, an important aspect of the genre, and they have much to do with the comprehensive way Meade's novel not only depicts but also participates in the marriage question, providing not just one model but two, as well as a cautionary tale in the Rosalind plot. Up until this point, Priscilla's plot has been the focus, and Rosalind's and Maggie's have functioned as subplots, counterpoints, background. But now Maggie and her courtship plot take center stage, quite literally.

I've left Maggie blushing, on stage, and about to begin her part in the play, and I must leave her there just a bit longer, while I fill in the gaps of her subplot. In considering the relationship of Meade's novel to Tennyson's poem, I've alluded to Maggie's academic talents, and I've indicated that the intellectual bond accounts for the friendship between Maggie, the heiress, and Priscilla, the penniless orphan. But the other important thing to know about Maggie is that she and Geoffrey Hammond (the Senior Wrangler who rescues Priscilla at the tea party) are in love; they met the summer after her first year at the college, and he proposed to her at the beginning of her second, asking her to marry him after she graduates from St. Benet's the following year. Maggie refused his proposal, not because she didn't love him, but because she believed that her best friend, Annabel Lee, loved Hammond herself. We learn very little about Maggie's second year at St. Benet's after she refuses Hammond; the novel opens on her third year at the college, which is Priscilla's first, and we're given only cryptic allusions to the previous year and the reasons for Maggie's moodiness. But it is clear that Hammond and Maggie have strong feelings for each other, though they are estranged, and when, late in the novel, we finally learn what has separated them, we also learn that "if she had loved Hammond a year ago her sufferings made her love him fifty times better now. . . . The thought of him mingled with her waking and sleeping hours" (137). Priscilla knows none of this, but she intuits that Maggie shares Hammond's feelings, and she sets out to unite her two friends by means of Tennyson. Inspired by the "stony (or was it yearning?) look in Maggie's face" as they rehearse, "when she spoke [her lines] to Maggie, she no longer felt like a feeble school girl acting a part. She thought she was pleading for Hammond" (78).[39]

So we have Maggie on stage, in the character of the Princess, blushing because she's caught sight of Hammond in the audience, about to be wooed by Priscilla, in the character of the Prince and, as she has done twice before in rehearsals, channeling Hammond. For "Priscilla, too," the narrator tells us, "had encountered Hammond's earnest gaze. That gaze fired her heart, and she became once again not herself but he. . . . She was Hammond pleading his own cause, she was wooing Maggie for him in the words of Tennyson's Prince" (160). The novel's production devotes its most sustained attention to the poem's courtship verses; it reproduces five stanzas from the Prince's "O Swallow, Swallow" song ("Fly to her, and pipe and woo her, and make her mine") as well as his pleading "I cannot cease to follow you" speech (Tennyson 4.97, 435, quoted in Meade 160). The novel reproduces the poem's lines accurately, but the narrator implies that Maggie's response is not quite by the book: "In the impassioned reply which followed this address it was noticed for the first time by the spectators that Maggie scarcely did herself justice. Her exclamation:

> "*I* wed with thee! *I*, bound by precontract
> Your bride, your bond slave!"

was scarcely uttered with the scorn which such a girl would throw into the words if her heart went with them," suggesting again that "Maggie was not merely acting her part, she was living it" (Tennyson 4.520–21, quoted in Meade 161, 159). In addition to the fact that these are the only lines we see Maggie utter in the play (effectively excising, then, all the Princess's speeches

39. The fact that Priscilla plays the Prince to Maggie's Princess is remarkable, to be sure, and it would be valuable to consider the cross-dressing involved in both novel and poem. Such wooing was commonplace, for Tennyson's poem was, as I discuss above, regularly performed in schools around the turn of the century. St. Benet's is also not the only fictional college to stage a production of *The Princess.* In Gertrude Fisher Scott's 1914 college novel, *Jean Cabot in Cap and Gown,* a performance of the poem is "the crowning event" of Junior Day (160). Priscilla's onstage wooing of Maggie also brings to mind a precursor scene in chapter 14 of *Villette* (also a school story), when Lucy, playing an "empty-headed fop," woos the "fair coquette," played by Ginevra in the vaudeville for the fête of Madame (203). Lucy's acting, like Priscilla's, is a kind of intervention in the courtship afoot offstage, but while Priscilla works to bring Maggie and Hammond together, Lucy confesses, "I hardened my heart, rivalled and out-rivalled him" (210). Both Ginevra and Maggie are very much aware of their suitors in the audience, too, but the sight of Hammond "disturb[s]" Maggie's "composure" (159), while Ginevra's response is, again, just the opposite of what we find in Meade: "such glances did she dart out into the listening and applauding crowd, that to me—who knew her—it presently became evident she was acting *at* some one" (210).

devoted to the reasons for founding her college, its curriculum, and its rules, not to mention all the speeches in which she resists the Prince's proposals), these lines are not, in Maggie's performance, an indignant, scornful rejection of the Prince but rather a foreshadowing of the end of the chapter, where we find her engaged to Hammond.

The portion of the play we as readers see (as opposed to the play we are meant to understand the audience at St. Benet's views) is almost entirely about marriage, then—the "older" students wishing for it, the Prince wooing the Princess, the Princess accepting the Prince. We are given a severely condensed version of Tennyson's poem, and the Princess herself is not only silenced but redrawn into a woman "conquered" by the Prince and eager to marry him. At this moment in the novel, the courtship plot intersects with the plot of curriculum and career, for Priscilla's efforts to bring together Maggie and Hammond, not only in the play but also when she shares with the Vice Principal Maggie's feelings for Hammond, give the narrator a chance to pontificate on the proper place for romantic interests in a school (story)—to make explicit the relationship between the two plots, we might say. What is more, Priscilla's revelations to the Vice Principal enable that figure of pedagogical authority to lend her aid to the successful conclusion of the courtship plot, indicating yet again that education does not stand in opposition to matrimony (in this novel or in Tennyson's poem, for that matter). Rather, there is a place and time for each, and, while, as Ida and Miss Heath make clear, there is no place for thoughts of matrimony in a women's college, especially one like St. Benet's ("where young women received the advantages of University instruction to prepare them for the battle of life"), that is not to say that those thoughts are antithetical to the academic endeavor (5). Indeed, Julia Bush reminds us that

> feminist and suffragist proponents of women's higher education frequently found themselves making a similar case for the compatibility of academic training and marriage. . . . On the eve of founding Girton College, the leading feminist Emily Davies wrote in *The Higher Education of Women* that "a liberal education and the pursuit of a profession are perhaps, on the whole, the best training that the conditions of modern society can supply for the special functions of the mistress of a household."[40]

Similarly, Elizabeth Wordsworth, founding principal of Lady Margaret Hall (1878) at Oxford, wrote, "We want to turn out girls so that they will be capable of making home happy."[41]

---

40. Bush, "'Special Strengths,'" 398.
41. Quoted in Percival, *The English Miss To-Day & Yesterday*, 173.

Four chapters before the girl graduates enact Tennyson's poem, Priscilla begs Miss Heath "to make [Maggie] marry Mr. Hammond at once." The Vice Principal refuses, saying that it is "far from me to say that I disapprove of marriage for our students, but, while at St. Benet's, it is certainly best for them to give their attention to other matters" (144). Or as Ida puts it, "Not for three years to correspond with home; / Not for three years to cross the liberties; / Not for three years to speak with any men" (2.56–58).[42] But Priscilla persists. "For most of us," she says, "but not for Maggie" (144). She goes on to explain that something is clouding Maggie's happiness, keeping Maggie and Hammond apart; all the girls can see it, but no one knows what it is. That Miss Heath truly does not disapprove of marriage "for our students" is borne out by the fact that she consequently shares with Maggie Annabel's dying words: "'Annabel said . . . tell Maggie not to mistake me. I am happy. I am glad she will marry'—I think she tried to say a name, but I could not catch it—'tell her to marry him, and that I am very glad'" (157). What is more, Miss Heath prefaces her revelation to Maggie with the assurance that "were [a girl at St. Benet's] to confide in the Principal of her college in case of any friendship developing into—into love, she would receive the deepest sympathy and the tenderest counsels that the case would admit of" (156–57). Immediately after Maggie gets this welcome (albeit long delayed) message, she goes on stage as the Princess, and we see that she is now ready to be courted—because of the combined efforts of Priscilla and Miss Heath.[43]

V. *THE PRINCESS*: A SCHOOL STORY

I began this essay by confessing that I've come to think of Tennyson's poem as a school story, and I've followed the logic of my own experience in organizing my analysis. That is, uncovering the relationship between *The Princess* and the schools (fictional and actual) it inspired first led me to think about the poem as a kind of school story. Those associations highlighted for me the fact that *The Princess* is not only about the school that Ida founds, but, further, that the focus is on school, not on the marriage that does not take place in the poem and is only implied when Ida leaves her college in shame. Similarly, in *A Sweet*

42. Bernard Bergonzi reminds us that "when Princess Ida welcomes the three supposed students to the college she sternly urges them to forget about men and thoughts of marriage [but] not, indeed, for good." He concludes that she thus "avoids the pathological anti-masculinism of some of the later suffragettes." "Feminism and Femininity in *The Princess*," 42.

43. Another essay might consider the role that Priscilla and Miss Heath play in Maggie and Geoffrey's courtship in light of Marcus's analysis of "how Victorian novels make female friendship the catalyst of the marriage plot." *Between Women*, 79.

Girl Graduate, the focus is on St. Benet's, not on the marriage that occurs after Maggie graduates from college with academic honors. Highlighting this marriage is to treat as foreground what the novel presents as background to Priscilla's bright future at St. Benet's. Highlighting the marriage of Ida and the Prince draws attention to what is represented as lamentable, if we share Walter's reaction to the medley ("I wish she had not yielded"), and inconclusive, if we look to what Best and Marcus call "the surface of the text" for evidence that Ida and the Prince do indeed marry. For "what is evident, perceptible, apprehensible . . . what is neither hidden nor hiding" at the end of the medley is that while in its last line the Prince asks Ida for her hand and for her trust—"Lay thy sweet hands in mine, and trust to me"—she does not respond (7.345).[44] The poem's next line is the first line of the conclusion, "So closed our tale."

Virginia Zimmerman suggests that "in Lilia, the frame's young feminist, we find the long results of time and Ida's work. She responds to the feminist position, but she does so with caution," and I would argue much the same thing about Meade's novel.[45] It—and its genre and the world it represents—too, is a result of Ida's work, and it too "responds with caution" to Ida's protofeminist vision, not inveighing against marriage, but clearly celebrating the interregnum of college. As one of the characters in the novel puts it,

> No life can be so absolutely delightful as that of a girl graduate at St. Benet's. The freedom from care, the mixture of study with play, the pleasant social life, all combine to make young women both healthy and wise. Ah, my love, we leave out the middle of the old proverb. The girls at St. Benet's are in that happy period of existence when they need give no thought to money-making. (48)

College is described here much as Ida describes it: as an important and pivotal moment in the development of a woman (and the development of a society, Ida would argue). Or, as Mavis Reimer puts it in her outline of the genre inaugurated by Meade, it is a "world apart." Reimer distinguishes this tradition of girls' school stories from a smaller, if more canonical, set of girls' school stories "that firmly bracket school life with domestic spaces towards which the girls inevitably move."[46] "Unlike more canonical girls' school stories," Reimer finds, Meade's novels "do not end with the girls leaving school" and returning to "a family home," whether that of her own family, a surrogate family, or the

44. Best and Marcus, "Surface Reading," 9.
45. Zimmerman, *Excavating Victorians,* 95.
46. Reimer, "Traditions," 218.

family she and her husband "will build together."[47] Rather, Meade's boarding-school stories and college novels "demonstrate [her] interest in the new, intellectual education for girls and women being theorized by first-wave feminists and put in place by such reforming headmistresses as Dorothea Beale and the principals of the new women's colleges at Oxford and Cambridge."[48] These novels do not end with a movement away from the space of that education; rather, Meade "hold[s] open the imaginative space she has created for her readers in the stories by refusing to return her scholars to an outside world."[49] While Maggie marries, the novel's last three paragraphs are devoted to Priscilla, who "was more than filling the place left vacant by Maggie" (163). "Everyone prophesied well for Priscilla in the future which lay before her," we are told, but that future lies outside the pages of the novel and is, indeed, very much the future (163–64).

At the end of *A Sweet Girl Graduate,* Priscilla is still in college. At the end of *The Princess,* Ida has yet to respond to the Prince's proposal. The endings of these two school stories thus reveal something crucial about the relationship between marriage and education. As I've been arguing, that relationship is not a binary; marriage and education are not positioned in opposition to each other. For some students, like Maggie, a college education precedes and prepares a woman for (a better, more equal) marriage,[50] while for others, like Priscilla, college has nothing to do with marriage. Her education is not positioned in opposition to marriage; it is unrelated to that institution. In this regard, I want to suggest, much like the frame's poet-speaker does in the last

47. Ibid., 218, 217.

48. Ibid., 218. Meade's college stories are part of the subgenre of school stories focusing on university life for women that flourished as Oxbridge slowly opened its doors to women. Anna Bogen notes that "throughout the early twentieth century, more and more novels about female undergraduates began to appear, their numbers eventually overtaking those about men in 1935 when four novels about Oxford women alone were published in the same year" (*Women's University Fiction,* 17). This subgenre includes series fiction, juvenile genre fiction, and more highbrow fiction by Vera Brittain, Virginia Woolf, and Rosamond Lehmann, among others. See Lindgren, Marchalonis, and Innes, as well as the Bryn Mawr Library's website, on the many series about American coeds from the 1870s to 1930s. See Reimer, Mitchell, and Bogen on juvenile genre fiction and Bogen on the more highbrow examples.

49. Reimer, "Traditions," 219.

50. We can imagine that Maggie will use her BA like Louise Creighton did. Creighton sat the first London University Higher Examination for Women, married a fellow of Merton College, and "before long was combining the onset of motherhood with authorship of a commissioned translation of Ranke and a history primer" (Bush, "'Special Strengths,'" 395). Or we can imagine for her L. M. Montgomery's Ruskinian vision of a college-educated wife: "If [sweet girl-graduates] marry, their husbands find in their wives an increased capacity for assistance and sympathy; their children can look up to their mothers for the clearest judgment and the wisest guidance" ("A Girl's Place," 148).

lines of the conclusion, that "maybe wildest dreams / Are but the needful preludes of the truth," that perhaps Ida's visionary institution was the necessary beta version, so to speak, of Girton and Newnham,[51] of institutions that prepared women both to support themselves should they not marry and to "increase the usefulness of women to the community as well as the consideration in which they are held," as Louise Creighton put it in her lecture "Home Life and the Higher Education of Women," going on to insist that "anything that will make her a more complete human being, will also make her a more helpful and stimulating companion to her husband and children."[52] Perhaps, then, it is most accurate to say that marriage has everything to do with education for women in that the first college for women—Queen's—was founded because it was becoming clear that marriage was not an option for all women; it offered education to women not in opposition but as an alternative to marriage. If we read the poem in this light—remembering, among other things, that the founders of Queen's turned to Tennyson and his poem as they developed the plans for their women's college—we can see the imbricated nature of these two institutions for women and attend to the interlocking, not the oppositional, pattern of their relationship, in the literature and the culture of the last half of the nineteenth century.

51. The narrator of Meade's novel certainly finds it so, describing Ida's college, as I note at the outset, as Tennyson's "vision so amply fulfilled in the happy life at St. Benet's" (158).

52. Quoted in Bush, "'Special Strengths,'" 397, 398.

CHAPTER 5

The *Longue Durée* of Political *Bildungsromane*

Putting George Eliot into Dialogue with Danish Television

LAUREN M. E. GOODLAD

> In [the Bildungsroman,] human emergence is . . . no longer man's own private affair. . . . He reflects the historical emergence of the world itself. He is no longer within an epoch, but on the border between two epochs, at the transition point from one to the other. . . . This transition is accomplished in him and through him. He is forced to become a new, unprecedented type of human being. . . . The organizing force held by the future is therefore extremely great here—and this is not, of course, the private biographical future, but the historical future.
>
> —Mikhail Bakhtin, "The *Bildungsroman* and Its Significance in the History of Realism," 23

THE CONFLICT between a heroine's vocation and the domestic strife it abets plays out against a background of historic change. Though her male foil is deeply scarred by personal tragedy, his narrative, like hers, weaves biography into a backdrop of social transition. In a second, contemporaneous work, an unrelenting commitment to duty divides the heroine from her loved ones while her male foil suffers baleful trial and disillusionment. Both works embed their doubled protagonists in densely multiplotted worlds. In doing so, both show that marriage—as in the oft-cited quotation from George Eliot's *Middlemarch* (1871–72)—is "the bourne" of "many narratives."[1]

In *The Novels of George Eliot* (1958), Barbara Hardy wrote that the author of *The Mill on the Floss* (1860), *Romola* (1862–64), *Felix Holt* (1866), and *Daniel Deronda* (1876) favored heroines in her quest for a "new kind of tragedy" so that gender itself—"the disability of being women"—would shape "the tragic suffering and redemption" that each novel achieves.[2] Though Eliot experi-

1. Eliot, *Middlemarch*, 890.

2. Hardy, *Novels of George Eliot*, 47.

mented constantly with hybrid genres, the tragic motifs that haunt these stories help to lay bare the "structural irony . . . between historical forces and the personal life."[3] Still, if Eliot's female *Bildungsromane* wax tragic, they do so within a larger complex of multiplot webs, marriage plots, and salient doublings. To "multiply plots," as Peter K. Garrett has written, is "to divide the fictional world," disrupt continuity, and "disperse the reader's attention." Multiplot works lack the kind of formal unity prized by many Modernists. Yet, for that very reason, they produce "generalizing effects" born of difference as well as likeness.[4]

Of course, while the two narratives sketched above feature cross-gender doublings, multiplot webs, and *Bildungsromane* blent with tragedy, neither derives from an Eliot work or even a Victorian novel. Both are acclaimed television series produced by the Danish Broadcasting Company ("DR"). The first is *Borgen* (2010–13), the fictional story of Denmark's first female prime minister and the close relationship she forms with her "spin doctor." The second is *Forbrydelsen* (also known as *The Killing* [2007–12]), a police procedural that, in its award-winning first season, pairs the stories of a self-sacrificing homicide detective and a principled politician locked in a tight campaign with an unscrupulous rival.

In describing these series in a volume on nineteenth-century marriage plots, I am thinking about the long afterlives of nineteenth-century fictional genres. The recent Victorianist interest in contemporary serials suggests the appeal of such transhistorical comparison: yet, despite their enthusiasm, Victorianists do not yet have a clear set of methods for studying the forms that interest them over long or discontinuous durations of time. It is sometimes alleged that Victorianists stay close to the seventy-odd years of the queen's reign because of the historicist methods that rose to prominence in the 1990s.[5] But since history neither begins nor ends with a single reign, I suggest that precisely *as* historicists Victorianists should explore how the genres populating their field develop over longer durations.

To be sure, genres themselves, as categories of analysis which extend as far back as Aristotle's *Poetics,* pose conceptual challenges. Tzvetan Todorov famously defined them as "horizons of expectation,"[6] a reception-oriented understanding of genres as pliable structures subject to contingency, metamorphosis, and hybridity. From this standpoint, genre is as much about the legibility of cues and conventions for particular audiences as it is about authors' intentions or critics' taxonomies. As Jonathan Culler writes, genres

3. Ibid., 22.

4. Garrett, *The Victorian Multiplot Novel,* 2.

5. For example, see Warhol, "Introduction: Genre Regenerated."

6. Todorov, *Genres in Discourse,* 18.

do not constitute "a set of rules" so much as a "background of conventions" against which the singularity of any given work stands out.[7] It follows that genres deriving from one set of circumstances may persist, mutate beyond recognition, or reclaim the limelight after a long hiatus. For much the same reason, generic archetypes such as tragedy or Bildungsroman may be more useful in highlighting the multiplicity *within* hybrid genres than in capturing any single work in its entirety. As Todorov writes, genres develop "from other genres": a "new genre is always the transformation of an earlier one, or of several: by inversion, by displacement, by transformation."[8] Such open-ended notions of what genre is and does testify to the social provenance of narrative.

This essay focuses on *Felix Holt, the Radical,* written in 1865 and published by William Blackwood & Sons as a three-volume novel the following year. I put *Felix Holt* into dialogue with *Borgen* and (briefly) *Forbrydelsen* for two main reasons. First, all three are species of the political Bildungsroman, a hybrid genre with genetic ties to the "condition of England" or "social-problem" novels that preceded it. In the form that Benjamin Disraeli popularized, a male "aristocrat of the younger generation . . . goes forth armed against" the "egotism" and "idleness of the privileged classes—his own people."[9] But whether in Disraeli's *Coningsby* (1844), Anthony Trollope's *Phineas Finn* (1867–68), or George Meredith's *Beauchamp's Career* (1874–75), political *Bildungsromane* transplant the marriage plot from the localized industrial conflicts of social-problem fiction to the broader terrain of national politics. Structurally, they turn successful courtship from a symbolic redress for class unrest into a character test for aspiring male leaders. As we shall see, *Felix Holt*—though often grouped with these political *Bildungsromane*—transforms the genre. Thus, while Disraeli's Young England trilogy advances a new Tory creed through charismatic leaders, and Trollope's Phineas narratives describe the pitfalls of parliamentary ambition, Eliot's comparatively female-centered and doubleplotted work incorporates elements of historical romance, tragedy,

---

7. Culler, "Genre: Lyric," n. pag. Compare to Todorov: in "order to be an exception, the work necessarily presupposes a rule"; moreover, "no sooner is" a new work "recognized in its exceptional status" whether commercial, critical, or both, than it "becomes a rule in turn." Todorov, *Genres in Discourse,* 15.

8. Ibid. Compare Fowler, *Kinds of Literature.*

9. Speare, *The Political Novel,* 61. Speare's *The Political Novel* remains the most thoroughgoing study of this topic, but see also Harvie, *The Centre of Things.* Bodenheimer defines *social-problem* or *industrial* fiction as works that focus on "specific social problems raised during the process of industrialization" (*The Politics of Story in Victorian Social Fiction,* 4). See also Williams's well-known chapter in *Culture and Society, 1780–1950,* and, more recently, Dzelzainis, who has identified the "social-problem or 'Condition of England' novel" as "centrally engaged with ideas of radicalism and reform" ("Radicalism and Reform," 428).

and naturalistic realism, which distinguish her political fiction from male-centered counterparts. Indeed, as Fred C. Thomson has shown, *Felix Holt*'s germ was the story of Mrs. Transome—a tragic plotline dominated by female adultery, secret illegitimacy, and violated patrimony. Only later, he surmises (in response to debates over the Second Reform Bill), did Eliot develop the idiosyncratic radicalism of her titular hero.[10]

To compare *Felix Holt* to *Borgen* is to bring Eliot's mid-Victorian novel into dialogue with a three-season-long television show that followed on the heels of DR's internationally renowned crime series *Forbrydelsen*.[11] By criss-crossing periods, media, and nations, this turn to long durations does more than enrich conventional genre histories. Just as important is to activate the socioformal lens of genre analysis as a way of contesting the disciplinary thinking that reflexively isolates Denmark's contemporary history from that of Victorian Britain. In fact, I will argue, Eliot's novels and Danish television share a common engagement in citizenship and social ontology which is mutually illuminating. Whereas *Felix Holt* strives to imagine collective civic life beyond the dominant individualism of its time, *Borgen* develops an Eliot-like tension between *Bildung* and tragedy which is only partly successful in negotiating the new neoliberal terrain.

I. POLITICAL *BILDUNGSROMANE* AND THE ADULTEROUS GEOPOLITICAL AESTHETIC

> This life at Transome Court was *not* the life of her day-dreams: there was dullness already in its ease, and in the absence of high demand; and there was a vague consciousness that the love of this not unfascinating man who hovered about her gave an air of moral mediocrity to all her prospects. . . . Somehow or other . . . it seemed that the higher ambition which had begun to spring in her was forever nullified. All life seemed cheapened.
>
> —George Eliot, *Felix Holt*, chapter 43

10. Henry reminds us that Eliot had put her narrative poem, *The Spanish Gypsy*, on hold while she wrote *Felix Holt* "and so was thinking deeply about the nature of both comic and tragic form and had reread Aristotle's *Poetics* in 1865. The challenge . . . was translating classically tragic . . . themes into a realistic novel with modern plots and characters" (*The Life of George Eliot*, 157). Norton describes Eliot as "intensely preoccupied with the formal problems of tragedy" ("The Aesthetic Education of Humanity," 6).

11. See Hammerich, *The "Borgen" Experience*, for the perspective of *Borgen*'s executive producer; for a scholarly account of both shows, see Redvall, *Writing and Producing Television Drama in Demark*.

In *The Victorian Geopolitical Aesthetic* (2015), Eliot's oeuvre provided an important test case for rethinking the conventional wisdom about mid-Victorian-era fiction. Comparing Eliot's marriage plots to Gustave Flaubert's, my goal was to break open the category of the "novel of adultery" so as to question the assumption that Victorian fiction was too stiflingly bourgeois to inspire challenge or critique. The tendency to divide British from Continental literature, I argued, obscures the variety and transnationality of nineteenth-century fiction. Against the common premise that French characters bring tragic conflicts to pass while British counterparts "retreat" into "private spheres to practice their ethically sanctioned negative freedoms,"[12] I proposed a means to reading works by Dickens, Trollope, Meredith, and others which was at once more "worlded" and more attentive to the conditions inciting certain formal experiments.

Eliot was a focal point because her immersion in Continental ideas inspired a prescient historical materialism. As she wrote in her notes on the "Historic Imagination," the abundance of writing on the world's great "turning-points" was either too abstract (in the mode of intellectual history) or too "picturesque" (like pure romance). What was needed, she believed, was fiction that captured the "pregnant movements of the past" through a dialectic of the imaginary and concrete.[13] From her translation of Strauss's historical Jesus in 1846, to the essay on "The Natural History of German Life" a decade later, Eliot's meditations on history foreshadowed her efforts to write what Georg Lukács later called "the historical novel of our time."[14] Hence, Eliot is part of a line of cultural critique which includes the proximate philosophies of Feuerbach, Hegel, and Marx; the critical materialisms of Auerbach, Bakhtin, Lukács, and Raymond Williams; and the *longue durée* of Braudel among others. Nonetheless, Eliot's historicism is by no means her singular contribution to novel form. Rather, to a degree that the catchall term "realism" obscures, Eliot's oeuvre is generically diverse, bold, and experimental.[15]

When Eliot began writing fiction, the nation whose history she sought to mediate was reinventing itself in response to political, economic, and imperial transformation (e.g., Michie, Hall). Like Trollope's contemporaneous Barsetshire series, Eliot's *Adam Bede* (1859) and *The Mill on the Floss* bear the impress of historical romance in answering worlds besieged by modernizing change with a vision of history's unifying power. In seizing courtship and marriage as flexible devices for exploring this morphing materiality, both authors exemplify Tony Tanner's claim that marriage is "the structure that maintains

12. Cohen, "Sentimental Communities," 108; cf. Moretti, *Way.*

13. Eliot, *Essays and Leaves,* 308.

14. Lukács, *The Historical Novel,* 350.

15. On this point, see also Kurnick, "Unspeakable George Eliot," 490.

the Structure."[16] Yet, in doing so, both wrote novels in which not merely characters but genres themselves came to occupy the historically charged "border between epochs" which Bakhtin aligns with the heroes of classic *Bildungsromane.*[17] Looking at Trollope's oeuvre, one perceives the shift from the world of Barsetshire—in which comedy leavens modern uncertainty—to the unremitting turpitude of later novels such as *The Way We Live Now* (1874–75). In answer to a growing financial economy, formalizing empire, and rising machinery for mass politics, Trollope's realism drifted from the quasi-providentialism of prolonged courtship narratives toward the dysphoric naturalism of broken marriage plots: for example, *The Eustace Diamonds* (1871–73), in which Lizzie's falseness hastens Sir Florian's passage to an early grave, or *The Prime Minister* (1876–77), which draws out the miserable coupling of Emily Wharton and Ferdinand Lopez. As the holistic social order shored up by comic irony in Barsetshire and elegized in *Adam Bede* gives way to the centrifugal and atomizing effects of speculation, exploitation, and "money from elsewhere,"[18] we discern the affective and material condition of the *adulterous geopolitical aesthetic,* a mode of naturalistic fiction which is less about infidelity *per se* (though there is plenty of it) than about the systemic corruption of bourgeois marriage as a paradigm-shaping "structure that maintains the Structure." As novels in this mode traffic in commodified wedlock, sexualized consumption, prostituted social bonds, and the breakdown of collective experience, they foreclose holistic world-making against the countervailing rise of an atomistic social ontology.

In its most familiar usage, adultery signifies a "violation of the marriage vows," the "sin or crime" entailed by this breach, and the "state or condition of having committed" this sin or crime.[19] Adultery thus enfolds a sexual act and a religious and civil offense as well as a metaphysical condition. Moreover, the Latin *adulterium,* from which the English "adultery" derives, denotes the "blending or mixing of different strains or ingredients"—thus expanding adultery through a homology that likens broken vows and profligate acts to the "debasement" or "corruption" of religious doctrines or material essences.[20] What adultery consistently signals is violation or breach: whether of a legal contract or sacred vow; one's mental or physical state of purity, fidelity, or innocence; or a material or spiritual essence. Flaubert and Trollope articulated this condition by turning to pervasively atomistic modes of naturalism.

16. Tanner, *Adultery and the Novel,* 15.
17. Bakhtin, "The *Bildungsroman,*" 23.
18. Williams, *Country,* 249.
19. *The Oxford English Dictionary Online,* s.v. "adultery," http://www.oed.com/.
20. Ibid.

As Harry Shaw writes of *Madame Bovary,* in terms that might also describe *The Eustace Diamonds,* the novel lacks "any 'common world' of intelligence" or clear connection to "the historical stream."[21] By contrast, Eliot persistently sought alternatives to such atomism, from the civic womanhood she depicted in *Romola,* to the Promised Land beckoning the title character of *Daniel Deronda.* This strong vein of antinaturalism, as well as the generic restlessness it provoked, was the flipside of Eliot's enduring faith in the redemptive powers of an ongoing history.

There are, however, two instances in which Eliot yielded to the naturalistic impulses of her times.[22] The best known is Gwendolen Harleth's "half" of *Daniel Deronda*—a narrative that leaves Grandcourt's young widow to atone in the purgatorial space of the adulterous geopolitical aesthetic. The type of this milieu is Gadsmere, a remote estate, "once rural and lovely, now black with coalmines," where Grandcourt's mistress resides with her illegitimate children. Redolent of a crumbling "structure that maintains the Structure," it is a place where pools of water are darkened by "overhung bushes" and the "naked roots" of untended trees. Grandcourt's illicit family shares this postlapsarian scene with the local miners. These toilers for the machine age, occulted by "diabolical" complexions and otherworldly gear, are indifferent to any but the "men of business" to whom their absent landlord has turned over his duties (ch. 30). I suggest that *Felix Holt* anticipates this Grandcourtian ruin and abandonment: the haunted space of Transome Court, first introduced in the prologue, establishes its secrets as the naturalistic vein in what we might conceive as the first political Bildungsroman to be shadowed by the adulterous geopolitical aesthetic. "As for the Transome business," the coachman says, "there had been ins and outs . . . so that you couldn't look into it straight backward."[23] The closing tableau—an image of "thorn-bushes" and "stems" that hide "human histories"—sets the stage for a new genre experiment while foreshadowing Gadsmere a decade later: then, as now, "these things are a parable" (10).

Like *Daniel Deronda, Felix Holt* foregrounds two kinds of plot: a dark adultery narrative that looks ahead to Gwendolen's dystopic wedlock, and a variation on political fiction which (like Daniel's exodus) speaks to the "pregnant movements of the past."[24] Significantly, this generic splicing yokes together two social ontologies that seldom cohabit: the atomistic aggregation

---

21. Shaw, *Narrating Reality,* 96.

22. Note that these mid-Victorian modes differ from Zola's more generically codified naturalism, including the signature focus on working-class environments.

23. Eliot, *Felix Holt,* 10. Cited parenthetically in the text hereafter, except where cited with another work.

24. Eliot, *Essays and Leaves,* 308.

of naturalism and the holistic collectivity of historical romance. This volatile juxtaposition exacts a formal price since the aesthetically powerful ontological solvent of naturalism hardly favors collective possibility. *Daniel Deronda* squares this circle with a title character whose doubled persona straddles two incommensurable worlds, one epitomized by Grandcourt and the other by Mordecai. Although *Felix Holt* lacks this formal device, we should nonetheless pause before construing Eliot's political Bildungsroman as the mouthpiece for a wholly conservative political creed.[25] We might recall that envisioning political possibility at a time when "reform" centered on the male franchise was somewhat like imagining it in Renaissance Florence, as Eliot had done in her previous novel. As Susan Winnett shows, the author of *Romola* saw that European literature needed "new legends to rescue female experience from the margins of narrative and to render it intelligible."[26] *Felix Holt* continues this work through its doubleplot: whereas Mrs. Transome's story looks ahead to Gwendolen in *Daniel Deronda*, Esther's choice of Felix looks back to *Romola*'s incarnation of republican virtue. In this way, *Felix Holt* mediates a discourse of radicalism which was still in flux.[27]

Consider what *Romola* brings to mind when we look at Ruth Yeazell's now classic essay on the role of heroines in political fiction. Likening *Felix Holt* to Disraeli's *Sibyl* and Gaskell's *Mary Barton*—two social-problem novels published more than twenty years earlier—Yeazell argues that the marriage plots in these works defuse the threatening politics they evoke: each "entertains the possibility of violence, even half-sympathizes with it, only to take refuge" in "female innocence" and stasis.[28] Such a reading confirms the binary logic that finds male characters advancing radical politics while female counterparts wage countervailing reactions through marriage and domesticity—precisely the gendered teleology *Romola* resists. From this outlook, Esther's *Bildung* becomes a diversion from Felix's politics, while Mrs. Transome's adulterous tragedy (a plotline unimaginable in *Sibyl* or *Mary Barton*) is mere background. Yeazell herself seems to notice these problems when she describes Esther as

25. Thus, the "Address to Workingmen, by Felix Holt," published after the passage of the Second Reform Act and written at Blackwood's request, is, to my mind, a generically distinct paratext, best understood as a separate work.

26. Winnett, "Coming Unstrung," 515.

27. As Gillian Beer writes, *Felix Holt* "looks at the contradictions within political radicalism, with its suggestion of uprooting and new beginnings, while assumptions" about the relationships "between men and women . . . remain unquestioned" (*George Eliot*, 133). The importance of gender was clear to no less a politico than John Morley, whose review described Eliot's subject as "the evil usage which women receive at the hands of men" ("*Felix Holt, The Radical*," 723).

28. Yeazell, "Why Political Novels Have Heroines," 130.

"the most conventional" of Eliot's heroines only to add that the character's renunciation of Transome Court bespeaks the author's "greatness."[29] One senses a similar ambivalence in another influential reading that groups *Felix Holt* with earlier works. According to Rosemarie Bodenheimer, *Felix Holt*, like Disraeli's *Sibyl* and Dickens's *Hard Times* (1854), is an industrial novel that portrays reform as an obstacle to coherent historical movement. Thus, while all of these works critique a deracinated status quo, their turn to history, Bodenheimer believes, is a rejection of politics which marriage helps to instantiate. *Felix Holt* is, thus, "obsessed" with the idea that "belief in change is blindness to continuity."[30] Or, more precisely, "Felix can change Esther, but his political actions effect nothing."[31] Such a reading never pauses to consider that political Bildungsroman distinguishes itself from industrial fiction by conceiving marriage as a sign of political maturity—not political escape.

In fact, Esther Lyon's severing of her ties to land is the most explicit "revolutionary" act in a novel that—as E. S. Dallas wrote in the *Times*—"touches on politics" without conforming to a straightforward political novel.[32] In renouncing her title to Transome Court, Esther resists her taste for refinement in favor of an adoptive father, artisan lover, and the "higher ambition" of a "life of privation" (407, 464). In *Sibyl*, by contrast, the heroine's working-class upbringing and noble birth incarnate the neofeudal bond between aristocracy and people which Disraeli had set forth in *A Vindication of the English Constitution* (1835). Sibyl confirms this Tory ideal when she marries the aristocratic Egremont.[33] Thus, when Esther chooses Felix over Harold, she reverses the pattern that finds Sibyl preferring a patrician paragon to his Chartist rival. What is more, no surprise ancestry or inheritance tempers the impact of Esther's decision; rather, Felix has *already* foresworn the profits of his father's quackery and chosen a "cravatless" artisan's lot over the "clerkly gentility" or physician's career his mother had urged (174, 64). When Rufus Lyon praises

29. Ibid., 142. See also Betensky, *Feeling for the Poor*; Lesjak, *Working Fictions*; and Livesey, *Writing the Stage Coach Nation*.

30. Bodenheimer, *The Politics of Story*, 209.

31. Ibid., 224.

32. Eliot, *Felix*, 464; Dallas rptd. in Carroll, ed., *George Eliot*, 264. The novel ought to have been named after its heroine, Dallas suggests, since "it is her story that . . . is chiefly engaged with, and Felix Holt is less interesting in himself than as being interesting to her" (266). As Speare notes, *Felix Holt*, unlike Disraeli-esque political fiction, lacks a leading protagonist "with a soul aflame to enter Parliament to right" working-class wrongs or awaken upper-class "consciousness of their national duties" (222).

33. *Sibyl* blends an industrial narrative with the political Bildungsroman Disraeli pioneered in *Coningsby*; Coningsby's marriage to Edith Millbank, the sister of a manufacturing friend, unifies landed and industrial elites. Gaskell's *North and South* (1850) offers a humbler variation on this industrial courtship plot.

"self-advancement," Felix retorts, "Let a man once throttle himself with a satin stock, and he'll get new wants and new motivations" until he ends "by collecting greasy pence from poor men to buy [himself] a fine coat and a glutton's dinner" (64). This repudiation of embourgeoisement, demagoguery, and the exploitation of labor takes the place of Chartism, trade unionism, or socialism in constituting Felix's radical bona fides. But whatever we make of the title character's politics, Esther's own "revolution" and "pledge" to "meet high demands" are never reducible to the choice of a husband (464–65) and, still less, to a depoliticizing transfer of "private for public transformations."[34] To the contrary, Esther's rejection of "moral mediocrity" confirms Bakhtin's claim that the Bildungsroman's development of human potential is no "private affair."[35] Placed at the "transition point" between a declining social order symbolized by the Transomes and a new order that has only begun to emerge, Esther, like Romola, "become[s] a new unprecedented type of human being" whose organizing force is "the historical future."[36]

Perhaps the most cogent generic marker in *Felix Holt,* therefore, is the lack of any deep spatial foundation to support this political *Bildung*—a sign of how the atomism of a naturalistic milieu seeps into multiple plotlines. Instead of an exceptional anchor to history like *Sibyl*'s Marney Abbey, Transome Court bodies forth the decay of the adulterous geopolitical aesthetic. The result is that Felix must "invent a new way of life" through force of character alone.[37] At the novel's close, he, Esther, and Rufus confirm this detachment from place by leaving Treby Magna for an unnamed town. In abandoning his childhood home, Felix severs himself from a material culture more hospitable to the "new prosperity of Dissent" than to civic aspiration (52). His closest tie—apart from a problematic mother and young foster child—is Rufus, a clergyman who relocated to Treby when doctrinal differences compelled him to vacate an earlier ministry. As the pastor of a chapel that goes by the telling name "Mal-

34. Yeazell, "Heroines," 131; cf. Lesjak, *Working Fictions,* 15.

35. Eliot, *Felix,* 407; Bakhtin, "The *Bildungsroman,*" 23.

36. Bakhtin, The *Bildungsroman,* 23. In a longer version of this essay, I emphasize Felix's status as artisan as opposed to the proletarian weaver his father was, the bourgeois tradesman his father became, or the aspiring professional his mother wished him to become. The novel pits Felix's J. S. Mill–like civic radicalism against prominent strains of radical individualism such as the free trade radicalism of Cobden and Bright, which premises social progress on an atomistic social ontology. The limitations of ontological atomism, including Locke's possessive individual or the *homo economicus* of Bentham's felicific calculus, eventually prompted Mill to abandon Benthamism. Mill's civic, social, and historically contingent variation on utilitarian ethics, and his revisions to the *Principles of Political Economy* (a book Eliot reread in preparation for *Felix Holt*) informed the intellectual fabric in which liberal collectivism, socialism, and the politics of the Labour Party emerged at the end of the century.

37. Bodenheimer, *The Politics of Story,* 221.

thouse Yard," the "odd-looking" Rufus is too "absent from the world of small facts" to develop strong bonds to local place. His French-speaking daughter, educated at a boarding school, "is not much liked by her father's church" (52). Thus, while Treby Magna bears the outward signs of a small town, *Felix Holt* is a provincial narrative about rootless exiles.

We can grasp the effects of this genre experiment by comparing Eliot's doubleplot to Flaubert's *Madame Bovary* (1856)—the defining adultery novel of its time. Miss Lyon's surname conjures the provincial mores called out in *Madame Bovary*'s subtitle (and later in *Middlemarch*'s), while her Gallicized refinement testifies to French nature and nurture.[38] To "God-fearing" Trebians, such Frenchness is a "melancholy vanity" likely to lead Esther "astray" (75). But from a narrative standpoint, her aestheticism is a generative force that must be harnessed to collective ends before it lapses into a Bovary-esque cult of the senses. According to Elizabeth Starr, Esther "performs all of the great tasks of the novel" once her "eye for aesthetic details" turns toward "Felix's idealism" and the cause of "social progress."[39] As she refuses to squander her acute "moral taste" by leading a "life of middling delights, overhung with the languorous haziness of motiveless ease" (426), Esther pivots from the Bovaryism of Transome Court to the heroism of *Romola*. Her marriage to an artisan whose radical ambitions go "a good deal lower down than the franchise" signals a coursing antinaturalism that turns female disability into female citizenship (264).

Still, the more obvious of Eliot's two Bovarys is Mrs. Transome, whose maidenhood conjures Emma-like desires for "dangerous French writers" and "sinful things" (29). When we first meet this bold figure of a new kind of tragedy, the narrator explains that the "early raptures" of (adulterous) motherhood "had lasted but a short time," giving way to bitter disappointments and the corrosive influence of "a hungry desire,"

> like a black poisonous plant feeding in the sunlight,—the desire that her first, rickety, ugly, imbecile child should die, and leave room for her darling [Harold], of whom she could be proud. Such desires make life a hideous lottery, where every day may turn up a blank; where men and women who have the softest beds . . . yet grow haggard, fevered, and restless, like those who watch

38. Rignall has also likened Flaubert's subtitle, "*Moeurs de Province*," to Eliot's "A Study of Provincial Life"; see *George Eliot, European Novelist.* The name "Esther" points to the fallen-woman subplot of *Mary Barton,* while the character's testimony on behalf of a future husband recalls Mary herself. On Gaskell's fallen-woman plot, see Anderson, *Tainted Souls and Painted Faces.*

39. Starr, "'Influencing the Moral Taste'" 56, 68.

> in other lotteries. Day after day, year after year, had yielded blanks . . . and all the while the round-limbed pet had been growing into a strong youth, who liked many things better than his mother's caresses . . . The lizard's egg . . . had become a brown, darting, determined lizard . . . Yet, she had clung to the belief that . . . the possession of this son was the best thing she lived for; to believe otherwise would have made her memory too ghastly a companion. (23–24)

Drawn from *Felix Holt*'s first chapter, the passage sets the stage for Eliot's most mordant adultery narrative, recalling that unusual blend of "tragic pity and critical disdain" which Erich Auerbach described in light of *Madame Bovary*.[40] By picturing Arabella Transome as a reckless gambler hankering after ruinous compulsions, the trope of the "hideous lottery" anticipates *Daniel Deronda*'s opening game of roulette. Already we sense the comeuppance awaiting an imperious woman who wagered her happiness on an illicit son—a "lizard's egg" who, like his father, has little interest in "living in the experience of another" (23).

To be sure, Mrs. Transome's weary dominion over her tenants is less pointedly banal than the life of a provincial doctor's wife. Whereas Flaubert's existential blankness accentuates the aestheticization of language, Eliot's focus on character upholds the moral force of art. Mrs. Transome's mental condition is an ominous dread rendered through chilling externalizations of psychic pain such as the "feeding" plant of desire and the "ghastly" companion of memory.[41] Nonetheless, what Arabella and Emma share is the female disability that imbues naturalistic narrative with its pathos: the "gravity of being caught up in history's workings."[42] Both novels capture the modern (female) condition through the aloof stance of naturalism, conveying "critical disdain" from a rigorous distance that ironizes tragedy on a quotidian scale.

Perhaps the most salient feature of Eliot's adultery plot, then, is searing tragic irony—an effect suitable to a milieu in which isolated characters lack connection to place, history, or an encompassing narrative web. By the time Arabella's toxic wish for her "imbecile" son's death comes to pass, the estate has been "burdened," leaving "no good prospect for any heir." Harold's need to "make a career for himself" thus redounds with irony. To his mother's chagrin,

40. Auerbach, "Serious Imitation," 433.

41. The point recalls Eliot's letter to Harrison, declaring that her way of "urg[ing] the human sanctities through tragedy" involved "terror" as well as pity (rptd. in Cross, *George Eliot's Life*, 2:483)—a formulation that echoes Aristotle's. But see also Norton on Eliot's preference for Schiller's theory of tragedy.

42. Auerbach, "Serious Imitation," 448.

he prefers the mentorship of an Armenian banker to his "high-born" cousin's diplomatic connections—a preference he is seen unknowingly to inherit from a man he regards as his social inferior (24). Meanwhile, the unscrupulous Jermyn has accelerated the ruin of a property already mired in lawsuits, shadowed by scandal, and sapped by the degenerate Durfey line. In a clear reprise of the naturalistic trope of "money from elsewhere," Harold, who is said to be "rich as a Jew" (194), uses mercantile wealth from "the East" to refurbish Transome Court (37). The crown of his Orientalized condition is his having purchased a "slave" who has borne him a son (421). From the standpoint of political fiction, therefore, Harold can neither rejuvenate Toryism like a Disraeli-esque scion, nor body forth a progressive alternative, like Meredith's hero in *Beauchamp's Career.* Whereas Felix determines to build a new polity from the bottom up, Harold talks vaguely of "abuses" (43). Like much else in the adultery plot, the main effect of his radical pose is to abash Arabella's pride in her Tory family, while proving once again that the "determined lizard" is his father's son.

If most of the dramatic power of *Felix Holt* thus derives from Mrs. Transome's adulterous tragedy, the narrator takes care to fuse the main lines of the doubleplot. Philosophically, the hinge is the vision of history which informs most of Eliot's writing, expressed in the narrator's oft-cited dictum "there is no private life which has not been determined by a wider public life" (50).[43] Formally, the same hinge pairs Arabella's downfall with Esther's *Bildung*—a contrast that distinguishes *Felix Holt* from an absolute naturalism like Flaubert's and enables Eliot (as she put it in a letter to Frederic Harrison) to "urge the human sanctities through tragedy."[44] As Robert E. Norton has argued, Eliot shared Friedrich Schiller's belief that the crux of tragedy was not (Aristotelian) catharsis but, rather, an extension of sympathy which animates one's "inner freedom to obey the promptings of duty."[45] *Felix Holt* enacts this enlargement of sympathy by enabling Esther to emancipate herself through tragic witness. As she happens upon the weeping Mrs. Transome, she apprehends "the dimly-suggested tragedy of this woman's life, the dreary waste of

43. The narrator's strongest endorsement of holism follows Rufus's idealistic objection to the secret ballot:

> What we call illusions are often, in truth, a wider vision of past and recent realities—a willing movement of a man's soul with the larger sweep of the world's forces—a movement toward a more assured end than the chances of a single life. We see human heroism broken into units and say, this unit did little . . . But in this way we might break up a great army into units; in this way we might break the sunlight into fragments. (184)

44. Rptd. in Cross, *George Eliot's Life,* 483.

45. Quoted in Norton, "The Aesthetic Education of Humanity," 9.

years." Her response, which borders on "horror," prompts Esther to renounce Transome Court in favor of the arduous freedom of building an unprecedented historical future (470). *Felix Holt* thus concludes by foreshadowing a collective citizenship distinct from the backward-looking organicisms of earlier social-problem genres.[46]

II. "DECENCY IN THE MIDDLE"

> Individualism, when it grapples with the facts, is driven no small distance along Socialist lines.
>
> —L. T. Hobhouse, *Liberalism*, 57

Although *Felix Holt* is hardly the most successful of Eliot's genre experiments, it is important to recognize that the ontological holism that Esther's "revolutionary" union prefigures was indeed a "pregnant movement" of nineteenth-century history. Indeed, the radicalism of skilled artisans like Felix reached its peak in September 1864, when the first Workingman's International was founded in London, just a few months after Eliot began working on her political novel (see P. Anderson). Hence, while Eliot herself feared franchise reform and did not endorse socialism, her political fiction singles out the same independent workingmen whose collectivist aspirations impressed Marx among others. By the time Eliot published *Daniel Deronda*, the proletarianization of labor was advancing apace and the First International had stalled. But with the late-century rise of New Liberalism and the Labour Party, collectivism became a prevalent force in British culture and politics. When Felix warns the

46. See also Kurnick, who proposes a "symptomatic displacement" between "the social suffering" implicit in political struggle and the stark "images of Mrs. Transome's psychological pain" ("*Felix Holt*: Love in the Time of Politics," 148). Lesjak's Arnoldian reading of *Felix Holt* does not consider the possibility that the stakes of the novel's vision of a unifying culture are democratic and civic rather than "national" per se (73). As Kucich shows, social-problem novels foster a "mid-century organic ideology" which "transformed paternalism into the ethical foundation for a social democratic politics" ("Appealing vs. Arguing in *Felix Holt*: From Paternalism to the Welfare State in Social Problem Fiction," n. pag.). In claiming that the generic hybridity of *Felix Holt* marks a difference from the organicisms of the past, my point is not to insulate Eliot's politics from charges of paternalism or conservatism; Betensky, for example, argues that Felix is, in effect, a middle-class character in a novel that substitutes a bourgeois vision of working-class politics for a "real" politics from below. But even granting this middle-class outlook, the novel's holistic social ontology is more future-oriented (if also more fragile) than the staid hierarchies of older organicisms. By affirming a holistic radicalism, instead of the dominant rights-bearing and atomistic variation espoused by Cobden and Bright, *Felix Holt* is timely, prescient, and progressive for the 1860s (in ways that anticipate the emerging social ontology necessary for collectivism).

election-day crowd that "ignorant power comes in the end to the same thing as wicked power" (249), he points to the difference between citizenship and a mere right to vote—predicting, in effect, that the atomistic radicalism of his day will acquire the latter without ensuring the former. Yet, within twenty years of *Felix Holt*'s publication, thanks in part to the advance of Hegel's philosophy, Continental ideas like those Eliot embraced helped to shape what would become the dominant ontology of British politics for much of the twentieth century.

In particular, British Idealists such as J. S. Mill's disciple T. H. Green and Green's disciple L. T. Hobhouse were drawn to the Hegelian notion of *Sittlichkeit* (ethical life) which holds that citizenship can reconcile individual liberty with communal participation. In a well-known speech from 1881, Green defined such freedom as "a positive power or capacity of doing" something "worth doing . . . in common with others" which "each man exercises through the help or security given him by his fellow-men, and which he in turn helps to secure for them."[47] By the time Hobhouse published *Liberalism* (1911), his influential account of what politics must achieve to deliver such "social freedom," a British mode of social democracy had begun to emerge.[48] It is worth noting, then, that Hobhouse admired Eliot's fiction—the intense moral freedom of which he preferred to the deterministic naturalisms of his own day.[49] What he especially commended was the "exaltation of self-sacrifice" as a "means not to salvation in another life but to social harmony in this life"[50]—in other words, the arduous work of assembling a holistic social ontology which Eliot's fiction identifies with the *Bildung* of civic heroines such as Romola and Esther.[51]

It is this focus on an ontological holism fostered by female citizenship which links Eliot's political fiction to millennial Denmark. As Shari Berman notes, the social democracy that developed in Europe at the turn of the twentieth century was neither a continuation of classical liberalism nor an unstable

47. Green, *Lectures*, 199.

48. Hobhouse, *Liberalism*, 48. The Labour Party eventually succeeded the Liberals as the main foundation for these political aspirations. On the advance of British collectivism, see Fraser and, from a literary perspective, Goodlad, *Victorian Literature and the Victorian State*; on the rise of more Germanic notions of individualism in Britain, see Lukes, "The Meanings of Individualism"; on Green's Hegelianism, see Wempe, *T. H. Green's Theory of Positive Freedom*. The social democratic century in Britain began in the prewar years and lasted until the 1970s and 1980s; see Ferrall, "From Wells to John Berger," 807.

49. Hobhouse, *World*, 34–35.

50. Ibid., 44.

51. As Kucich notes, Eliot's fiction "powerfully influenced" Hobhouse "from his career's beginning until its end"; he suggests that *Felix Holt* most actively promotes "a welfare ethos" by sustaining a "centralist" organicism ("Appealing vs. Arguing").

compromise between the latter and Marxism. Rather, social democracy is a politics in its own right, which reverses classical liberalism by subjecting economic forces to the democratic control of a sovereign citizenry. To do so, it convenes a public that, ideally, is socially cohesive without privileging any particular group, class, race, or ethnicity. To American eyes, Denmark's status as one of the world's most economically fair, gender-equal, "happy," and sexually open-minded countries likely suggests social democracy of the highest order.[52] During the 2016 presidential election, Bernie Sanders upheld Denmark as a role model that has "gone a long way to ending the enormous anxieties that comes [*sic*] with economic insecurity."[53] Danes themselves hastened to explain that "social democracy" is a misleading term given the prevalence of business-friendly neoliberal reforms since the 1980s as well as the challenge of immigration in a state often thought to rely on ethnic homogeneity.[54] According to Ashley Lavelle's *The Death of Social Democracy* (2008)—which discusses Sweden but not Denmark—the embrace of neoliberalism after the collapse of the postwar economic boom has left social democratic parties without a progressive agenda. Though social democratic politicians continue to seek parliamentary office, they lack a firm commitment to restraining capitalism.[55] Is Lavelle's assessment too bleak to describe a Danish political condition that continues to deliver equality and social welfare despite the advance of privatization and technocracy? Although this essay can only ponder that question, what is clear is that cynical power-seeking is a dominant theme in *Forbrydelsen*—especially in the doubleplotted first season that oscillates between political Bildungsroman and police procedural.

Looking for generic clues, we recognize the show's Sarah Lund as the type of gritty "hard-boiled" detective who has embodied modern alienation ever since Raymond Chandler and Dashiell Hammett popularized the form. As Jason Mittell notes, *Forbrydelsen* amplifies this "genre mixing" by "placing a female protagonist at the center" of "a traditionally masculinist genre story."[56]

---

52. Berman, *Understanding Social Democracy.* On happiness see, for example, "World Happiness Report 2015 Ranks Happiest Countries."

53. Moody, "Bernie Sanders's American Dream," n. pag.; cf. Sanders.

54. Moody, "Bernie Sanders's American Dream." Denmark's neoliberal reforms center on political trade-offs of the kind that the increasingly polarized two-party structure of American politics seldom generates. As Sørensen notes in his work on Danish universities, the introduction of market incentives yielded cost savings that benefited higher education (as well as "tax reductions" and the "development of a very active and aggressive foreign policy"; "Visiting the Neo-Liberal University," 7). Danish universities remain relatively well funded, but the new managerial systems of control have diminished shared governance and academic freedom.

55. Lavelle, *The Death of Social Democracy*, 14.

56. Mittell, *Complex TV*, 251. Of course, Eliot herself pioneered this technique when she put Romola at the fore of a historical romance—a genre hitherto manned by the likes of Waverley.

Yet, even as a female hard-boiled detective in a naturalistic procedural, Lund's characterization stands out for its originality. In the words of actor Sophie Grabøl, the character is an "isolated person unable to communicate"—a challenge she met by performing the part as if Lund were "a man."[57] By twinning this complex procedural with political Bildungsroman, *Forbrydelsen*'s award-winning first season pairs an implacable female dick's determination to solve her case with a male politician's fall from innocence. Over the course of twenty episodes, Lund contends with the pressures of a high-profile rape and murder, the victim's grieving family, internal police politics, a byzantine conspiracy, and multiple threats to her life—all of which exact a punishing toll on her and her family. In the adjacent political narrative, the ambitious Troels Hartmann learns too late that the cost of winning Copenhagen's mayoralty is devastatingly high. Though he is cleared of any crime, Hartmann, whose name bespeaks his aspiration to ethical integrity, must break off his engagement to a colleague whom he can no longer trust. In the end, he realizes that he is as morally compromised as the cynical career politician he fought to replace.

Forbrydelsen renders the cold naturalism of this doubleplot through an almost total absence of daylight: each episode opens with a lingering shot of Copenhagen lit up against a nocturnal November sky. This Danish heart of darkness creates an inauspicious climate for domestic bliss. Like Hartmann, Lund abandons her plans to remarry and, even more concerningly, neglects her adolescent son. But whereas Hartmann believes he is a better man until the very last moment, the illusionless Lund knows that the consuming demands of detective work will always trump private matters such as family or even her own career. This grim self-knowledge endows Lund with a stoic gravitas that positions her as a kind of Deronda to Hartmann's Gwendolen in a story that offers no exodus for either.[58] Although both plots are intermittently tragic, only Hartmann experiences a life-changing fall. Lund, whose

---

Injecting the nonconformist Lund into the politically sensitive bureaucracy of Danish policing, *Forbrydelsen* also recalls Ian Rankin's Rebus series which, as John Scaggs notes, puts a "rule-bending individualist" of the hard-boiled cast into a set of procedural conventions intended to emphasize teamwork, paperwork, and other routines. *Crime Fiction*, 90.

57. Anthony, "*The Killing*," n. pag. Space does not permit a full discussion of the "Nordic noir" investment in heroines who answer to the psychic perils of (female) detective work with spectacular emotional control—what for Lisbeth Salander, the title character of Stieg Larssen's *The Girl with the Dragon Tattoo* (2008), derives from a long history of abuse, and for Saga Noren of the Danish-Swedish collaboration *The Bridge* (2011–present) suggests a neurological difference compounded by childhood trauma. On the recent trend for emotionally damaged female detectives, who are paired with emotionally gifted male partners, see Kornfield, "Re-Solving Crimes."

58. That said, at the close of *Forbrydelsen*'s third season, Lund, who breaks the law to fulfill her duty, leaves Denmark behind her.

fully fledged ethos thus recalls Felix Holt's, establishes herself as a professional able to weather adversities that would destroy a less single-minded figure. While *Forbrydelsen*'s Denmark is too fallen to save, Lund's victories on behalf of truth constitute her as a lone public citizen in a naturalistic wilderness.

In turning to *Borgen*, it is important to distinguish DR's political series from the worldwide enthusiasm for Nordic noir which *Forbrydelsen* intensified. Whereas crime genres have proven transcultural appeal, few imagined that a show about Danish politics would garner audiences outside Scandinavia.[59] Steeped in its contemporary moment, *Borgen* addresses a nation of citizens who increasingly experience themselves as consumerist strivers, or, still worse, victims of a society infiltrated by immigrants and the politically correct elites who enable them. This crisis of Danish mettle plays out against world financial crisis, deepening neoliberalization, and American hegemony. Yet, also profoundly antinaturalistic, *Borgen* expresses a measure of idealistic "faith in the possibility" of the "collective good" of the kind that Hartmann's story nullifies.[60] Thus, like Eliot's *Middlemarch*—another antinaturalistic serial narrative that places a public-spirited woman at the fore of a complex social location—*Borgen* proposes that despite the clear limitations of individual moral acts, the morality of individuals is indispensable to collective progress. Indeed, Hobhouse's ontological linkage between social harmony and individual sacrifice constitutes what we might call the Eliotic thematic of *Borgen*'s variation on the political Bildungsroman.[61]

To be sure, *Borgen* has its share of cynics: most especially, Michael Laugesen, the champagne-sipping Labour leader who gleefully pees on Parliament before reinventing himself as a tabloid provocateur.[62] Contemptuous of such

---

59. The name *Borgen* itself marks the show's particularity, since it is the familiar moniker for the Danish Parliament. Roughly signifying *castle* in English, *Borgen* derives from Christiansborg Palace, which is both the monarch's residence and the site of Parliament. While *Forbrydelsen* and *Borgen* were both produced by DR and bear the stamp of its "dogmas," the two shows had separate creative teams. *Borgen* was still in development when *Forbrydelsen* began to air in 2007. The latter's landmark success in Britain occurred in 2011, after *Borgen*'s first season had aired domestically. *Forbrydelsen*'s reception in the United States was slowed by AMC's Seattle-based version of the show, *The Killing* (2011–13).

60. Hammerich is citing one of creator Adam Price's original concept papers for the show. *The "Borgen" Experience*, 44.

61. *Borgen*'s social ontology is, to some degree, an expression of DR's public service mandate which, as Redvall notes, emphasizes the ethical and social potential of television storytelling.

62. While riveting in depicting the realpolitik particular to parliamentary coalitions, *Borgen* is a decidedly more Eliotic narrative than Netflix's *House of Cards* (2013–)—an American series (loosely based on a UK precursor) more interested in the pleasures of venality than the art of the possible. According to another early concept paper, the original inspiration for *Borgen* was *The West Wing* (1999–2006); see Hammerich, *The "Borgen" Experience*, 40. The analogy

naïve notions as democracy, Laugesen declares that a "tiny privileged circle of people rule Denmark," a system that suits him just fine so long as he is one of them. But while Laugesen's antics play out across all three seasons, *Borgen* is more interested in lesser sinners like Kasper Juul, the shrewd "spin doktor" whose lack of center bespeaks a traumatic childhood, and Torben Friis, the television news producer wedged between adhering to journalistic ideals and pleasing his neoliberal bosses. That these male figures command so much sympathy despite their flaws highlights the show's pointed reliance on women for its vision of a better Denmark. Whereas Birgitte Nyborg hopes to revitalize the nation's politics, Katrine Fønsmark, an ambitious young newscaster, defends the integrity of the fourth estate with the help of Hanne Holm, her battle-worn mentor.

Crucial to this regeneration is *Borgen*'s conviction of "Decency in the Middle"—the title of the show's first episode. When we first meet Nyborg, she is the leader of *De Moderate,* one of several minority parties that have splintered from the establishment politics of Labour (based on Denmark's real-life Social Democrats) and the Liberals (a center-right party based on the real-life Venstre). When Liberal PM Lars Hesselboe embroils himself in a scandal involving purchases for his wife on a government credit card, the unscrupulous Laugesen overplays his hand while Nyborg's heartfelt appeal to citizenship yields a win for her party. The way is paved for the Moderates to invite Labour and the Greens to join Nyborg's coalition. In the show's first two seasons, Nyborg learns to negotiate crises, mediate disagreements, and execute her role as a forward-thinking head of state. While she believes that "democracy is a dialogue," she learns that governing a democracy is also about the need to decide and act. The ministers in her own coalition require constant vigilance, since these ambitious politicians crave power for themselves and their parties. When necessary, Birgitte seeks counsel from outside experts, including her husband, Phillip Christensen, a former CEO and lecturer in international finance. Above all, she relies on media adviser Kasper Juul. Though his "spin" rests on shaky civic principles, and is shot through with personal tragedy, he is, ironically, the only character she can trust to keep her political interests in mind.

As leader of *De Moderate,* Nyborg resists the neoliberal status quo neither through staunch Leftism or populism but, rather, through a centrist vision of "broad compromise" which entails crossing party lines to create lasting

---

is misleading, however, because the focus on a female prime minister and the accompanying emphasis on private life make the two shows markedly different.

change.[63] As a progressive, Birgitte supports the Green Party's Left agenda: but as prime minister, she believes that scaled-down reforms won partly through tolerable concessions to the Right are the best way forward. Old-school Leftism like that of her mentor Bent Sejrø is superseded with little nostalgia. Instead, "decency in the middle" entails steering the best possible course between the Right's market fundamentalism and the old Left's dream of a postcapitalist socialism. Thus, while Birgitte is neither a heartless technocrat nor cynical elitist, in "The Last Worker," a season 2 episode, she looks on as Labour ousts an older leader who has risen from the rank and file. And while Birgitte keeps her distance from American influence, she finds her own reasons to increase military spending and stay the course in Afghanistan. Only xenophobic anti-immigrant policies, which offend her vision of a tolerant Denmark, evince a more assertive Leftism from this consummate pragmatist.[64]

Then too, "Decency in the Middle" is not only Nyborg's political creed. It is also the formal structure of many *Borgen* episodes—a feature that, in resembling the writerly qualities of multiplot fiction, distinguishes the show from soap opera. Committed to preserving Denmark's welfare state during a time of austerity, Nyborg expands education through reduction of early retirement. Advised to turn a blind eye to American use of Greenland to transfer illegal detainees, she visits Denmark's former colony and grants more autonomy to its indigenous government. Faced with a powerful businessman's call for intervention in an African civil war, she determines to broker peace. Such persistent emphasis on the center may remind U.S. viewers of Barack Obama's bid for a "grand bargain" (though the tactic works differently in a governing coalition that, by definition, has the votes to decide).[65]

It is all the more ironic, therefore, that, while female statesmanship calls forth arts of compromise which Birgitte eagerly masters, marriage and motherhood turn out to be absolute and unyielding. What begins as an idyllic domestic partnership gradually founders until it crashes with inexorable force. Birgitte's unexpected rise to power, we learn, has occurred at an inopportune moment. Having agreed to spend five years each supporting one another's

---

63. The show's focus on the "middle" anticipates mainstream discourse about our own political malaise, such as Tony Blair's 2017 call for a unified "center."

64. Compare to Shari Berman, who notes that increasing multiculturalism means that today's social democracies must be built on the relatively inclusive grounds of "shared value and responsibilities"—not appeals to race, ethnicity, or exclusive cultural qualifications. *Understanding Social Democracy*, 24.

65. On Obama's "grand bargain" see, for example, Wallsten, Montgomery, and Wilson, "Obama's Evolution: Behind the Failed 'Grand Bargain' on the Debt." A less novelistic aspect of the show's complexity is the way that news coverage of the political narrative provides not only another plotline but also an analogue for the viewer's television experience.

careers, Phillip is at the end of his stint as primary caregiver when Birgitte gets the chance to become prime minister. When she asks if he is willing to make this sacrifice, he replies that no man wants to keep his wife from seizing such an opportunity. But as viewers can see, most of the men *Borgen* depicts would never marry politicians in the first place—men like Hesselboe, whose neglected wife triggers the scandal that elevates Birgitte to power. Still, if we trust in Phillip's readiness to endure a few more years in academia, it is because we feel his pride in his wife's achievements, perceive his self-confidence, and, above all, believe these loving partners will find their own "decency in the middle."

That this turns out to be far from the case seems, at times, like a contrivance. Why does this wealthy professional couple lack domestic help? Alternatively, we might point to Birgitte's failings: consumed with affairs of state, she is too distracted to give her family the attention they need. On at least one occasion she forgets that however much power she wields in Borgen, in her own castle she is part of a couple that has thrived on equality. "I love my wife," Phillip tells her in one episode, adding that he is less sure about "that Prime Minister lady." It is also possible that Phillip himself is "a chilly monolith of passive-aggressive blame targeted at the doubts of working women."[66] The possibility arises when Phillip loses his interest in sex as he begins to feel like an accessory to his wife's official life. The man who starts the season by joking that he looks forward to "blowjobs" from the prime minister ends up rejecting precisely that offer. It is only later, when he tells Birgitte that he has agreed to become the CEO of a major corporation, that he rediscovers his passion. Explaining why he has taken on the kind of position he had agreed to forgo, he tells her, "I wanted it"—speaking a Danish word that sounds like "lust." We get the idea. The problem is that when Katrine's reporting reveals that Birgitte's defense minister has been accepting gifts from a military contractor, Phillip's position as the new CEO for a company that supplies parts becomes a liability, leading Birgitte to ask him to resign. Furious, he disappears. "I felt like breaking something," he tells her later, admitting that he has had an affair.

As Birgitte's old friend Bent reminds her, most politicians' marriages are a disaster: his advice is to make the kind of "arrangement" he has with his wife. Eager to save the marriage, Birgitte urges Phillip to weather the storm until they can repair the relationship—during which time she will accept his need for "intimacy." But when Kasper advises a televised interview to quell rumors about the marriage, Phillip, unwilling to play his part in a sham, asks for a divorce. Birgitte opens Parliament with the best speech Denmark has

66. I am grateful to Ted Underwood for permission to quote his online comment.

heard for decades, assuring Danes that "they are better than they think they are" and echoing a famous inaugural address: "Ask not what your country can do for you—ask what you can do for your country." As a newscaster remarks, Nyborg's first year in power has proved her to be a "resolute and realistic PM."

Replete with tragic irony, *Borgen* proffers a charismatic leader who can unify an entire country around a vision of shared civic life but cannot figure out how to meet her family's needs. In this millennial variation on the adulterous geopolitical aesthetic, the same woman who achieves "broad compromise" in the public realm fails to mend tears in her own marriage. Though such paradoxes are plausible, they push the show uncomfortably close to Anne-Marie Slaughter's much-discussed thesis that feminism has fatally encouraged women to believe they can "have it all."[67] It is remarkable, then, that rather than turn this challenge into an issue for politics—for example, by developing a story about a policy to aid working families who need counseling or care—*Borgen* heightens the pathos: in effect, portraying marital breakdown as a tragic necessity for political leaders (especially women). In this way, though *Borgen,* like *Felix Holt,* offers female citizenship as an alternative to the male-centered political Bildungsroman, it does so to decidedly different effect.

For example, when Birgitte, learning of Phillip's affair, repels his outstretched arms and falls, she cuts her eye. The prime minister's appearance on television must conceal the evidence of her battering. Whereas Denmark sees their stalwart *Statsminister* shot from the right, viewers of *Borgen* see her head on and know what she suffers. The same tragic irony determines Birgitte's somehow forgetting that her husband wants a job, not a mistress. Thus, her attempt at compromise—hatched from vague notions about what male politicians have done—merely confirms Phillip's sense that his wife has become someone else. Yet, when season 2 opens several months later with the children living in Birgitte's custody, Phillip somehow fails to realize that she has made the kind of changes which would have precluded the rift; instead, he presses her to finalize the divorce. The episode opens with Birgitte wearing body armor as she visits troops in Afghanistan and closes with her breaking down in Phillip's arms. Shot from above, she tells him, "I don't want to divorce you." These pointed contrasts recur throughout the second season. As Nyborg grows into an ever more confident leader, Phillip's new relationship with a pediatrician takes a private toll. Accidentally overhearing the couple's giddy banter, the shaken prime minister must cancel a plan to meet Phillip's new

67. Slaughter's controversial 2011 article, "Why Women Still Can't Have It All," provoked numerous online criticisms (e.g., Linda Hirshman, "A 'Very Hostile' Response to Anne-Marie Slaughter"), a book-length reformulation of the argument (Slaughter, *Unfinished Business*), and, most recently, a cluster of replies in the Winter 2017 issue of *Signs.*

"*kæreste*." When her daughter Laura calls to assure her that Cecilie is really nice—she cooks Mexican food and plays Pictionary—Birgitte is once again reduced to tears. To be sure, the purpose of this spectacle is not (or not intentionally) to humiliate a formidable female character but, rather, to dramatize the tension between the success of political *Bildung* and the pathos of broken private life. Still, the comparison to *Felix Holt* is telling: whereas Arabella suffers for ill-fated selfishness, Birgitte pays a comparable cost for political ambitions that ultimately benefit Denmark.

Borgen's multiplot structure amplifies these effects by making Nyborg the emblem of the countless professional women whose sacrifices point the way to a better Denmark. There is Hanne Holm, the pioneering journalist who built a career as a foreign correspondent while her ex-husband raised the daughter who no longer talks to her. Holm's inspiring alliance with Katrine is shadowed by episodes of alcoholic ruin. Though Katrine herself is too young for such wear, by season 3 she is raising a child whose father is the incorrigible Kasper. When the little tot cries for his grandma as his mother cares for him, we laugh—but we also worry. We do not want Katrine to end up drinking or her child to grow up feeling abandoned (like Sarah Lund's son in *Forbrydelsen*).

Significantly, the original concept for *Borgen* centered on the moral effects of political compromise. But as research revealed "the incredible personal costs" of high political office—and DR responded by calling for more focus on "private lives"—the concept changed. Instead of asking whether it is possible to maintain power while staying true to one's own "political and personal morality"—a question that *Forbrydelsen*'s political plot also pondered—a rather different question came to the fore: "Is it possible to maintain power and stay true to yourself?"[68] Reading between the lines of this carefully gender-neutral phrasing, we perceive that the real question seems to be "Is it possible for a *female politician* to maintain power and stay true to her (female) self?" Another key revision turned Birgitte's husband from a man already weary of his wife's career to a supportive paragon[69]—the kind of husband who would be terrible to lose. Hence, "Can a female politician maintain power without losing the husband she loves?" In yet another tweak, the alcoholic journalist was changed from a man to the female Hanne. In other words, "Can *any* woman flourish in a demanding career while enduring 'incredible personal costs'"? Thus, while no concept paper ever articulates the point, *Borgen* is as much about the "disability of being women" as any Eliot novel; only the message is decidedly Slaughter's focus on women's "still" not "having it all."

68. Hammerich, *The "Borgen" Experience*, 52.

69. Ibid., 47.

Toward the end of season 2, Laura suffers from anxiety attacks and must be hospitalized. As Birgitte and Phillip pull together to support their daughter, each recognizes a part in triggering the crisis. A friendly doctor assures Birgitte that Laura did not become ill because her mother became prime minister. Yet, she also articulates a Slaughter-like take on the professional woman's paradox in a nutshell: "You can't work 24 hours a day and be a good mother—but you can't stop working." When Birgitte confesses that she finds running Denmark easier than family life, a priceless moment follows in which the shrink, dragging on a cigarette, says, "Welcome to the club." In the end, however, *Borgen* confirms the logic of "Why Women Still Can't Have It All" without offering any corresponding effort to counter or question a material condition that (allegedly) draws professional women into an unlivable contradiction.

At the end of season 2, Laura must leave the hospital because of intrusive paparazzi; Birgitte responds by finding a way around the demand that both motherhood and profession be all or nothing. She determines to put Denmark on hold, taking a leave of absence to care for her child. A month later, Phillip watches as Birgitte's political rivals criticize her for dereliction of duty. In the richest of ironies, Hesselboe—who lost an election because of his distressed wife's expenses—complains that Danes need the best prime minister, not the best human being. Earlier in the episode, Birgitte reproaches Phillip for the first time: "It takes time to find the right balance. We had to invent it." "You were weak, and you quit. You let me down." Listening to Hesselboe boast about neglecting his wife when the country needed him, Phillip realizes that she is right. The season closes with him ending the relationship with Cecilie while Birgitte calls an election. Viewers are left to ponder whether the next season will feature a male Bildungsroman in which the prime minister's husband, like Esther in *Felix Holt,* develops into an "unprecedented" subject whose organizing force is the historical future—in this case, an ambitious man who refuses to make his powerful wife suffer for her public success.[70]

What *Borgen* gives us instead is the mastery of its dispersive storytelling—the way that particular events or themes cut across the zones of a storyworld to ramify ethical, political, and aesthetic perception. In doing so, the show offers a televisual variation on the multiplottedness of *Middlemarch.* In particular, Birgitte's doubling with Kasper—the Lydgate to her Dorothea—substitutes an indispensable "spin doktor" for Eliot's story of fallen medical aspiration. We are reminded that *Middlemarch* also shows us how the "catastrophe" of failed marriage takes many forms. As the narrator tells us, many "middle-aged men"

70. Instead, at the start of season 3 we learn that the marriage is over: Phillip and Birgitte remain friendly, he is single, and she has moved on to a new relationship.

who long ago accustomed themselves to the grind of professional life, "once meant to shape their own deeds and alter the world a little." Lydgate, of course, "did not mean to be one of those failures." A would-be hero, he chooses medical research to achieve "intellectual conquest and the social good," not to keep a family in bourgeois comfort.[71] Lydgate's tragedy is, thus, the fatal attraction that leads him to a "moral mediocrity" that Esther eludes when she chooses Felix over Harold.

Borgen glimpses a comparable story of failed professional idealism in its focus on Torben Friis in season 3. Harried by a cocky young supervisor obsessed with ratings and gimmicks, the newsman discovers that he is no longer "sexy" enough to get a new job. The compensatory office affair that follows reiterates a familiar theme by leaving Torben's colleague, Pia, disappointed in the end. But the prolonged focus on Torben's enervated masculinity, as he chafes under the yoke of neoliberal reforms, is also freshly illuminating—prompting us to wonder if *Borgen* makes women the primary bearers of social change because it imagines the pains of their gendered experience as the best preparation for neoliberalism's relentless assaults on civic life. By contrast, Kasper, a serial philanderer, is a surprisingly static character who is never prompted to consider whether his private troubles—rooted in childhood sexual abuse—impact his efforts on behalf of Birgitte's political vision.[72] In the case of Phillip, *Borgen* is even more reticent. Is his life as a CEO in banking worth the price of losing Birgitte? Does he regret having failed to "invent" the balance that might have helped his family to thrive? Would Denmark's citizenry prefer such a partner to their usual diet of spin-doctored spouses? The show's palpable indifference to these questions helps to explain why no one writes articles titled "Why Men Still Don't Have It All"—even in Denmark.

Borgen thus reinforces a gendered division between public and private which derives from classical liberalism—a division, moreover, that Eliot's novels contest and that social democracy's collective politics and shared sacrifice promises to eradicate. As such, *Borgen* naturalizes a particular way of organizing social life that insulates (male) civic duties from a space of care which

---

71. Eliot, *Middlemarch*, 140.

72. The secret tragedy of childhood sexual abuse, depicted through melodramatic flashbacks, was another tweak to the show's original concept. Although it offers a compelling spectacle of male suffering, Kasper's private trauma freezes him in perpetual adolescence without exacting any noticeable professional toll. Instead, his "traumatic childhood" helps to "explain his cynicism" while enabling the character to "evolve" into someone who believes in Nyborg's political mission (Hammerich, *The "Borgen" Experience*, 56). For Kasper, in other words, the neoliberal split between public and private life is professionally productive. By contrast, when Katrine becomes Birgitte's spin doctor in season 3, a female pattern recurs in which professional overwork threatens maternal bonds without becoming a topic for political redress.

remains stubbornly feminized. Rather than create the male *Bildung* that might enable Phillip or Kasper to evolve into citizens who politicize their domestic choices and help to prefigure new kinds of social life, *Borgen* turns these men into minor characters.

This makes *Borgen* something of a conundrum. At a time when American television favors larger-than-life male characters such as Tony Soprano and Walter White, *Borgen* creates female characters who are rarely overshadowed by the men in their lives. It evokes the persistent sexism of one of the world's most gender-equal countries. Over and again we witness the pats on the bottom, the patronizing remarks, the scorn heaped on feminism, age, "goody two shoes," and so on. But the writers of this show—who, like the writers of *Forbrydelsen,* all happen to be men—unwittingly create a trap.[73] In their imaginary pantheon, Danish women take on moral and political struggles of which, men, apparently, are no longer capable. Thus, while the intention is clearly otherwise, *Borgen* installs a new kind of double standard: it conjures women's exemplary civic passion and then demands full access to the resulting pathos as the inevitable "private" tragedies ensue.

One is prompted to wonder how Sarah Lund would look if she paused to weep over every lost love before entering dark buildings armed with a flashlight. In fact, there are moments throughout *Forbrydelsen* which gesture toward this very perception—but the conventions of hard-boiled guarantee that Sarah's suffering will be rigorously curtailed. To think about what the relaxation of this double standard would look like in a political drama, we might imagine a show in which scenes of Hesselboe's private despair follow each glib remark and slippery maneuver.[74] It is worth reflecting, then, that the real-life female prime minister of Denmark, Helle Thorning-Schmidt, who rose to power less than a year after *Borgen* first aired (as a Social Democrat, not a moderate), is still married. So too is Angela Merkel, Europe's most powerful leader.[75] Thus, while *Borgen*'s creators altered the original concept to produce a drama centered on personal costs, the inital plan to focus on the moral effects of political compromise might well have provided a more realistic window into Denmark's condition.

73. Note, however, Camilla Hammerich's role as executive producer.

74. The closest approximation notably concerns a male politician, Troels Höxenhaven, who pays a tragic price for his life of closeted homosexuality.

75. Likewise, Margaret Thatcher, Britain's first female prime minister, remained married until her death. Thorning-Schmidt's British husband, the son of former Labour Party leader Neil Kinnock, may perhaps have helped to inspire the British architect with whom Birgitte develops a relationship in the show's final season. It is interesting to contemplate whether the show's writers had in mind Merkel's husband, an academic, and Thatcher's husband, a businessman, when they made Phillip both an academic and a businessman.

When Birgitte fires her mentor Bent at the end of season 1 despite years of friendship, he tells her she is "good at separating things." In fact, neoliberal work discipline insists on such compartmentalization. Pressed on relentlessly by newfangled metrics and fiscal demands, we learn late in the game what is left for our friends, loved ones, and fellow citizens. This is the tragic irony of many neoliberal lives. At its most Eliotic, *Borgen* rallies against the atomization and compartmentalization of the neoliberal lifeworld to propose a "Common Future" in shared civic life. But when the show dwells on the suffering of its female leaders while occluding the private worlds of their cynical male rivals, it falls into a kind of cliché. By shielding such men from the camera's gaze, it endows them with a political edge that may compensate for the moral high ground they're denied.

In fact, inventing "the right balance" is not simply a question of how much time married professionals spend at home. By the same token, shared civic life requires more than political trade-offs between Right and Left (though that may make sense as a starting point). The dramatic tension *Borgen* seeks between the optimism of political *Bildung* and the pathos of private tragedy is thus everywhere latent in the neoliberal storyworld: including the workers who have lost their access to high-paying jobs and the immigrants who have yet to find a voice in that tiny circle that rules Denmark. Perhaps in making tragic irony a cathartic emotional valve for viewers in search of political alternatives, Denmark's writers are even "better than they think they are." At the very least, a good start for meditating this *Borgen* from below is the long history of the political Bildungsroman which Eliot's fiction opened up to contemplation at the dawn of the social democratic era.

CHAPTER 6

'Til Death Do Us Part

Marriage, Murder, and Confession

MARLENE TROMP

> It is a very melancholy reflection . . . to consider the number of instances of . . . domestic murders that have disgraced the domestic and private history of this country.
>
> —Chief Baron of the Exchequer Pollack[1]

> I can scarcely conceive of a crime of greater enormity or one of deeper dye.
>
> —Baron Rolfe

SCHOLARSHIP ON marital violence has primarily focused on men's physical assaults on their wives or common-law partners. Examining such abuse has given us a richer sense of Victorian marriage and its terms across the classes. The aspect of this violence, however, that we have neglected in our increasingly nuanced analysis is retributive violence of women abuse victims—women who struck back against their husbands and the institution of marriage they inhabited. This is surely, in part, because it is far easier to locate stories about women who killed their children and themselves in an attempt to escape a violent marriage or about husbands who murdered their wives (indeed, these stories litter the papers) than it is to find those in which women are charged with committing mariticide. When stories of mariticide are told, however, they are told obsessively and with rich commentary, running in papers across the United Kingdom. Examining these tales and their articulation provides new texture to our analysis of Victorian marriage and the Victorian marriage plot, as well as the social politics of its representation.

When we explore how women, who struck back against oppressive systems with murderous rage (or calm preparation) fared in both the social and legal

1. Sir Frederick Pollock, Baronet, Lord Chief Baron Exchequer of the High Court, as quoted in "Crown Court, Saturday. Poisoning a Husband."

landscape, we begin to understand the broad spectrum of ways that such violence was understood and articulated. Women who opposed male authority—and not all mariticides did so—were often swiftly condemned and executed. Those who seemed submissively to inhabit the role of the good wife—particularly when the man had failed to fulfill his role—were sometimes given shockingly light sentences when they confessed to murder. Indeed, the perpetrator's confession, whether occurring before the sentence or after, served as one of the critical components in righting the image of the "murderess" and restoring her "proper" gender identity, as well as restoring a sense of social order. If she had usurped a masculine role or failed to properly refeminize herself in confession, however, her elimination from the social order altogether was the likely outcome.

The ritual of confession is a critical component of this process and reflects in fascinating ways upon our study of literature as an avenue for exploring the nineteenth century. In *The History of Sexuality: An Introduction,* Michel Foucault argues that the confession became vital to Western culture in the nineteenth century. He understood this practice as a means of articulating sexuality, but his argument pertains just as powerfully to the articulation of gender in a period in which the power relations of marriage—intimately predicated upon notions of gender—became increasingly contested. Confession, he argued, produces "intrinsic modifications in the person who articulates it: it exonerates, redeems, and purifies him." Significantly, however, he also noted that "the agency of domination does not reside in the one who speaks (for it is he who is constrained), but in the one who listens and says nothing."[2] As he explains it, "The confession is a ritual of discourse in which the speaking subject is also the subject of the statement; it is also a ritual that unfolds within a power relationship, for one does not confess without the presence (or virtual presence) of a partner who is not simply the interlocutor but the authority who requires the confession."[3] In this process, Foucault suggests, the truth of the confession is "scientifically validated," and the confession is no longer a test, "but rather a sign," and it made in the nineteenth century the subject of the confession a "scientific discourse."[4]

Confession, then, became a way to restore the socially proprietous femininity of a woman who engaged in one of the most destructive, antipatriarchal acts: mariticide. Just as critically, it reinforced the power of the listening culture at large to define gendered norms. The murderess's confessional, which became a genre with its own particular codes and structures in the nineteenth

2. Foucault, *History of Sexuality,* 62.

3. Ibid., 61.

4. Ibid., 67.

century, effectively situated her gender and, further, was broadly dispersed outside of the prison and courtroom. Such confessionals infected those narratives—fictional and nonfictional—that depicted gender disruptions. The Victorian marriage plot, which we have begun to read as increasingly complex and vexed and to which this volume is dedicated, might be read, against this backdrop, as another means of narrating properly restored femininity to Foucault's silent, listening audience—a move that situated the figures in the fiction as powerfully as it situated the readers themselves.[5]

To explore these issues, I examine four cases that occasioned voluminous news coverage from the 1840s through the 1860s, the period when the first domestic violence laws were debated and passed, when access to poison underwent a shift, and when capital punishment was becoming increasingly polemical (especially for women). With this argument, I revise Martin J. Wiener's important analysis of gendered violence. He has argued that, as a perceived danger of men's violence became a serious Victorian concern, there was a concomitant reduction in anxieties about women's violence. "In a Victorian moral climate every day more concerned to tame men than women, the 'intimate danger' in public nightmares was now likelier to come from a man" than a woman.[6] I would argue that, instead, women's potential danger often required urgently public redress. Judith Knelman in her comprehensive study of murderesses, *Twisting in the Wind*, makes claims similar to Wiener's. "Whereas murder by a man frightened the public," she remarks, "murder by a woman, unless it could be explained by insanity, aroused indignation."[7] I would contend that, while the arc of these arguments is keen, they do not capture how and why some women were perceived as threats to be executed and others released for the same crime. Wiener's attention to broadsides alone made him more likely to encounter those women who were executed for their crime, rather than redeemed, and this skews his analysis. Moreover, both Wiener and Knelman focus on cases where women were convicted of murder rather than crimes like manslaughter. The greater digital availability of nineteenth-century newspapers and ease of searching them makes discovering a broader range of cases possible and can help us nuance our analysis.

---

5. This argument might be read, then, as a reconfiguration of Nancy Armstrong's classic argument in *Desire and Domestic Fiction* about the function of domestic fiction in disciplining the reader. Armstrong doesn't speak of confession or Foucaultian confession and its role in thus situating the reader and composer/speaker's gender identity.

6. Wiener, "Alice Arden to Bill Sikes," 202. While Wiener's assessment discusses a number of women executed for mariticide and thus clearly perceived as a threat, he still argues that there was a "diminishing fear of women" (203) and focuses, instead, on men who were perceived to pose the greater danger.

7. Knelman, *Twisting in the Wind*, 6.

One startling case of this type involved Sarah Westwood of Burntwood, Staffordshire. The Westwoods had been married for twenty years, and Sarah was the mother of eight children. In November 1843 Sarah prepared her husband John gruel for midday meal.[8] He called for a bible to read the family verses—an almost novelistic domestic scene—but soon began to feel unwell with stomach cramps and vomiting. He was dead by 9:00 pm. The consistent narrativizing of this prelude to murder suggests how significant telling the story of this normative structure *was* to the events that led to her execution. Indeed, such narratives help us understand patterns in fiction, as well as to better read the historical record. Westwood's undoing of the gendered norms of domestic marriage was her own undoing as much as the act of murder itself.

Even her choice of poison as a murder weapon undermined the domestic scene. Knelman contends that poisoners were the most threatening of murderesses, and I would argue that their exploitation of feminine foodways and domesticity to perpetrate often-undetectable mariticides shocked Victorian gender norms as much as an act of physical violence and made these cases particularly compelling. This was a choice that enough women made to produce significant mariticide anxiety. James Whorton suggests that there was a Victorian perception that arsenic was uniquely attractive to women and posed a particular threat to husbands.[9] He reports that, while 90 percent of spousal murders overall were uxoricide (husbands murdering wives), 55 percent of (*known*) mariticides were poisonings.[10] So pressing was the anxiety about arsenic that, in the wake of several poisoning cases, Parliament crafted the Arsenic Act of 1851, which legally compelled closer regulation and tracking of arsenic sales, a move that suggests that mariticide and women's potential for violence and disruption of gender codes more broadly was more present than we have previously acknowledged.[11]

The Westwoods seemed like a troubling case of apparent marital bliss gone badly awry. Though many people had believed them to be a happy couple, near neighbors and family members had witnessed their rows about their tenant, Samuel Phillips, with whom Sarah was accused of having an affair. These disagreements sometimes became fistfights. Charles Dawson, a neighbor and

8. As I am referring to married couples who share a last name, I adopt a standard of referring to spouses by the first name for clarity and brevity.

9. Whorton, *Arsenic Century*, 21.

10. Ibid., 34.

11. There were, of course, other poisons, but arsenic took a primary place in the scientific study of poisons as well as in cultural consciousness. It was associated with women's autonomy and violence, in part, because it was believed to be an abortifacient.

friend, explained that John, Sarah, and he had all exchanged blows in an out-and-out melee. The outcome, with even the most robust working woman in a battle of strength against two working men, was no surprise. Ultimately, they "knocked her down" and—literally—"left her lying in the road."[12] When John and his perceived rival, Phillips, fought, Sarah urged Phillips on. One witness had heard Sarah tell John she would rather "beg her bread from door to door" than live with him anymore. Sarah was a woman who fought back.

Her wishes, however, were certainly not the ones that mattered the most. With a host of children, a marriage bond, and no access to divorce,[13] she had very little hope of ending her unhappy marriage. While her husband could have cast her off, if he had chosen to do so—without a loss of status or income—she did not have this option. Nor would she have retained custody of her children if she had chosen to walk out. Beating a wife into physical submission and leaving her in the road, but still expecting her to return home to make the family dinner, was not far enough outside the norm to elicit a public response or remedy. This was just as true for a working-class woman as it was for a middle- or upper-class woman (who would order dinner preparation, rather than standing in the kitchen herself) until the Divorce Act of 1857, which legislators saw primarily as a remedy for working-class women.[14] Under these circumstances, it may be that Sarah felt that her husband's death was the only way out of this situation.

Witnesses testified about Sarah's visit to a chemist with a local folk-healer, Hannah Mason (ironically, Samuel Phillip's mother), that was followed by an independent visit of her own. Her own children gave evidence about the gruel she had prepared and their father's reactions, and medical experts testified about John's dying symptoms and the postmortem on the corpse. Mr. Chevas,[15] the surgeon responsible for the initial examination of the body, remarked in stunning terms that "the quantity of arsenic in the stomach was so great that it

---

12. "Assize Intelligence," December 30, 1843, 4.

13. Prior to the Divorce Act of 1857, divorce was only available as an act of Parliament, and then only to women in dire circumstances: adultery plus either incest, desertion, or extreme cruelty.

14. In *The Private Rod,* I explain that women of all classes faced the threat of domestic violence and that legislation was targeted to the "roughs," whom Parliament believed were the likely perpetrators of such violence against women. Fiction, I argue, helped create a paradigm shift in which middle- and upper-class women could be understood as subject to marital violence.

15. Nicholas Corder, who had access to the Salt Library and Shire Hall Library in Stafford, is likely correct when he reports that the surgeon's name was "Chavasac" in *Foul Deeds and Suspicious Deaths in Staffordshire & The Potteries.*

could be removed from the [lining of the organ] with a spoon." His chemical assessment was confirmed by that of professional analytic chemists.[16]

Though Sarah had entered an emphatic "not guilty" plea, the jury quite swiftly condemned her. The reading of the verdict was punctuated by Sarah's hysterical sobs, but this was the only time the press reported her weeping. It wasn't simply motive or opportunity that made it so easy for the jury to send a woman, wife, and mother to the gallows on circumstantial evidence. In spite of her fervent insistence upon her innocence (even up to the moment of her death), Sarah Westwood was already guilty: she had violated gendered Victorian behavioral expectations with her alleged affair and her forceful, even violent, resistance to her husband's authority. Her refusal to bow down under the weight of his death with a sorrowful posture and confession of sins against her husband made her less feminine, less wifely, and less womanly. The act of poisoning could be read as merely an extension of this violence, not just against her husband but against the social codes for wives and marriage. Certainly, the woman who metes out violence against violence becomes a nearly unreadable figure, one to be erased.[17] Judith Knelman agrees, describing such women murderers in stark cultural terms, noting that "murder by a woman was so unthinkable in the patriarchal ideology of Victorian England that it had to be explained away as the action of a whore, witch, monster, or madwoman."[18] We could hardly imagine *Oliver Twist*'s Nancy, for example, returning Bill's blows in the moments before her death and still retaining the reader's sympathy. Sarah's violations easily overwhelmed any doubts about her guilt in the murder case and can help us imagine how we might read fiction more critically against this backdrop.

Not one of the dozens of papers all across the UK who printed the story on Sarah's conviction and death sentence lamented the outcome, in spite of anxieties about both execution and women on the scaffold. The presiding judge, Baron Rolfe, described her crime as uniquely disturbing: "You have been guilty of the crime of willful murder; and that against one whom it was your duty to have cherished and protected instead of injured and attacked. I can scarcely conceive of a crime of greater enormity or one of deeper dye."[19] Sarah Westwood maintained her innocence to the last—in spite of confess-

16. "Assize Intelligence," December 30, 1843, 4.

17. See Auerbach, *Woman and the Demon*, 89. In Auerbach's classic words, Sarah Westwood became more demon than woman. Woman became angelic, in Auerbach's formulation, in part through the establishment of their counterpart, demonic womanhood. She argues that "these interdependent and mutually sustaining character types infuse restrictive social categories with the energy of the uncanny" (9).

18. Knelmen, *Twisting in the Wind*, 230.

19. "Assize Intelligence," December 30, 1843, 4.

ing at a final communion. Her refusal to supply the normalizing comfort that would have come with her confession seemed to enrage the public, who wholly accepted her guilt. She was hanged without public protest and before a very large crowd. No public voices advocated for Sarah Westwood.

In a case that might appear, on its face, to be very similar, Catherine Foster was convicted of her husband's poisoning murder and hanged just three years later in 1846. However, rather than a long and fruitful marriage that ended in a tawdry sea of violence like the Westwoods', Catherine had employed arsenic to rid herself of her husband when she and John were newlyweds. The Fosters had been married only three weeks—ten days of which Catherine had been out of town. Though her trial occurred in the wake of Sarah Westwood's largely uncontested case and while the memory of it was still fresh in the British imagination, Catherine's case produced enormous public consternation and distress—not only regarding the death penalty but about Catherine's execution in particular. What made these cases so different in the public consciousness is striking.

Catherine and John had known each other from childhood, and he had long been attached to her. People observed his attachment and admired it, though she did not return his affection. His feelings were the pivotal component of their relationship. Catherine might have believed that she would be liberated from their relation when she went off to service at sixteen, but John "frequently visited her." Perhaps she felt her only choice was a more dramatic escape, so she planned to go to her aunt's in Pakenham, a village nearly a hundred and twenty miles distant.

At the announcement of this news, however, "the lover became most desirous that the marriage should take place [because] he fancied that . . . he might lose his prize. . . . He earnestly urged [her mother to let them] be married at once."[20] "Her mother consented to her being immediately united."[21] Later, critics confessed that her mother "urged her into the match . . . against her will."[22] The couple was married and moved in with Catherine's mother—perhaps a means of ensuring the girl's fidelity to a bond she had not wished to make.

Catherine took her planned trip, and, given the outcome, one can only imagine her desperation as she approached her home with the man to whom she had unwillingly been wed. On the day of the murder, Catherine prepared one dumpling for her little brother and herself, and another for her husband. Not long after, John fell ill with vomiting and severe stomach cramps. By that evening, he had perished. The first doctor who saw him thought he had died

20. "Law and Assize Intelligence," 19.

21. "The Late Poisoning Case in Suffolk," 8.

22. "The Late Murder of a Husband by His Wife Three Weeks after Marriage," 2.

of cholera—a reasonable theory that should make us (and made the Victorians) wonder how many other deaths were hidden in this way. However, when the chickens in the yard also died suddenly after eating from the dust heap where she had disposed of the vomit, people became suspicious, and Catherine was arrested. "But for the death of the fowls," one London paper recorded, "a cruel and revolting murder would, in all probability[,] have been buried in the grave."[23]

When John's body was exhumed by the crown for a postmortem, Catherine visited a neighbor's, where she admitted that "had she gone to [the nearby city of] Bury before her marriage, she never would have had him."[24] Had she an anchor in any other landscape or the freedom to escape, in other words, she might have avoided the marriage. She later said that she only wanted to be able to go back into service and to be away from him. The newspaper's evident discomfort with the young girl's enforced marriage may have been partly a consequence of new narratives of forced marriage in the broader world. The 1840s saw a flood of women's travel literature—Sophia Poole, Harriet Martineau, and Florence Nightingale—that spoke about the "degraded and bestialized" marriage of the East. These pieces explicitly condemned the "soul-killing" tedium of women in marriage that rendered women prisoners and sexual slaves.[25] Catherine's marriage echoed, perhaps too closely, the state of women in the harem, unsettlingly suggesting that a prior failure underwrote the murder, that both a personal and social harm preceded her immoral act. Jill Matus notes, "The vehemence with which some female visitors respond to the perceived immorality of the Eastern marital systems and the subjection of Eastern women signals an anxious desire to distance and distinguish their own world and their place in it from what may in some ways look uncomfortably similar at home." Indeed, their articulation of the enforced marriage "disclose[s] the instability of dominant ideological formulations" of marriage in Britain.[26] The "simple story" of Sarah Westwood's villainy and gender noncomformity made her an unsympathetic figure on the gibbet. Catherine Foster's tale, however, was more vexed.

Though Catherine was sentenced to death, and Judge Baron expressed his complete concurrence with verdict—"your heart and mind went along with your hand, and . . . the poison was placed in that food for the deliberate purpose of procuring the death of an individual with whom you had so lately formed at the altar of God a connexion the most sacred which can

23. "Lloyd's Weekly Newspaper," 7.

24. "The Late Poisoning Case in Suffolk," 8.

25. Matus, "The 'Eastern-Woman Question,'" 69–70.

26. Ibid., 76, 81.

exist on earth between man and woman"—he did not offer the unbending and flat assertion that had accompanied Sarah Westwood's sentence. The tensions between Catherine's youth, beauty, and femininity on one hand and the murder and deception on the other, particularly alongside the childless and compelled marriage, disturbed social norms in the way that Sarah Westwood's case did not.[27] Indeed, during the sentencing, "the learned Judge['s] voice was at times almost inaudible from emotion," straining, perhaps, between these two poles that seemed so far apart, not only in Catherine but in the culture at large. The *Times* wrote, "She is not yet 18 years of age, her appearance is somewhat good looking. . . . Her countenance pourtrays [*sic*] not the slightest hardihood, or anything indicating her to be a person likely to commit such a crime."[28] Violent, unfaithful Sarah could be a murderer; she was a throw-away woman, one whose ascent to the scaffold did not disturb cultural norms. Catherine, it seemed, could not so easily be marked as a failure in femininity, and her case hauntingly suggested a poor girl trapped in an unwanted union. Her case disturbed the cultural narratives of marriage and of the execution of the mariticide.

After her conviction, Catherine fully owned the crime in writing, requesting that it only be published after her execution, and this text had significant implications for her depiction. *The Times* meditated at length on the happy fact of her confession:

> If there be any one thing less painful than another in recording circumstances connected with deeds of a character so appalling as the crime we were last week called upon to report, it is the duty of assuring the public that the force of circumstantial evidence has not betrayed the judgment of the jury, but that their verdict is confirmed by the full confession of the prisoner. . . . With a conscientious man summoned to arbitrate on so serious a question, confidence in his own good intentions, purity of motive and respect for justice, can hardly, at all times, bear him up against the lingering doubt which the lack of decided and irresistible proof is calculated to encourage, however close and convincing the testimony upon which the verdict is founded; and it is, therefore, highly desirable that, on all such grave occasions, opportunities should be afforded to the culprit to confess the offence, and thereby relieve the minds of his or her judges of that painful

27. Strangely, her grandfather was executed for a murder, which he had attempted to render as an apparent suicide by hanging, and her father was supposed to have murdered another man for his money, though he was acquitted of the crime. This man, too, was found hanging from a direction post without marks on his neck. "Confession of Catherine Foster," 2.

28. "The Murder by Poisoning.-Sudbury, Dec. 1," 5.

> sense of the possibility of error which a death punishment for an unadmitted malefaction is so capable of inspiring. Since her conviction and sentence, and return to gaol, the unhappy prisoner, Catherine Foster, has. . . . made a full confession of her guilt in writing.[29]

Remarkably, the papers did not simply print this confession. They printed *three* full versions of it: one reportedly written in her own hand; a confessional letter to her mother, supposedly carried in her bosom at her execution; and a confession transcribed by her religious advisors, which was widely reprinted. These documents served the very ends the *Times* hoped to achieve and much more, and, I would argue, they played a key role in the events that occurred in their wake.

The first document reportedly said, "i must confess that i ame gilty veary gilty of this awfal criame and well dearserves the death that i ame condamed to die. . . . it is riten veary bad sir but i did it as i could."[30] Her avowal of her weakness and insufficiency underscores and repentance for her failure helps to expiate her sin, reinforcing the propriety of normative wifehood—indeed, returning her to proper womanhood before her death. Her transcribed confession went even farther. Provided as a result of the urging of Reverend Ottley, her own parish minister, it gave details of the crime that were uncertain in the trial, absolving everyone else of responsibility and explicitly relieving the distress of the jury and judge in sentencing this attractive seventeen-year-old girl to hang: "I deserve the death I am condemned to die [and I have] no complaint to make of any witness that appeared against me on [*sic*] my trial."[31]

This confession helped to bring her visible appearance into alignment with her relationship to cultural values. Indeed, we might wonder what the outcome of her case might have been had her confession appeared earlier. Her revelation of wrongdoing, her self-condemnation, not only comforted the distressed courts—distressed, no doubt, because of the tension between her feminine identity and her behavior and the implied critique of her marriage in particular and marriage more broadly—by valorizing her murdered husband ("I had no cause of complaint against my husband. He was always good and kind to me.") and by rendering a dramatic return to the angel of the house through her communion with the very angels themselves: "I hope, though the merits and blood of my Saviour, and a sincere repentance of this and all my sins, to obtain forgiveness of God, and to be received by him into heaven."[32]

---

29. "The Acton Murder," 7.
30. "Execution of Catherine Foster," 2.
31. "Confession and Execution of Catherine Foster," 8.
32. Ibid.

The letter to her mother was the coup de grace, absolving the entire culture in its gender-norming socialization and absorbing all the blame into her singular person: "I had every attendance that could ever be[,] both for body and soul." More significantly, this letter absolved marriage more broadly, by exonerating hers in particular. She suggested that her death and ascendance to heaven would literally restore their marriage, indicating her belief that she would see the "dear creature I have injured: and the years that I might have spent in pleasure with him on earth, I hope I shall rest with him in Heaven."[33]

Of course, we cannot know whether these documents ever existed, beyond the hopeful reporting of the *Times,* but even if they were journalistic fantasies, they speak to the culture's hunger for such narrative absolution. Indeed, the excessiveness of these confessions is as striking as Sarah Westwood's blank refusal to supply one. Reverend Ottley, Catherine's confessor, delivered a sermon on her execution to a church that was "crowded to overflowing, and the churchyard was so full that it was difficult to reach the doors."[34] He pointed to an "all-seeing God" and to the inevitably of sin's discovery (certainly not something about which Victorians were generally confident) as well as to God's agents, the courts. Significantly, however, he also disavowed that Catherine had been guilty of crimes other than those to which she had confessed. He urged people to reject the rumors of the sexual improprieties that marred Sarah Westwood's case. He traced the murder to the "original" sin of lying at the altar of God during her wedding. The foundationally tainted marriage ended in murder, but Catherine had confessed to her sins and atoned for it with her death. The resolution of her sin and her exploitation as an object lesson seemed to restore cultural values.

Ironically, these tensions made her execution widely distressing. Several petitions were circulated and delivered to the Home Secretary. As *Lloyd's Weekly* reported it, "Her unhappy position has not failed to arouse the sympathy of many benevolent people in this town. Three memorials on her behalf are on course of signature in the country": one saying execution was "unchristianlike," one appealing for mercy on the grounds of her age and sex, a third, by the women of Suffolk, appealing to the Queen for clemency.[35]

While a reprieve was not granted, a sympathetic crowd of ten thousand people appeared at her execution.[36] The *Morning Post* lamented that her execution had not been "clean": "the sufferings of the unfortunate creature were prolonged for a very considerable space of time, and the assembly was so

33. Ibid.

34. "Execution of Catherine Foster," 2.

35. "The Acton Murderess," 2.

36. "Execution of Catherine Foster," 3.

struck and horrified thereby that they called out, 'Shame, shame—murder, murder'"—a reference to the violence of the execution, not the act that had sent Catherine to the gallows in the first place.[37] Their defense of her on the scaffold echoed their call for the commutation of her death sentence in the wake of her confession.

By making her confession, Catherine Foster restored moral order, marriage, and gender relations. Mariticide, which upended these structures, could be regularlized and normalized, but there were social costs. Sarah Westwood's villainy unsettlingly suggested that women were capable of like violence. Whereas Westwood made women dangerous, hard, and threatening, and suggested a failure in the culture, Catherine Foster made an individual woman weak and erring, but refeminized women as a class. Her confession made her the object of sympathy, which also helped create a shift that made executions of women for mariticide more vexing. If a woman could be cleansed, then she could be saved; indeed, she must be saved to reinforce the gendered norms that suggested that the husband and the state cared for the wife.[38] This became the narrative of marital violence for which the culture hungered, in fiction as in life, as gender became an increasingly vexed category.

In contrast, the Westwood case offered a dramatic miscarriage of confession that illustrated her unworthiness in the system the judge was arbitrating. In passing the sentence of death, the judge asked "whether she had anything to urge stay of execution," and she claimed to be pregnant. The judge instantly impaneled a "jury of matrons" and a medical professional, who contradicted her statement. This claim of pregnancy was reported from Leeds to London as an appalling falsehood—perhaps earning even more press coverage than the murder itself. This moment of perceived duplicity, Sarah's lies about her femininity and maternity in place of her confession, made her execution the only way to right the social order. It also gave the public comfort that she was not a woman whose life they wished to preserve, hardly a woman at all. The contrast provided by the execution of Catherine Foster may have had an impact on the cases that followed—both when a woman was executed and when a woman was reprieved.[39]

---

37. "Imperial Parliament," 2.

38. See my argument in *The Private Rod* about Caroline Norton's and Francis Power Cobbe's articulation of the state's role in protecting women in a brutal marriage when the husband has failed.

39. A very famous case that I do not address here is that of Sarah Chesham, who poisoned two of her sons, her husband, a neighbor's husband, and, likely, a paramour's illegitimate child. I offer a detailed analysis of Chesham and these murders in "Throwing the Wedding Shoe: Foundational Violence, Unhappy Couples, and Murderous Women."

Like Sarah Westwood, Elizabeth Martha Brown did not supply the confessional correction that might have saved her life. When she angrily killed her husband John Anthony Brown with a hatchet (1856), she suffered the highest penalty of the law in spite of the increasing distress over execution and the execution of women especially. "Martha," as she was known, had met John when they were fellow servants on a farm, and, at the time of the murder, they had been married for five years. He was only nineteen, and she was forty. There were stories, particularly given their age difference, that she had paid £50 to entice him into the marriage. As a carrier, he frequently traveled, and his absence gave him ample opportunity to court other women. Martha had, in fact, overheard him in an amorous encounter with Mary Davis, another local woman. The day of the murder, he had been working with his horse and cart and a professional colleague in a neighboring community until about four o'clock in the afternoon. On their homeward journey, they had encountered the object of John's affection, Mary Davis. They traveled in her company, and then he and his working partner stopped at a public house and played skittles and drank until midnight. After a gap of two hours, a neighbor heard him come by her house at two in the morning. Another heard screams between two and three a.m. Martha called upon her closest neighbor at five a.m.

Martha explained that John had been kicked by a horse at about two in the morning but managed to make his way home. As a good wife, she said, she had helped him into the house. She wasn't able to go for help, however, because John held her fast for two hours. He had eventually weakened enough that she could loosen his grip, and she had come away to get help. Problems were immediately evident in her story. Though he had massive wounds on his head, John had no blood on his shirt, suggesting that he had not been upright after the injury; nor was there any blood on her clothes, or in the foyer, hallway, or on the road, which her story would have required—just in the spot where he lay when his body was examined.

In the trial, Richard William Broster, a local surgeon, testified to the severity of the wounds. John, he explained, had a wound over the right eyebrow, and the bones of the nose were broken. There was a grievous wound on top of his head and a wound behind his ear, the frontal and occipital portions of the skull were fractured, and several pieces of bone were driven into the brain. The wounds, Broster felt, were made by a blunt instrument, like the back of a hatchet, not a horseshoe, as Martha had suggested.[40] Broster also argued that

40. "Assize Intelligence," July 26, 1856, 2.

John couldn't possibly have walked or talked with such injuries, "even with the assistance of [his] wife."[41]

In the wake of Martha's conviction and death sentence, Reverend De La Foss pleaded with Martha to confess, and, in an echo of Sarah Westwood's deplored post-conviction falsehoods, Martha responded, "The horse did not do it. He fell down the stairs." This was so obviously a fallacious explanation for his injuries, even to a person with no medical training, that it occasioned a public outcry. *The Morning Chronicle* called her "horribly obdurate [because] she had added another lie to the many accounts she has given of this sad tragedy."[42]

Ultimately, Martha offered a final confession that shifted the terms by which she was understood. She painted herself as a forbearing sufferer in the wake of his infidelity, violence, and cruelty. She claimed that she had made him dinner, waited patiently for him to return home, but, upon his arrival, he verbally abused her, kicked her chair out from under her, and "struck me a severe blow on the side of my head, which confused me so much I was obliged to sit down." He then horsewhipped her. She called, "If you strike me again I will cry 'Murder.' He retorted, 'If you do I will knock your brains out though the window . . . I hope I shall find you dead in the morning.' He then kicked me on the left side."[43] In an "ungovernable passion on being so abused and struck," she seized the hatchet and hit him. She emphasized her long-suffering feminine passivity and the severity of the abuse, which she suggested temporarily clouded her judgment. "I had never struck him before, after all his ill-treatment; but when he hit me so hard at this time I was almost out of my senses, and hardly knew what I was doing."[44]

The addition of this confession, which restored her femininity and her role in the domestic scene, hit all the high points of the desirable confession. His behavior, in this context, seemed to merit a defensive response, and one letter to the Editor of the *Times* expressed this thought. "The wretched woman confessed her crime, but unfolded such a tale of illtreatment [*sic*] as has excited the sympathies of almost every one, and there is but one general feeling in the country, and that is, that the wretched woman has been unjustly executed. . . . the unfortunate slayer of her brutal husband pays the dreadful penalty of the law. . . . Martha Brown is a murdered woman."[45] It was difficult, however, with three confessions—at least two of which she admitted were false—to know

41. Ibid.
42. "The Broadwindsor Murderess," 5.
43. "Execution of Elizabeth Martha Brown," 2.
44. Ibid.
45. Cox, "The Late Execution at Dorchester," 9.

whether to believe these final words. Some sources suggested that there had even been a confession prior to her last in which she claimed to have murdered John in his sleep.

These multiple confessions divided the public. Another letter to the editor complained that the more sympathetic reader foolishly believed the "wretched woman's 'confession,'" and condemned an "implicit reliance upon the 'tale of ill-treatment' which that alleged confession is supposed to unfold."[46] This reader dismissed the confession as illegitimate. Without a "reliable" confession, Brown could not be reclaimed to proper womanhood. Strikingly, however, a minister commenting on the complexity of the case believed she would have been reprieved if the final confession had been her only words on the case—even if it meant *seeking* information to exonerate her. "Had she from the first *confessed the truth and shown the slightest sorrow,* it is very possible that an effort would have been generally made to find circumstances in her bloody deed sufficiently extenuating to justify a remission of her sentence."[47]

The divided confessions in her case certainly contributed to the carnivalesque atmosphere of her execution before thousands. Her husband's abuses and her narrative of feminine passivity discomfited the public, but her unclean spirit and body, which had remained tainted by her lies, seemed to deserve execution. The local paper made this connection explicit: "After a few convulsive struggles of the body, her spirit, *with all its dread secret workings,* has gone to stand before that dread tribunal, whose verdict is final and sentence just."[48] The secrets that had remained with her damned her in the public eye, as much as her tale of woe unsettled the audience. The crowd seemed to respond to this tension. Rather than the sympathetic onlookers Catherine Foster had at her death, "many of the 'roughs,' as they are termed appeared to forget the solemnity of the event then about to transpire, and amused themselves in lewd jocularity and vulgar jests."[49] Her ignominious end was witnessed by Thomas Hardy, only sixteen years old at the time, who was haunted by the beautiful form of Martha's corpse twisting on the rope, an experience that helped shape his novel *Tess of d'Urbervilles,* with its sympathetic and tragic murderess, who struggled to tell the truth.

It might seem impossible that a proper confession could free the murderess, but in Agnes Osbaldeston's 1866 case, it did. Not only did she not face execution, her sentence was remarkably light, though she was found guilty of the crime. Her immediate confession and feminine remorse—precisely what

46. Mallett, "The Late Execution at Dorchester," 9.

47. Malan, "The Late Execution at Dorchester," 7.

48. "Execution of Elizabeth Martha Brown," 2; emphasis added.

49. Ibid.

the press had called for in Brown's case—recuperated her sufficiently to save her life. While she threw a knife at her violent, unemployed husband, she immediately ran to his side to nurse him. She was released from prison shortly after the assizes. The perceived "cold-bloodedness" of Brown and the distress, femininity, and confession of Osbaldeston were greater differences in their case than the behavior of their husbands—both of whom were abusive and provocative.

George Osbaldeston had worked at a factory, but "in consequence of ill health, he had merely looked after the house, while his wife and two of his sons went to a cotton factory and earned the money requisite to keep him and all of them."[50] Their lodger had said George "did nothing for a living[, but Agnes] went to work every day."[51] George's perceived abandonment of his breadwinning role, particularly while he continued to abuse his wife, made him seem as if he were reaping the benefits of masculinity without the social work that was expected to precede it. Indeed, a local paper described him as a "man of idle and worthless habits [who] ill-treated the prisoner, who was the main support of the family."[52]

That night, the couple had exchanged insults, then he "struck her several times on the face and knocked her down. She got up, sat on a chair, and afterwards he kicked her." Strikingly like the scene Martha Brown had described, Agnes Osbaldeston's case differed in others' attestation to George's failures and her submission to him. These witnesses saw Agnes humbly submit to his abuse this night and many nights prior. Worse, when Agnes began preparing a meal for her son, George threatened to beat her again. Indeed, her son testified that his father had beaten his mother before for "giving [him] food."[53] His beatings were so severe that they had often confined her to bed for days and weeks, but this couldn't prevent her from feeding her child, an act that her maternal role demanded. "At last Mrs. Osbaldeston, who had in the meantime received more abuse, said, holding in her hand a knife with which she had been cutting some bread, 'If you strike me again I'll send this knife through you.' Osbaldeston here got up from his chair and struck his wife on the head with his fist, and she then hit him on the side of the neck with a [common table] knife." "I threw the knife; I did not mean to hurt him, him, God knows."[54] Several witnesses testified that George had backed Agnes into a corner to beat her again when she threw the knife that ended his life. These

50. "A Man Murdered by His Wife," 9.
51. "Lancaster Assizes," 6–7, 7.
52. "Local News," 3.
53. "Lancaster Assizes," 6–7, 7.
54. "A Man Murdered by His Wife," 9.

threats were a serious danger to her life. Their lodger, John Sumner, asserted that as soon as George was injured, Agnes knelt down by his side and said, "Oh, what have I done? Oh, George have I killed thee?"

While the courts and the media both wanted to condemn her violence, in spite of the abuse she suffered, his failings as a husband had clearly preceded her failure as a wife. One remarked, "She threw the knife at him whilst they were both in an excited state[. Though] there were mitigating circumstances, there was nothing to justify the act."[55] The Judge, too, described the circumstances of George's death as modulated by his violence. "She had been subject to great ill treatment at her husband's hands [and] was [not] aware of the serious injuries she was inflicting."[56] Agnes's immediate confession of the crime, however, owning the responsibility of the act—from the moment it occurred to the legal proceedings—permitted her reclamation to womanhood and restored her proper femininity the moment it had been undermined by her aggression. Her sentence was a stunning *four days* in addition to the few months she had been in prison awaiting the assizes on the grounds of his perceived failure and her perceived innocence in the case. Such a brief sentence indicates a far more complex sensibility about mariticide than we have previously described.

Overall, these cases suggest several important things about domestic violence and marital relations in the mid-nineteenth century, which was a terrain of shifting marital law and gendered expectations in marriage. First, women did not simply cower under the hands of violent or abusive husbands but sometimes fought back—even planning and executing retribution. Some used physical violence and weapons, as cases like Brown's and Osbaldeston's indicate. Mariticide was not simply the perceived "feminine" act of poisoning but could be violence that disrupted the very terms of feminine identity. Second, it was not acts of "domestic murder," as described by the Lord Chief Baron, that produced the national disgrace but women's resistance to the norms of patriarchal authority and the law that was unsettling, and this made confession a critical part of the stories the press told about murder in the nineteenth century. Grappling with this more nuanced backdrop can give us a richer understanding of the fiction of the period.

Murder is not only an individual act, but a social one. The murderer and her or his victim are situated in social contexts in spite of and in the wake of the homicide. They have roles that maintain a system of relations in the social fabric, often hierarchical ones. Of course, when the relation between

55. "Lancaster Assizes," 6–7, 6.

56. Ibid., 6–7, 7.

the murderer and her victim is marriage, the death of the husband cannot be divorced from the social critique that is implied, not perhaps of their marriage alone, but of marriage overall in that context. Sukanya Banerjee, in her study of English-language novels of conjugality in India, the divorce laws, and Indian Mutiny, suggests that British anxiety about conjugal loyalty was key in this moment in history.[57] Infidelity to the norm is evidenced not just by illicit intercourse but also in these acts of murder and their implicit disruption of gendered identity. Anxiety about righting the gendered propriety of the wife was paramount in murder cases, even when a woman was found guilty of the crime. The courts and the media were adjudicating these cases in a far more complex context than we have previously recognized, and women who struck their husbands with deadly violence were moving through a cultural milieu desperately trying to normalize gender roles in marriage and marriage itself. Those women who failed to expiate their sins with a prompt and feminizing confession were likely to go to the gallows to be swiftly dispatched into the afterlife. In some cases, however, it was more expedient to situate the flaws elsewhere, so as to maintain and affirm gender norms and matrimony. The threat murderous wives proposed was not just to husbands but to faith in a culture's narrative of marriage. A better understanding of these complexities should help us chart more carefully how marriage and the marriage plot evolved over the century. The foregoing cases suggest that sensation fiction's depiction of women murderers in the 1860s and 1870s, which rarely featured poisonings, was not fantasy but a serious cultural concern—and not just about the murderesses themselves but about the entire social system they inhabited. Moreover, it suggests that the confessions (like Lady Audley's, for example) may not have simply been narrative twists but critical cultural phenomenon, broadly recognized by the readers as a part of restoring gender and restoring the speaker's value, even while stretching the limits such gender norms imposed.

57. Banerjee, "Troubling Conjugal Loyalties."

CHAPTER 7

Marriage, Modernity, and the Transimperial

SUKANYA BANERJEE

FAIRLY EARLY on in Mary Elizabeth Braddon's *Aurora Floyd*, the narrator remarks: "Now my two heroines being married, the reader versed in the physiology of novel writing may conclude that my story is done."[1] Indeed, coming as it does upon the heels of the wedding ceremonies of both the female characters of the novel, the eponymous Aurora Floyd and her cousin Lucy Graham, the narrator's comment pointedly draws attention to what may seem a structural anomaly. Rather than gradually building towards a wedding that marks its denouement, the novel truncates such a trajectory by marrying off its female characters to men of their choice before even a third of it is over. This seemingly premature turn of events may well befuddle the reader. Yet, as the narrator famously interjects, "must the play needs be over when the hero and heroine have signed their names on the marriage register? Does a man cease to be, to do, and to suffer when he gets married? And is it necessary that the novelist, after devoting three volumes to the description of a courtship of six weeks' duration, should reserve for himself only half a page in which to tell us the events of two-thirds of a life time?" (163).

The narrator's preoccupation with the aftermath of marriage in *Aurora Floyd*, which was serialized in 1862 and published as a single volume in early

1. Braddon, *Aurora Floyd*, 163. All references to the novel are to the Oxford edition and are parenthetically cited in the text.

1863, is not idiosyncratic. Appearing as part of what Braddon called her "pair of bigamy novels"[2]—*Lady Audley's Secret* being the other one—novels such as *Aurora Floyd* discard the telos of courtship in favor of another kind of marriage plot inasmuch as the plot now begins and ends with marriage, often the same marriage (as in the case of *Aurora Floyd*). Even if the novel ends with its primary character(s) remarrying (*The Woman in White* or *East Lynne*) or with the marriage of a different set of characters altogether (*Lady Audley's Secret*), the marriage marking the end of the novel serves mainly to offset the failures of the "initial" marriage that much of the novel depicts. In other words, even as the event of marriage—a wedding—features at the end of these novels, it is the long-drawn-out *relationship* of marriage—its promises, betrayals, hopes, and despair—that demands the reader's attention. An unhappy marriage now draws extended commentary upon itself, and the temporal framework of marriage, rather than that of courtship, overtakes the temporality of the novel. Such a temporal restructuring also widens the affective ambit of the novel, for rather than focusing on the question of romantic love, our attention now extends to what supposedly holds a marriage together: conjugal loyalty.

But how is conjugal loyalty articulated, and what are its generic implications in terms of the marriage plot? It is in addressing these questions that this essay proposes how conjugal loyalty in fact mediates the vexed relation between marriage and modernity in the mid-nineteenth century. But in so doing, it looks to how a grammar of loyalty is constructed anew over the course of the nineteenth century rather than being always-already available. While loyalty is hardly a novel concept, it performs, I suggest, a novel function in the nineteenth century. Given that loyalty is usually associated with feudal notions of allegiance and servitude, it may well seem misplaced in a political and social order that is more laterally inclined (at least ostensibly so).[3] But even as the sheer verticality of pivotal relationships—such as between Lord and Servant; King and Subject; God and Man; Husband and Wife—was, from the seventeenth century onward, increasingly leveled (which is to assume that we take a Whiggish view of history), concepts of faithfulness, obedience, and constancy that characterized those relations remained indispensable in cementing the social and political configurations of the nineteenth century—such as that of the state, the family, and the economy—in ways that attempted to coalesce a viably "modern" idiom of loyalty. Loyalty in the nineteenth century, then, is about negotiating modernity but, perforce, with an old set of

---

2. Braddon referred to the two novels as her "pair of Bigamy novels" in a letter to Edward Bulwer-Lytton. Quoted in Wolff, *Sensational Victorian*, 154.

3. See Pateman, *Problem of Political Obligation*; see also McCormack, "Rethinking 'Loyalty.'"

tools. Marriage, predictably, featured as a key site for this particular negotiation not least because it naturalized hierarchical relations, and the marriage plot in sensation novels—the genre of study in this essay—bears witness to this burden. The "sensation-marriage plot," I argue, becomes an important site for assembling loyalty.

Of course, marriage constitutes the dominant plotline of Victorian novels in general, and much of what I have described could well be applied to most novels. But the novels I have mentioned so far are distinct inasmuch as they not only put marriage at the front and center of the plot but also focus on failed, mistaken, or troubled marriages. In so doing, they performed a reparative function. However, as we know, they were pejoratively referred to as "sensation novels."[4] Significantly, it was very common for sensation novels of the 1860s to deploy the bigamy plot to depict marriage, a preference that was not lost on Victorian literary critics.[5] But as Maia McAleavey notes, it is hardly the case that bigamy was the exclusive preserve of sensation novels. McAleavey argues for the prevalence of bigamy plots across a range of genres extending before and beyond sensation novels of the 1860s.[6] Yet, as she also concedes, the 1860s witnessed a profusion of bigamy novels.[7] As many as eight of the novels reviewed by Henry Mansel in his influential review of the genre, in 1863, dealt with bigamy.

Expectedly, scholars have queried the heightened focus on frayed, troubled, or—more significantly—bigamous marriages in the early 1860s.[8] But in rehearsing that discussion, I also ask: Why does bigamous/multiple marriage become the stuff of sensation (understood as genre?) And, equally important, can the morphology of the marriage plot in sensation novels be understood or contained within the geopolitical realm of Britain alone?[9] I should concede at

---

4. Combining elements of melodrama, the gothic, crime reportage, and domestic realism, sensation novels seemed to revel in bringing the seamy underside of domestic life to light. While their preoccupation with lurid details of murder, intrigue, and adultery did not endear them to the literary establishment, one of the reasons they enjoyed immense popularity was that they dealt with a topic that was the subject of public and legislative debate: marriage. See Brantlinger, "What Is 'Sensational'"; Gilbert, *Companion to Sensation Fiction*; and Mangham, ed., *Cambridge Companion to Sensation Fiction*, among others.

5. In his review of a selection of sensation novels, Henry Mansel noted, "Of particular offences, which are almost always contemporary and sometimes personal, undoubtedly the first place must be given to Bigamy." Mansel, "Sensation Novels," 490.

6. McAleavey, "The Plot of Bigamous Return," 93.

7. Ibid., 112.

8. For an engaging discussion on this topic, see Hager and, more recently, McAleavey, *The Bigamy Plot*.

9. In her reading of realist texts, Lauren Goodlad, for instance, pushes for a considerably broader framework in what she terms a "geopolitical aesthetic." See especially n16 (*Victorian Geopolitical Aesthetic*, 12).

the outset that my answer to the latter question is, as this essay will make clear, "no." Using the sensation-marriage plot as an example, this essay also takes as its objective the task of etching a framework for literary analysis that is irreducibly transimperial. However, in so doing, I do not seek to merely place the sensation novel within a wider geospatial context, for, methodologically, such a move often relies on an additive logic of inclusiveness that remains highly arbitrary and can also bypass any reconceptualization that the transimperial can proffer. Rather, by focusing on the marriage plot in a novel such as *Aurora Floyd,* I want to consider how "marriage"—reconfigured now more in terms of loyalty—renders the turn to the transimperial as something more than an option.[10]

In what follows, I first trace how marriage became the crucible for the modern in interlinked ways in *both* mid-Victorian England and India. Then, in examining the role played by sensation in marking the embrace between marriage and modernity in each of these sites, I read *Aurora Floyd* alongside Bankim Chandra Chatterjee's *Rajmohan's Wife* (1863), the first Indian novel in English. Significantly, *Rajmohan's Wife* was serialized in Bengal in the same year in which the publication of bigamy novels apparently peaked in England.[11] While it is tempting to make note of this similarity in terms of a parallelism, I prefer to think about it in terms of an intersecting contemporaneity. This alternative framing limns the transimperial in ways that deflect the tendency to mark the non-English/non-West in terms of the civilizational "other" marked by lag or stasis, a tendency that contemporary Victorian scholarship amply recognizes in its inadequacy and ideological freightedness and continually needs to deflect, not least by nominating more heteroglossic objects/subjects of study. But the final value of locating the study of conjugal loyalty within a transimperial framework of analysis lies not so much in its emphasis on the contemporaneity of production as in our understanding of the "contemporaneity of effects."[12] In other words, the transimperial alerts us to the nested nature of the differentiating logic that the modernizing rhetoric of marriage deploys, such that reading *Aurora Floyd* alongside *Rajmohan's Wife* is not just about asserting the contemporaneity of literary production—and thereby widening the literary canvas—but also about accounting for the resonance of a discursive strategy of representation writ large across and through

10. I prefer the extended, if somewhat clumsy, nomenclature of the "sensation-marriage plot" to the more tidy "bigamy plot" because my focus is not exclusively on bigamy (or its discovery) but on the kinds of questions about marriage that the bigamy plot in sensation novels throws up.

11. Fahnestock, "Bigamy," 56.

12. My thanks to the editors of this volume for suggesting this phrase to me.

interlinking constituencies of empire, an interlinking that may well explain why such strategies of representation in many ways remain unsuperseded.

I

In discussing the rising popularity of sensation novels in the 1860s, it is hard to miss the connection between the genre's preoccupation with marriage and the promulgation of the Matrimonial Causes Act of 1857, which made it easier to file for divorce, a process that had earlier required ecclesiastical appeal or a special act of Parliament that entailed considerable expenditure.[13] But though women could apply for *divorce avinculo* (that allowed for marriage afterwards), they could do so only on grounds of the husband's aggravated adultery, that is, adultery that was compounded by bigamy, incest, gross cruelty, and desertion, whereas in what critics refer to as a "double standard," all that was required for men to apply for divorce was proof of the wife's adultery alone.[14]

By wresting marriage away from ecclesiastical authority, the Matrimonial Causes Act (also known as the Divorce Act) seemed to signal "the long-dreaded fall into modernity."[15] For those who feared that the act threatened to destroy the divine sanctity of marriage, the specter of the adulterous woman now acquired an even more resonant charge (because adultery by the wife provided the easiest legal option for dissolving a marriage). Although what constituted adequate proof of adultery could not readily be established, adultery became a matter of public and legal discourse in ways that normativized conjugal loyalty, which was now visibly embodied by monogamy.[16] Of course this did not rule out the possibility that monogamous marriages could be adulterous, but precisely because that possibility could never be ruled out (or conclusively proved), bigamous marriages now offered proof of what could not otherwise be ascertained about monogamy.[17] In other words, the "secu-

13. Anne-Marie Beller's caveat on the ascending popularity of sensation novels is instructive, for as she notes, the sensation novel did not merely explode into the literary scene in the 1860s as is commonly attributed; rather, by the 1860s there was "more of a dawning recognition on the part of critical commentators and the middle-class press that this type of fiction had gradually been gaining momentum for several years and was now popular to a worrying degree." "Sensation Fiction," 8.

14. Shanley, *Feminism*, 38.

15. Chase and Levenson, *Spectacle*, 188.

16. As Winifred Hughes notes, "Bigamy . . . has the advantage of making sexual offense into an actual crime." *Maniac*, 31.

17. The stance on bigamy was also a response to the Divorce Act, for marriage after divorce was widely considered bigamy.

larization" of marriage meant that conjugal relations were now rendered most legible through the filter of monogamy, whereas bigamy and infidelity, though not necessarily cognate, were now made so through the singularizing logic of conjugal loyalty.

Therefore, ironically enough, even as divorce became more accessible after 1857, it was bigamy that was more commonly thematized, and sensation novels with their fragile marriages and bigamous plots can be seen as orchestrating the delicate balance between marriage and modernity. By 1865 Geraldine Jewsbury stated that bigamy had become such a conventional plotline that readers might soon tire of it.[18] But if sensation novels of the day did indeed succeed in rendering the bigamy plot an overly familiar one, then it is worth considering the work that the novelization of bigamy was performing vis-à-vis the prevalence of bigamy in England, where bigamous arrangements were not unusual, especially among migrant working-class populations. Indeed, they were considered socially acceptable—and often even received the benefit of legal doubt—provided concerned parties admitted to the truth of the situation.[19] Sensation novels, on the other hand, marked bigamy in its exorbitance—either as a sign of depravity or a product of incredible circumstance—removing bigamy from the realm of the everyday. By narrating bigamy either as the product of an elaborate plot of deception or accidental misinformation about the existence of a living spouse, sensation novels allowed readers to engage with the fascinations of bigamous situations but from a distance: the safe, normativizing distance of bourgeois monogamy.[20] Such an effect was also in tandem with Darwinian theories, such as those propagated by John McLennan, for whom monogamy, as represented by (middle-class) British Victorians, marked an evolved stage of civilizational development from a prior state of promiscuous cohabitation.[21] The subject of bigamy—or polygamy—in *non*-English contexts had begun to be taken up in many periodicals, some of which even regularly serialized sensation novels. An installment of Ellen Wood's immensely popular *East Lynne*, for instance, appeared in the same issue of the *New Monthly Magazine* that carried a censorious article on polygamy among Mormons.[22] Writings from colonies such as Natal in the 1850s and 1860s also indicate how the colonial state developed a vocabulary of barbarism through its labeling

18. Fahnestock, "Bigamy," 56.

19. Frost, "Bigamy and Cohabitation," 292. For a similar observation with reference to "incest," see Corbett, *Family Likeness*, 5–16.

20. Fahnestock, "Bigamy," 65.

21. Stocking, *Victorian Anthropology*, 204.

22. Wynne, *Sensation Novel*, 80–81.

of indigenous marriage practices, such as that of polygamy, as "heathenish."[23] Clearly, monogamy served as a marker of modernity and Englishness, aligning them together in ways that also charted a defined path to civilizational development.

Yet the attempt to modernize marriage was hardly restricted to England alone. Marriage was also the site of fervent reform, particularly in mid-nineteenth-century India. Responding to universalist ideals transmitted through Western-style education as well as to an internal realignment of the familial unit, the native (male) intelligentsia seized upon marriage—and the question of the woman's status within it—as a site to announce its arrival into a bourgeois modernity.[24] The practice of sati or widow immolation had been outlawed in 1829, and in 1856 the legislation of the controversial Hindu Widow Remarriage Act legalized widow remarriage.[25] Incidentally, the Hindu Widow Remarriage Act occasioned some of the same misgivings that were to attend the passing of the Divorce Act in England the following year. In both cases critics of the proposed legislation emphasized, albeit for different reasons, the indissolubility of the marital bond. Such opposition notwithstanding, the legalization of widow remarriage received enthusiastic support from reform-minded Indians, many of whom also took up the case against polygamy. In Bengal, male polygamy was notably prevalent, especially among Kulin Brahmin families.[26] But from 1855 onwards, a section of middle-class Indians as well as members of the landed elite repeatedly petitioned the British government in Bengal to curb the practice.[27] Even as the colonial state refrained from issuing any legislation on the matter until as late as 1872, the outcry against polygamy did not lose momentum. What could not be eliminated by statute became the topic of censure in the public sphere, a process in which literary production played a key role. In 1863 an article in the Bengali-language weekly from Calcutta, *Somprakash*, stated with considerable impatience: "The

23. Tallie, "Queering Natal," 175.

24. For an illuminating discussion of the reconfiguration of marriage and conjugality in nineteenth-century Bengal and Tamil Nadu, see Majumdar, *Marriage and Modernity*, and Sreenivas, *Wives, Widows, Concubines*, respectively.

25. In the context of marriage reform, it is important not to view the colonial state necessarily as a modernizing agent. Nor should we assume that the question of women's rights was necessarily the guiding force for native male reformers. For a nuanced analysis of the various constituencies involved in reconfiguring marriage, see Sarkar, *Hindu Wife, Hindu Nation*, ch. 7.

26. Even within Brahmins, kulin brahmins evidently represented a higher subsection. The prevalence of polygamy among kulin brahmins was a result of their endogamous attempt at preserving caste rank and privilege.

27. For details of native petitions to the Bengal government against polygamy, see *Annual Report*, 44–45.

sooner polygamy is banished from the country the better."[28] The impatience was not without cause, for as early as 1853 Kali Chandra Ray, a wealthy landlord, had announced a competition to select the best Bengali-language play on the evils of polygamy, and the winning play, Ram Narayan Tarakratna's *Kulin Kul Sarbasva,* was staged to popular acclaim in Calcutta in 1857. Contemporary Bengali playwrights made a name for themselves by writing plays on the topic of marriage. Even when not dealing with polygamy, they satirized other characteristics of contemporary marriages, such as the fairly common practice of elderly men marrying much younger women.[29]

That mismatched matrimonial alliances became the subject of popular satire indicates the extent to which the emphasis on monogamous marriage was also an emphasis on marital companionability, which underwrote the "new conjugality" that Indian male reformers began to craft and claim as their own.[30] Conventional practices had allowed the conjugal couple very little—if any—contact with each other until the consummation of the marriage, and, even so, conjugal intimacy or friendship was heavily punctuated by an overriding sense of familial duty and obligation. The redefinition of conjugality, on the other hand, emphasized a "conscious partnership" in terms of mutual friendship, love, and sexual fidelity, encouraging an "impression [at least] of equality in marriage."[31] Consequently, the marital ideal was now presented in terms of a monogamous fidelity that marginalized nonmonogamous connubial practices otherwise extant across various classes and castes. Conjugal loyalty emerged as the keystone of this new marital ideal, combining as it did Victorian notions of companionate marriage with a selective recall of (mostly Hindu) religiocultural markers of female chastity. The discussion on polygamy, then, was folded into a larger discussion of marital fidelity.

Given this trend in the conversation, it is not surprising that in the early 1870s, the Calcutta public was all agog with two adultery cases that were taken to court, and a spate of popular plays depicted the details of the cases as gleaned from ongoing court proceedings as well as newspaper gossip.[32] *Queen vs. Nobin Chandra Banerjee,* which was tried in 1873 and even involved a mur-

---

28. *Somprakash,* August 3, 1863. The word used for polygamy is "bahubibaha," which refers to marriage to more than one spouse, thereby referring to bigamy as well as polygamy. Translation mine.

29. Examples include Michael Madhusudhan Dutt's *Buro Shaliker Ghare Ron* (New Feathers on an Old Bird), 1859, and Dinabandhu Mitra's *Biye Pagla Buro* (The Old Man Lusting for Marriage), 1866.

30. See Chakravarti, "Changing Notions," 309.

31. Borthwick, *Changing Role,* 150.

32. For an elaboration of the "scandal" surrounding these cases, see Sarkar, *Hindu Wife, Hindu Nation,* ch. 4.

der, was a cause celebre. Nobin Chandra, who worked at a military press in Calcutta, was guilty of murdering his wife, Elokeshi, who had stayed behind in the family home in the outskirts of Calcutta and was reportedly having an affair with the powerful head priest of the local temple. Upon hearing of the affair, Nobin Chandra murdered his wife in a fit of rage and, interestingly enough, turned himself in to the authorities. The case made its way to the Calcutta High Court, and Nobin Chandra was sentenced to life imprisonment. The priest, who was also convicted, was fined and sentenced to three years of rigorous imprisonment. The trial attracted considerable public interest, with crowds gathered at the court, and people passing judgment on whether it was the husband (the murderer) or the priest (the seducer) who deserved the harsher sentence. The trial inspired nearly two dozen plays, and the performance of one of them, Lakshmi Narayan Das's *Mohanter E Ki Kaaj?* (What Did the Priest Do?), even secured the early fortunes of a fledgling theater company.[33] As Tanika Sarkar rightly notes with regard to these plays as well as the trial, "while the drama closely followed and modeled itself on trial sense, the trial itself was theatrical enough to be consumed as drama."[34]

This intertextuality between court, newspaper, and popular literature will strike a chord for those familiar with the intimate relation between sensation fiction and divorce court proceedings in 1860s England.[35] I invoke the reference to sensation literature purposefully, for while satire was a popular literary mode in Bengali literature of the time and easily lent itself to thematizing the ills of contemporary marriage, it is significant that at this moment sensation emerges as a genre particularly attuned to depicting the nuances of changing ideas of conjugality. Although drama and poetry were the predominant literary forms,[36] Bengali authors were increasingly taking to the novel, and the first Indian novel in English, *Rajmohan's Wife* (1863), authored by someone who is now hailed as the pre-eminent novelist not only of nineteenth-century

33. Ibid., 60.

34. Ibid., 74. The other adultery case that provoked similar interest was what came to be known as "The Great Adultery Case" of 1876, in which a young woman, Khetramoni, was accused by her husband of having an affair with her uncle. While the trial was avidly followed by the press and was the subject of public discussion, it generated fewer plays than did the earlier Elokeshi case (involving the priest).

35. See Leckie, *Culture and Adultery*.

36. It is worth noting that the plays on the adultery cases were not considered "high drama" both because of their theme and their provenance (the playwrights were often from a lower-caste background and did not belong to the established literary milieu). It is interesting, then, that *Rajmohan's Wife*—which anticipates these plays in terms of their topical interest—is written by Bankim (who belonged to an upper-caste/class background) and serialized in an English-language periodical, which would have undoubtedly endowed the novel with a certain cultural cachet.

Bengal but India as well, Bankim Chandra Chatterjee, not only deals with marital infidelity but also does so in a generic mode that is unmistakably that of sensation.[37]

II

In tracing the particular logic of sensation that becomes crucial to the question of conjugal loyalty, however, let us return to *Aurora Floyd.* Given that bigamy was cast in non-English terms, it is not surprising that descriptions of Aurora Floyd in Braddon's novel are replete with non-English, or, to be more specific, non-Western, references. The unconventional and strong-willed daughter of a wealthy banker, Aurora is likened to Cleopatra, Semiramide (empress of Nineveh), or expansively referred to as an "Eastern empress" (41). In what the novel describes as a misguided act of youthful infatuation, Aurora had secretly married her father's horse-trainer, James Conyers. Although their marriage precedes the timeline of the novel, we are told that Aurora left Conyers soon after the marriage. The novel has a very contemporary setting in which divorce is mentioned several times and is very much a legal option, but Aurora chooses to abandon her marriage and keep it a secret in order to avert the shame that divorce proceedings might bring upon her father. It is only after she receives news of Conyers's death that she consents to marry John Mellish, a wealthy landowner, who is not told of her previous marriage. But the information regarding her first husband's death turns out to be false. Conyers is still alive, and Aurora's well-kept secret of her prior marriage to him is on the verge of being revealed when Mellish employs him to work in his stables.

Even as Aurora's bigamy is revealed only later in the novel (when we get to know that she was previously married to Conyers) and therefore contributes significantly to the narrative suspense, her appearances in the novel are marked from an early stage. Upon seeing her for the first time, one of her early suitors, Talbot Bulstrode, likens the enchanting quality of her beauty to the intoxicating effect of a narcotic Indian brew, "*bang* [*sic*]," that he had tasted while on military duty in India.[38] *Bang,* in referencing India in the novel, also metaphorizes its early depiction of Aurora. Enamored of Aurora's charms, Bulstrode successfully proposes marriage to her. As the narrative describes,

---

37. For an extended reading of *Rajmohan's Wife* as a sensation novel, see S. Banerjee, "Troubling Conjugal Loyalties."

38. For a discussion of the ways in which the iconography of the Indian Revolt of 1857 informs *Aurora Floyd,* see Tomaiuolo, "Sensation Fiction."

Bulstrode had "accepted the cup of *bang* which the siren had offered, and had drained the very dregs thereof, and was drunken" (73). At this point, the reader is unaware of Aurora's marriage to James Conyers. But here, as elsewhere in the novel, "India" provides an associative logic that seems to anticipate Aurora's guilt. It provides ground for suspecting Aurora's fidelity even as *she* refuses to divulge details of her past, a refusal that also results in Bulstrode nulling their engagement.

Aurora eventually marries John Mellish, who has no qualms in accepting her enigmatic past, or that Aurora remains enigmatic about her past. Aurora's marriage to Mellish, however, takes place within the first third of the novel, thereby indicating not so much a closure as a prelude. This is just as well because much of the novel's narrative energy is directed towards removing the "stain" of Aurora's bigamy. The conclusion of the novel, which finds a considerably subdued Aurora monogamously wedded to John Mellish, reclaims her with an assurance born from expunging those qualities that marked her as non-English, as "Indian." The final scene of the novel restores Aurora, John Mellish, and their infant child to a familiar object-world of colonial commodities, where "bang" no longer functions as a metaphor for Aurora. Instead, happily ensconced as the rightful mistress of Mellish Hall, Aurora is reinstated in a familiar subject position, as but the English consumer of "chillis preserved in vinegar, guava-jelly, the strongest Jamaican rum" that an uncle purveys for her from the Caribbean (458).

What is notable about this reinstatement of the familiar subject-object relationship with relation to the colonies—or of Aurora's status as a monogamous wife—is that it is made possible by a murder plot. In other words, it is through the investigation of a murder bearing a relatively legible trail of evidence that the novel is able to pronounce Aurora's fidelity (which has been put in doubt by her "accidental" bigamy) and her Englishness. Incidentally, Aurora's first husband, Conyers, is the one who is murdered on the Mellish estate, and Aurora is wrongly suspected of the crime. And it is by exculpating Aurora of the crime of murder that her "crime" of bigamy is obliterated. If in the English imaginary, bigamy helped decipher and criminalize the otherwise more opaque sexual offense of adultery, then in *Aurora Floyd*, murder serves as proxy for bigamy.[39] It is not surprising, then, that the "sensation-marriage plot" often involves a murder mystery replete with blackmail, intrigue, and (shoddy) detective work. While the literary establishment of the day reviled sensation novels for their overreliance on plot—Mansel spoke for many liter-

39. A similar proxy function is evident in Braddon's other "bigamy novel" as well, in which Lady Audley, who knowingly commits bigamy, is also guilty of the attempted murder of her husband, and unraveling the latter crime becomes a way of bringing the former to light.

ary critics when he commented: "A sensation novel, as a matter of course, abounds in incident. Indeed, as a general rule, it consists of nothing else"[40]—this excessive plotting can be seen as key, and not extraneous, to the question of conjugal loyalty underwriting the marriage plot.

But the murder plot becomes important for reasons other than providing a legible trace for sexuality. Jonathan Loesberg notes how the thick emplotment characteristic of sensation novels, which comprise a concatenation of seemingly random events, captivates readerly interest to the extent that the climax of the novel is often "detached" from the primary themes that the novel began with.[41] Indeed, in *Aurora Floyd*, the narrative momentum of the "whodunit" soon overrides the question of Aurora's fidelity. As we get immersed in keeping track of possible clues—a missing button here, marked currency notes there—Aurora's enigmatic past and her imputed infidelity seem quite beside the point. Moreover, that Aurora is hounded by Stephen Hargraves, "Softy," who turns out to be Conyers's murderer, deflects attention from her own bigamous "guilt." Hargraves, who worked on the Mellish estate, had been plotting revenge on Aurora ever since she had spiritedly horsewhipped him for harming her beloved dog. His festering grievance against Aurora seems ominous:

> "Shall I tell you," [Hargraves] says, "what it is I'm afraid of? . . ." It isn't Mrs. Mellish. It's myself. It's *this,*"—he grasped something in the loose pocket of his trousers as he spoke,—"it's *this.* I'm afraid to thrust myself a-nigh her, for fear I should spring upon her, and cut her thro-at from ear to ear." (191)

The thinly veiled sexual violence implied in these lines along with Hargraves's later accosting of Aurora makes the reader root for her throughout the murder investigation without even knowing whether she committed Conyers's murder. Because of the nested nature of the plot, the "stain" of Aurora's bigamy ceases to be, and the alluring "Eastern enchantress" (41) now becomes the guileless Englishwoman who needs to be saved from the likes of Hargraves (and the long hand of the law). It would not be incongruous, and certainly not anachronistic, to suggest that the narrative logic marshaling sympathy for Aurora is the same that garnered sympathy for hapless Englishwomen raped by leering Indian mutineers in narratives circulating about the so-called Indian Mutiny of 1857.[42] The novel paves the way for such a reading by deliberately invok-

40. Mansel, "Sensation Novels" 486.

41. Loesberg, "Ideology of Form," 130.

42. For an analysis of the depiction of Englishwomen in English accounts of 1857, see Paxton and Sharpe. That *Aurora Floyd* should replay some of the anxieties and misgivings generated by 1857 on the part of the British brings home the point that Christopher Herbert makes

ing the Mutiny. In the final chapter, Hargraves is eventually arrested after a scuffle with Bulstrode, who warns him: "You'd better not trifle with me, . . . I've been accustomed to deal with refractory Sepoys in India" (454). So, by the end of the novel, we get to a point where Aurora's one-time suitor who could not accept her enigmatic (bigamous) past now vanquishes the character who threatens to expose her and cause bodily harm (Hargraves is more menacing because he has advance knowledge of Aurora's marriage to Conyers). Loesberg is certainly on the mark in insisting that the "plot detachment" of sensation novels—signaled here in *Aurora Floyd* by a detour or "degeneration" into a murder plot—should not be read in terms of lapse or failure.[43]

But whereas Loesberg reads the detachment as indicating a "willed nonseriousness," I prefer to read it in terms of the effects it generates.[44] The intricacies of the murder plot and, more important, its navigation of our emotional response, offer a necessary corollary to depictions of loyalty inasmuch as murder provides a readily available moral calculus that loyalty cannot. Loyalty, as Derrida leads us to consider through a discussion of faithfulness in his deeply meditative *Gift of Death,* bears an angular relation to ethics. It calls for sacrifice or acts of commission that often exceed the moral and ethical code.[45] It is this compromised relation with ethics that makes loyalty paradoxical and even morally ambiguous despite being couched in terms of duty, obedience, and sacrifice.[46] While Derrida places his discussion in the realm of religious faith and responsibility, other commentators on loyalty have also noted its inher-

---

in *War of No Pity.* Along those lines, it is important to keep in mind Marlene Tromp's reading of the novel, which provides a layered account of Aurora's interaction with Hargraves and the complex ways in which the novel deals with the question of the female body (Aurora's body) being subjected to physical violence. In Tromp's reading, Aurora is not simply the hapless victim of male violence (*Private Rod,* ch. 3).

43. Loesberg, "Ideology of Form," 133. In a different but related vein, Hughes notes that murder is important in sensation novels, for it "acquires a certain legitimacy . . . with the vaguer, weaker, less legally punishable sins of the flesh." *Maniac,* 32.

44. For Loesberg, the "willed nonseriousness" encodes a strategic ambivalence to changing class relations and class mobility, which, according to him underpins the plot of sensation novels ("Ideology of Form").

45. Derrida, *Gift of Death,* 72.

46. Derrida develops this thesis around the example of Abraham's sacrifice of his son Isaac as an act of faith to God. As he puts it: "Abraham's decision is absolutely responsible because it answers for itself before the absolute other. Paradoxically it is also irresponsible because it is guided neither by reason nor by an ethics justifiable before men or before the law of some universal tribunal" (ibid., 77). Derrida's discussion is in reference not only to man's relation with God but to all humanity, for the point of his argument is that "God as the wholly other, is to be found everywhere there is something of the wholly other. And . . . each of us, everyone else, each other is infinitely other in its absolute singularity" (78).

ent paradoxes—and dilemmas—in terms of the social relations and familial ties that it forges.[47]

In the historical context of the English family, which was being reconfigured from the eighteenth century onwards in response to increased mobility, capitalist modes of transaction, and changing laws of female inheritance, the discomfiting question posed by loyalty was whether loyalty to one's spouse trumped loyalty to one's natal family. In her study of eighteenth-century novels, Ruth Perry notes how marriages transacted to appease familial expectations are weighed against those occasioned by romantic love in ways that pit conjugal loyalty against consanguineal loyalty.[48] While Perry provides illuminating examples from eighteenth-century novels, the dilemma that she points to courses through the marriage plot of sensation novels as well, even as sensation novels—also referred to as "railway novels"—remain resolutely immersed in their specific moment of technomodernity. The plot of *The Woman in White* hinges on the fact that Laura Fairlie's father betrothed her to the villainous Percival Glyde when she was very young. In *Aurora Floyd*, the reason Aurora does not divorce her first husband is that she is loath to drag her father, a reputed and well-liked banker, through the infamy of divorce proceedings (355). Her loyalty to her father/patrimonial name, in other words, stands in the way of her marriage to Bulstrode, to whom she is attracted. Although we get no indication of such an attraction to Mellish, Aurora accepts his proposal of marriage namely because Mellish asks no questions about her past. Bigamous marriage, then, is not just about providing a legible register for adultery as suggested earlier; rather, depicting more a predicament than choice, it accommodates different orders of loyalty, consanguineal and conjugal.[49]

But the dilemmas posed by loyalty are hardly resolved at the end of the novel, which finds Aurora monogamously wedded to Mellish. Is Mellish important because he helps preserve the secret of her first marriage/father's name? Does the absence of an erotic relation between him and Aurora not matter? Does consanguineal loyalty actually win over conjugal loyalty in a novel that is about a twice-married woman? Even as the sensational aspect of the novel makes the depiction of bigamy an unexceptional element of the

47. See Gert, "Loyalty and Morality."

48. Perry, *Novel Relations*, 5.

49. In a different but related context, Corbett notes a similar dynamic in her insightful reading of cousin marriage in Jane Austen's novels. She notes, for instance, that "the narrative voice of *Mansfield Park* implies that marriage should support rather than nullify sibling ties; indeed, the ideological framework even for so-called companionate marriage encouraged the creation of new affinal bonds of comparable strength to consanguineal ones" (40). For a powerful reading of what she describes as "familiar marriage" (in contrast to romantic marriage), see Schaffer, *Romance's Rival*.

marriage plot, it is the narrative excesses of sensation—its assemblage of melodrama, mystery, and detection—that blunt those questions, which are never quite resolved but are at least vivified through the bigamy plot. Loyalty, in other words, finds its apt narrative vehicle in sensation, which can articulate its dilemmas while also eliciting an emotional response that absorbs their characteristically unyielding nature. What this also means is that bigamy is not simply a plot feature that can be detached in its non-Englishness in novels like *Aurora Floyd.*

But how is conjugal loyalty even articulated in a novel that is about bigamy? While it is Aurora's fidelity that is ostensibly under scrutiny, I would like to shift attention to Aurora's second husband, John Mellish, who evades critical attention inasmuch as he is depicted as "stainless" and "pure."[50] Unlike Bulstrode, who is unable to accept Aurora's silence about her past, thereby "fall[ing] away from Aurora at the first trial of his faith" (234), Mellish succeeds in such a trial through his willingness to take Aurora at her word (or lack thereof). However, even as Mellish marries Aurora with a "loyal and pure affection" (142) and for the most part ignores the incriminating evidence mounting against her during the murder case, the novel appears fairly ambivalent about this dispensation of loyalty. Mellish is often described as childish (310), and his love for his wife apparently "touches upon the boundary line which separates the sublime from the ridiculous" (324). If Mellish is the "loyal spouse," then the novel stumbles in providing an adequate idiom for his loyalty. Loyalty seems stuck somewhere between faithfulness and devotion on one hand and companionability and discernment on the other. The novel cannot quite amalgamate both, and it is as if bigamy is the narrative outcome of this incomplete amalgamation.

Significantly, Mellish's relation with Aurora is expressed in remarkably nonerotic terms. Although towards the end of the novel Aurora's name is cleared of the murder, and she is relieved that "her faithful husband [still] loved her as devotedly and tenderly as ever" (416), Aurora exists more as a distant "object of [Mellish's] faith and his worship" (334). Their relationship has none of the sexual tension marking her interactions with Bulstrode, who, even later in the novel, well after he has been married (to Aurora's cousin, Lucy), cannot but recall their broken engagement without "a sharp thrill of pain," which, the narrator notes, "though short-lived," can possibly be read as an "infidelity to Lucy" (350). Mellish's feelings towards Aurora, however, are placed along an entirely different register. Not only is his unswerving faith in

50. McAleavey, *Bigamy Plot,* 155. McAleavey's reading of the novel focuses on the relation between the bigamy plot and the courtship plot, arguing how while the bigamy plot upholds the conventions of the narrative of courtship, it ultimately subverts it.

Aurora's innocence situated in terms of affection and worship that are erotically bland, but also it is cast in terms of a loyalty that is linked to that of his ancestors, who were Royalists during the Civil War (394). That loyalty is "best" embodied by Mellish—a character who inhabits an explicitly feudal world and is described as "strictly conservative" (335)—seems to place it outside the decidedly modern setting of the novel.

Yet I hesitate to posit loyalty as inherently out of step with modernity. In terms of the novel, I would also hesitate to place conjugal loyalty along a spectrum that increasingly tempers devotion with discernment or faithfulness with companionability. Such a spectrum suggests a teleology that can overlook how loyalty, as it is rearticulated in response to the modern, is always processual, *continually* negotiated through a balancing act between the customary and the contractual.[51] Such a balancing act becomes a constitutive feature of modernity, which places the *im*balance of loyalty—fanaticism, "slavish" devotion—in the realm of the unmodern. In the context of conjugal loyalty, the "sensation-marriage plot" dramatizes this balancing act, or, more important, sensationalizes the nondramatic aspect of it.

Loyalty most often gains reckoning through acts of disloyalty, which are relatively more spectacular; consequently, it is disloyalty that garners critical scrutiny, whereas loyalty remains in shadow.[52] The marriage plot in sensation novels, as we know, is thematically primed to portray infidelity, but its structure, as I have tried to show, enables a contemplation of loyalty itself. In so doing, a novel such as *Aurora Floyd* also indicates how the balancing act that loyalty necessarily entails also posits a differential grammar of modernity. What appears as a temporal anomaly with reference to Mellish is compounded in the case of Lucy, Aurora's cousin, and the woman whom Bulstrode (Aurora's original suitor) eventually marries. Lucy had been in love with Bulstrode though she knew he loved her cousin. When Bulstrode proposes to Lucy after abandoning his engagement with Aurora, Lucy is happy to accept. Their marital life is contented and fulfilling, but Lucy's unswerving love for Bulstrode is hardly described in salutary terms: "It was a part of [Lucy's] nature to love in a reverential attitude. To sit at her sultan's feet and replenish his chibouque; to watch him while he slept, and wave the punkah above his seraphic head; to love and admire and pray for him,—made up the sum of her heart's desire" (348).[53] Although it is Lucy and Mellish's "loyal" love that evidently holds their

51. The idea of the customary and the contractual is from Allen, "When Loyalty," 293.

52. Oath-taking, be it in the context of marriage or citizenship, is a visible form of pledging loyalty, but it does not necessarily demonstrate loyalty.

53. For an engaging reading of Lucy that goes beyond expected conventional observations of her pliancy, see Curtis, "Espaliered Girl."

respective marriages together, the novel, in driving home the importance of the adjudicatory nature of loyalty, projects its lack (as evinced in Lucy's and Mellish's unquestioning devotion) either onto a Royalist past, or, more vividly, as in this scene with Lucy, onto a geotemporal "elsewhere," which is unmistakably orientalist (or Indian).[54] Perhaps loyalty necessitates such a projection; perhaps such an "elsewhere" allows for an articulation of loyalty even as—or because—it, in its modern incarnation, is otherwise always seeking a more calibrated idiom.

III

"India," then, imputes Aurora's lack of fidelity while also signifying loyalty's "excess" on the part of Mellish and Lucy. Evidently, it marks the limits of loyalty. But if "India" emerges as the figurative limit, it is also important to push the analysis further, for critical analysis too often stops at the point where the East/colony/orient is seen as marking the limit, howsoever figurative it may be. In the context of conjugality, especially, the figurative tends to be mistaken for the literal, a misrecognition that is perhaps the residual effect of the fact that from 1860 onwards, marriage, as Kathy Psomiades points out, presented not so much an indirect way of talking about "political life in disguise" as much as "a theoretical tool for thinking about political life."[55] Psomiades's reference point is anthropological theory, and she is right to suggest that rather than reading the marriage plot through an anthropological lens, we should consider how novels of the 1860s were instrumental in circulating and even consolidating the evolutionary narrative of marriage in anthropological accounts, be it Henry Maine's *Ancient Law* (1861) or John McLennan's *Primitive Marriage* (1865).[56] In this light, the bigamy plot of sensation novels can very well be seen as engaging in an anthropological boundary-drawing. But bigamy had a literary as well as sociological bearing in England, and, as I have attempted to show, even at the level of plot, it cannot be so easily resolved or isolated in terms of its "non-Englishness."[57] In fact, the "non-English" is integral to the sensation-marriage plot, and the challenge of a transimperial

54. The scene is generally orientalist in setting, but in suggesting its Indianness, I take my cues from the words "chiboque" and "punkah."

55. Psomiades, "Marriage Plot," 58.

56. Ibid., 57.

57. Dan Bivona and Eileen Cleere have recently shown how mid-Victorian writers and novelists referred to polygamous practices in non-English contexts (such as Mormon polygamy) to unhinge or question the primacy of monogamy in an English context. These examples are important, for they offer a variegated sense of the English discourse on monogamy. How-

analysis is not only to probe its centrality at a conceptual (rather than only representational) level but also to push beyond reading the "non-English" in its figurative dimension alone.

In attempting to do so, it is worth paying heed to what Prathama Banerjee offers by way of a comparative strategy. As Banerjee, a historian, usefully suggests, "contemporanising is an act that seeks to set up unlikely relationships, alignments and exchanges across what conventionally appear as *parallel* histories, distant lands, mismatched times, and mutually untranslatable languages."[58] Quite surprisingly, even as there is a robust body of scholarship on transatlantic Victorianism—indeed of transatlantic sensation fiction—the scope of that scholarship rarely extends laterally across empire; in other words, it rarely takes the transimperial turn. To be sure, Victorian studies has taken due note of the inextricable relation between colony and metropole as well as of the impact of empire on "domestic" literary production, in both material and thematic terms. There is valuable scholarship, too, on writings by Britons in different parts of the empire. But the growing attention to non-English writers, literary or otherwise, seems largely limited to those who could claim mobility in the nineteenth century. Speaking of Indians, for instance, it is writers such as Rammohun Roy, Toru Dutt, Cornelia Sorabji, Pandita Ramabai, Behramji Malabari, or Rabindranath Tagore who draw easy attention, namely because of their connection with the imperial metropolis.

Important as it is to make note of this variegated metropolitan presence and literary production, it is worth keeping in mind that such an endeavor not only privileges mobility but also singularizes colonial figures, which is to say that they are viewed in terms of (and because of) their exorbitant biographies. *Systems* of colonial literary production—be it in terms of literary history, thematic preoccupations, stylistic innovations—tend to get overlooked in ways that mark off the colony, casting it in all-too-familiar frames of lag or lacuna.[59] By contemporanising, that is, by arguing for a coevality that is usually not accorded to the episteme of the colonial, a transimperial frame of analysis posits, instead, an *inter*related plane of modernity without flattening the differences between the colony and metropole or suggesting equivalence between the two. The relation between colony and metropole is presented not so much

ever, the easy association between polygamy and non-English or non-Western contexts needs to be tweaked as well.

58. P. Banerjee, "The Politics of Contemporanising"; emphasis added.

59. By referring to "systems" rather than to individual writers, I am not arguing here for a practice of "distant reading" that Franco Moretti advocates in *Distant Reading*. Rather, my focus is on the *ecology* of colonial literary production, which gets abstracted when authors come into visibility by dint of their metropolitan presence, a result largely of our reliance on the critical lens provided by cosmopolitanism, migrancy, or diaspora.

in terms of "influence" (familiar as Bankim Chandra Chatterjee, the author of *Rajmohan's Wife*, may have been with British sensation fiction),[60] nor is it read in terms of an alternate or belated modernity as much as a proximate commonality that is underwritten by the shared, fraught, and evolving relation with modernity in *both* sites. For the purposes of this essay, the idealization of monogamous marriage as a mark of the modern in both Victorian Britain and Bengal (the seat of the British Empire in India) has offered an important node for contemporanising and the sensational marriage plot a heuristic for and evidence of the transimperial.

I close therefore with a brief discussion of Bankim Chandra Chatterjee's *Rajmohan's Wife*, reputedly the first Indian novel in English, which, as mentioned earlier, is "sensational" in form and theme, weaving together elements of melodrama, suspense, and the supernatural in a plot that centers on the adulterous Matangini (the eponymous protagonist). As a reading of *Aurora Floyd* indicates, the sensation-marriage plot, navigating as it does the entangled relation between marriage, modernity, and conjugal loyalty, generates a differential logic, an "elsewhere." But reading *Aurora Floyd* alongside a novel such as *Rajmohan's Wife* in terms of a contemporaneity not only demystifies the "elsewhere" but also helps follow through with this logic in all its abiding effects.

Rajmohan's Wife is set in rural Bengal—not very far from Calcutta, though—and centers on the eighteen-year-old Matangini, the eponymous Rajmohan's wife. The contemporary setting of the novel enables it to focus on an iteration of the family that is fairly novel: the conjugal family. True, Matangini lives with her husband (Rajmohan) as well as his widowed aunt and sister, but this represents a condensed family structure (unlike that of a joint family), one in which the conjugal couple takes center stage. It is beyond the scope of this essay to dwell at length on the main plot involving Matangini and her husband, Rajmohan, but to put it briefly: Matangini, who is unhappily married to the disreputable and churlish Rajmohan, becomes aware of his implication in a plot to steal, among other things, a contested will, from the house of her brother-in-law, Madhav. Upon meeting Madhav to warn him of the impending theft, Matangini also confesses her love for him. As it transpires, both Madhav and she had been in love since childhood but did not marry perhaps because of the impermissibility of romantic love in marriage negotiations among "respectable" classes. Despite professing her love to Madhav, Matangini promises never to see him again, and resumes her role as "Rajmohan's wife." The novel frames her return to Rajmohan in terms of a fidelity to

60. See S. Banerjee, "Troubling Conjugal Loyalties," 486n13.

her marriage vows. Notably, however, such loyalty has very little to do with Rajmohan as a person, a figure whom Matangini seems to hold in very low esteem. If Matangini chooses to overlook Rajmohan's many flaws, then her "return" to him bespeaks a nondiscerning devotion that seems antithetical to the idea of a companionate marriage. The novel fails to provide an idiom of loyalty that is commensurate with the ideals of the new mode of conjugality that it gestures towards. And though the novel dispenses with Matangini, who, rather predictably, dies young, the lack of an adequate referent for loyalty actually presses home its importance in fashioning a bourgeois conjugality in a context where it is the conjugal couple, rather than the extended family, that assumes center stage.

That conjugal fidelity was deeply entwined with new ideas of companionate marriage is made evident by the subplot of the novel, one in which Matangini plays a tertiary role. While *Rajmohan's Wife* itself has not received much critical attention overall, there has been no commentary at all on its subplot, which deals with bigamy. As it turns out, the mastermind behind the attempted robbery at Madhav's house was his cousin, Mathur, who wanted to defraud Madhav of his inheritance. Contrary to popular opinion and literary trends in Bengal in which the urban, Western-educated native male, the *babu,* was the object of satire for his pretensions and/or profligacy (a literary trend that Bankim contributed to as well), in *Rajmohan's Wife* it is Mathur, the uneducated rural landowner, who is cast in a negative mold. In contrast to Madhav, who has attended college in Calcutta, is depicted as reading English books, and is mindful of the propriety of social relations (despite being in love with Matangini, he is respectful of her wish to return to Rajmohan), Mathur represents a predatory, grasping feudal order that is contemptuous of legal process. Upon realizing that Matangini was responsible for thwarting the attempted robbery, Mathur has her abducted and imprisoned in a stronghold in the dungeons of his house.

If Mathur epitomizes villainy in the novel, it is significant that he is also a bigamist. Bigamy (or polygamy) was not illegal, and the novel plays on familiar misogynist humor in commenting: "Mathur Ghose . . . had the good fortune or misfortune of being blessed or incommoded by double ties of matrimony, and was the master or slave of both of [his] wives."[61] But the humor seems more a ruse for the novel's more trenchant critique of bigamy because Mathur's bigamous status is attributed to his immoral character rather than to an established social practice. The virtuous Madhav, on the other hand, is monogamous, or virtuous on account of being monogamous. In what can be

61. Chatterjee, *Rajmohan's Wife*, 78. Further references to the novel are cited parenthetically.

seen as a familiar Victorian motif, the novel links virtue with domesticity. Madhav's otherwise well-appointed, peaceful home (94–95) stands in marked contrast to the internal squabbles (between the co-wives) besetting Mathur's house, which is also described as "a genuine specimen of mofussil magnificence united with a mofussil want of cleanliness" (73). The bigamous household is a dirty, querulous, and unhappy one. Evidently, the domestic ideals of a Victorian colonial modernity stand in to perform a somewhat admonitory function as the novel takes aim at the entrenched patriarchal prerogative of bigamy.

In his 1879 Bengali-language essay, "Samya" (On Equality), Bankim had listed the "right of men to have several wives" as a grievous inequality against women, stating, "it cannot be in accord with ethics for any person to have the right to take several spouses."[62] However, unlike antipolygamists, such as Ishwarchandra Vidyasagar, who sought legislative intervention, Bankim, like many others, wanted to rely on native initiative and awareness alone. He was confident that "[polygamy] will surely disappear as a result of good education."[63] It is not difficult, then, to surmise the pedagogical work that *Rajmohan's Wife* potentially performs. In what seems befitting, Mathur dies at the end of the novel. He commits suicide just as he is about to be arrested. Significantly, he is charged with criminal conspiracy; he cannot, of course, be charged with bigamy. It is as if Mathur's connivance in stealing the will from Madhav's house serves as proxy for his bigamy: if the murder charge had served to exculpate Aurora of bigamy in *Aurora Floyd,* then here the charge of criminal conspiracy serves to seemingly indict Madhav for it. Evidently, the generic elements of sensation help in negotiating the bigamous turn in both novels. But, given that bigamy did not require proof nor even count as an offense in the novelistic (or extranovelistic) world of *Rajmohan's Wife,* it is only by reading a novel such as *Aurora Floyd* in tandem with *Rajmohan's Wife* that we can follow, and gauge the broader implications of, bigamy being literarily moralized in Bankim's novel as well as the world it inhabited.

Mathur's bigamy is destructive in its voraciousness, whereas Matangini and Madhav, who are eminently suited for each other, nonetheless adhere to their respective marriage vows in ways that singularize loyalty. Yet, even as this more defined conjugal loyalty bespeaks a bourgeois self-fashioning that is important in securing Matangini's and Madhav's respective marriages—and, as the novel would have us believe, the social order itself—*Rajmohan's Wife* is unable, as is *Aurora Floyd,* to depict loyalty as fully commensurate with

62. Chatterjee, "Samya," 105. According to literary convention, I refer to the author by his first name.

63. Chatterjee, "Polygamy," 77.

companionability. This inability may speak to the historical moment that both these novels occupy in an unfolding narrative of bourgeois marriage. Or, as discussed in relation to *Aurora Floyd,* this inability serves as a stark reminder of the fraught nature of loyalty itself. In either case, the absence of an articulable referent for conjugal loyalty generates a very tangible outcome. On one hand, we witness a literary preoccupation with conjugal *in*fidelity, as in *Rajmohan's Wife* (and indeed in British sensation fiction). On the other hand, from the late 1860s onwards in Bengal, there is a marked preoccupation with the long-established virtues of the *patibrata*—the devoted wife marked by her hyperbolic declarations of faithfulness and husbandly devotion.[64] Although *Rajmohan's Wife* does not valorize such a figure, Bankim goes on to invoke this earlier ideal, stating in "Samya" that "This Aryan ethic of devotion to the husband is very beautiful: on account of it the Aryan household is as full of happiness as paradise."[65]

While the *patibrata* was to gain relevance in nationalist iconography later in the century, it enables here a reconfiguration of conjugal loyalty in a familiar language of patriarchal excess, if only to vivify modern notions of monogamous marriage. Significantly, such reconfigurations invoked religiomythological figures—such as that of Savitri—to meld wifely devotion, strength, and purity "as primary markers of [a new] *Hindu* compatibility."[66] Nonmonogamous marriage, then, is marked as unmodern, castigated as un-Hindu. This is to say that if conjugal loyalty, as emblematized by monogamy, became the standard-bearer of modernity, then it commandeered a decidedly Hindu cast of figures as proof and object of a Bengali/Hindu modern, in contradistinction to polygamous practices that were readily identified as Muslim.[67] The imputedly nonmonogamous Muslim male was framed as one whose loyalty (and modernity) was rendered suspect, as in nationalist invocations towards the end of the nineteenth century, such as Bankim's much-cited novel *Anandamath* (1882).

---

64. See, for instance, Devi, *Patibrata Dharma.* I bring out this point further in "Troubling Conjugal Loyalties."

65. Chatterjee, "Samya," 100.

66. Chowdhury-Sengupta, "Return of the Sati," 42; emphasis added.

67. The perception was that polygamy had scriptural sanction for Muslims, whereas it was more of a customary practice for Kulin Brahmins. However, although Muslim reformers in nineteenth-century Bengal began to question polygamy (Amin, *World of Muslim Women,* 67–70) and its scriptural sanction was also subjected to debate (ibid., 4), Muslims were kept at bay in the late nineteenth-century nationalist discourse that modeled itself along "Hindu" monogamous lines. For a sense of the robust debate among Indian Muslims on the subject of polygamy in the late nineteenth and early twentieth century, see also Alam, "Polygyny, Family, and Sharafat."

The figure of the "disloyal Muslim" emerges, then, as a corollary to the orientalized "elsewhere" of *Aurora Floyd*.[68] And while we continue to grapple with the perniciousness of both these projections (of loyalty) in a wider context and at multiple levels, the working of the "sensation-marriage plot" on a transimperial canvas also points to the interrelatedness and systematicity—and therefore the abiding resonance?—of these projections. Equally, if not more, important, the fact that reading *Aurora Floyd* in tandem with *Rajmohan's Wife* reveals a narrative logic that is startlingly similar also signals to us that to read sameness is not always to succumb to the logic of homogenization.[69] Rather, in this case, it is to acknowledge the expansive sweep of capitalist modernity that nominates the (heteronormative) familial unit—as emblematized by the monogamous family—as one of its key sites of reproduction. To fail to grasp this expansiveness as a matter of transimperial contemporaneity would be to fall too readily for the conventional geotemporal ramifications of the Victorian marriage plot.

68. For a discussion of the figure of the "disloyal Muslim" and the Indian polity, see Pandey, "Can a Muslim Be an Indian?"

69. For an elaboration of this point in the broader context of anthropological frameworks for studying culture, see Visweswaran, *Un/Common Cultures*.

PART III

BEYOND COUPLING

QUEER, COMMUNAL, TERTIARY

CHAPTER 8

"Even Supposing—"

Reading/Writing Outside the Marriage Plot in Dickens Fan Fiction

HOLLY FURNEAUX

THE CLOSING DASH of Dickens's *Bleak House* (March 1852–September 1853) offers an invitation to choose your own adventure, to fashion Esther's thoughts, "even supposing—," to reader requirements.[1] As a final sentence of a Victorian novel by the author whose name has become synonymous with the Victorian period, it is not what the reputation of the genre leads us to expect. Readers and writers from Dickens's time to ours have chafed against the apparent constraints of the novel form, with its tidy, normalizing closure structures. As E. M. Forster famously put it, "if it was not for death and marriage I do not know how the average novelist would conclude."[2] W. Somerset Maugham wrote of the apprehension caused by attempting a novel that ends "neither with a death nor a marriage":

> Death ends all things and so is the comprehensive conclusion of a story, but marriage finishes it very properly too. . . . When male and female, after whatever vicissitudes you like, are at last brought together they have fulfilled their biological function and interest passes to the next generation.[3]

My thanks to David Clark, Martin Willis, and the editors of this volume for their generous insights at draft stage and help in developing this essay.

1. Dickens, *Bleak House*, 989.
2. Forster, *Aspects of the Novel*, 67.
3. W. Somerset Maugham, *The Razor's Edge*, quoted in Roof, *Come as You Are*, i.

More recently work in queer narratology has critiqued what Judith Roof calls the "heterosexually friendly shape" of narrative, pointing out the novel's structural reinforcement of a narrowly constrained way of being through the (almost) inevitable working towards the marriage plot in an ideological alignment of narrative, capitalist, and biological function.[4] As Roof explains, a dominant "reproductive narrative trajectory . . . insists on a plot impetus towards 'joinder or synthesis,'" and D. A. Miller characterizes coupledom culminating in marriage as cultural ur-narrative, a story "that one hardly exaggerates in our culture to call *the* story."[5]

Dickens's novels certainly contain capitulations of the nuptial and fatal variety. Esther's closing dash, however, directs us to other readerly possibilities in the invitation to imagine beyond the text, an impulse Dickens actively encouraged through serial publication and his own reanimation and repurposing of characters. This incitement of creative response is visualized in Robert Buss's painting *Dickens' Dream* (1875, the best-known example from a plethora of similar early Dickens pictorial mash-ups), which shows characters from across Dickens's career interacting above the sleeping author.[6] A wealth of multimedia work from Dickens's period to our own testifies to the potency of Dickens's characters and plotlines as independent of the forms in which they first appeared. These forms typically disrupt narrative and marital convention, and they have the capacity to challenge the heterosexual assumptions underpinning traditional novel structures. This essay places twenty-first-century Dickens fan fiction, with its strong slash lines (male/male and female/female), sexual plurality beyond the unit of the couple, and affectionate shipping (relationship bonding) of particular figures, in a longer history of readers' creative responses.[7] I argue that the content, form, and mode of publication

4. Roof, *Come as You Are*, xxxii.

5. Ibid., 112; Miller, *Bringing Out Roland Barthes*, 45. In their summary of the field, Robyn Warhol and Susan Lanser characterize "feminist and queer narrative theorists" as working to "identify and demystify the workings of those norms ["social systems, cultural practices"] in and through narrative, and expose the dominant stories keeping the binaries in place." *Narrative Theory Unbound*, 8.

6. For a discussion of Buss's painting and many similar visual works see Litvack, "Dickens's Dream."

7. The term *slash* refers to the erotic pairing of same-sex characters and was first widely used to describe fan responses to *Star Trek*, notably Kirk/(slash)Spock. For the genesis of slash fiction and early scholarly and fan responses to it see Jenkins, *Textual Poachers*, ch. 6; and Green, Jenkins, and Jenkins, "'Normal Female Interest in Men Bonking.'" There is a useful glossary of fan-works terms at http://fanlore.org; "Shipping in fandom is the act of supporting or wishing for a particular romantic relationship—that is, a het (different-sex), slash (male/male), femslash (female/female), or poly (three or more partners) ship—by discussing it, writing meta about it, or creating other types of fanworks exploring it." http://fanlore.org/wiki/Shipping. This and all subsequent online references accessed October 1, 2015.

of Dickens's work offer incitements to creative extension and that fan authors work collaboratively with Dickens in their development of queer plotlines that depart from the marital closure closely associated with the Victorian novel.

Readers over the last 180 years or so have made imaginative use of Dickens's figures, both playfully and to fulfill deep emotional needs. Fan fiction shares William Makepeace Thackeray's hunch that "it is the unwritten part of books that would be the most interesting," adding to and meshing material at least loosely related to a source narrative, often described by fan writers as "canon."[8] As Anne Jamison outlines, reciprocity and readership are as important components in fan works as source material; fan fiction is not "just writing stories about existing characters and worlds—it's writing those stories for a community of readers who already want to read them, who want to talk about them, and who may be writing them too."[9] Communities of Dickens fans gather on internet platforms such as FanFiction.net, which describes itself as the "world's largest fan fiction archive and forum" and includes, as of October 1, 2015, 578 Dickens-inspired pieces. Archive Of Our Own (AO3), an "archive for transformative fan works" with a sister academic journal and historical fan-works archive, has a similar number of Dickens-related works, 512, as of the same date. In the context of fan fiction, this is quantitatively a relatively niche activity; a search for Harry Potter material returns 77,096 hits on FanFiction.net and 85,870 on AO3. Nonetheless, the still considerable imaginative investment in Dickens represented by these short works and the often lively discussions surrounding them offers a qualitative, previously untapped, resource through which creative, emotional, and political responses to Dickens can be explored.

Fan author Laura Schiller's response to *David Copperfield* on FanFiction.net is concerned, as is typical in fan writing, with multiplied possibility and plurality. Schiller's "Undisciplined Hearts" is a miscellany in twelve short parts that recalls the seriality of the novel's original publication and the featuring of key characters out of context in visual creations like Buss's *Dickens' Dream.* It plays upon David's diagnosis of his disastrous marriage to Dora as "the first mistaken impulse of an undisciplined heart" to consider the range of romantic impulses in the novel and the rarity of the happy couple in Dickens's work.[10] The parts each take a pairing, incorporating the touching and very straight David/Agnes—in which Agnes scolds her adoring narrator husband for making her seem too good to be true: "Really, Trotwood! . . . Must you make me out to be completely flawless? No reader will believe this"—and the

8. Thackeray, quoted in Brewer, *Afterlife of Character,* 1.

9. Jamison, *Fic,* 36.

10. Dickens, *David Copperfield,* 643.

similarly moving Agnes/Dora. The latter features a stolen kiss between these two women, both very aware of the other's physical appeal to the man they will both marry: "With no warning, Dora's tiny hands are on her shoulders and Dora's lips are brushing hers. She tastes like strawberries."[11] Schiller's miscellany encapsulates a guiding principle of fan fiction: that possibilities will proliferate rather than compete. Showing Agnes in joyful marriage to David in no way disqualifies Agnes/Dora, David/Uriah, and David/Steerforth action in other vignettes.

In this genre's preference for the brief (including the popular drabble form, strictly defined as 100 words but often used less precisely to refer to very short pieces like those that make up "Undisciplined Hearts"), the in-progress, and the multiple, fan fiction breaks formally with the closure devices of the realist novel. It often breaks thematically with those devices too, querying the deaths and marriages meted out in canon, and, as we shall see further, questioning the concept and content of the happy ending. Whatever the emotional and erotic orientation of the characters represented, fan fiction can be considered a queer impulse from a narratological point of view, as it refuses the apparent authority of a definitive ending and turns away from the future-oriented drive of single narrative lines towards the proliferation of multiple moments or temporalities. Roof has recently revised her thinking on narrative's heteroideology via a discussion of the plenitude of variants of Red Riding Hood. Through a systems analysis of multiple versions, she explores the "possibility that desire might torque away not just from the heteronormative and heteroreproductive but also from urges towards completion, satisfaction, and quiescence—in other words from ends themselves."[12] Roof's thinking resonates with recent work, particularly that of Lee Edelman and Judith Halberstam, on queer temporalities not governed by cultural logics of progress and completion. These ideas are related to critiques, made by Sara Ahmed, Lauren Berlant, Heather Love, and others, of the narrative prescriptions we live by which hold that the good life story must include marriage, productivity, and reproductivity.

In fan fiction, queer narratological possibilities combine with the genre's strong tradition of representing desires beyond dyadic heterosexuality. The significant proportion of Dickens fan works that consider same-sex bonds, bisexuality, and sexual plurality beyond the couple compose the archive for this essay. Queer readers and readings use Dickens aftertexts to respond to

11. Laura Schiller, "Undisciplined Hearts," FanFiction, August 15, 2012, https://www.fanfiction.net/s/8432759/1/Undisciplined-Hearts.

12. Roof, "Out of the Bind," 49. For an overview of scholarship, notably that of Judith Halberstam and Lee Edelman, on queer temporalities not oriented by narratives of futurity, see Warhol and Lanser, eds., *Narrative Theory Unbound*, 8.

the heterosexist structures of narrative and society—exposing, denaturalizing, critiquing, transforming—working with Dickens as co-producers, to at least some degree, of potentially sustaining queer imaginaries. As the first piece of research, so far as I know, that takes seriously recent Dickens fan fiction as a form of creative-critical work, this essay makes a new contribution to Dickens studies and endeavors to reshape that field to include fan writing. What follows also seeks to extend understandings of the counterfactual, and to draw out the interrelationships between fan fiction, theories of queer temporality, and projects concerned with affect and public feeling (including work by Sedgwick, Ahmed, Berlant, and Ann Cvetkovich). Drawing these threads together, I propose that Dickens fan fiction offers forms of reparative writing and reading.

I. DWELLING ON/WITH DICKENS: PORTABILITY, SERIALITY, COUNTERFACTUALITY

Current Dickens fan fiction is part of a long and continuing history of Dickens's "portability," which Juliet John defines as "the ability of his novels and indeed his image, even during his lifetime, to travel across various media and national boundaries, and after his death, across different time periods."[13] This phenomenon is not unique to Dickens, as David Brewer's exploration of readers' "imaginative expansion" of eighteenth-century characters such as Richardson's Pamela shows, but Dickens's own active role in presenting his work as eminently portable has contributed to its particular reach.[14] Carrie Han uses the term *continual reading* for the endless forms of textual and extratextual engagements with Dickens work, noting that he explicitly "invites readers to imagine details and events that haven't yet been narrated."[15] Dickens continually reanimated his characters for his own purposes, most notably in the repeated living-out of Sikes's murder of Nancy in the public readings that

13. John, *Dickens and Mass Culture*, 15. As John argues, "The translatability of Dickens's works and image across multiple media has arguably been more crucial to his continued ability to establish a long-term mass cultural presence than have sales of the novels." For a related discussion of portability, see Plotz, *Portable Property*. Both John and Plotz use the term *portable*, with its connotations of "property," to capture the combined, often inextricable, creative and commercial impetuses in the nineteenth-century novel and various repurposings of it.

14. Brewer uses "imaginative expansion as an umbrella term for an array of reading practices in eighteenth-century Britain by which the characters in broadly successful texts were treated as if they were both fundamentally incomplete and the common property of all." *Afterlife*, 2.

15. Han, "Pickwick's Other Papers," 19, 20.

shortened his life, and, for example, in the resurrection of Pickwick and the Wellers to help sales of *Master Humphrey's Clock.*[16] In his interrelated careers as serial novelist, public reader of his own work, editor, and journalist, Dickens encouraged his readers to re-encounter characters as old friends. In the April 30, 1859, issue of his journal *All the Year Round,* for example, Dickens invokes without explanation the quietly heroic minor character of Cousin Feenix, who stands by his disgraced relative Edith Dombey in *Dombey and Son* (October 1846–April 1848), in the entirely different context of a journalistic account of class and temperance.[17] The entire lack of context supplied suggests that Dickens was confident that regular readers would readily recognize and appreciate the characteristics of this figure. Amy Cruse's classic account of Victorian reading practices offers a wealth of evidence that Dickens's first readers incorporated his characters into their mental landscapes as personal acquaintances, and this form of readerly relationship persisted through the 2012 bicentenary of Dickens's birth, with many readers turned writers discussing the parallels with Dickens plots and characters in their own lives.[18]

This sense of dwelling with Dickens's characters is intensified by the serial form, as Thomas Arnold anxiously observed in an 1839 sermon in which he described periodical fictions as "dwelling upon the mind, and distilling themselves into it, as it were drop by drop," "possess[ing] it so largely, colouring even, in its many instances, its very language and affording frequent matter for conversation."[19] As Arnold's worried reference to the "conversation" generated by serial reading suggests, possession by parts was often experienced in company. That company of fellow readers might be actual or an imaginative "imaginary community," to extend Benedict Anderson's valuable term for the

---

16. In ch. 2 of *Queer Dickens,* I discuss Dickens's repurposing of characters from *The Pickwick Papers.* Maureen England has considered Dickens's own reuse of the character of Sairey Gamp (the fragment "Mrs Gamp and the Strolling Players" was as far as he took the idea for a new travelogue voiced and apparently authored "by" this character) in the context of mass produced Dickens spin-offs from sheet music to toby jugs. "The Curious Case of Dolly Varden," paper given at the 2015 BAVS conference, Leeds.

17. [Charles Dickens], "The Poor Man and His Beer," *All the Year Round,* April 30, 1859, 13. I came across this reinvocation of Cousin Feenix in a collaborative reading of the serialization of Dickens's *A Tale of Two Cities* in the journal that tried to replicate the serial experience by following the weekly rhythms and reading the fiction in the context of the journal's other contents. See https://dickensataleoftwocities.wordpress.com for the project blog, including the discussion of this character in week 1.

18. Cruse, *The Victorians and Their Books;* Justin Cartwright, for example, "Dickens: Nightmare Before Christmas," 36–37. Also broadcast by BBC Radio 3 as part of *The Writer's Dickens* series, December 23, 2011.

19. Thomas Arnold, quoted in Winter, *The Pleasures of Memory,* 87.

sense of virtual community generated by synchronous periodical reading.[20] Various scholars have noted that the gaps between installments also encourage the imaginative independence of characters as readers dwell upon the reported activities of their favorites and project possible plotlines for them. As Ben Winyard puts it in a reflection on reading Dickens by parts, "the serialised novel gives us formal spaces or gaps between installments that encourage the proliferation of imaginative surpluses," "spaces that facilitate discussion, analysis, ambiguity, deviation and fantasy."[21] Linda Hughes and Michael Lund argue that this sustained affective engagement made for a different sense of an ending: "Although the happy ending certainly had a resonance over time for Victorian readers after the novel concluded, modern evaluations of the text have given too much weight to this small part of the total event." Serial readers looked forward to "possible (probable) renewed engagement later (in other novels)."[22] For those frustrated by the heteroideology of narrative, most firmly secured by the novel's typical marital closure, serial fiction provided opportunities for counternarrative lines—extrapolations that looked backwards and sideways as well as forward.

Jennifer Hayward's description of the "unique reading practices and interpretative tactics" to which serials give rise sees this form as a direct invitation to fan fiction: those practices and tactics "include collaborative, active reading, interpretation, prediction, occasional rewriting or creation of new subplots, attempts to influence textual production."[23] In his analysis of responses to the TV serial *Twin Peaks,* pioneering fan-works theorist Henry Jenkins recorded a Dickensian sensibility within experiences of interactivity. As an alt.tv.twinpeaks member put it, "back in Lit class we talked about how Dickens wrote his books in instalments and sometimes wound up changing his original plan because of the feedback he got . . . I wonder how much we are writing our own show."[24] Given the widespread teaching of Dickens with reference to part publication, which contributes to the typical comment in the UK that "if Dickens were alive today he'd be writing for *Eastenders,*" readers make connections between the Victorian serial novel and interactivity and see contem-

---

20. Anderson, *Imagined Communities.* As Anderson puts it, a reading public may "never know most of their fellow-members, meet them, or even hear of them, yet in the minds of each lives the image of communion" (15).

21. Winyard, "'May We Meet Again.'"

22. Hughes and Lund, *The Victorian Serial,* 44, 289.

23. Hayward, *Consuming Pleasures,* 4.

24. Jenkins, *Fans, Bloggers, and Gamers,* 128. Jenkins also cites fans using Dickens's unfinished *The Mystery of Edwin Drood* as one key to *Twin Peaks* mysteries, 127. For notable examples of Dickens changing his plans in response to readers' letters, see Slater, *Charles Dickens,* 301, 516–17.

porary participatory fan culture as part of a long-established practice.[25] While twenty-first-century audiences rarely read Dickens in serial installments, the contemporary encounter with Dickens's work shares dimensions of seriality—this encounter takes place by segment and over long duration even if it is not sequential in the manner of a part-published novel—through cumulative exposure to a combination of forms including text, heritage, TV, film, and conversation.

Readerly fantasy work is also encouraged by the explicit fascination in Dickens's fiction with what might have been. As Andrew Miller has recently argued, Dickens's work is deeply concerned with the optative and counterfactual, the conditional alternative possibilities of roads not traveled and choices not made, as articulated in *Great Expectations* by Pip:

> That was a memorable day to me, for it made great changes in me. But, it is the same with any life. Imagine one selected day struck out of it, and think how different its course would have been. Pause you who read this, and think for a moment of the long chain of iron or gold, of thorns or flowers, that would never have bound you, but for the formation of the first link on one memorable day.[26]

While lives and the realist novel are shaped by the parameters of birth, death, and, in many cases, marriage, the novel form also invests great energy in imagining alternative courses of events were these things not so. In the optative mode Pip enters here, attention is shifted from the boundaries of life and death, beginning and end, to the boundaries of right and left: "It is not just that my life will come to a stop, be limited in the future, but that it is limited now, at every moment." Miller argues that "the optative is not merely the chance preoccupation of some novelists; it is an intrinsic feature of realistic representation."[27] And, I add with the arguments of queer narratology in mind, the forms of the optative in which the novel invests offer counterbalance to the restrictions of its narrative heteroideology. As Miller's reading of *Great Expectations* elucidates, counterfactual possibilities exceed the constraints of capitalism ("no longer determined by inheritance, anyone might have expectations, might hope to exchange a life as a blacksmith's apprentice,

---

25. Emphasizing the connections between current and Victorian networks and distribution networks, Jay Clayton suggests that "if Dickens were sitting before a computer screen today, he would not be surprised at what his browser revealed. The global network, the commercial crassness, and the dizzying pace of both technology and the imagination were all discernible in the nineteenth-century world of cyberspace." *Charles Dickens in Cyberspace*, 10.

26. Dickens, *Great Expectations*, 72.

27. Miller, "'A Case of Metaphysics,'" 782.

say, for that of a gentleman"), of marriage (visions of marriages made and not made are an occasion for the optative "fundamentally at work in Dickens's fiction"), and of reproduction (a concern with child lives that might or might not have begun or ended is the third feature of Dickensian and realist counterfactuality that Miller identifies).[28]

Serialized novels also have a particular relationship to the counterfactual and to queer forms of temporality in which the imaginative spaces in between installments take on greater significance than narrative resolution. The optative content of Dickens's work presents itself very clearly in a serial reading, as I have found over the last year and a half in reading *Our Mutual Friend* (May 1864–November 1865) month by month as part of Birkbeck College's collective reading project. The Rokesmith/Harmon/Handford plot at the center of this novel, which lives out the fantasy "what if I had died but could still observe the behavior of those dear to me?" perhaps singles out *Our Mutual Friend* as the ur-text of the counterfactual. In one of the in-person events to accompany the largely online experience, a group of serial readers got together in January 2015 at about the novel's halfway point. We noted how the January 1865 installment, the ninth part, weaves a web of featured characters' fantasies. In this installment Dickens finally reveals the Rokesmith/Harmon connection. Having decided that John Harmon should remain dead, the character once known by this name makes his feelings for Bella clear under the alias of John Rokesmith, secretary. A counterfactual intuiting of what Harmon would have done follows:

> Ah! What a *different life* the late John Harmon's *if* it had been his happy privilege to take his place upon that ottoman, and draw his arm about that waist, and say, "I hope the time has been long without me? What a Home Goddess you look, my darling!"[29]

Though Harmon is given the opportunity and resources to live his fantasy life more fully than others, Dickens devotes his narrative energy to imagining alternative existences for many of the characters in this installment. Jenny encourages Lizzie to use her old skills of seeing alternative lives in the fire to imagine being a lady, a socially plausible match for Eugene, "only as a fancy, and for instance" (343), while Pleasant Riderhood looks at the sky above the "reeking street," and "may have had some vaporous visions of far-off islands in the southern seas or elsewhere (not being geographically particular), where it

28. Ibid., 785–87.

29. Dickens, *Our Mutual Friend*, 368; emphasis added. Cited parenthetically in the text hereafter.

would be good to roam with a congenial partner among groves of bread-fruit, waiting for ships to be wafted from the hollow ports of civilisation. For sailors, to be got the better of, were essential to Miss Pleasant's Eden" (346). This particular vision of exotic wealth and agency over men and their money clearly recalls Bella's November installment imagining "all sorts of voyages for herself and Pa," picturing herself married to a "merchant of immense wealth" (315). There are gendered arguments to be made about the way in which a male character lives out his own fantasy life and death while the women figures are left dreaming. And all these examples show the ways in which the counterfactual exposes and denaturalizes the social structures of class and marriage, measuring a gap (shown to be larger for women than men) between life choices imagined and those available. This halfway point in the novel contextualizes the revelation of Harmon's multiple identities with a layering of counterfactual fantasies, an incitement to the serial reader dwelling, for instance, on Pleasant Riderhood's warm, lush bread-fruit dreams to more thoroughly imagine alternative departures for her narrative. To extend Miller's argument, counterfactual possibilities are intensified by the serial form, as readers play out alternative plot trajectories for characters in vibrant ways often not fully superseded by the resumption of the Dickens-authored plot.

In a talk at Birkbeck prior to the publication of his article, Miller also gestured towards the queer possibilities of the counterfactual. He began the talk with George Stanley's poem "Veracruz," in which the speaker imagines himself in an alternative family:

> . . . I wished my father had come back to San Francisco
> armed with Brazilian magic, & that he had married
> not my mother, but her brother, whom he truly loved.[30]

Dickens's fiction encourages this kind of connection with its many forms of non-maritally or biologically related family, intermarriages to the sister of a beloved male friend (such as John Westlock's marriage to his close friend's sister, Ruth Pinch, in *Martin Chuzzlewit*), and imagined or actual sibling doubles (such as Steerforth's fantasy of David Copperfield's sister, Smike's immediate love for Kate Nickleby, and near-identical twins Helena and Edwin Landless in *Edwin Drood*). The memorable same-sex intimacies of Dickens's fiction com-

30. https://www.poetrysociety.org/psa/awards/frost_and_shelley/shelley_winners/2006/; Andrew Miller, Birkbeck Forum for Nineteenth-Century Studies, January 26, 2012, http://www.cncs.bbk.ac.uk/thursday-26-January-2012-a-case-of-metaphysics-counterfactuals-realism-great-expectations.

bine with its optative content and serial form to work against the narrative constraints of the novel form to provide rich ground for queer co-production.

II. QUEER DICKENS CO-PRODUCTIONS

Queer Dickens fan fiction has a long history. As Kim Edwards has showed, the unfinished *Mystery of Edwin Drood*, which continues to incite fan works that offer continuations and solutions to the mystery, inspired early lesbian completions.[31] Other Victorian authors suggested that Dickens titles be incorporated into queer libraries.[32] These queer readings/writings are continued today on fanfic forums, with content covering the whole Dickens canon. *A Christmas Carol* and *Oliver Twist* are particularly well represented on the two fan writing forums I have studied closely, due to their wide dissemination as "culture texts," to use Paul Davis's term.[33] This familiarity means that characters from these novels are most likely to be slashed with other fandoms such as Sherlock. Scrooge, the Cratchits, Oliver, and the Artful Dodger experience autonomy even beyond the range of other Dickens fiction, something less common in treatments of other Dickens titles. Fan authors often acknowledge the potency of the transformation of Dickens into culture text, citing one or more adaptations as source text and identifying inspiring film and TV versions as ways into reading Dickens. In some cases the adaptations themselves offer queer interpretative lines that fan fictions develop.[34]

---

31. Edwards discusses Elizabeth Newton's 1878 *A Great Mystery Solved: A Sequel to "The Mystery of Edwin Drood"* (published under the pseudonym Gillian Vase), which expands on the passionate intimacy of Helena and Rosa in Dickens's novel, in "Unnameable Desire," 178.

32. I consider the inclusion of Dickens in early twentieth-century queer bibliographies in *Queer Dickens*, 9.

33. Davis, *The Lives and Times of Ebenezer Scrooge*. Davis uses the term *culture text* to describe the ways in which particular Dickens texts permeate everyday life in Britain and America via their diffusion through a range of nonliterary media.

34. See especially discussions around the 1998 BBC serial of *Our Mutual Friend*. Following a post titled "Five reasons why Mortimer Lightwood and Eugene Wrayburn are unbelievably gay" on the queer fandom discussion site Almost Canon, one respondent says: "And give the BBC credit where it's due, the subtext is there in abundance in the 1998 TV adaptation," "if anything, those two get more screen-time together in the show than they do in the book." Brewsternorth, May 28, 2008, http://almost-canon.livejournal.com/1952.html. Other readers of Eugene/Mortimer works note that this miniseries brought them to the novel; see, for example, Bangela's comment on Zlot's "Two Men in a Boat," Archive of Our Own, August 25, 2013, http://archiveofourown.org/works/141813. In their account of fan fiction as reading collectively, Hellekson and Busse discuss how "other versions of the same story may be just as important to the fan artwork as the primary source." *The Fan Fiction Studies Reader*, 21.

Schiller's "Undisciplined Hearts," discussed in this essay's opening, is representative of a genre of Dickens fan works that posit multiple narrative lines alongside one another. Other examples include Tom Cranver's "Five Ways Smike's Story Could Have Ended" and ct010124's "Pairings That Will Never Happen in ATOTC." Cranver's variations posit Smike's potential deaths at the sadistic Dotheboys Hall and survivals—longing in vain for Nicholas's return at the Crummles theater, living with the benevolent John Browdie, recovering from the illness that kills him in canon, and returning to London with Nicholas. Nicholas reassures him that a romance with Kate Nickleby is not necessary for their sense of brotherhood—"As far as I'm concerned, you're part of our family already"—and the closing tableau is of their emotional and physical intimacy:

> "You have been kinder to me than anyone in the world," Smike said, and he rested his head on Nicholas's breast. Nicholas moved his hand to stroke Smike's hair. They stayed like that all the way to London.[35]

The patterning of Smike's experience of violence from the Squeers family and then nursing and gentleness from Nicholas shares a hurt/comfort structure popular in erotic fan fiction, and these elements recur in *Nickleby*-inspired fan works, which also cite Dickens's treatment of Smike's fantasy of Nicholas's sister.[36] Halfhardtorock's sexually explicit work is headed with a Smike-voiced summary—"'There could be nothing hurtful about having Nicholas inside me'"—and plays on the Kate/Nicholas/Smike triangle, reassigning the roles of husband and wife to Smike and Nicholas.[37] Ingridmatthews's Smike/Nicholas story begins with a direct Dickens quotation:

> "Is she like you?" inquired Smike.
>
> "Why, so they say," replied Nicholas, laughing, "only a great deal handsomer."
>
> "She must be *very* beautiful," said Smike, after thinking a little while with his hands folded together, and his eyes bent upon his friend.[38]

35. Tom Cranver, Archive of Our Own, April 4, 2010, https://archiveofourown.org/works/77771.

36. Cicioni examines the hurt/comfort tradition in slash fiction as "the eroticisation of nurturance." "Male Pair-Bonds," 162.

37. Halfhardtorock, "Four Times," Archive of Our Own, August 4, 2015, https://archiveofourown.org/works/4499838?view_adult=true.

38. Ingridmatthews, "In the Pauper's Court," Archive of Our Own, January 5, 2010, https://archiveofourown.org/works/45851, and Dickens, *Nicholas Nickleby*, 359.

Direct quotations from Dickens are often noted in writers'/readers' discussions identifying queer elements from canon. These discussions establish a layering of co-production, with fan writers positioning themselves in a creative partnership with Dickens, Dickens readers, and their own readers, who, in some cases, have requested the production of fan works addressing particular scenarios.

The preoccupations of these works also parallel those of academic scholarship on queer Dickens. The Agnes/Dora section of Schiller's "Undisciplined Hearts" offers another version of the kind of argument made in Sharon Marcus's *Between Women* about the plurality of desire that comes into view in Agnes and Dora's ready understanding of each other's appeal to David.[39] And there are particular resonances with my work's emphasis on the tender erotics of care and nursing in Dickens's fiction and the proliferation of Smike/Nicholas, Herbert/Pip, hurt/comfort narratives in fan fiction. Both Marcus's work and my own offer alternatives to an established critical practice of finding same-sex desire in Dickens where it appears in the forms of aggression and asociability. As I have argued elsewhere, Eve Sedgwick's early work on violent erotic contact between men in Dickens's fiction was a major influence on a line of paranoid (to use the terms of Sedgwick's later thinking), antihomophobic reading of Dickens in which homoeroticism could only register through devices of punishment and shame.[40]

It has taken academic criticism some time to respond to the encouragement, given particularly in Sedgwick's later work, to move beyond an exclusive hermeneutics of suspicion. Fan works, however, have more readily explored the erotic potential of both violent and healing encounters. Fan writing offers forms of what Marcus calls "just reading," making visible "what texts present on their surface but critics have failed to notice."[41] This interpretative approach is often highlighted in discussions of fan works by reference to canon; personalized_radio for example writes *A Tale of Two Cities* fan fiction from the perspective that "carton/darnay/lucie . . . is basically canon to me anyway."[42]

39. As Marcus puts it, "Agnes can sympathise and thus complete David's love for Dora because she decides to love the same woman he does," while Dora shares a desire "with her husband: to have chosen Agnes as her first spouse." *Between Women*, 88–89.

40. I discuss the potent critical legacy of Eve Sedgwick's 1985 *Between Men: English Literature and Male Homosocial Desire* in *Queer Dickens*, 14–16. Sedgwick offered a critique of her own paranoid approach in the introduction to *Novel Gazing: Queer Readings in Fiction* (1997; she expands on this material in *Touching Feeling*, 2003), outlining an alternative practice of paranoid/reparative reading, which I discuss more fully in the development of this essay.

41. Marcus, *Between Women*, 75.

42. Personalized_radio, comment on "A Tale of the Darnay's and Their Sydney," Archive of Our Own, September 29, 2014, http://archiveofourown.org/works/2349035?view_adult=true. In

Shared interpretations are perhaps particularly pronounced in queer Dickens fan fiction and recent queer Dickens scholarship because both fields of endeavor are often deliberately and self-consciously entered as ways of working collaboratively with Dickens to tease out the present but overlooked queer content of his canon.

While fan-fiction responses build on the suggestions and subtexts (to use the term popular in fan-writing forums) of Dickens's work, they also work out frustrations with canon and its narrative conventions. Many queer responses to Dickens's fiction share an interest in revisiting endings found to be unsatisfying and in sustaining characters whose plots are curtailed in Dickens's work by the closing structures of death and marriage. The charisma, early death, and narrative dexterity of Sydney Carton, who creatively inserts himself into another man's life and then death, have resulted in a proliferation of *Tale of Two Cities* fan fiction in which Sydney is not dead. These include Penthesilea's "Hero's Footsteps," in which a mashup with the Scarlet Pimpernel results in Sydney's last-minute rescue from the guillotine.[43] Some works allocate him a form, albeit a tragic one, of the heterosexual romance plot, through the love of the seamstress he befriends at the guillotine.[44] Others play on the potential erotic energies of Carton's triangulation with his physical double Charles Darnay, and Lucie Manette, whom they both love. Fan fiction works through various configurations of this trio, with many stories focusing on Sydney/Darnay and envisaging contexts for their realization and/or revelation of their feelings for each other. In "Alternative Scene" Starry_Neko_Maid, for example, has Sydney out himself to an unconscious Darnay just before he takes his place for execution, while in another work the same author gives substance to Dickens's establishment of a ghostly family of choice through Sydney's final vision of himself as part of the Darnay family, through a plot in which Darnay dreams that baby Sydney is actually the child of himself and Sydney.[45]

---

the tongue-in-cheek "Five Reasons why Mortimer Lightwood and Eugene Wrayburn are unbelievably gay," Casablancagirl presents the overtness of Dickens's same-sex pairings as making writing of/on slash redundant: "You know, I could write a thousand page book on the slashiness of Our Mutual Friend, but I can't be bothered. If anyone hasn't read it, read it now, because it's about as canon as nineteenth century literature gets. Even more canon than Herbert/Pip (Great Expectations) who are also pretty canon." Almost Canon, May 28, 2008, http://almost-canon.livejournal.com/1952.html.

43. Penthesilea, "Hero's Footsteps," FanFiction, April 18, 2002, https://www.fanfiction.net/s/728296/1/Hero-s-Footsteps.

44. For example, Little Lotte's "The Seamstress," FanFiction, May 20, 2002, https://www.fanfiction.net/s/787451/1/The-Seamstress.

45. Starry_Neko_Maid, "ATOTC Drabbles," Archive of Our Own, June 8, 2015, http://archiveofourown.org/works/4097521/chapters/9230737, and "The Beauty Underneath," Archive of Our Own, September 6, 2015, http://archiveofourown.org/works/4739318.

Personalized_radio's "A Tale of the Darnay's and their Sydney" is tagged for "BDSM (Bondage, Dominance and submission, Sadomasochism) Threesome, F/M/M two doms one sub" and combines the pleasures of erotic creativity with an interest in Dickens's psychological characterization of Sydney as, finally, suicidally self-abnegating. Readers responded warmly to personalized_radio's representation of Sydney's difficulty in accepting love, and of his love for both Darnay and Lucie. As LifeLover commented, "Sub!Sydney. Of course—pretty much canon. Heartbreaking his belief of that they shouldn't 'bother' with him. Or that he's in love with both of them (also canon!)."[46] LifeLover also noted the rarity of "happy, bdsm oT3 (one true threesome) fic," calling for more works to give Sydney a happy ending.

Fan-fiction responses to *Our Mutual Friend* (1997) are similarly concerned with providing more fulfilling endings for beloved characters. Mortimer/Eugene fan fiction is typically written from a position of concern for Mortimer, in response to a shared desire within these online communities of authors to provide a happier ending for this admired figure. As Rachel McMillan put it on the DickensBlog, "Somebody, somewhere, should give one half of this magnificent duo a chance at more life: a life beyond that final Tremlow [*sic*] handshake and the retreat back to the Temple. But at any rate—long live Mortimer and Eugene: one of Dickens' definitive friendships and certainly one of the strongest in Victorian literature."[47] Fan fiction supplies this wish with varied online afterlives envisaged for Mortimer. In "The Winning of Mortimer" Dickensian812 creates Rebecca Wrayburn to offer a possibility already outlined by Dickens in the context of other novels. Steerforth's vision of David Copperfield's nonexistent younger sister, for example, or Smike's compulsion to love Kate Nickleby as a result of his intimacy with her brother Nicholas, as explored in various Smike/Nicholas works): "Eugene Wrayburn's little sister hasn't seen Mortimer Lightwood in years. But she hasn't forgotten."[48]

Several AO3 authors explore a scenario concisely expressed by the summary line "Mortimer wonders whether Eugene still needs him after Lizzie has taken his place."[49] Rather than Lizzie displacing Mortimer, these authors imagine their unity in shared love for Eugene and suggest enabling emotional and practical arrangements between the trio.

---

46. LifeLover, comment on "A Tale of the Darnay's and Their Sydney," Archive of Our Own, September 29, 2014, http://archiveofourown.org/works/2349035?view_adult=true.

47. Rachel McMillan, "Mortimer and Eugene: A study in friendship," Dickensblog, February 11, 2012, http://dickensblog.typepad.com/dickensblog/2012/02/mortimer-and-eugene.html.

48. Dickensian812, "The Winning of Mortimer," FanFiction, March 11, 2012, https://www.fanfiction.net/s/7914100/1/The-Winning-of-Mortimer.

49. Deanna (Sweetsorcery), "Sources of Light," Archive of Our Own, December 21, 2009, http://archiveofourown.org/works/33509.

In "Sources of Light" Deanna (Sweetsorcery) navigates the interlocking claims of relationship at the shattered Eugene's bedside through the growing trust developed between Mortimer and Lizzie:

> "He will be quite himself again soon," he assured her awkwardly. "You have cared well for him."
>
> "As have you," she hurried to say. "Please, do not feel as though you are intruding. Come and see him, and sit with him, whenever you wish. You have many years of close friendship with Eugene, and he loves you dearly. He has spoken much of you during his waking times, and while I hope you do not find me presumptuous, I feel I have come to know you a little, through him."

Lizzie and Mortimer then work together to care for the man they both love, neither excluding the other, and Eugene looks forward to being sufficiently restored to join them, describing them both as "my family." Another story, Zlot's "Two Men in a Boat," introduces a sexual relationship to Eugene and Mortimer's joyful times on the river, bachelor cottage, and lighthouse fantasies. Here Eugene's marriage to Lizzie is predicated on their understanding that his relationship with Mortimer will continue: "I am certainly aware of how little I merit such devotion as you are capable of, dear boy. But . . . I desire no essential change in our relation."[50] Readers responded particularly enthusiastically in their comments to the line "She is one-half my heart, one-half my soul. And she has graciously permitted me to dispose of the other half as I choose." As one reader describes it: "The happy ending seems very true to the book; after all, Eugene does (in canon) declare his love for Mortimer and Lizzie at pretty much the same time. It's wonderful—and, I think, very much in the spirit of Dickensian alternative families—to see the m/m and m/f relationships as collaborating, not competing, in the end. Did you ask M. R. F. [Eugene's ironic way of referring to "my respected father" in the novel] for his blessing too?"[51]

The warmth of these online communities is also in a Dickensian spirit, as writers and readers establish an active, emotional engagement, similar to the kind of personal relationship that Dickens worked so hard to achieve with his public. Two of these stories were written in direct response to calls on the site for Eugene/Mortimer content and presented as yuletide gifts to other readers. The etiquette of both fanfic sites I have quoted from is only to post positive or

50. Zlot, "Two Men in a Boat," Archive of Our Own, December 20, 2010, http://archiveofourown.org/works/141813.

51. Rose71, comment on ibid., December 28, 2010; see also lionpyh, comment on ibid., May 7, 2012.

constructively critical response, so authors can improve their writing in a supportive environment. Writing in thanks for Zlot's "Two Men in a Boat," AO3 member Bangela describes the formation of virtual community and the pleasure of fan fiction as a realization and confirmation of one's own fantasy life:

> One of the most wonderful things about the Internet is that you can find others that accurately put into words what you've seen in your own imagination but couldn't articulate. I first discovered *Our Mutual Friend* as a BBC miniseries and I immediately went to the library and borrowed the book—I was 13 years old. I never returned the book (shame!) but I read it many times over the years. The most compelling relationship in the book, for me, was of course Eugene Wrayburn and Mortimer Lightwood. I worried about Mortimer after Eugene and Lizzie were married. Thank you for writing a happy ending for all three of them.[52]

I experienced similarly generous dynamics of storytelling and community in my own, and so far only, production of a form of fan fiction. A Twitter character project accompanied Birkbeck's serial reading of *Our Mutual Friend,* in which participants tweeted monthly about their designated character's action that month in miniature installments of 140 characters or less. I had the pleasure and responsibility of embodying Mortimer Lightwood, my own favorite Dickens character and a figure who has been central to me personally and professionally. In the fraught penultimate installment when Mortimer believes Eugene's narrative will end in the combined closure of marriage and death, Lizzie Hexam tweeted comfort: "I hope I do not intrude upon @OMF_Mortimer's space at the bedside. I know how dearly loved Mr Lightwood is by my beloved @OMF_Eugene."[53] Thank you, Lizzie.

III. FAN FICTION AS REPARATIVE READING

Academic and fan studies of fan works have long been concerned with the extent to which the genre is resistant to or complicit with cultural norms.[54] This question is particularly urgent in studies of slash fiction, where arguments about the genre's potential for subversion of heteronormativity are

52. Bangela, comment on "Two Men in a Boat," August 25, 2013.

53. @OMF_Lizzie, Twitter, October 4, 2015, 1:28 p.m. See the tenth-anniversary edition of *19: Interdisciplinary Studies in the Long Nineteenth Century* 21 (2015), http://www.19.bbk.ac.uk, for reflections on experiences of rewriting Dickens's characters in the Twitter serial.

54. Hills, *Fan Cultures,* gives an overview of the academic focus on "'resistant' or 'complicit' readings," xi.

offset by the concern that it operates primarily as a fantasy outlet without effecting real-world change.[55] Debate also centers around who are appropriate producers and consumers of slash fiction (heterosexual women were initially deemed to be the primary producers, although more recent accounts note the proliferation of writers and perspectives and the limited value of interrogating the writers' own sexual identifications) and whether it fetishizes homosexuality.[56] These controversies continue, as demonstrated by the ongoing response to effingdeixis's 2013 Tumblr essay, "Dear 'Slash' Fandom," and the to-date two thousand responses to it, arguing whether or not slash is "about selfishly seeking validation for private homoerotic fantasies of fictional characters" or concerned with "the advancement of queer representation in the media." The essay writes against the shaming of slash fans and instead presents slash as "something special, something new, something . . . hopeful."[57] Sedgwick's account of paranoid/reparative reading offers a both/and alternative to these oppositional either/or standoffs. Paranoid/reparative reading as a practice of nondualistic thought allows both possibilities to be held in tension or balanced against one another so that adjudicating between the resistant or complicit becomes redundant, as do questions like "How subversive is slash?" Paranoid/reparative reading gives equal space to the competing affects—notably shame and hope—circulating in slash practices.

Sedgwick's account of the reparative project builds on Melanie Klein's work on infant separation trauma. Extrapolating from Klein's account, Sedgwick proposes a wider context, continuing through adulthood experiences of pain and loss, in which it becomes possible "to use one's own resources to assemble or 'repair' the murderous part-objects into something like a whole. . . . Once assembled to one's own specifications, the more satisfying object is available both to be identified with and to offer one nourishment and comfort in turn."[58] This process resonates with Jenkins's account of fan practices. Focusing on TV serial fans as "consummate negotiating readers," Jenkins argues that

> fan critics work to repair gaps or contradictions in the programme ideology, to make it cohere into a whole that satisfies their needs for continuity and emotional realism. Fandom is characterised by a contradictory and often

55. See, for example, Cicioni's conclusion to her essay on m/m works subtitled "How Subversive Is Slash?," 174–75.

56. For a recent version of this debate, see cantpronounce's Tumblr essay "Fetishising Homosexuality" and responses to it: 387 in May 2015, as documented at http://fanlore.org/wiki/Fetishizing_Homosexuality.

57. See effingdeixis, "Dear 'Slash' Fandom," Fanlore, May 7, 2013, http://fanlore.org/wiki/Dear_%22Slash%22_Fandom.

58. Sedgwick, *Touching Feeling*, 128.

> highly fluid series of attitudes toward the primary text, marked by fascination as well as frustration, proximity as well as distance, acceptance of program ideology as well as rejection.[59]

This proliferating fan work of "repair," in which insufficient fragments are fashioned into more satisfying fuller forms, is inspired by, as Jenkins notes, a mixture of feelings and contradictory attitudes. This thinking also coheres with Sedgwick's theorization of "a reparative impulse" as "additive and accretive. Its fear, a realistic one, is that the culture surrounding it is inadequate or inimical to its nurture; it wants to assemble and confer plenitude on an object that will then have the resources to offer to an inchoate self."[60] Extending Sedgwick's work, a number of recent studies of affect and public feeling have pointed to the ways in which limited narratives for what count as the good life produce an inadequate culture that refuses to nurture and does violence to lives lived on different lines, particularly those that turn away from the supposed happy-ending scripts of marriage, productivity, and reproductivity.[61] Dickens fan fiction, particularly slash fiction, draws out the material present in Dickens's fiction and augments it, responding to a paucity of sustained queer canonical literature and to the inadequate, inimical nature of traditional heterosexist narrative and social structures. Dickens slash works, with their emphasis on plurality, the rewriting and evasion of endings that conventionally close down and contain erotic and narrative possibilities through marriage and death, create resources for lives, sex lives, and fantasy lives lived differently. They create, to use the title of a major fanworks project, an "archive of our own," and attest, to use Sedgwick's terms, to "the many ways selves and communities succeed in extracting sustenance from the objects of a culture—even of a culture whose avowed desire has often been not to sustain them."[62] Fan works extract sustenance not from forms of repair that tend towards completion or finality but from a plenitude and proliferation of parts.

Ann Cvetkovich builds on Sedgwick's work to characterize reparative reading as "affectively driven, motivated by pleasure and curiosity, and directed toward the textures and tastes, the sensuous feel, of one's objects of study."[63] Cvetkovich explores the reparative possibilities of various craft forms, including written forms that prioritize immediacy, and the "rough

59. Jenkins, *Fans, Bloggers, and Gamers*, 111.

60. Sedgwick, *Touching Feeling*, 149.

61. See especially Ahmed, *The Promise of Happiness*; Berlant, *Cruel Optimism*; and Cvetkovich, *Depression: A Public Feeling*.

62. Sedgwick, *Touching Feeling*, 150–51.

63. Cvetkovich, "Public Feelings," 462–63.

draft" such as diary keeping or blogging.[64] Much of the fan fiction examined here is presented as a provisional, draft form, open to revisiting and rewriting in response to comments. Fan work, motivated as its designation suggests by powerful feelings including pleasure and curiosity, offers a form of tactile encounter with other authors in the writing and editing activities of actual or virtual cutting, pasting, and brushing up against other texts. Writers of, and reader respondents to, Dickens slash eschew master narratives, instead creating plenitude through a bricolage or story patchwork.

It is not just that thinking about the reparative can help us to better understand the dynamics of fan fiction; engagement with fan fiction can also give us a model for how reparative reading and writing works. For some time academics have been reaching for a reparative critical mode. Cathy Davidson and Jessamyn Hatcher see Sedgwick's work as inspiring a quest: "We are seeking a post-Foucauldian model of criticism based on the complexity and interdependence of power and resistance, coupled with an awareness that aesthetic expression is never monolithic and unambiguous."[65] Their search parallels the quest for modes that deprivilege the imposed certainty of narrative structures complete with endings in marriage or death and for means of calling into question cultural scripts for the good life lived to this formula. Rebecca Solnit finds forms of critical hope in John Keats's "negative capability" and Virginia Woolf's embrace of not knowing, using these authors to advocate a countercultural mode that celebrates "the meandering, the digressive, the exploratory, the numinous, the uncertain."[66] These are features and principles of fan writing, and characterize nondualistic approaches to that work.[67] Dickens fan fiction takes pleasure in the spaces opened up by the suspension of a finite, certain ending. As a body of work it shows the restrictiveness both of critical and narrative traditions, offering instead affectively powerful queer experiments with life stories not lived by cultural ur-narratives of marriage, progress, reproduction, or conclusion. Reparative reading, queer temporality, critiques of prescribed affects linked to limited life scripts (compulsory happiness realized in marriage, for example), and fan fiction are projects with similar, and sometimes overlapping, stakes and potentials for reinventing the narratives we

---

64. Cvetkovich, *Depression*, 192.

65. Davidson and Hatcher, *No More Separate Spheres*, 14.

66. Solnit, "Woolf's Darkness."

67. Notably in *Fic* Jamison catches herself out in urges to categorize—"It's fiction, it's theory, no wait—since when do I think that's an either/or question" (10)—and points to ways in which "fanfiction blurs a whole range of lines we (mistakenly) believe to be stable: between reading and writing, consuming and creating, genres and genders, authors and critics, derivative and transformative works" and "increasingly offers a space where gender, like sexuality, is not an either/or phenomenon" (6–7, 19).

live by. These projects also share an investment in affective transformation, by which emotions are no longer directed along dominant narrative lines but are reoriented, so that competing and mixed feelings can be recognized and lived and broader understandings and experiences of love become possible.

Fan works are often produced and consumed in love—a term less familiar in the academy than it might be, used by Sedgwick—via Klein—to characterize the reparative, and used frequently in fan forum comments in relation to Dickens and Dickens-inspired works. Padfoot Reincarnated's story of Herbert's nursing of the burned Pip, "Faithful Attendant," was greeted with thanks and some relief. Chanting the Mantra was one of many to find in the story a sense of community with its author a resource to "satisfy one's own specifications," to use Sedgwick's terms, commenting: "This is wonderful. I love this story, its so great to see another Pip/Herbert slash fan." Retired Indefinitely and others, on the other hand, voiced a strong emotional response to the story's reinstatement of a Pip/Herbert emphasis, which was felt to have been straightened out by Dickens's revisions to the ending of *Great Expectations*: "Much love for writing such! :D I swear they belong together; I've got nothing against Estella or Clara . . . but the original ending was much better for the book! :D."[68] Responses like these sum up the ways in which this growing archive is felt to provide emotional resources and attest to the continuing power of Dickens's characters to inspire creativity and create bonds between unmet readers. Bangela (on Zlot on Dickens) gets the last word: "When I was younger I never in my wildest dreams thought a place like AO3 could exist. Finding it is like thinking you are alone in a dark room but when the light goes on you see that your friends are there with you."

68. Reviews for "A Faithful Attendant," FanFiction, https://www.fanfiction.net/r/3511295/.

CHAPTER 9

Disabling Marriage

Communities of Care in Our Mutual Friend

TALIA SCHAFFER

OUR MUTUAL FRIEND (1865), as its title indicates, is centrally concerned with social relationships. But a mutual friendship—a network of multiple, coexisting, amicable relationships—is a complicated matter. In this essay, I argue that *Our Mutual Friend* develops its ideal relationships through caregiving communities, and I argue, further, that such mutual caregiving friendship is what *Our Mutual Friend* advocates as the real basis of marriage. As I have argued elsewhere, Victorian novels depict disability not as a medical deficit but as a social advantage.[1] Someone in need accrues a community of caregivers, a loving social network that is highly attractive to outsiders. Moreover, disabled sociality trains characters in the feelings that make marriage work. In *Our Mutual Friend*, Eugene Wrayburn and Lizzie Hexam initially set about relationships the wrong way, and only through experiencing care relations do they learn the mutual consideration, trust, and respect necessary for a good marriage.

Such affective re-education is fundamental not only to the marriage plot but also to the reader's experience. We too get retrained; we too learn to care in particular ways. To trace these dynamics, it will help to consider *Our*

I'm grateful to the anonymous readers, Jill Galvan, and Elsie Michie for their perceptive comments on earlier drafts of this essay, and to the members of Dickens Universe in 2014 for their enthusiastic response to an earlier version of this argument. I also thank Oxford University Press for permission to republish some of the material from *Romance's Rival*.

1. See Schaffer, *Romance's Rival*.

Mutual Friend's care-based marriage in relation to Victorian nursing practices and the theoretical structure of "ethics of care," as well as the discursive elements of Dickensian sentiment.

In Dickens's novels, and indeed in Victorian fiction more generally, conditions are ideal for the formation of care communities. People are bound into small communities observing one another's behavior, vast numbers of the population have no gainful employment and therefore have leisure to care for one another, caretaking is profoundly approved of, and nursing occurs within the home, not the institution. In Victorian fiction, care really does take a village. After all, Victorian fictions, according to Martha Stoddard Holmes,

> normalize and valorize relationships built on vulnerability and need. While dyads of care are a common character development structure, ensemble plots construct disability as a feature of community life. . . . Thematically, the fictions engage disability as a force that brings people into a wide range of complex relationships, transforming social institutions like marriage in the process.[2]

If Victorian marriage depends on disability, as Stoddard Holmes writes, it is no wonder that care is central.[3] Brigid Lowe argues that "the mid-Victorian realist novel is the medium par excellence for an exposition of a sympathetic politics of care, and an effective vehicle for the perpetuation of the conditions for its realization."[4]

In many Victorian novels, the impaired suitor has a retinue of caretakers: servants, nurses, parents, siblings, friends.[5] Not surprisingly, isolated people tend to be drawn to this social world. Lizzie Hexam is just one of many rootless orphans: Jane Eyre, John Halifax, Ruth Hilton, Isabel Archer, Amy Dorrit, Caroline Helstone. All lose their parents and are estranged from any guardians or siblings they may have. They find a new community by affiliating with a disabled individual: Eugene Wrayburn, Phineas Fletcher, Thurstan Benson, Ralph Touchett, the feverish Arthur Clennam, the injured Robert Moore. These are not all marriages in a legal sense, but they function narratively like marriages, with some combination of deep affective ties, shared property, and lifelong cohabitation. In these novels, a vulnerable woman finds

---

2. Stoddard Holmes, "Victorian Fictions," 30.

3. Care ethicists have used Victorian novels. Carol Gilligan invoked *The Mill on the Floss* when she first delineated the theory in *In a Different Voice* (1982), and Nel Noddings described *The Way of All Flesh* in *Starting at Home* (2002).

4. Lowe, *Victorian Fiction*, 241.

5. For an expanded definition of this marriage plot, see *Romance's Rival*.

a social home in joining a disabled man's community of care, and a lonely man finds a quasi-spouse.[6] These were communities formed of especially chosen friends. Miriam Bailin writes, "Often, rather than reuniting kin, illness summons a society suited to one's own specifications and substitutes for the coercions of blood and marriage a physical tie as voluntary as friendship and as essential as survival."[7]

In the middle-class, nineteenth-century family, women nursed sick family members at home. Functions we would today outsource to hospitals, institutions, and schools were instead handled (as best they could be) by amateur family members and servants within the domestic realm. "Every woman, or at least almost every woman, in England has, at one time or another of her life, charge of the personal health of somebody, whether child or invalid,—in other words, every woman is a nurse," Florence Nightingale wrote.[8] Bailin explains that

> nursing was repeatedly invoked to verify in a way no other activity apparently could the genuineness of one's affections, the essential goodness of one's character. In a characteristically Victorian adaptation of the moral assumptions underlying the previous century's cult of sensibility, the shedding of tears over human distress was not in itself sufficient to attest to one's benevolence but required instead the practical demonstration of compassion that nursing affords.[9]

The female mission extended beyond nursing to include succoring the poor, teaching children, and offering religious guidance. From material gifts to more tenuous "influence," women were in charge of improving others' lives. Trained to the "practical demonstration of compassion," in Bailin's words, Victorian middle-class women would have had a strong reaction to accounts of dying children, starving waifs, suffering animals. Dickens, when mobilizing readers for social reform, was writing to an audience accustomed to alleviating others' pain. He had a great deal invested in training his readers to channel their activity properly, to read rightly.

Today, theorists are still asking whether reading can factor into "practical demonstration[s] of compassion." Does fiction immerse the reader in fantasy

6. Of course, this can be painful, as in Craik's *A Noble Life*, where the Earl cannot marry the woman he lives with and loves. The disabled man still does not get a full relationship. It is, however, arguably better than being written out of the narrative completely.

7. Bailin, *The Sickroom*, 19.

8. Nightingale, *Notes on Nursing*, v.

9. Bailin, *The Sickroom*, 11. For accounts of the affective pleasures of illness in the Victorian period, see Bailin and Frawley, *Invalidism and Identity*.

in lieu of real social action, or does the intensity of fiction motivate readers to act in the world?[10] Mary-Catherine Harrison argues that characters come to stand as synecdoches for larger types; reading about Tiny Tim, for instance, trains a reader to want to help all disabled children.[11] However, this question assumes that reading is a passive activity, with the reader unable to act until the reading experience ends. Victorians did not necessarily share this expectation of silent, passive, private reading.

Indeed, Victorian readers might have wanted to act on behalf of a specific person in the midst of reading, to help Tiny Tim himself, instead of later generalizing the lesson of Tiny Tim to real children. Such a reader might yearn for a kind of interactive reading. Indeed, active, pragmatic, inclusive reading experiences were common in nineteenth-century culture. Victorian readers read aloud to people who would comment along the way, wrote reviews that urged characters to behave differently, and attended dramatic versions of beloved sentimental stories like *East Lynne, A Christmas Carol,* and *Uncle Tom's Cabin.* It's not that Victorian readers believed these characters were real and could somehow benefit from their advice, but rather that there seemed no particular reason to discontinue the habit of active intervention just because the characters were fictional. The fact that famously sentimental tales got dramatized is no coincidence. Sentiment was particularly irksome to caregivers, as we shall see, provoking an especially urgent desire to insert oneself into the story.

We can help understand this urge through the modern theory of "ethics of care," a feminist philosophy developed over the past fifty years by scholars like Nel Noddings, Virginia Held, and Eva Feder Kittay. Ethics of care argues that humans are, in Held's words, "relational and interdependent, not the individualistic autonomous rational agents of the perspective of justice and rights."[12] We can only live insofar as we depend on others; no newborn can survive on its own, and none of us would be alive today if we didn't depend on others to grow our food or build our homes. Thus care is an ongoing, universal network, in which we are constantly involved. Care relations become especially visible in cases of disability. The disabled person and the caretaker (the cared-for and the carer) offer models of the kind of intimate dependency on which all human relations depend, and in these situations, it is often the disabled figure who becomes exemplary and teaches others how to care. *Our Mutual*

10. See Harrison, "The Paradox of Fiction." Suzanne Keen (*Empathy and the Novel*) is skeptical that fiction influences our real-world behavior at all, although psychologists Kidd, Ongis, and Castano ("On Literary Fiction") argue that reading literary fiction does produce improved empathy.

11. Harrison, "The Paradox of Fiction."

12. Held, *The Ethics of Care*, 72.

Friend charts such an experience. In this novel, Dickens constructs marriage as a care relation in which a disabled woman, Jenny Wren, has a crucial role in retraining and mediating Eugene's and Lizzie's feelings. In *Our Mutual Friend,* marriage is about consolidating community, not forming a private dyad, and marital love means caregiving tenderness, not erotic passion.

This marital model challenges half a century of literary-critical norms. Ever since Ian Watt published *The Rise of the Novel* in 1957, literary critics have tended to read the novel as the story of the individual's growth, maturation, and autonomy.[13] The marriage plot supposedly requires the individual to choose a uniquely suitable partner and experience the thrill of being chosen. Desire thus ratifies one's individuality. In *Desire and Domestic Fiction,* Nancy Armstrong builds on Watt's idea to stress the particular importance of the female individual as corroborated through marriage.[14] In Victorian marriage plots, however, such individualist desiring subjects are often dangerous as well as charismatic: Rochester, Willoughby, Wickham, Stephen Guest. Eugene Wrayburn begins as this kind of lover—someone whose intense desire singles out another person for an exotic shared future life, swept away from all other ordinary social ties into a blissful private haven of mutual adoration.

However, the dangerous desiring lover is not the only marital option. He often competes against a well-known local connection, a cousin or a neighbor or family friend. In lieu of desire, this man offers esteem, trust, and a future characterized by companionship, continuing social networks, and meaningful work: St John, Colonel Brandon, Mr Collins, Philip Wakem. If the romantic lover is associated with modern individualism, the familiar lover derives from a history of traditional relationality. In choosing between her suitors, the woman is actually deciding what kind of future she wants to live. Sometimes the romantic lover can be reformed into a familiar suitor; this occurs with Rochester and Eugene Wrayburn, as suffering teaches the man to be a patient, kind, tender participant in care relations and finally therefore worthy of marriage. In this novel, then, marriage does not confirm the unique modern selfhood of its participants. Rather, *Our Mutual Friend* regards individual desire as a problematic delusion that needs to be recalibrated into a communal, companionable experience.

In Eugene's case, what makes him require care is a trauma that renders him nonverbal and immobile, core competencies that must now be provided by others. But other fictional characters experience milder, more common, chronic conditions, from Jenny's bad back to Venus's weak eyes. Indeed, as disability studies scholars often point out, we will all be disabled if we live long enough. Everyone has experienced periods of illness or injury, a body that

13. Watt, *The Rise of the Novel,* 177.

14. Armstrong, *Desire and Domestic Fiction,* 4.

does not fit the spaces designated for it, a cognitive orientation that means ordinary tasks are a struggle. Everyone who has been shorter or taller or wider than the norm, had to use crutches, tried to read with dyslexia, gone to work while ill, been pregnant on public transit, knows what it feels like to need help—a lived experience that disproves the unrealistic assumption that everyone is or ought to be fully able at all times.

For Victorians, of course, bodily impairments were far more visible, common, and intractable than they are today. They accepted impairment as an ordinary variant of human experience, whereas we tend to view it as a catastrophic error to be fixed by medical intervention. This modern attitude is called the medical model: the idea that the body (or brain) is flawed and must be fixed. Disability scholars espouse the social model instead: people become disabled by entering an environment that is not designed for their needs. Although the social and the medical model disagree on where the problem lies, they both focus on something that has gone wrong, whether it is a person's legs or a staircase.

By contrast, ethics of care is primarily interested in the quality of a relationship between people, and it is suprisingly indifferent to the question of why care might be needed, or even whether it is genuinely needed at all. One can need care because of one's age, status, or situation: a penniless orphan, an elderly woman, an infant, a second-language learner, a person who feels sad, would all be legitimate recipients of care. The primary examples in ethics-of-care theory are parenting, teaching, and nursing, and because ethics of care is a feminist idea—a way to grant the significance of women's heretofore slighted activities of caregiving—care ethics makes a point of prioritizing maternal relations.[15] Children, parents, students, and teachers practice care as a sustaining way of life, not because something has gone wrong. In ethics of care, then, one need not be disabled. Everyone needs care, and everyone gives care, enmeshed in a fluid network of multiple interactions.

Such a network grows increasingly complicated the more people that get involved. While care ethicists often imagine the simplest model, a partnership between a cared-for and a carer, Victorian novels tend to chart the dynamics of larger communities of care. In Dickens's vivid versions of such networks, a neglected child might find help from a neighbor, an aunt, a local shopkeeper, a servant, the servant's brother—and the child's innocent admiration may sustain them in return for their protection, affection, or shelter. Care communities are not determined by gender, marital status, class, or relationship. They extend beyond nuclear families and private couples. Therefore, such communities offer alternative ways of organizing social experience in texts.

15. For examples of maternalist emphasis in ethics of care work, see Noddings's *Starting at Home*, Ruddick's *Maternal Thinking*, and Held's *Feminist Morality*.

That means they offer a kind of egalitarian freedom in the midst of what otherwise tend to be heavily hierarchical, heteronormative, essentialist, strictly regulated behavioral expectations. The members of such care communities are not merely minor characters assisting the main figures towards marriage (for instance) but actually substantive entities in themselves. Care ethicists emphasize case-by-case, particular treatments in lieu of universalist abstractions.[16] Each figure in a care community matters. In *Our Mutual Friend*, Eugene's care community comes to include Jenny, a disabled doll's dressmaker, and Sloppy, a cognitively impaired foster child, as well as his same-sex friend Mortimer.

The care community in Victorian fiction has three key qualities. First, it is reciprocal: everyone cares for everyone else. Within the care community, everyone is equal and appreciated. Second, it is discursively regulated: people must ask to join, and negotiate the terms under which they stay or leave. For instance, Mortimer invites Jenny to join Eugene's care community, and she agrees. Third, care is an act—one can give care without really caring.[17] Care is a performative act inasmuch as acting as if one cares can make it true.

Dickens explores the performativity of care in the scene where the men resuscitate Rogue Riderhood: "Everyone present lends a hand, and a heart and soul. No one has the least regard for the man; with them all, he has been an object of avoidance, suspicion, and aversion; but the spark of life within him is curiously separable from himself now, and they have a deep interest in it, probably because it *is* life, and they are living and must die."[18] As life gradually returns, the four rough sailors weep at the miracle, shaking hands and sobbing. However, "as he grows warm, the doctor and the four men cool. As his lineaments soften with life, their faces and their hearts harden to him" (441). Riderhood's resuscitation is the first of three near-death caregiving scenes I will examine, and it is the one that most dispassionately registers the way that care can operate without real feeling.

This efficacious, uncaring care is one end of a spectrum whose other endpoint is helpless sentiment. Sentiment, in Dickens, is a peculiarly passive form of sympathy. Most scholars trace Victorian sympathy to its eighteenth-century origins in theories of moral sensibility (especially those by Kant, Smith, and Hume), but we can understand it differently if we see sympathy as the under-

16. See for instance Bowden, *Caring: Gender-Sensitive Ethics* and Nel Noddings, *Caring: A Feminine Approach*, 5.

17. As a nursing home director points out, "carers [must] avoid 'personal feelings' getting in the way of a professional approach." Sevenhuijsen, *Citizenship and the Ethics of Care*, 2. The same is true for teachers or daycare providers. They can't show their real preferences or real irritations—they have to treat all their wards the same way.

18. Dickens, *Our Mutual Friend* (New York: Penguin Classics, 1997), 439. Further references are to this edition and are noted parenthetically in the text.

lying feeling that might emerge in various contemporary forms of emotional expression.[19] Sympathy can provoke active care, but sympathy can also spill into an inefficacious, self-indulgent feeling that has no effect in the world. Rogue Riderhood's resuscitation is a startlingly antisentimental scene inasmuch as it shows caring as a mere automatic reflex that ebbs as the subject recovers. But sentiment occurs in the opposite of the Riderhood resuscitation: unavailing sorrow. Sentiment means despair over a decline with no possibility of recovery; it is emotion expended in futility. We care for people whom we cannot help, fictional characters preordained to live out their allotted pain. And if we are habitually irritated by sentiment, it might be not because of sentiment's excessive feeling but because that feeling remains useless, a surge of emotion with nowhere to go.

Little Johnny's death is textbook sentiment. Betty Higden reacts to Johnny's decline:

> To conceal herself in sickness, like a lower animal; to creep out of sight and coil herself away and die; had become this woman's instinct. To catch up in her arms the sick child who was dear to her, and hide it as if it were a criminal, and keep off all ministration but such as her own ignorant tenderness and patience could supply, had become this woman's idea of maternal love, fidelity, and duty. (321)

This kind of ignorant instinct leads to tragedy. The doctor reminds us that "this should have been days ago. Too late!" (325). Johnny dies because Betty experiences a sorrow that forestalls "ministration": sentiment.

This passage uses an omniscient narrative voice that makes authoritative moral assessments. The analytic distance here encourages the reader to stand back and view Betty not as a fellow being but rather as a kind of specimen: "this woman" (twice repeated). Similarly, when Eugene is at his worst, he watches Jenny crying over her alcoholic father. "Eugene Wrayburn saw the tears exude from between the little creature's fingers as she kept her hand before her eyes. He was sorry, but his sympathy did not move his carelessness to do anything but feel sorry" (523). Once again we have the generalizing language about subjects ("the little creature") combined with narrative disapproval, as if individuation was incompatible with torpid sorrow. Indeed, when Dickens specifically uses the term *sentiment,* he does so in the context of deploring the indistinguishability of the dead. We should identify their graves, he argues,

19. Important work relating nineteenth-century sentimentality to its eighteenth-century philosophical roots includes Greiner, *Sympathetic Realism*; Kaplan, *Sacred Tears*; and Festa, *Sentimental Figures.*

> so that the soldier, sailor, emigrant, coming home, should be able to identify the resting-place of father, mother, playmate, or betrothed. For, we turn up our eyes and say that we are all alike in death, and we might turn them down and work the saying out in this world, so far. It would be sentimental, perhaps? But how say ye, my lords and gentlemen and honorable boards, shall we not find good standing-room left for a little sentiment, if we look into our crowds? (507)

"Sentiment" is connected to the fear of indistinguishable stasis. What does it mean to be "all alike," to be "this woman," a "creature"? *Our Mutual Friend* is a novel full of generic types: the cherub, the schoolteacher, the pardner, the Secretary, t'other gentleman, Boots, Brewer, and the Buffer. Sentiment means suffering a promiscuous sympathy, immured in a depressive state, lost in the crowd. A mutual friend is meaningless if everyone is already the oldest friend, as Twemlow finds at the Veneerings' dinner table. Yet the alternative may be no better. Who would endorse individuation if it is associated with the dangerous predatory desires of a Eugene Wrayburn (always identified by his full name)?

This is a question for the critic, as well as the characters. In moving away from the individualist readings advocated by Watt and Armstrong, towards a more relational, communal understanding of the novel, might we lose our critical edge, merely merging into the crowd of weeping readers that supposedly awaited word of Little Nell on the docks of New York?[20] Emma Mason has argued that sentiment, which demands personal feeling, irritates us because we are committed to a calmly analytical stance as critics.[21] We might resent sentiment not only because it pushes us towards an involvement we find unprofessional, but also because it insists we participate in a déclassé mass movement, a crowd of the undifferentiated ignorant, people like Betty Higden, like "a lower animal," operating from "instinct."

Our Mutual Friend offers an alternative in two other near-death scenes, which use a very different rhetorical structure. John Harmon tells himself,

---

20. Nicola Bown, however, argues powerfully for the humane benefits of such merging into the crowd: "When we cry at the death of Little Nell, 'we are involved.' Through the 'movements' of emotion through our bodies we come nearer to the grief and sorrow of all those in the past who mourned their own and others' children through the death of Dickens's heroine. Weeping at her death collapses the distance in time and circumstance between us and them, and allows us sympathetically to share their emotional world" ("Introduction: Crying Over Little Nell"). Carra Glatt, however, claims persuasively that there were no crowds awaiting the news of Nell's fate. In my view, this makes the Little Nell story all the more compelling as an example of sentiment; it is a cultural myth generated to testify to the imagined power of mass sentiment ("When Found, Make a Note Of").

21. Mason, "Feeling Dickensian Feeling."

"This is John Harmon drowning! John Harmon, struggle for your life. John Harmon, call on Heaven and save yourself!" (363). When Lizzie rescues the drowning Eugene Wrayburn, she prays, "Now, merciful Heaven be thanked for that old time, and grant, O Blessed Lord, that through thy wonderful workings it may turn to good at last! To whomsoever the drifting face belongs, be it man's or woman's, help my humble hands, Lord God, to raise it from death and restore it to some one to whom it must be dear!" (683). The person in need, bereft of human help, invokes God as the ultimate carer, and the divine sponsorship lends strength to do the necessary, though unimaginably difficult, action. Both John Harmon and Lizzie must deliberately swallow their panicky horror, subordinating feeling to activity.

In the most astounding act of caregiving in the novel, Lizzie deliberately beats back her sentiment. Allowing herself just one "terrible cry" when she recognizes the mutilated face as Eugene's, Lizzie manifests nearly supernatural strength as she lashes the body to the line, rows him in, and carries him into the inn (684). This rescue helps transform Eugene's feeling towards her from a kind of sexual obsession towards what Twemlow, rightly, calls "feelings of gratitude, of respect, of admiration, and affection" (796).

Jenny Wren, on the other hand, seems a sentimental subject, given her perpetual suffering, which makes us want (in vain) to alleviate it. However, Jenny is, it turns out, one of the most active figures in the novel, and, as I shall argue, not particularly pitiable in certain respects. Jenny is simply the most visible figure in a narrative full of nonnormative people, from the cognitively impaired Sloppy to the amputee Wegg to the "disfigured" and "mutilated" Eugene Wrayburn at the ending, none of whom are particularly good subjects for sentimental sympathy. If, however, we read Jenny, Sloppy, and Wrayburn in ethics-of-care terms, then instead of diagnosing their incapacity, we ask about how they care for one another.

Care ethicists often assess whether care is appropriately respectful, or whether it is, rather, a form of domination over someone powerless to fight back. Bad care can abuse or damage the cared-for. People can give or demand care for many reasons besides love, ranging from automatic duty, to pay, to a desire for power over someone else. Bad care relations, too, can deplete and exploit the carer. As Kittay notes: "Care is a costly morality: costly in the personal and emotional resources it demands and in the time it consumes (time that cannot be devoted to investing in a career or advancing oneself materially)."[22] Victorian fiction often highlights bad relations. In *Our Mutual Friend*, Jenny Wren is verbally and sometimes physically abusive of her father,

22. Kittay, "When Caring Is Just," 272.

while Lizzie suppresses her own needs to accede to her father's demands. Accustomed to self-erasure, Lizzie says that she wants to "give herself up to another," as she says, enunciating a particularly damaging element of Victorian femininity and a particularly bad kind of care (384). Eugene Wrayburn's relation to his own father is characterized by intensive mutual resentment. This is a novel in which paternal relations are, more often than not, traumatic.

Luckily, bad parent–child care can be overridden by a more egalitarian care relationship in adult life. Good care is the kind of relationship that Jenny Wren enacts and teaches to both Eugene and Lizzie that makes them capable of marrying one another. It is a relation characterized by mutuality, by concern for the other, and by affection for multiple people rather than desire for one. It is for that reason that Lizzie and Eugene can only marry once Eugene himself becomes disabled. Disability enables him to become a person who needs and appreciates care. It moves him into an alternative form of relationship that the novel presents as the most constructive mode of personhood.[23] It reprograms the hostile, destructive relations of parental bad care into a more nurturing form of love. And it does so through respecting that person's ability to navigate relations.

In her enormously influential account of the homoerotic dynamics of *Our Mutual Friend* in *Between Men*, Eve Kosofsky Sedgwick writes: "Dickens makes no attempt to disguise the terrible diminution in [Lizzie's] personal stature as she moves from being the resentful, veiled, muscular, illiterate figure rowing a scavenger boat on the Thames, to being a factory worker in love, to being Mrs. Eugene Wrayburn *tout court*."[24] She loses her own identity, Sedgwick insists. But this is only tragic if the achievement of a full individuality is the aim of the novel. If the aim of the novel, on the other hand, is to get Lizzie away from her rough, exploitative, and often cruel father and brother, and the watermen and schoolteachers with whom they socialize, into the company of people who will respect and cherish and care for her, then her final situation is fairly good. If the aim of the novel is to replace an unsatisfactory family with a chosen social network, Lizzie succeeds.

While male sexuality in Victorian fiction is often seen as frighteningly predatory, male sociality offers a safer and more egalitarian basis for a rela-

23. Space forbids a discussion of the Harmon plot in *Our Mutual Friend*, but I note briefly that the Wilfer and Harmon families demonstrate bad forms of care. Mrs. Wilfer's hostile domination and Reg Wilfer's self-erasure create a pathological pattern followed by Lavinia and George. John Harmon's sustained trickery of Bella in her most intimate private life, aided by the Boffins, turns a care community into a communal victimization. Arguably, it is only the Boffins who demonstrate a genuinely mutual and egalitarian marriage through much of this novel.

24. Sedgwick, *Between Men*, 178.

tionship. When Eugene is able-bodied, he aggressively pursues his lower-class love, in spite of his friend's remonstrances and her own misery. When he tracks Lizzie to her refuge, she has to repeatedly implore him to stop putting his arm around her waist (674, 675). Eugene seems bent on a seduction plot, almost against his own will—it is "out of the question to marry her," Eugene reminds himself, in the "wickedness" of his thoughts, just before Headstone assaults him (292–93).[25] Only traumatic injury reforms him and frees the woman. Once the man requires care, Lizzie Hexam can initiate contact, soothing and ministering to the men's bodies. Lizzie "drew her arm under his head, and laid her own head down upon the pillow by his side" (734). Instead of the stark choice of either responding to or refusing male sexual overtures, the woman can generate touch herself, in a different way. The relationship becomes mutual, respectful, and egalitarian, instead of a stalker pursuing a victim.

The narrative's emphasis on affectionate contact does not necessarily mean that the marriage will be sexless. Indeed, in nineteenth-century fiction, disabled male bodies were often hypersexualized rather than desexualized, like Quilp, a demonically perverse male dwarf.[26] Female disabled bodies were also often sexualized. As Stoddard Holmes points out, quite often the disabled woman is "too feeling, too expressive, and potentially too sexual for matrimony."[27] I am not arguing that Eugene and Lizzie enter a de-eroticized marriage but rather that, in this novel, desire is a poor motive for marriage, and caring tenderness is far better.

Marriages based primarily on mutual care, not desire, can accommodate nontraditional unions. Any couple will work: siblings, cousins, same-sex friends. So long as one needs care, their loving cohabitation is not in the least controversial. If the issue is the quality of care between two people, not their biological relationship or marital status, then all relationships—adoptive, sexual, companionable, professional, and marital—are simply enunciations of the same fundamental principle of care. Anyone can mother: anyone can husband: anyone can friend. Everyone can nurse. This substitutability can produce radically democratic, modern relationality, as Holly Furneaux has argued in her account of the way disability allows Dickensian characters to construct their own queer family organizations.[28]

---

25. Hilary M. Schor clarifies that Wrayburn is "clearly bent on seducing, if not raping her." *Dickens*, 182.

26. See Kelly Hager's memorable discussion of Quilp's sexual aggression in *Dickens and the Rise of Divorce*.

27. Stoddard Holmes, *Fictions of Affliction*, 39.

28. Furneaux, *Queer Dickens*. See especially ch. 5, "'It is impossible to be gentler': The Homoerotics of Nursing in Victorian Culture," 177–211.

We see Dickens favoring relationality over eroticism in the union between Jenny Wren and Sloppy that seems imminent at the end of the novel. *Our Mutual Friend* critics tend to agree that Jenny is the one exception to the general rule that "sexuality is inaccessible to disabled people, who are culturally enjoined from reproducing their defect"[29] and that physically disabled characters "are removed from the sexual economy."[30] Consequently, they have applauded Dickens's provision of a marriage plot for Jenny. Jenny is, according to Helena Michie, allowed an erotic future denied to the other female characters.[31]

While it does seem significant that Jenny is depicted as marriageable, I would argue that what makes this relationship viable is not her sexuality but her sociality. Jenny proves herself worthy of marriage because she becomes a notable caregiver, and in *Our Mutual Friend,* caregiving is the core quality for a good marriage. Jenny and Sloppy's relationship shows very little sense of mutual physical attraction—if anything, it shows mutual physical revulsion. Jenny warns Sloppy to close his mouth more when he laughs, and Sloppy evades Jenny's query about whether he likes how she looks. There is, however, a strong sense of mutual care, as Sloppy offers to make items for Jenny and Jenny to sing for Sloppy in return.

Care relations can queer normative assumptions about the novel, and one thing they challenge might be our assumption about which characters matter. In *The One vs. the Many,* Alex Woloch describes the novel's protagonist as struggling for character-space against a horde of minor characters.[32] What happens, however, if we conceptualize the characters in a novel not as major or minor, but rather as egalitarian members of a community? In a care community, everyone is important. In reconceptualizing the novel in this radically democratizing way, we would not dismiss Sloppy and Jenny as minor characters, grotesques, or comic sidekicks.

The members of this relationship come together from two experiences of care communities. Like Eugene and Lizzie, they have had abusive parental relationships in early life, and had to be retrained in better care relations. Sloppy is an abandoned, neglected, illegitimate, and cognitively disabled teenager, whom Betty took in from the poorhouse (199–200). In return for her care, he runs the mangle for her and reads the paper aloud. When the Boffins offer to adopt him, Sloppy refuses, thinking first of his care responsibilities: "'Oh, mum!—But there's Mrs. Higden,' said Sloppy, checking himself in

29. Klages 77, cited in Schotland, "Who's That in Charge?"
30. Schillace, "Curing 'Moral Disability,'" 37, 588.
31. Michie, "Who Is This in Pain?" 212.
32. Woloch, *The One vs. the Many.*

his raptures, drawing back, and shaking his head with very serious meaning. 'There's Mrs. Higden. Mrs. Higden goes before all'" (332). Sloppy cheers up only when he finds a way to work for both Betty Higden and the Boffins simultaneously. Sloppy's disability, combined with his poverty, requires others to care for him. Their care makes him grateful enough to demand to work for them in turn. Sloppy requires care because he is both impoverished and disabled, but his extraordinary capacity for labor allows him to offer a compensatory care in return.

Similarly, Jenny Wren initially suffers from a toxic filial relationship. Jenny acts as parent for her own father, her "bad boy."[33] This tragicomic role reversal is actually not that different from Betty Higden and Sloppy's far more positive relationship; Sloppy, too, is the child but plays the role of the parent, working hard to provide for the elderly individual in the home. In this respect alcoholism and aging respectively have much the same role in shifting the burden of care to those whose own impairments might normally make them the cared-fors.

However, Jenny gets retrained by her friendships, while Sloppy gets retrained by his adoptive mother. Sara D. Schotland argues that "in *Our Mutual Friend,* Dickens presents a dynamic relationship in which the disabled person slips in and out of the role of care receiver and caregiver."[34] Jenny cares for Lizzie—combs her hair, counsels her, gives her a place to live, and helps facilitate her move to the paper mill. She also has a mutually beneficial relation with Riah, who nurtures her when she purchases waste fragments, and whom she accommodates when he is fired from Pubsey & Co. Schotland sums up: "As in the case of her relationship with Lizzie, the dolls' dressmaker is first presented as requiring the help of the able-bodied, but then becomes the protector."[35] Jenny finally transfers her attention to a peer, Eugene, where she outdoes both Lizzie and Mortimer:

> It was amazing through how many hours at a time she would remain beside him, in a crouching attitude, attentive to his slightest moan. As he could not move a hand, he could make no sign of distress; but through this close watching (if through no secret sympathy or power) the little creature attained an understanding of him that Lightwood did not possess. Mortimer would often turn to her, as if she were an interpreter between this sentient world and the insensible man; and she would change the dressing of a wound, or

---

33. On Dickens's childish men, see Nelson, *Precocious Children*, 53–54.
34. Schotland, "Who's That in Charge?"
35. Ibid.

> ease a ligature, or turn his face, or alter the pressure of the bedclothes on him, with an absolute certainty of doing right. (720)

In this description of caregiving, Dickens stresses Jenny's intensive observation and swift movements. Like a reader, Jenny remains attentive, achieving understanding through her close watching, sympathy, or power; but unlike a reader, Jenny can take action. Jenny is the only person who can decode Eugene's incoherent muttering to supply the missing word, "wife," thereby indeed acting like a writer, not just a reader. By supplying Eugene's dialogue, she facilitates Eugene's marriage plot, translating his inarticulate yearning into legitimate marital intention.

Thus Jenny and Sloppy's union makes sense for a number of reasons. Impoverished teenagers, adopted by the kindly Boffin/Wilfer/Harmon/Wrayburn care community, they must still make their own economic way through their manual dexterity in small craft practices. Both care for their own carers. Both find their own impairments spurs to better work habits—Sloppy works instead of sleeping, and Jenny uses the time when ordinary children would have played to practice her craft instead. As a result, both become exceptionally accomplished in their jobs. Desire may or may not be present, but it is certainly not the deciding factor in their relationship, which seems instead to be based on shared habits of caring, class position, and laboring.

We might ask whether this pair is disabled at all. Jenny's impairment mainly seems to function as a rationale for not answering the door. For Jenny has no trouble crutching her way around London, dodging the horses, visiting Fledgby and Riah, taking her dolls for sale, and visiting Eugene at the site of his attack. As Sloppy remarks when Jenny demonstrates her crutch, "it seems to me that you hardly want it at all" (788). It is true that she has a spinal impairment, but her environment does not disable her. Jenny's bad back and queer legs do not inhibit necessary functions. Rather, they work to excuse her from tiresome social rules like standing to greet a guest, they gift her with empathy for others who are suffering, and they collude to keep her indoors where she can be more productive. Jenny's physical situation is not necessarily fortunate, or pain-free, but in her particular environment it might not be disabling.

A similar case might be made for Sloppy, whose cognitive disability does not inhibit his mobility, his literacy, or his judgment. If anything, Sloppy, who never needs sleep, who is enormously tall and strong, who can do the police in different voices, and who can eat prodigious quantities, seems almost excessively abled. Like someone in a wheelchair who is disabled at a staircase but extra mobile on a ramp, Jenny and Sloppy manifest different capacities in different environments. In this respect *Our Mutual Friend* demonstrates the social model—the idea that the disabling factor is one's environment, not one's body—a century before disability scholars invented the term.

In fleeing to Jenny, Lizzie puts herself in relation with a loving disabled woman, instead of two dangerously sexualized men, Bradley Headstone and Eugene Wrayburn. To read from Lizzie's point of view allows us to see her as more than simply a conduit, a pawn between men, or an alienated piece of property. Sedgwick notes that "Charley's offer of Lizzie to his schoolmaster represents the purest form of the male traffic in women," but Lizzie never does get trafficked, since she refuses to be transferred to Headstone.[36] Rather, from Lizzie's point of view, this is a novel in which a woman rejects the male suitors available to her, choosing instead to construct an alternative social realm and cohabit with an alternative kind of partner. Her care relation with Jenny in turn can be transposed back on the eventual marriage, reforming and improving it, so that Eugene Wrayburn becomes remodeled on this better predecessor.

For Jenny Wren is, as she announces frequently, "the person of the house."[37] The appellation means that, legally speaking, she is the householder, who would be paying taxes and voting, had those civic responsibilities been accessible to her—but in a deeper sense, that she is gifted with a kind of personhood that others lack. To feel pain that allows you to imagine and then alleviate others' suffering is to be a "person." This is a gender-neutral position, in the radically egalitarian sense characteristic of ethics-of-care narratives; men, women, mothers, fathers, children, husbands, wives, all are equivalent and interchangeable in a system where relationships are predicated on care. Thus it is possible to be a "person," escaping the constraints of gender. (As the narrator remarks when we first see Jenny, she is "a child—a dwarf—a girl—a something"—her femininity is the third of four terms, by no means the most important [222].)

When Lizzie and Jenny cohabit, their mutuality is obvious in a small incident. Jenny, loosening Lizzie's hair, "so managed a mere touch or two of her nimble hands, as that she herself laying a cheek on one of the dark folds," reveals Lizzie's face to the firelight, and once Lizzie confesses her love for Eugene, Jenny cries in pain—"but not the old pain" while she "folded [her hands] around Lizzie's neck, and rocked herself on Lizzie's breast" while praying for her fantasized angelic children to come console Lizzie (342, 344).

---

36. Sedgwick, *Between Men*, 167.

37. See pp. 222, 224, 232, 239, 241, 243 for examples.

This complex scene reveals considerable physical intimacy—the two young women are locked together in an intimate embrace, stroking each other's hair—and there is more than a suspicion that the "pain" Jenny feels derives from the confirmation that Lizzie wants Eugene rather than herself. Although it is rarely read as scene of same-sex desire, the hair scene is certainly amenable to such a reading. However, Lizzie's breast is maternal as much as, or more than, anything else. Their bodies are entangled as if their identities have merged and become interdependent. As Sharon Marcus has argued, female friendships need not always be cover stories for same-sex desire, but quite often function to facilitate heterosexual marriage for the main character.[38] Jenny and Lizzie's relationship clearly functions this way. Both had been in damagingly askew care relations with fathers, and it is their female friendship that teaches both of them the mutually considerate care they will need to marry.

Same-sex care relations teach kindly loving in this novel. If Lizzie learns this kind of relation from Jenny, Eugene similarly acquires it from Mortimer. In a scene just as intimate as the hair scene, the wounded Eugene lies in bed, pleading, "touch my face with yours, in case I should not hold out till you come back. I love you, Mortimer" (723).[39] Yet in both cases, this expression of same-sex love occurs in the context of the declaration of heterosexual desire. Eugene is asserting that he wishes to marry Lizzie, just as Lizzie, in the hair scene, confesses that she loves Eugene. In other words, the same-sex beloved kisses and hugs in the moment of the symbolic transfer of the affections to the other-sex lover, as if teaching the kind of affection that would be needed in the future heterosexual relationship.

This reading is supported by the fact that Lizzie and Eugene solemnize their wedding as a communal event: "As the bridegroom could not move his hand, they touched his fingers with the ring, and so put it on the bride. When the two plighted their troth, she laid her hand on his, and kept it there" (732). Eugene's illness has created a community of care around Eugene—Mortimer, Jenny, Bella, and Lizzie all participate in enacting his wishes, like prostheses, acting as his hands when he cannot use those hands himself. Indeed, when Eugene decides to marry Lizzie, one would expect the proposal to be sealed with a kiss. But Eugene makes the proposal through Mortimer's voice, and it is Jenny who, "for the first time, kissed him on the cheek, and kissed the poor maimed hand that was nearest to her" (722).[40] From the moment Jenny

38. Marcus, *Between Women.*

39. Furneaux reads this scene as highly homoerotically charged, arguing that the relationship between Eugene and Lizzie pales by comparison. *Queer Dickens*, 101–2.

40. Wedding scenes where the groom lies near death are not uncommon in Victorian fiction; we might think of Charlotte Yonge's *The Pillars of the House* (1873), in which Wilmet marries John Harewood, and *Dracula* (1897), in which Mina marries Jonathan Harker.

solicits Lizzie's private feelings in the hair scene, to the nuptial kiss, Jenny is "participating in the birth of a courtship as someone with a right to be there," in Stoddard Holmes's words.[41]

Finally, the Eugene–Lizzie union is one in which sex is somewhat irrelevant. When Eugene states that he wishes to marry Lizzie, he vows that the marriage will make him "more at peace" and complete his "reparation" (722). Such language does not sound particularly erotic, and, given that Eugene's entire body is bound in bandages and he needs round-the-clock nursing, this is not a union that will be consummated any time soon. After their wedding ceremony, "he mustered strength to move his wounded head a very little way, and lay it on her bosom." This is not a sexualized contact; it is a "refuge that I have so ill deserved" (734). In this respect Eugene exactly emulates Jenny. Both lay their heads on Lizzie's breast, but both identify it as a maternal haven, not a sexualized incitement. *Our Mutual Friend* offers a vision of communal, care-based social relations as a better basis for marriage than individualist, desire-driven marriage.

One of care's fundamental tenets is that carers need to imagine themselves into the mindset of the cared-for. "Motivational displacement," as Nel Noddings calls it, means that the carer must be willing to suspend her own wishes in order to fulfill another's ideas.[42] Jenny demonstrates this perfectly when she crouches by Eugene's bedside, watching intensively, so that when he evinces discomfort she can intuit exactly what he needs. However, in reading, only the first part of that process is available to us. We can know what a character wants but we cannot give it to her. How, then, can the reader find emotional satisfaction? How can we channel our sympathy into a real act, avoiding the futile, passive, generalizing flood of sentiment?

Dickens works through the problem of the passive reader in two scenes that frame *Our Mutual Friend*. The "Society" around Lady Tippins hears the core story of *Our Mutual Friend* itself, focalized through Mortimer Lightwood. In chapter 2, "The Man From Somewhere," Mortimer tells the story of the Harmon family. While dinner guests ask him questions, they are essentially passive spectators who regard it as entertainment. Twemlow, though privately dismayed, remains silent. Mortimer and Eugene themselves are bored observers of their own lives. "'Then idiots talk,' said Eugene . . . 'of Energy. If there is a word in the dictionary under any letter from A to Z that I abominate, it is Energy'" (29–30). The final chapter, "The Voice of Society," reassembles the same group, with Mortimer again as the raconteur to a group of largely passive guests—but the great difference this time is that Twemlow speaks back. A resisting reader, Twemlow forcibly inserts himself into the

41. Stoddard Holmes, *Fictions of Affliction*, 58.

42. Noddings, *Caring*, 16–18.

narrative, insisting that Eugene was right. This unexpected defense electrifies Mortimer, who then pursues a bond with Twemlow. The contrast between these dinner parties shows that Dickens finds it crucial to act, to intervene, or, to use the terms from Jenny's sojourn with Eugene, to be "attentive" enough to be "an interpreter between this sentient world and the insensible man" (720).

Twemlow testifies, accurately, to Eugene's "feelings of gratitude, of respect, of admiration, and affection" for Lizzie, fighting the idea that Lizzie is a generic item, a mere female waterman, factory girl, or mechanism for turning beefsteak into labor (796). The dehumanizing generalizations associated with sentiment can have no place in a novel endorsing the care community's values: one should look at particular cases instead of abstracting generally, and each person is as important as any other. Their love comes from care. Eugene tells her, "Out of your compassion for me, in this maimed and broken state, you make so much of me—you think so well of me—you love me so dearly" (735). How, he wonders, "shall I ever pay all I owe you?" and realizes "it would require a life, Lizzie, to pay all; more than a life" (734–35). The basis of their marriage is caregiving. She has saved his life; he gives her his life. She has showed such compassion and love he can do no more (or less) than reciprocate.

This is the meaning of marriage: care—the intimate relation between a cared-for and his carer that can flower into "gratitude, respect, admiration, and affection," a marriage that is not about romantic love or individuation but rather about a tender trust and an intimate kindness. Steeped as it is in care relations, *Our Mutual Friend* envisions marriage as the ideal union of feeling and doing, caring while caregiving, for which disability may well be the best possible teacher. Because some form of performative carework is necessary to form this tie, the reader cannot have precisely such relationships with the characters. Reader, we cannot marry him. Rather, what Dickens wants is for us to be like Twemlow in the final chapter, speaking back to the author, asserting real values, insisting on the best readings: a form of critical care that Victorians may well have felt to be the best possible relation between ourselves and the novel.

CHAPTER 10

Extra Man

Dining Out Beyond the Marriage Plot in Our Mutual Friend

HELENA MICHIE

"EXTRA MAN," the term that names this essay, suggests for me the problems and possibilities of superfluity on several levels. It is a phrase not quite discarded from an earlier joint lifewriting project with Robyn Warhol for which we found ourselves trying to articulate an identity for our subject, Sir George Scharf, a Victorian bachelor and diner-out. Although we came to know through seventeen years of research much more about Scharf than what he ate for dinner at country houses, London lodgings, and restaurants, we wanted to retain our initial sense of him as a social and professional diner—but we came up against the poverty of descriptive terms for those for whom eating is a central activity. We wanted an identity category that suggested a connection between our emerging sense of Scharf's complicated sexual identity and his dining without using one as a euphemism for or displacement of the other. "Extra man," our primary term for Scharf during the long middle of our project—and his life—was inspired by my rereading of *Our Mutual Friend* and by the character Mr. Twemlow, the unmarried, poor relation of a lord and a guest at all the novel's many dinner parties. Twemlow's undermotivated ubiquity at upper-class dining tables forcefully reminded me of Scharf's: Scharf's scrapbooks and diaries—the latter full of triumphant notations of his friendships with aristocrats—seemed to me, perhaps fancifully, to be written in what is of course absent in *Our Mutual Friend*: the first-person Twemlow.[1]

We do not know how Scharf's hosts constructed their guest lists. They might have begun with Scharf, added him in at the end as a gendered makeweight, or thought of him—despite our (affectionate) sense of his probable tediousness as a companion—as central to an amusing evening. We know from his diaries and correspondence that he valued after-dinner conversation with lords and ladies and perhaps especially with lords, although he never repeated for posterity a single bon mot or story. Surely, we thought, Scharf was in some sense out of place at these gatherings of dukes and baronets, even if he always seemed to have a place at the table. Unlike Twemlow, of course, Scharf was not a poor relation of the aristocracy descending the social scale; he was an ambitious professional man whose presence at dinner parties signaled a rise in status.[2] Perhaps we could think—again fancifully—of Scharf and Twemlow passing each other on the social scale, pausing as it were to dine—and to dine again.[3]

And in that passing one might recognize the figure of the "extra man," a figure that would, in the thirty years after the deaths of Charles Dickens and Scharf, become so necessary to the turn-of-the-century hostess. In part because of its anachronism, Robyn and I finally rejected "extra man" as the titular term for Scharf and for the book about him, substituting "bachelor" on the front cover while keeping "extra man" alive in the text as one of many possibilities for understanding Scharf.[4] The superannuated term has, however,

---

1. Starting in the late 1850s, George Scharf's diaries for a given year end with a summary of the year's landmarks. These would often include mentions of titled "friends" or patrons. See, for example, his entry for 1860 looking back on 1859, written from the house of the Duke and Duchess of Marlborough and noting increasing intimacy with Lord and Lady Stanhope and Lord Overstone (Scharf, Personal diaries, 1 January 1860). See Michie and Warhol, *Love among the Archives*, 75–78, for discussion of the genre of the year-end summary and its relation to social class.

2. We might also think of Scharf and Twemlow as "professional diners-out," a phrase Robyn and I thought we had coined until we came across it in several etiquette books. For example, the author of *Habits of Good Society* warns that single men routinely invited to mixed dinner parties "run the risk of being known as professional diners-out, like the *convivœ* of Rome, so that it is a greater charity not to invite them too often" (302).

3. The point here is not to suggest that Scharf was influenced by Charles Dickens or Dickens by Scharf, although they did know each other, as everyone seemed to know Dickens and almost everyone seemed to know Scharf. Rather, I am interested in how a juxtaposition between these two men, one historical and one fictional, can illuminate the insufficiencies of the marriage plot in its literary and cultural manifestations. For Scharf and the marriage plot, see Michie and Warhol, *Love among the Archives*, 62–111.

4. For a discussion of the process of "identifying" Scharf, see ibid., 5–15. For a discussion of the bachelor figure in Victorian literature, see Snyder, *Bachelors, Manhood, and the Novel*. As

continued to haunt me with its limits and possibilities, with its ability not only to challenge the marriage plot from within its privileged domestic spaces but also to produce its own wry commentary on singleness, coupledom, and community.

While readings of *Our Mutual Friend,* beginning with Eve Sedgwick's exemplary exploration of the novel's homosociality, have charted the novel's ambivalence about the marriage plot, even queer readings have tended not to see it as a novel of singleness, lingering instead in the idiom of doubling and pairing so that even the novel's proto-homosexual characters Eugene Wrayburn and Mortimer Lightwood become subject to an unexamined discourse of coupling.[5] Even readings freed from certain kinds of textual constraints tend to think of the novel in the idiom of matchmaking; Holly Furneaux's essay in this volume notes that writers of fan fiction seem to glory in pairing up unlikely—or at least uncoupled—characters in the novel: "As Rachel McMillan put it on the DickensBlog, 'Somebody, somewhere, should give one half of this magnificent duo a chance at more life: a life beyond that final Tremlow [*sic*] handshake and the retreat back to the Temple. But at any rate—long live Mortimer and Eugene: one of Dickens' definitive friendships and certainly one of the strongest in Victorian literature'" (185). If in McMillan's comments "life" and "liv[ing]" are equated with the possibility of coupledom, then in *Our Mutual Friend* we see those connections examined and explored, made and unmade. Thinking about Twemlow in a tradition of extra men is a way into the complex negotiation of the human and the inhuman, the communal and the singular, and the paired and the single staged at the many dining tables of Dickens's last complete novel.

Twemlow is introduced during the novel's very first dinner party at the "bran-new" home of the novel's parody of nouveau-riche social climbers. He is the subject—if that is the right word here—of one of Dickens's most extended and fantastic metaphors:

> There was an innocent piece of dinner-furniture that went upon easy castors and was kept over a livery stable-yard in Duke Street, St. James's, when not in use, to whom the Veneerings were a source of blind confusion. The name of this article was Twemlow. Being first cousin to Lord Snigsworth, he was in frequent requisition, and at many houses might be said to represent the

---

with the extra man, the bachelor figure, according to Katherine Snyder, relies on an ambiguous and paradoxical relationship to "marital, familial, and domestic ideologies." As she notes, "bachelors were seen as both proper and improper to conventional married, bourgeois domesticity" (19).

5. For the germinal reading, see Sedgwick, *Between Men,* 161–79, esp. 165–69.

> dining table in its normal state. Mr and Mrs Veneering, for example, arranging a dinner, habitually started with Twemlow, and then put leaves in him, or added guests to him. Sometimes, the table consisted of Twemlow and half-a-dozen leaves; sometimes, of Twemlow and a dozen leaves; sometimes, Twemlow was pulled out to his utmost extent of twenty leaves. Mr and Mrs Veneering on occasions of ceremony faced each other in the centre of the board, and thus the parallel still held; for it always happened that the more Twemlow was pulled out, the further he found himself from the centre, and the nearer to the sideboard at one end of the room, or the window-curtains at the other. (6)

Both ubiquitous and peripheral, Twemlow is part of the furniture of the social class to which he belongs. The grander the party, the less central he is, although he is in some sense foundational—always present and always accounted for.

On the surface the passage enacts a dehumanizing process we might call lignification, or the turning of people into wood.[6] The passage begins as if this process has already been completed, as if the tenor and the vehicle of the metaphor have been so collapsed that all marks of comparison have been rendered unnecessary. As we pursue this extended metaphor, however, we might come to realize that it does not work perfectly: Twemlow is simultaneously the table (he is pulled out) and the person sitting at it (he is further from the center). To understand the passage we must see Twemlow simultaneously as a person and as a thing, straddling the divide between the human and the nonhuman, between dead wood and the strangely animate wooden "leaves" of upper-class dining tables. Life and humanity (not quite the same thing) pass back and forth between the diner and the table. When the passage finally does grant humanity to Twemlow, it does so incompletely and grudgingly. Even when the "innocent piece of dinner-furniture" becomes a "he" in the third sentence, Twemlow is not fully an individual; his existence is dependent—grammatically as well as financially—on his relationship to Lord Snigsworth.

This passage becomes even more complicated when we realize that it is an extended metaphor for extension itself. By the time of *Our Mutual Friend*'s

6. I borrow (and extend) the term from plant biology, where "lignify" has the following technical meaning: "to make or become woody as a result of the deposition of lignin in cell walls." *American Heritage Dictionary of the English Language*, 5th ed., s.v. "lignify," 2016, accessed July 5, 2017. *Wiktionary* broadens the definition: "Turning into wood; the process of becoming ligneous." *Wiktionary*, s.v. "lignification," accessed July 5, 2017, https://en.wiktionary.org/wiki/lignification.

publication, Victorian writers on interior design were beginning to reject the massive dining room table with its mechanical extenders in favor of smaller, lighter tables that could be put together as needed. Although the Veneerings seem to follow a newer fashion in dining *à la Russe* (more on this later), their table may be as old fashioned and as stiff as Twemlow himself.

Importantly for the purposes of this essay, Twemlow's exile on "occasions of ceremony" to the edges of the dining room—to the "sideboard" or the "window-curtains"—is calibrated specifically in terms of the marriage that gives meaning and shape to the table. This is, after all, the crucial function of the "extra man": to throw marriage into relief. At larger parties, Mr. and Mrs. Veneering "face[]" each other (for better and for worse) "in the centre of the board," their position articulating the centrality of their marriage to the social world of the novel's upper class. Twemlow's symbolic banishment in, but not from, the room helps define him against both the Veneerings and their other guests—against marriage and other forms of coupling supported by the imperatives of dinner parties and novels. Flanked at various dining tables by Eugene and Mortimer, by Boots and Brewer, by the "mature young lady" and the "mature young gentlemen," Twemlow becomes an extra—although by no means extraneous—man, a figure for radical singleness (10).

To say that Twemlow is single is both to state the obvious and to indulge in understatement. We have only to glance at him in his own home, preparing to enter society to be faced with his profound detachment from the world of couples. Dickens describes Twemlow preparing, halfway through the novel, to attend the Lammles' anniversary dinner:

> The estimable Twemlow, dressing himself in his lodgings over the stable-yard in Duke Street, Saint James's, and hearing the horses at their toilet below, finds himself on the whole in a disadvantageous position as compared with the noble animals at livery. For whereas, on the one hand, he has no attendant to slap him soundingly and require him in gruff accents to come up and come over, still, on the other hand, he has no attendant at all; and the mild gentleman's finger-joints and other joints working rustily in the morning, he could deem it agreeable even to be tied up by the countenance at his chamber-door, so he were there skillfully rubbed down and slushed and sluiced and polished and clothed, while himself taking merely a passive part in these trying transactions. (408)

While in the previous passage Twemlow was compared to a "piece of dinner-furniture" stored above the stable until rolled out when needed "upon easy castors," here he is compared to his disadvantage to animals who have human "attendant[s]" to dress them before they leave home. The passage seems to express envy, on Twemlow's behalf, for the possibility of human touch, however rough or even violent. Twemlow inspires pity for being unattended by servants, perhaps even for being unattended by a master, another form of coupledom that mitigates the loneliness of other figures in the novel such as the spinster teacher Miss Peecher and her pupil Marianne.

This essay follows Twemlow from the stable to the novel's many dining tables, and lingers at the mahogany, among silver ice buckets and camels, and around pyramids of fruit and flowers, in order to think through the novel's complicated relationship to marriage, humanity, and community as they are embodied in what I am calling the novel's linked projects of lignification and reanimation. The first section of this essay, "Lignification," looks at how the novel stages the confusion between humans and things, and at how the novel's table scenes can be read through a philosophical tradition that privileges the table as a place to think through that confusion. The second section, "Singularity," looks at the entanglement of humanness and marriage, and at how the novel, through its very grammar, questions not only what is human but also whether humans are single or double. In this section as in the previous one, I propose Twemlow as a figure for the grammar and the ethics of singularity. The final section, "Reanimation," looks to the end of the novel and to Twemlow's transformation from woodenness to humanity, from a piece of table to a gentleman—still indicatively singular but very much alive.

I. LIGNIFICATION

What is it about tables? And when, in fact, is a table, well, just a table? The answer to the latter question might be both "always" and "never." The table, it seems, has long held a privileged position in Western philosophy, where it is both—and sometimes simultaneously—an example of the real, the self-evident, the quality of thingness-itself, and the support for cultural grand (and often abstract) narratives. If we tell at least one kind of story of Western philosophy, then we can see the table emerging as a kind of model organism, the way fruit flies are for geneticists, or nuns for historical demographers and early endocrinologists.[7] It appears with special frequency in two different dis-

---

7. For a discussion of the value of drosophila to genetic research, see, for example, Beckingham et al., "Drosophila Melonogaster," 1–2. Nuns and monks have been used since 1746 to study life expectancy. More recently, they have been used specifically to study gender and longevity. As Marc Luy puts it, "populations of monks and nuns live under similar conditions,

cussions: those about form and those about commodities—in other words, the Platonic and the Marxist traditions. When Plato expounded his theory of ideal forms, he turned to tables and beds (or couches) as examples; and although in book X of the *Republic* he spends more time with beds than with tables, interpreters of Plato have tended to eschew the bed in favor of the table.[8] The table appears in discussions of idealism, and it becomes the canonical example of the difference between ideal forms and specific instantiations such as the "Dining Table" or the "Operating Table."[9] In his history of Greek Philosophy, G. W. F. Hegel uses the table and the wood from which it is made to discuss Anaxagoras's ideas of intrinsic and extrinsic form.[10] Bertrand Russell returns to the table to undermine ideas of reality outside perception.[11]

Perhaps most pertinent to the tables in *Our Mutual Friend* is the philosophical tradition that places them in the context of commodity and exchange. Isobel Armstrong invokes the Podsnaps' dining room table when she discusses Karl Marx's theory of the commodity gone awry. In a comparison of tables in Marx and Hannah Arendt, Armstrong notes that for Marx the table is an example of a useful object, grounded in the reality of common life, turned by capitalism grotesquely into a commodity: "Notoriously . . . against Plato's table

---

so they provide a near-perfect sample to try to understand the biological versus environmental factors in life expectancy." "A Matter of Lifestyle."

8. See, for a foundational example, the debate between Diogenes and Plato as rendered by Silvia Montiglio. Diogenes objects, "Plato, I see table and cup, but in no way tablehood and cuphood." Plato answers, "This is because you have the eyes to see . . . cup and table, but not the understanding to see tablehood and cuphood." Montiglio, *Wandering in Ancient Greek Culture*, 182.

9. Ibid. Benson, *A Companion to Plato*, 218.

10. Hegel, *Greek Philosophy*, 94.

11. Bertrand Russell offers a very sensual engagement with the table worth quoting here:

> To make our difficulties plain, let us concentrate attention on the table. To the eye it is oblong, brown and shiny, to the touch it is smooth and cool and hard; when I tap it, it gives out a wooden sound. Any one else who sees and feels and hears the table will agree with this description, so that it might seem as if no difficulty would arise; but as soon as we try to be more precise our troubles begin. Although I believe that the table is "really" of the same colour all over, the parts that reflect the light look much brighter than the other parts, and some parts look white because of reflected light. I know that, if I move, the parts that reflect the light will be different, so that the apparent distribution of colours on the table will change. It follows that if several people are looking at the table at the same moment, no two of them will see exactly the same distribution of colours, because no two can see it from exactly the same point of view, and any change in the point of view makes some change in the way the light is reflected. (*The Problems of Philosophy*, 8–9)

For a sustained discussion of Russell's table metaphor, particularly as it influences Virginia Woolf's use of the image in *To the Lighthouse*, see Banfield, *The Phantom Table*, 53–55.

as ideal form, Marx puts a common wooden table, which, ordinarily standing with its feet on the ground, upends itself and adopts fancy ideas when it 'steps forth as a commodity,' inverting its whole being. Once the table derives its value not from use but from comparison with other commodities in order to establish its exchange value, it stands on its head (with its legs in the air, Marx implies)."[12] This is not Plato's ideal form of a table, but rather a table with "fancy ideas" or fancies attributed to the exchange system of capitalism and perhaps also somehow to the perversity of the table itself, which might, during a dinner, say, of capitalists, suddenly produce a version of itself covered in silver camels, as at the Veneerings' home, or chassed silver ice buckets, as at the Podsnaps.'

Armstrong contends that Arendt's treatment of the table is very different from Marx's. For Arendt, who is interested in the relationship between humans and things, the table is once again the exemplary object. Like other objects, but more obviously, its place is between people: "To live together in the world means essentially that a world of things is between those that have it in common, as a table is located between those who sit around it."[13] A table defines those who sit around it as a community, even as human beings, simultaneously participating in the production of humanness and breaking down the dichotomy between things and people. The table can of course fail in its function to produce community; in such instances, Arendt argues, the table itself becomes visible as a thing—as we see during the Podsnap dinner party when the table ornaments, so carefully described, fail to produce a sense of community in the ill-assorted group of diners-out. The world of things, of which tables are an example, "relates and separates men at the same time."[14]

The more benign idea of the table as creating community has passed into popular culture and specifically into the discourse of American nostalgia. Medical and parenting websites feature blogs with titles such as "Whatever Happened to the Family Meal?" supported by statistics about the benefits that accrue to children who eat regularly with their parents.[15] The dinner table has a specific role to play in this imaginary. The *Aha Parenting* website features an article titled "Dinner: 30 Minutes to a More Connected Family" with an

12. Armstrong, "Bodily Things and Thingly Bodies," 22.

13. Quoted in ibid., 24.

14. Ibid.

15. Sweat, "Whatever Happened to the Family Meal?" For an account of the healthfulness of family dinners, see Davis, "Family Dinners Are Important," which claims that "when families dine together, they tend to eat more vegetables and fruits—and fewer fried foods, soda, and foods with trans fats, research shows. When younger kids frequently eat dinner with their families, they are less likely to be overweight than other children." One feature of many of these articles, including Sweat's, is the importance of a certain kind of formality, including setting the table.

epigraph attributed to Doris Christopher: "*The table is where we mark milestones, divulge dreams, bury hatchets, make deals, give thanks, plan vacations, and tell jokes. It is also where children learn the lessons that families teach: manners, cooperation, self-control. Values. Following directions. Sitting still. Taking turns.*"[16] This table, like Marx's commodity, is full of ideas. It also, like Arendt's, has an odd ontological status as both thing and human. The table is not literally where we mark milestones—that is, we do not usually chalk those milestones on the table's surface, rendering the table simply a thing. Instead, the table implies and gains meaning from the fact of human presence at or around it. Tables can serve as national as well as familial metonymies; as I write this I am acutely aware that I have heard many times recent presidential election campaign candidates quoting (or misquoting) a line from Ronald Reagan's farewell speech from the Oval Office: "All great change in America begins at the dinner table." That table, whether the massive piece of Victorian furniture or the folksy piece of Reaganite Americana, bears a cultural burden heavier than the Podsnaps' elaborate silver plate.

The formal dining tables in *Our Mutual Friend* are Marx's commodities gone wild. They reflect—in all senses—the excesses of Victorian capitalism. Dickens's description of the Podsnaps' silver plate almost literally undermines the aura of the household position to display its economic base: "Hideous solidity was the characteristic of the Podsnap plate. Everything was made to look as heavy as it could, and to take up as much room as possible. Everything said boastfully, 'here you have as much of me in my ugliness as if I were only lead; but I am so many ounces of precious metal worth so much an ounce;—wouldn't you like to melt me down?'" (131). The Podsnap and Veneering centerpieces would also have reflected other cultural changes associated with, but perhaps not reducible to, their relation with capitalism. Both the Veneerings and the Podsnaps have obviously taken on the new fashion of service *à la Russe,* in which plates were handed around by servants, making possible the satiric glories of the Veneering's butler, the Analytical Chemist. In contrast with the earlier service *à la Française,* in which dishes of food were laid out on the table (often in carefully regulated patterns) so that guests could help themselves and each other, in service *à la Russe* the center of the table was emptied of food. This, of course, left an ornamentation vacuum soon to be filled with epergnes, vases, salt cellars, and other decorative objects, some of which included edibles and some of which did not. The switch to the new fashion was not without its detractors. When Alfred, Lord Tennyson's friend

16. "Dinner," n. pag., original emphasis.

Arthur Henry Hallam gave a dinner party *à la Russe* in 1848, his guests "giggled" because they came down to find "nothing on the table, not even soup."[17]

Interestingly, the Dickenses themselves embraced *à la Russe* service quite early. The famously acerbic Jane Carlyle was very critical about the Dickens's dining arrangements:

> The dinner was served up in the new fashion—not placed on the table at all—but handed round—only the desserts on the table and quantities of *artificial* flowers—but such an overloaded dessert! Pyramids of figs raisins oranges—ach! At the Lady Ashburton dinner served on these principles there were just *four cowslips* in china pots—four silver shells containing sweets, and a silver filigree temple in the middle! But here the very candles rose each out of an artificial rose! Good God![18]

Marx would not, we assume, have approved of Carlyle's class snobbery or her idea of simplicity (*only* "a silver filigree temple in the middle!") but he would, we assume, have recoiled with her from the further introduction of artifice. Clearly—at least by the exacting standards of Carlyle—the Dickenses had some Veneering in them. Moreover, the center of the table, denuded of food, is clearly a fraught space: the items one places there say much about one's class, status, and commitments.

Less well known than the debate over kinds of service is what seems to be a related discussion among arbiters of dining etiquette that centers on the importance of the "mahogany" of the table itself.[19] "Mahogany" by the Victorian period became a metonym for the act of dining—in particular, of dining out. Alexis Soyer is only one example of a writer proposing going back to an earlier tradition of removing the tablecloth at the end of dinner. In his compendium of letters from a "Modern Housewife," he has a "Mrs. B" explain: "In laying the cloth, we place it over the baize, and remove it after dinner, as Mr. B. says he likes to see the mahogany, for when he asks a City friend to come and put his feet under the mahogany, it looks rather foolish if he never sees it."[20] Exposing the bare table—"the mahogany"—at the end of the dinner is a sign of hospitality, while covering it up with expensive bric-a-brac suggests concern for display over care for the comfort of the guests.

---

17. Colquhoun, *Taste,* 252.

18. Rossi-Wilcox, *Dinner for Dickens,* 184; original emphasis.

19. For a discussion of cultural and literary association with mahogany, see Freedgood, *The Ideas in Things,* 30–54.

20. Soyer, *The Modern Housewife,* 398.

If Dickens was to some extent implicated in the ostentation that proceeded from new styles of dining, then he was of course very critical of (and very funny about) how commodities take on lives of their own. In *Our Mutual Friend,* the silver plate takes on a life denied to the diners who use (or, more accurately, are used by) it. As we have seen, the plate actually "addresses" the diner ("'wouldn't you like to melt me down?'"). Later in the same passage, Dickens shows the various silver pieces speaking to each other:

> A corpulent straggling epergne, blotched all over as if it had broken out in an eruption rather than been ornamented, delivered this address from an unsightly silver platform in the center of the table. Four silver wine coolers, each furnished with four staring heads, each head obtrusively carrying a big silver ring in each of its ears, conveyed the sentiment up and down the table, and handed it on to the pot-bellied silver salt cellars. All the big silver spoons and forks widened the mouths of the company expressly for the purpose of thrusting the sentiment down their throats with every morsel they ate. (131)

It is easy and inviting to see the Podsnap and the Veneering (very different) silver as reflective of something like character read as mere reflections; these ugly silver surfaces mirror the Podsnaps' prejudices and moral failings. Read differently, against the grain of lignification but as part of the same process, we see how life is granted to wood and silver in a way that it is not granted to human flesh. The epergne resists any easy notion of "ornament[ation]" that would keep it in the object world; instead it seems to have skin that has "broken out" from diseases—or perhaps out of its own formal qualities. Articulate as well as animate, the silver communicates across internal categories, forming a community that mimics and thus mocks the human community around the table. The four wine coolers suggest a particularly grotesque parody of coupling as they form a hideous matched set, with their four heads and two "big silver ring[s]" apiece. Unlike the diners in Arendt's example, the dining tables of Dickens's novel do not confer humanity and community; instead, they undermine the distinction between the human and the nonhuman.

The almost gothic animation of tables and their things has its counterpart in *Our Mutual Friend* in the lignification of the people who collect around and use these objects. Twemlow is not the only human being in *Our Mutual Friend* turned by lignification into furniture: when the novel's hero, John Harmon, applies for the job of secretary to Mr. Boffin, Dickens draws out over two chapters the comic possibilities of a category error. As we find out later, Boffin has always thought of a secretary as something "mostly mahogany, lined with green baize and leather, with lots of little drawers in it" (179). It is this misconception that produces Boffin's amazed reaction to Harmon's first proposal:

> "If you would try me as your Secretary—"
> "As *what?*" cried Mr Boffin, with his eyes wide open.
> "Your Secretary."
> "Well," said Mr Boffin, under his breath, "that's a queer thing!" (96; original italics)

John Harmon is, like Twemlow, a "queer thing" caught between the human and the wooden, the animate and the dead. While the lignification of Harmon in this scene is comic, Boffin's later treatment of his secretary as a functionary is not—at least until we realize that it is part of a conspiracy between employer and secretary to test Bella's character.

The process of lignification is not merely a characterological one: the book itself suggests a metonymic intimacy between people and the things they use, people and their work. The name of the piece of furniture derives from the name of the person using it; this is a common form of worker-for-tool metonymy that Dickens employs critically in many of his novels—the opening of *Bleak House,* for example, refers to lawyers and judges as "maces, bags, and purses."[21] In *Our Mutual Friend* the worker-for-tool metonymy becomes comically attached to a conjugal metonymy: Pleasant Riderhood will not marry the articulator of human bone, Mr. Venus, because, she does not wish "to regard [her]self, or to be regarded, in that bony light" (84).

We see lignification at work in another marginally human figure: the Podsnaps' daughter, Georgiana. Like Twemlow's and Harmon's, her relationship with wood is both metaphoric and metonymic. Like Twemlow, she is first introduced into the text through extended metaphor: she is both her father's exemplary "Young Person" and—like her mother, but in miniature—a "rocking horse" (129). The glimpse into her childhood that Dickens offers suggests a woodenness by "association":

> Podsnap's young person was likely to get little good out of association with other young persons, and had therefore been restricted to companionship with not very congenial older persons, and with massive furniture. Miss

21. Dickens, *Bleak House,* 16. Of course it is in *Bleak House* that we find the entirely admirable and human Matthew Bagnet, whose nickname is "lignum vitae," "in compliment to the extreme hardness and toughness of his physiognomy" (499). *Lingnum vitae* means "wood of life" and identifies Caribbean trees of the *Guaiacum* family. "Life" here refers to the trees' medicinal uses.

> Podsnap's early views of life being principally derived from the reflections of it in her father's boots, and in the walnut and rosewood tables of the dim drawing-rooms, and in their swarthy giants of looking-glasses. (130)

Georgiana's life is close to being no life at all; it is not so much that she *is* furniture than that she is defined by it. In the story of her (non)childhood, even wood loses its distinctive properties, as the "walnut" and "rosewood" become merely reflective surfaces equivalent to mirrors and, more frighteningly perhaps, to "her father's boots." Although wood in *Our Mutual Friend* can become part of the body, as in the case of Silas Wegg's leg, it is most often associated with tables of various kinds, as if humanness is both granted by the act of sitting at a table (or a desk, or a secretary) and endangered by that proximity. While I have more to say later about those characters who seem most vulnerable to lignification, I want at this point to think of it as a foundational process of Dickens's novel that underwrites its central concern with the difference between the dead and the alive, the human and the nonhuman.

II. SINGULARITY

Our Mutual Friend was of course written at a time of especially strict social rules regulating dining for the upper classes. As consumers of neo-Victorian films or books know all too well, dinner guests "went down" to the dining room in order of status and left the table in gendered groups. In between, there were rules about how much to eat and drink, whom to converse with, and what topics constituted appropriate dinner conversation. There were also rules about whom to invite. For mixed-sex dinner parties, the author of *Habits of Good Society* warns, it was considered rude to "ask a man without his wife"; he assumes that "the chief point is to invite men and women—an equal number of each of course—who can *talk*."[22] He notes, however, that "there are indeed some privileged persons like myself, agreeable old bachelors, who, being free from encumbrance and full of talk, are always welcome and generally wanted."[23] Robert Kemp Philp recommends "an equal number of ladies

22. *The Habits of Good Society*, 302–3.

23. *The Habits of Good Society*, 302. It is difficult to say how gender-balanced actual Victorian dinner parties tended to be. Of course there were many dinners to which women were not invited. At these all-male affairs, which the author of *Habits* calls "bachelor" dinner parties, the rules were a little looser. We see what happens when women are invited to previously all-male dinners in chapter 4 of Margaret Oliphant's *Miss Marjoribanks*. Scharf hosted only all-male events in his lodging, although of course the larger dinners at great houses included both men and women.

and gentlemen," as well as a variety in age and profession.[24] In *Our Mutual Friend,* the Veneerings—and presumably others—follow the rule to invite wives, who appear in parentheses when Twemlow ponders how he became the Veneerings' "oldest friend" and most frequent guest:

> Twemlow had first known Veneering at his club, where Veneering then knew nobody but the man who made them known to one another, who seemed to be the most intimate friend he had in the world, and whom he had known two days—the bond of union between their souls, the nefarious conduct of the committee respecting the cookery of a fillet of veal, having been accidentally cemented at that date. Immediately upon this, Twemlow received an invitation to dine with Veneering, and dined: the man being of the party. Immediately upon that, Twemlow received an invitation to dine with the man, and dined: Veneering being of the party. At the man's were a Member, an Engineer, a Payer-off of the National Debt, a Poem on Shakespeare, a Grievance, and a Public Office, who all seemed to be utter strangers to Veneering. And yet immediately after that, Twemlow received an invitation to dine at Veneering's, expressly to meet the Member, the Engineer, the Payer-off of the National Debt, the Poem on Shakespeare, the Grievance, and the Public Office, and, dining, discovered that all of them were the most intimate friends Veneering had in the world, and that the wives of all of them (who were all there) were the objects of Mrs Veneering's most devoted affection and tender confidence. (7)

Taking advantage of the worker-for-tool metonymy once again to dehumanize the male guests, Dickens mechanically (and parenthetically) supplies them all with wives and the Veneering dining table with a matched set of couples. While I spoke earlier of other kinds of couplings at the table, including Mortimer and Eugene, these are clearly part of the novel's and dining etiquette's heterosexual imaginary. This is one of many moments where Twemlow ponders his place at the table and beyond.

If the table is structured by pairing and around the central—if problematic—marriage of the Veneerings, then the novel itself is structured by the problem of couples. This is most evident in the climax of the novel's marriage plot: the dying and delirious Eugene's talismanic discovery of the word "wife," a word that of course has the power to bring him back from the dead in a crucial moment of the novel's project of reanimation. Twemlow is not only separated from such a plot, such an ending, but also rhetorically punished

24. Philp, *The Domestic World,* 217.

for imagining that he might be part of one as he contemplates his role in the horrific Lammle wedding:

> So, Twemlow goes home to Duke Street, St James's, to take a plate of mutton broth with a chop in it, and a look at the marriage-service, in order that he may cut in at the right place to-morrow; and he is low, and feels it dull over the livery stable-yard, and is distinctly aware of a dint in his heart, made by the most adorable of the adorable bridesmaids. For, the poor little harmless gentleman once had his fancy, like the rest of us, and she didn't answer (as she often does not), and he thinks the adorable bridesmaid is like the fancy as she was then (which she is not at all), and that if the fancy had not married some one else for money, but had married him for love, he and she would have been happy (which they wouldn't have been), and that she has a tenderness for him still (whereas her toughness is a proverb). Brooding over the fire, with his dried little head in his dried little hands, and his dried little elbows on his dried little knees, Twemlow is melancholy. (118)

Both the ironic syntax of asides and the sentiment it embodies are, I think, unusual for Dickens. Taken together, the parentheses that interrupt this paragraph and Twemlow's marriage-plot fantasies are absolutely devastating. With some verbs in the present, some in the subjunctive, and others in various past tenses, they cover all temporalities and foreclose all possibilities of marital happiness as well as a conventional marriage plot. Twemlow has only to imagine a constituent element of the marriage plot to have it undermined by the ruthless and insistent voice of the narrator. Like Twemlow, the reader is forbidden the easy pleasures of the romance plot, the easy syntax of coupling.

If radical singleness is inscribed at the level of syntax, then it also works its relentless critique at the level of grammar. In *Our Mutual Friend* the difference between being single and being paired becomes, temporarily, a grammar lesson. The teacher of that lesson is the reluctantly single Miss Peecher, who uses her pupil Mary Anne to spy on Bradley Headstone. Miss Peecher disguises her interest in Headstone by pretending that her concerns are strictly pedagogical. When Mary Anne, speaking of Lizzie, says, "They say she is very handsome," Miss Peecher puts her pupil through a catechism about the use of "they"; this lesson prompts Mary Anne's confession that she might mean just one person: "I don't know if I mean more than her brother himself." Miss Peecher presses home the crucial difference between singular and plural pronouns: "Now pray, Mary Anne, be careful another time. He says is very different from they say, remember. Difference between he says and they say? Give it me." Mary Anne responds with the correct answer: "One is indicative mood, present tense, third person singular, verb active to say. Other is indicative mood, present tense, third person plural, verb active to say" (220). It is in Miss Peecher's painful interest to distinguish the singular from the plural, the single from the paired. In the grammar of *Our Mutual Friend,* she is / will be single in both the present and the future tense. As I suggested earlier, however, Miss Peecher's singleness within the marriage plot is not (quite) the same as singularity: paired with Mary Anne, she forms one of Dickens's affiliative or metonymic households that serve as alternatives to marriages and traditional families.

As we have seen, the "unattended" Twemlow has no such household, no such option. The novel ends—to the frustration of at least one writer of fan fiction and Mortimer fan—with the newly singular Mortimer leaving Twemlow at his (stable) door. The very last words of *Our Mutual Friend* are: "Mortimer sees Twemlow home, shakes hands with him cordially at parting, and fares to the Temple, gaily" (820). While readers of the homosexual plot tend to focus on Mortimer, I, of course, am thinking of Twemlow left behind at the entrance to his lonely lodgings. Mortimer and Twemlow pass each other as Mortimer goes "gaily" on to a destination and perhaps a plot of his own, while Twemlow stays at "home," not even the agent or the grammatical subject of the novel's final verbs. For all that happens in the novel, Twemlow remains single and singular.

III. REANIMATION

Although this moment of parting—Mortimer's with Twemlow, the readers' with the novel—leaves Twemlow where he started, I would argue that he does partake of the novel's reanimation project in a limited way. In a novel where one marriage-plot hero fakes his own death and stages his own reappearance, and where the other rises from his deathbed in response to the word "wife," reanimation and marriage are closely linked. Twemlow, unmarried, follows a slightly different path away from thingness and woodenness to a singular humanity. By the long middle of the novel, we might think of Twemlow finding a vocation—ironically, or, at least, appropriately—as a sort of secretary, a keeper of secrets.

The novel initially forbids him a work plot as it denies him a marriage plot:

> So Twemlow trips with not a little stiffness across Piccadilly, sensible of having once been more upright in figure and less in danger of being knocked down by swift vehicles. To be sure that was in the days when he hoped for leave from the dread Snigsworth to do something, or to be something in life, and before that magnificent Tartar issued the ukase, "As he will never distinguish himself, he must be a poor gentleman-pensioner of mine." (409–10)

Like the passage about Twemlow's ancient romance, this one invokes past desires—in this case, for work. This desire, has been forestalled as Twemlow stiffens into uselessness. Ironically, Twemlow has managed to "be something"—although not, perhaps, "to be something in life."

The novel and Mrs. Lammle eventually give him work to: he must warn Georgiana away from the marriage with Fascination Fledgby and in the process keep the secret of Mrs. Lammle's role in the plot to forward that marriage. He must be, in effect, a secretary. Of course the novel does not name him as such: over time Twemlow takes up and asserts the identity of "gentleman," as distinct from the "gentleman-pensioner" of the previous passage. To be a gentleman is, however, to keep promises and secrets. When, for instance, Mrs. Lammle begs Twemlow not to "betray [her] confidence" about the Georgiana plot, Twemlow responds formulaically: "madam, on the honour of a poor gentleman" (417). By naming himself a "gentleman," albeit a "poor" one, Twemlow relies on the connection between secret keeping and his class identity—an identity that is ironically undermined by the associations of secrets with domestic service and domestic furniture.

By the end of the novel, Twemlow no longer uses "gentleman" defensively. Indeed, his final act in the novel is to shame Podsnap through a cascading repetition of the word as he defends Eugene's decision to marry Lizzie:

> "Pardon me, sir," says Twemlow, rather less mildly than usual, "I don't agree with you. If this gentleman's feelings of gratitude, of respect, of admiration, and affection, induced him (as I presume they did) to marry this lady—"
>
> "This lady!" echoes Podsnap.
>
> "Sir," returns Twemlow, with his wristbands bristling a little, "YOU repeat the word; I repeat the word. This lady. What else would you call her, if the gentleman were present?"
>
> This being something in the nature of a poser for Podsnap, he merely waves it away with a speechless wave.
>
> "I say," resumes Twemlow, "if such feelings on the part of this gentleman, induced this gentleman to marry this lady, I think he is the greater gentleman for the action, and makes her the greater lady. I beg to say, that when I use the word, gentleman, I use it in the sense in which the degree may be attained by any man. The feelings of a gentleman I hold sacred, and I confess I am not comfortable when they are made the subject of sport or general discussion." (819)

In defending Eugene as a "gentleman," Twemlow echoes his earlier use of the term to describe himself. Repeatedly identified in the novel by the narrator as the "poor gentleman" or "the old gentleman"—and, as we have seen, by Lord Snigsworth as a "gentleman-pensioner"—Twemlow jettisons qualifiers to make the term available not only to Eugene but also to himself. Gentlemen, of course, ideally do not work for pay; their work is to be—perhaps even to be "something in life." Faithful keeper of the novel's secrets, no longer wooden or stiff or a piece of furniture, Twemlow comes alive on the novel's last page—only to be left alone and singular.

Although in the ending to *Our Mutual Friend* Dickens does produce a genre-confirming number of couples, probable and improbable, conventional and potentially subversive, he resists the impulse to convert all singularity into coupledom.[25] In their very different ways, Georgiana Podsnap, Mortimer Lightwood, Miss Tippins, and Mr. Twemlow cannot be absorbed by the marriage plot. Georgiana's singleness seems singularly passive: rescued from a marriage to Fascination Fledgby, she retreats from the action of the novel as "a credulous little creature" who still believes in her "friend," Mrs. Lammle (626). Mortimer suffers the fate of many a proto-homosexual bachelor of Victorian fiction, playing the role of best friend to a married couple. Miss Tippins is perhaps the most revolutionary figure of the three: she remains resistant to coupledom by continuing to live out the fantasy of having insistently multiple lovers although she is also continuously framed as a grotesque. It is Twemlow who is allowed to be both human and single, Twemlow who is allowed to participate in the reanimation process that usually depends on marriage. Left alone at the stable door, Twemlow remains tied to the nonhuman, both to animals and to wood, but he is given a life and work to do in it. Of course, Twemlow is also a prop to the marriage plot. Like the extra man at the dinner table, Twemlow is both odd man out and a social necessity: his singleness defines others as encoupled; his gentlemanliness consists of filling himself with other people's plots, other people's secrets. *Our Mutual Friend* experiments as, I believe, no other Dickens novel quite does, with the limits of the marriage plot and its hegemony over categories of the human.

25. For a positive view of Jenny Wren's marriage to Sloppy, see Sara D. Schotland's essay "Who's That in Charge?" calling Dickens "ahead of his time" for "providing a suitor" for his crippled heroine and envisioning for her "a reproductive future" (n. pag.).

AFTERWORD

Real Figures

MARY JEAN CORBETT

> So that was the Lighthouse, was it?
>
> No, the other was also the Lighthouse. For nothing was simply one thing. The other Lighthouse was true, too.
>
> —Virginia Woolf, *To the Lighthouse*

IN THE brief thirteenth chapter of the first section of *To the Lighthouse*, while strolling the lawn of the house in the Hebrides, Lily Briscoe, the artist, and William Bankes, the scientist, "turned and saw the Ramsays. So that is marriage, Lily thought, a man and a woman looking at a girl throwing a ball."[1] Compared with what readers have seen up to this point in the novel concerning not "marriage" in general but one complex marriage in particular, this view is stark and simple. Lily at once composes the triptych she calls "marriage" as a familial scene—father, mother, daughter. And its elements are both like and unlike those of the tableau she has been painting all afternoon, of "Mrs. Ramsay reading to James" (55), to which she will return once more, a decade or so later, upon coming back to the house in the final section of the novel.

That actual canvas had already provoked the scientist's curiosity: "Simple, obvious, commonplace, as it was, Mr. Bankes was interested. Mother and child then—objects of universal veneration, and in this case the mother was famous for her beauty—might be reduced, he pondered, to a purple shadow without irreverence" (55–56). Evoking both the domestic intimacies of the Impressionists Berthe Morisot and Mary Cassatt and those same subjects as very differently treated by Woolf's sister Vanessa Bell, Lily's painting is no portrait: it "was not of them, she said. Or, not in his sense," "the question being" instead,

1. Woolf, *To the Lighthouse*, 75. Cited parenthetically in the text hereafter.

from both an aesthetic and a scientific point of view, "one of the relations of masses, of lights and shadows" (56). Surely Woolf would have said the same of *To the Lighthouse* itself, which unmistakably renders the biographical data of Leslie and Julia Stephen's marriage, and of their youngest daughter's complex ambivalence toward them, yet is not a portrait of them, or their marriage, or their family, at least not in any straightforward, literal, representational way.

Representing mother and child in explicitly antirealist terms, posing the relations that the painting configures as a "question" to be solved rather than as a sight to be mimetically reproduced, Lily's painterly vision eschews portraiture in favor of abstraction in a characteristically modernist mode. But just after she visually composes the scene that "is marriage," something else takes place in or just beyond her consciousness, an experience that the narrative voice casts as not unique to Lily alone, evoking as it does a key feature of the nineteenth-century novel. As she and William continue walking towards the Ramsays,

> suddenly the meaning which, for no reason at all, perhaps as they are stepping out of the Tube or ringing a doorbell, descends upon people, making them symbolical, making them representative, came upon them, and made them in the dusk standing, looking, the symbols of marriage, husband and wife. Then, after an instant, the symbolical outline which transcended the real figures sank down again, and they became, as they met them, Mr. and Mrs. Ramsay, watching the children throwing catches. (75)

Like the "ordinary sight" of "a girl in patent leather boots" and "a young man in a maroon overcoat" converging "at a point directly beneath [her] window" that both inspires and emblematizes Mary Beton's meditation on the so-called androgynous mind in the final chapter of *A Room of One's Own* (1929), in this moment the "real figures" of "husband and wife" are indeed made figurative.[2] They are made, that is, to typify something larger than themselves, something that, to use Woolf's word, "transcended" them. In both the novel and the prose polemic, that something is an institution as heavily laden with metaphorical freight as any other we might name.

For if the Ramsays and their daughter here symbolize "marriage," then marriage, too, symbolizes, or is believed to symbolize, as we know from the last several generations of feminist scholarship on nineteenth-century fiction and as the essays in this volume readily attest. At least since the publication of Eve Kosofsky Sedgwick's *Between Men* (1985), marriage has been understood

2. Woolf, *A Room of One's Own*, 95.

as being always already about something else in addition to itself, being both symbolic and literal. It stands in for another social formation, like the consolidation of a homosocial public sphere; or enacts another cultural narrative, as in "the terrible diminution" of female agency accomplished by the marriage of Lizzie Hexam to Eugene Wrayburn in *Our Mutual Friend* (1864–65).[3] A few years later, Nancy Armstrong's *Desire and Domestic Fiction* (1987) reinforced this disposition toward reading marriage as about something else in addition to pure hetero romance, arguing that Elizabeth Bennet's possession of "essential qualities of mind," gendered feminine, when united to Darcy's materially abundant possessions, enabled the consolidation of class hegemony.[4] After Armstrong, marital happy endings marked ideological triumphs most critical feminist readers would no longer applaud.

In a different vein, the Latin Americanist Doris Sommer's analysis of the cultural and political work of "national romances" in *Foundational Fictions* (1991) initiated an important strand of scholarship on the symbolic capacities of marriage: there heterosexual marriage figures as a trope of reconciliation between conflicting entities rendered separate and unequal by gender. In the Anglo-Irish tradition, national tales by Maria Edgeworth and Sidney Owenson, which Katie Trumpener has exhaustively studied in *Bardic Nationalism* (1997) and to which Ian Duncan alludes in his important essay in this volume on Germaine de Staël's *Corinne* (1807), constitute what I have called "allegories of union." From their different ideological positions, Edgeworth and Owenson construe the marriage between Irish heroine and English hero as both the medium for settling the conflict between the nations which the protagonists represent and the crucible for forging a symbolically hybrid transnational identity. Within this frame, the feminized figure of the Irish heroine *cum* wife remains the subordinate element, as in Duncan's analysis of the gendered asymmetry that emerges when Staël appropriates the *Bildung* plot of *Wilhelm Meister's Apprenticeship* (1795–96), available primarily if not exclusively to men, for her artist-heroine. Whereas "Staël, repossessing a role newly invested with the universal project of *Bildung*, indicts the marriage plot as a betrayal of her heroine's full and harmonious development" (17), Duncan writes, sundry heroines in the English tradition yet undergo that "terrible diminution" as a function of the national/marital plot. Later in the century, however, as Lauren M. E. Goodlad's reading of *Felix Holt* (1866) as political Bildungsroman deftly illustrates, the marriage plot that features so centrally in condition of England fiction can be repurposed for other collective ends.

3. Sedgwick, *Between Men*, 178.

4. Armstrong, *Desire and Domestic Fiction*, 4.

The valences of the plot differ, then, depending on where, when, and through what lens we look. On the earlier end of the long nineteenth century, the philosophical anthropology of the late Enlightenment, which on Duncan's account secured the primacy of the novel in its anthropomorphic focus, cast women as incapable of achieving species-being. At the same time, the genre constructed, and was constructed in light of, hierarchies of race and nation that situated other humans and all nonhuman animals as similarly debarred from either moving up the great chain or moving forward progressively in time. By the end of the century, however, not only have the anthropological terms changed, as Kathy Alexis Psomiades shows here and elsewhere; so have the experiential ones.[5] Precisely at the historical moment when at least some Englishwomen could be construed as having more choice or agency—in ending a marriage by divorce or, in Marlene Tromp's fascinating study, by murder; in getting an education and perhaps a job, a husband, and/or a family thereafter, as in Kelly Hager's perceptive reading of Meade's use of Tennyson; in refusing heterosexual arrangements altogether and entering into other forms of affiliation and intimacy that anticipate the online communities Holly Furneaux discusses—a new plot emerges. Modernity is sutured to monogamy, as Sukanya Banerjee's analysis demonstrates, and defines a clear mode of progress in the English and Indian bigamy novels she explores. In Psomiades's reading of *She* (1886–87) and *Tess of the d'Urbervilles* (1895) in this volume, "older, earthier plots of literal battle and quest" coexist with "late, cerebral, figurative versions" (62) of the same, even as "the mythic plot"—conceived as an emblem of the complex entanglements of realism with sexuality at century's end—"erases the features of choice, consent, agency that mark the realist marriage plot" (64).

From a different angle, terms like "choice, consent, agency," closely aligned as they are with the liberal subject, may obscure other formations at work that do not invoke either the literal or symbolic twoness of marriage or threeness of family and that do not privilege middle-class women's access to and achievement of liberal autonomy. In her critique of Sedgwick's point regarding Lizzie Hexam's unfortunate fall into marriage, Talia Schaffer convincingly argues that such an end registers as unfortunate, or even oppressive, only if we construe the achievement of autonomous selfhood as the really desirable goal, extending her argument in *Romance's Rival* (2016) as to how marriage facilitates the development of broader intersubjective relations to recast this as a defining trait of both Victorian marriage and Victorian fiction. We may

5. In addition to Psomiades's essay in this volume, see "Heterosexual Exchange" and "The Marriage Plot in Theory."

thus instead read Lizzie's marriage to Eugene, mediated by her connection to Jenny Wren, as a crucial but not totally dominant element in the construction of a beloved community that instantiates relations of care among kin and non-kin. In this light, *Our Mutual Friend* values affective bonds both between men, per Sedgwick, and between women, with Sharon Marcus's groundbreaking book of that name providing a crucial touchstone for Schaffer's work, as for my own.

This, then, could all look much less like loss than gain, with heterosexual marriage understood as one tool among others for forging a nondyadic relationality that implicitly critiques liberal autonomy and rationality. Taking this approach would potentially enable readers to break "the mesmerizing focus of the 'subject-constitution' of the female individualist," in Gayatri Chakravorty Spivak's memorable words from another crucial feminist intervention of the 1980s.[6] From an evolutionary perspective that similarly challenges the pre-eminence of the liberal individual and his or, by century's end, her development, Elisha Cohn shows how late-century novelists including Olive Schreiner, Mona Caird, and Thomas Hardy deconstruct concepts of choice and agency, subordinating the little lives of their protagonists to the much larger and longer flow of deep time. The marriage plots of *The Story of an African Farm* (1883) and *The Daughters of Danaus* (1894) are thus as "fatal" for their female protagonists as *Corinne*'s is for hers—but not for the same reasons. Ultimately, then, the differences between the rebellious Corinne and the equally resistant Lyndall and Hadria come to seem like effects of the shifting meanings and functions of marriage and its plots in and over time.

•

When Woolf looked back at marriage as (she thought) it was, what did she see? To be sure, she clearly understood its symbolic valence as a mode of naturalizing gendered inequalities for domestic and/or imperial ends. Through the figures of Mr. Ramsay, so fond of chanting Tennyson's "The Charge of the Light Brigade," and his no-less-imperializing wife, confident that "an unmarried woman has missed the best of life" (53), she represents a particular idea of Victorian marriage: its presumably gender-exclusive roles, its reproductive fecundity, its coercive force, all the stereotypical features associated with the nineteenth century that Woolf was to mock the very next year in *Orlando* (1928). Yet the transiently "symbolical" or "representative" status of the Ram-

6. Spivak, "Three Women's Texts," 237.

says' union, as impersonally observed by the narrator, competes with other ways of thinking about or visualizing intimate relations that do not conform to "Victorian" type.

Although Woolf may have perceived such relations as "modern," members of the novel's older, late Victorian generation are not debarred from engaging in them. Among "those unclassified affections" that Mrs. Ramsay identifies—"of which," the narrator tells us from her point of view, "there are so many" (106)—we can locate William Bankes's feelings for her:

> For him to gaze as Lily saw him gazing at Mrs. Ramsay was a rapture, equivalent, Lily felt, to the loves of dozens of young men (and perhaps Mrs. Ramsay had never excited the loves of dozens of young men). It was love, she thought, pretending to move her canvas, distilled and filtered; love that never attempted to clutch its object; but, like the love which mathematicians bear their symbols, or poets their phrases, was meant to be spread over the world and become part of the human gain. So it was indeed. (50–51)

Bankes's feelings for his old friend's wife, no less complex than his feelings for that friend himself, seem something other than possessive or sexual, or so at least Lily interprets them even as she shares them. She characterizes those feelings as impersonal, a somewhat paradoxical affect in light of the specifically embodied experience that "rapture" connotes: we might recall here the earlier scene in which Mrs. Ramsay feels "the rapture of successful creation" (42) after satisfying her husband's desire for sympathy, a sexually charged event that leaves her physically spent with "scarcely a shell of herself left for her to know herself by" (41).

But Lily perceives William's affection, by implicit contrast with Mr. Ramsay's coercive demand for attention, as enlarging rather than exhausting. "That people should love like this, that Mr. Bankes should feel this for Mrs. Ramsay (she glanced at him musing) was helpful, was exalting" (51)—in its lack of possessiveness, its orientation towards "the world," and the contribution it makes to "the human gain." Bankes's expansive "rapture" and Lily's appreciation of it directly counter the thrust of the narrowly nuclear formation Woolf's North Pargiter would identify in *The Years* (1937), for example, where "thirty years of being husband and wife" boil down to his aunt and uncle not being "interested in other people's children. . . . Only in their own; their own property; their own flesh and blood, which they would protect with the unsheathed claws of the primeval swamp," in a passage that demonstrates Woolf's capacity for primitivizing modern marriage.[7] Yet whatever else we might say about Mrs. Ramsay's mania for the marriage plot, at least Paul Rayley and Minta Doyle's engagement immerses her, too, in "that community of feeling with other people which emotion gives as if the walls of partition had become so thin that practically (the feeling was one of relief and happiness) it was all one stream, and chairs, tables, maps, were hers, were theirs, it did not matter whose" (115–16). Personal or individual happiness becomes a shared public affect.

Chief among Lily's own "unclassified affections" is her feeling for the Ramsays: to borrow James's way of regarding "the Lighthouse" once he finally reaches it, this is not "simply one thing" (189). More closely allied by the narrative with Cam and James than any of them knows, Lily finds early on that she must look down, "purposely, for only so could she keep steady, staying with the Ramsays. Directly one looked up and saw them, what she called 'being in love' flooded them" (50). Unable otherwise to maintain the impersonal appreciation she associates with the love that does not seek to "clutch its object," Lily must turn away. Like praising Mr. Ramsay's boots, or composing a scene, this becomes one of her chief strategies for preserving the aesthetic and emotional distance she seems to require. Having secured "her own exemption from the universal law" (53)—an exemption that her "Chinese eyes" (29) arguably signify from the start[8]—Lily successfully resists the heterosexual imperative seemingly foundational to Woolf's view of Victorian marriage. Her resolute singleness would appear to ratify the extension of the liberal ideal of individual and aesthetic autonomy to the middle-class woman. At novel's end, she achieves her "vision" (211), just as Mr. Ramsay and his two youngest children reach the lighthouse. All these narrative facts indicate that for the post-Victorian novelist, as Rachel Blau DuPlessis argues in *Writing beyond the Ending* (1985), the heroine's plot need not end in either marriage or death—or in a marriage that is death.

Yet Lily's affective situation radically shifts when she draws near enough for physical contact and does quite literally clutch *her* object, "her arms round Mrs. Ramsay's knees, close as she could get":

> What art was there, known to love or cunning, by which one pressed through into those secret chambers? What device for becoming, like waters poured into one jar, inextricably the same, one with the object one adored? Could the body achieve, or the mind, subtly mingling in the intricate passages of

---

7. Woolf, *The Years*, 338, 341.

8. On this point, see Seshagiri, "Orienting Virginia Woolf": "Woolf secures a new English feminism by attributing non-Western characteristics and perspectives to Lily, whose 'little Chinese eyes' exclude her socially and elevate her artistically" (67).

> the brain? or the heart? Could loving, as people called it, make her and Mrs. Ramsay one? for it was not knowledge but unity that she desired, not inscriptions on tablets, nothing that could be written in any language known to men, but intimacy itself, which is knowledge, she had thought, leaning her head on Mrs. Ramsay's knee. (54)

Seeking to overcome the distance that she otherwise wants to maintain, the physical "intimacy" and bodily contact represented in this moment convey the "mingling" especially of women's bodies that, as Marcus has illustrated, Victorian fiction so graphically portrays: not just Lizzie Hexam and Jenny Wren, but Dorothea Casaubon and Rosamond Lydgate, or Diana Warwick and Emma Dunstane, or Rachel West and Hester Gresley. That mingling is, in this case, both desired and feared. "Unity" with another, as putatively exemplified in heterosexual marriage, may well entail a loss of individual identity or erosion of boundaries, at least from Lily's perspective. She "led her victims, Lily felt, to the altar," comparing Mrs. Ramsay's marriage-making power to a witch's "spell" (103). Mrs. Ramsay herself invokes this same image when she ordains that "these lovers, these people entering into illusion glittering eyed, must be danced round with mockery, decorated with garlands" (102).

But nothing is, of course, simply one thing. And so the critique of heterosexual marriage and its plots in *To the Lighthouse* nonetheless proceeds: even as Lily's thinking about same-sex "intimacy" reconfigures some of the conventional meanings of Victorian marriage within a new frame, her terms would have struck Victorian readers as very familiar and, perhaps, familial. The wish to become "one with the object one adored," for instance, so as to become "inextricably the same," surely recalls the mixed figure of "one flesh," which grounded the spiritual, social, and biological meanings of marriage in the bodily contact of sexual intercourse, whereby two (and usually many more than two) become one.[9] That the Ramsays and their daughter at one moment symbolize and represent "marriage" to Lily, while at another she conceives them quite differently, suggests a comparable interplay of literal and symbolic in a single multivalent figure, like James's golden bowl.

But even in symbolizing the two made one by marriage who yet decidedly remain two, the Ramsays bear their burden of representativeness very lightly. "Meaning" arbitrarily or fortuitously "descends upon" them as if from on high, in the passage I cited above, momentarily endowing them with a "symbolic" function; but "the symbolical outline" just as quickly "sank down" as it had risen up. For all the weight this couple shoulders in the novel—and in the

9. I develop this point at length in *Family Likeness*, esp. 64–65.

tradition of the nineteenth-century novel that *To the Lighthouse,* like other fictions in Joseph Allen Boone's "counter tradition," brings to a close—the figurative language Woolf uses to describe the coming and going of "meaning" is not especially heavy. Darkness and light can both descend upon and sink down; the same could be said of fog, or mist, or dew. The novel conveys the temporary, transient quality of the "symbolical" function ascribed to the Ramsays' marriage via the weightlessness of these atmospheric entities. Those actual human events associated with marriage in this novel—sex and reproduction, to be sure, but also conquest, war, death—weigh on it a good deal more heavily. "In an instant," then, both Lily and the narrative voice thus acknowledge the cultural work that marriage has done, and continues to do, as a site at which the "simple, obvious, commonplace" stuff of ordinary life becomes a vehicle for multiple meanings in different historical moments.

BIBLIOGRAPHY

"The Acton Murder." *The Times,* April 8, 1847, accessed June 26, 2015. *The Times Digital Archive.*

"The Acton Murderess." *Lloyd's Weekly London Newspaper,* April 18, 1847, accessed June 4, 2013. *19th Century British Library Newspapers: Part II.*

Adams, James Eli. "Woman Red in Tooth and Claw: Nature and the Feminine in Tennyson and Darwin." *Victorian Studies* 33, no. 1 (1989): 7–27.

Ahmed, Sara. *The Promise of Happiness.* Durham, NC: Duke University Press, 2010.

Alam, Asiya. "Polygyny, Family, and Sharafat: Discourses amongst North Indian Muslims, circa 1870–1918." *Modern Asian Studies* 45, no. 3 (2011): 631–88.

Allen, R. T. "When Loyalty No Harm Meant." *Review of Metaphysics* 43, no. 2 (1989): 281–94.

Almost Canon. http://almost-canon.livejournal.com. Discussion forum.

Amin, Sonia Nishat. *The World of Muslim Women in Colonial Bengal.* Leiden: Brill, 1996.

Anderson, Amanda. *Tainted Souls and Painted Faces: The Rhetoric of Fallenness in Victorian Culture.* Ithaca, NY: Cornell University Press, 1993.

Anderson, Benedict. *Imagined Communities: Reflections on the Origin and Spread of Nationalism.* London: Verso, 1983.

Anderson, Perry. "Internationalism: A Breviary." *New Left Review* 14 (2002): 5–25.

Annual Report on the Administration of the Bengal Presidency for 1863–64. Calcutta: Military Orphan Press, 1865.

Anthony, Andrew. "*The Killing*: Meet Sophie Grabøl, the Star of the Hit Danish Crime Thriller." *The Guardian,* March 12, 2011, https://www.theguardian.com/tv-and-radio/2011/mar/13/the-killing-sofie-grabol-sarah-lund-interview?INTCMP=SRCH.

Archive of Our Own. https://archiveofourown.org. Open source repository for fan fiction contributed by users, created in 2008 by the Organization for Transformative Works.

Armstrong, Isobel. "Bodily Things and Thingly Bodies: Circumventing the Subject-Object Binary." In *Bodies and Things in Nineteenth-Century Literature and Culture,* edited by Katharina Boehm, 17–44. New York: Palgrave Macmillan, 2005.

Armstrong, Nancy. *Desire and Domestic Fiction: A Political History of the Novel.* New York: Oxford University Press, 1987.

"Assize Intelligence." *The Bristol Mercury,* July 26, 1856, accessed August 16, 2014. *19th Century British Library Newspapers: Part II.*

"Assize Intelligence." *The Morning Chronicle,* December 30, 1843, accessed August 16, 2014. *19th Century British Library Newspapers: Part II.*

Auchmuty, Rosemary. *A World of Girls: The Appeal of the Girls' School Story.* London: Women's Press, 1992.

Auerbach, Erich. "On the Serious Imitation of the Everyday." In Gustave Flaubert, *Madame Bovary,* translated by Eleanor Marx Aveling and edited by Margaret Cohen, 423–49. New York: Norton, 2004.

Auerbach, Nina. *Woman and the Demon: The Life of a Victorian Myth.* Boston: Harvard University Press, 1992.

Bailin, Miriam. *The Sickroom in Victorian Fiction: The Art of Being Ill.* Cambridge: Cambridge University Press, 1994.

Bakhtin, Mikhail M. "The *Bildungsroman* and Its Significance in the History of Realism (Toward a Historical Typology of the Novel)." In *Speech Genres and Other Late Essays.* 2nd ed. Translated by Vern W. McGee, 10–59. Austin: University of Texas Press, 1986.

Banerjee, Prathama. "The Politics of Contemporanising: Some Notes." http://mail.mail.sarai.net/pipermail/reader-list_mail.sarai.net/2011-March/028141.html.

Banerjee, Sukanya. "Troubling Conjugal Loyalties: The First Indian Novel in English and the Transimperial Network of Sensation." *Victorian Literature and Culture* 42, no. 3 (2014): 475–89.

Banfield, Ann. *The Phantom Table: Woolf, Fry, Russell, and the Epistemology of Modernism.* Cambridge: Cambridge University Press, 2000.

Barash, Carol L. "Virile Womanhood: Olive Schreiner's Narratives of a Master Race." In *Speaking of Gender,* edited by Elaine Showalter, 269–81. New York: Routledge, 1989.

Beale, Dorothea, Jane Frances Dove, and Lucy Helen Muriel Soulsby. *Work and Play in Girls' Schools, by Three Headmistresses.* 1898. London: Longmans, Green, 1901.

Beckingham, Kathleen M., J. Douglas Armstrong, Michael J. Texada, Ravi Munjaal, and Dean A. Baker. "Drosophila Melonogaster: The Model Organism of Choice for the Complex Biology of Multi-Cellular Organisms." *Gravitational and Space Biology* 18, no. 2 (2005): 1–13.

Beer, Gillian. *Darwin's Plots: Evolutionary Narrative in Darwin, George Eliot, and Nineteenth-Century Fiction.* 2nd ed. Cambridge; New York: Cambridge University Press, 2000.

———. *George Eliot.* Bloomington: Indiana University Press, 1986.

Beller, Anne-Marie. "Sensation Fiction in the 1850s." In *The Cambridge Companion to Sensation Fiction,* edited by Andrew Mangham, 7–20. Cambridge: Cambridge University Press, 2013.

Benson, Hugh H. *A Companion to Plato.* NY: Blackwell, 2005.

Bergonzi, Bernard. "Feminism and Femininity in *The Princess.*" In *The Major Victorian Poets: Reconsiderations,* edited by Isobel Armstrong, 35–50. Lincoln: University of Nebraska Press, 1969.

Berlant, Lauren. *Cruel Optimism*. Durham, NC: Duke University Press, 2011.

Berman Shari. *Understanding Social Democracy*. Washington, DC: Friedrich Ebert Foundation, 2005.

Bernstein, J. M., ed. *Classic and Romantic German Aesthetics*. Cambridge: Cambridge University Press, 2003.

Bernstein, Susan David. "Designs after Nature: Evolutionary Fashions, Animals, and Gender." In *Victorian Animal Dreams: Representations of Animals in Victorian Literature and Culture*, edited by Deborah Denenholz and Martin A. Danahay, 65–79. Aldershot, England: Ashgate, 2007.

Best, Stephen, and Sharon Marcus. "Surface Reading: An Introduction." *Representations* 108, no. 1 (2009): 1–21.

"The Best Thing in a Girl's Life": Early Women's Colleges in Fiction and Fact. Canaday Library, Bryn Mawr College, 2009, http://www.brynmawr.edu/library/exhibits/BestThing/bibliography.html.

Betensky, Carolyn. *Feeling for the Poor: Bourgeois Compassion, Social Action, and the Victorian Novel*. Charlottesville: University of Virginia Press, 2010.

Bittel, Helen. "Required Reading for Revolting Daughters? The New Girl Fiction of L. T. Meade." *Nineteenth Century Gender Studies* 2, no. 2 (2006), http://www.ncgsjournal.com/issue22/bittel.htm.

Bivona, Dan. "Richard F. Burton, Polygamy, and the Worlding of the American West." *Yearbook of English Studies* 41, no. 2 (2011): 73–93.

Blair, Tony. "Against Populism, the Center Must Hold." *The New York Times*, March 3, 2017, https://www.nytimes.com/2017/03/03/opinion/tony-blair-against-populism-the-center-must-hold.html?_r=0.

Blau DuPlessis, Rachel. *Writing beyond the Ending: Narrative Strategies of Twentieth-Century Women Writers*. Bloomington: Indiana University Press, 1985.

Boase, George Clement. "Hall, Anna Maria." In *Dictionary of National Biography*, 1885–1900, Volume 24, edited by Leslie Stephen and Sidney Lee, 54–55. London: Smith, Elder & Co., 1890.

Bode, Christoph. "Absolut Jena: A Second look at Lacoue-Labarthe's and Nancy's Representations of the Literary Theory of *Frühromantik*." In *Romanticism and Philosophy: Thinking with Literature*, edited by S. Laniel-Musitelli and T. Constantinesco, 19–39. Oxford: Routledge, 2015.

Bodenheimer, Rosemary. *The Politics of Story in Victorian Social Fiction*. Ithaca, NY: Cornell University Press, 1991.

Boes, Tobias. *Formative Fictions: Nationalism, Cosmopolitanism, and the Bildungsroman*. Ithaca, NY: Cornell University Press, 2012.

Bogen, Anna. *Women's University Fiction: 1880–1945*. London: Pickering & Chatto, 2013.

Boone, Joseph Allen. *Tradition Counter Tradition: Love and the Form of Fiction*. Chicago: University of Chicago Press, 1987.

Borgen. Directed by Søren Kragh-Jacobsen and Rumle Hammerich. Denmark: Danish Broadcasting Company (DR), 2010–13.

Borthwick, Meredith. *The Changing Role of Women in Bengal, 1849–1905*. Princeton, NJ: Princeton University Press, 1984.

Boumelha, Penny. *Thomas Hardy and Woman: Sexual Ideology and Narrative Form*. Sussex: Harvester, 1982.

Bowden, Peta. *Caring: Gender-Sensitive Ethics*. London: Routledge, 1997.

Bown, Nicola. "Introduction: Crying Over Little Nell." *19: Interdisciplinary Studies in the Long Nineteenth Century* 4 (2007), https://doi.org/10.16995/ntn.453.

Braddon, Mary Elizabeth. *Aurora Floyd.* Edited by P. D. Edwards. Oxford: Oxford University Press, 1996.

Brantlinger, Patrick. "What Is 'Sensational' about the 'Sensation Novel'?" *Nineteenth-Century Fiction* 37, no. 1 (June 1982): 1–28.

Brewer, David. *The Afterlife of Character, 1726–1825.* Philadelphia: University of Pennsylvania Press, 2005.

"The Broadwindsor Murderess." *The Morning Chronicle,* July 26, 1856, accessed August 16, 2014. *19th Century British Library Newspapers: Part II.*

Brontë, Charlotte. *Villette.* 1853. Harmondsworth: Penguin, 1979.

Bush, Julia. "'Special Strengths for Their Own Special Duties': Women, Higher Education and Gender Conservatism in Late Victorian Britain." *History of Education* 34, no. 4 (2005): 387–405.

Caird, Mona. *The Daughters of Danaus.* 1894. New York: The Feminist Press at the City University of New York, 1989.

———. *The Morality of Marriage and Other Essays on the Status and Destiny of Woman.* London: George Redway, 1897. Reprint, Cambridge: Cambridge University Press, 2010.

Campe, Rüdiger. "Form and Life in the Theory of the Novel." *Constellations* 18, no. 1 (2011): 53–66.

Carroll, David, ed. *George Eliot: The Critical Heritage.* 1971. New York: Routledge, 2005.

Cartwright, Justin. "Dickens: Nightmare Before Christmas." *Independent,* http://www.independent.co.uk/arts-entertainment/books/features/dickens-nightmare-before-christmas-6279773.html.

Cave, Terence. *Mignon's Afterlives: Crossing Cultures from Goethe to the Twenty-First Century.* Oxford: Oxford University Press, 2011.

Chakravarti, Sambuddha. "Changing Notions of Conjugal Relations in Nineteenth Century Bengal." In *Mind, Body, and Society: Life and Mentality in Colonial Bengal,* edited by Rajat Kanta Ray, 297–330. Calcutta: Oxford University Press, 1995.

Chapman, Alison. *Networking the Nation: British and American Women's Poetry and Italy, 1840–1870.* Oxford: Oxford University Press, 2015.

Chase, Karen, and Michael Levenson. *The Spectacle of Intimacy: A Public Life for the Victorian Family.* Princeton, NJ: Princeton University Press, 2000.

Chatterjee, Bankim Chandra. "Polygamy." In *Sociological Essays: Utilitarianism and Positivism in Bengal,* translated and edited by S. N. Mukherjee and Marian Maddern, 70–77. Calcutta: Rddhi-India, 1986.

———. *Rajmohan's Wife: A Novel by Bankim Chandra Chatterjee.* 1864. Edited by Meenakshi Mukherjee. New Delhi: Ravi Dayal, 1996.

———. "Samya." In *Sociological Essays: Utilitarianism and Positivism in Bengal,* translated and edited by S. N. Mukherjee and Marian Maddern, 83–112. Calcutta: Rddhi-India, 1986.

Chowdhury-Sengupta, Indira. "The Return of the Sati: A Note on Heroism and Domesticity in Colonial Bengal." *Resources for Feminist Research* 22, no. 3–4 (1993): 41–44.

Chrisman, Laura. "The Imperial Unconscious? Representations of Imperial Discourse." *Critical Quarterly* 32, no. 3 (1990): 38–58.

Christ, Carol. "Victorian Masculinity and the Angel in the House." In *A Widening Sphere: Changing Roles of Victorian Women,* edited by Martha Vicinus, 146–62. Bloomington: Indiana University Press, 1977.

Cicioni, Mirna. "Male Pair-Bonds and Female Desire in Fan Slash Writing." In *Theorising Fandom: Fans, Subculture and Identity,* edited by Cheryl Harris and Alison Alexander, 153–77. Cresskill, NJ: Hampton, 1998.

Clayton, Jay. *Charles Dickens in Cyberspace: The Afterlife of the Nineteenth Century in Postmodern Culture.* Oxford: Oxford University Press, 2003.

Cleere, Eileen. "Chaste Polygamy: Mormon Marriage and the Fantasy of Sexual Privacy in *East Lynne* and *Verner's Pride.*" *Victorian Studies* 57, no. 2 (2015): 199–224.

Cohen, Margaret. "Sentimental Communities." In *The Literary Channel: The Inter-National Invention of the Novel,* edited by Margaret Cohen and Carolyn Dever, 106–32. Princeton, NJ: Princeton University Press, 2002.

Colquhoun, Kate. *Taste: The Story of Britain through Its Cooking.* New York: Bloomsbury, 2007.

Condorcet, Marie-Jean-Antoine-Nicolas Caritat, Marquis de. *Outlines of an Historical View of the Progress of the Human Mind.* Philadelphia: Carey, 1796.

"Confession and Execution of Catherine Foster." *The Times,* April 19, 1847, accessed June 26, 2015. *The Times Digital Archive.*

"Confession of Catherine Foster." *The Bury and Norwich Post, and East Anglian,* April 7, 1847, accessed August 16, 2014. *19th Century British Library Newspapers: Part II.*

Corbett, Mary Jean. *Allegories of Union in Irish and English Writing, 1790–1870: Politics, History, and the Family from Edgeworth to Arnold.* Cambridge: Cambridge University Press, 2000.

———. *Family Likeness: Sex, Marriage, and Incest from Jane Austen to Virginia Woolf.* Ithaca, NY: Cornell University Press, 2008.

Corder, Nicholas. *Foul Deeds and Suspicious Deaths in Staffordshire & The Potteries.* Barnsley, South Yorkshire: Wharncliffe, 2006. Ebook.

Coward, Rosalind. *Patriarchal Precedents: Sexuality and Social Relations.* London: Routledge, 1983.

Cox, H. N. "The Late Execution at Dorchester." *The Times,* August 13, 1856, accessed August 16, 2014. *19th Century British Library Newspapers: Part II.*

Cox, R. G. *Thomas Hardy: The Critical Heritage.* New York: Barnes & Noble, 1970.

Cross, J. W. *George Eliot's Life as Related in Her Letters and Journals.* Vol. 2. New York: Harpers, 1885.

"Crown Court, Saturday. Poisoning a Husband." *The Bury and Norwich Post, and Suffolk Herald,* August 6, 1851, accessed August 16, 2014. *19th Century British Library Newspapers: Part II.*

Cruse, Amy. *The Victorians and Their Books.* London: George Allen and Unwin, 1935.

Culler, Dwight. *The Poetry of Tennyson.* New Haven, CT: Yale University Press, 1977.

Culler, Jonathan. "Genre: Lyric." In Warhol, ed., *The Work of Genre,* http://quod.lib.umich.edu/cgi/t/text/text-idx?c=acls;idno=heb90055.0001.001;rgn=div3;view=text;cc=acls;node=heb90055.0001.001%3A5.1.1.

Curtis, Jeni. "The Espaliered Girl: Pruning the Docile Body in *Aurora Floyd.*" In *Beyond Sensation: Mary Elizabeth Braddon in Context,* edited by Marlene Tromp, Pamela K. Gilbert, and Aeron Haynie, 77–92. Albany: State University of New York, 2000.

Cvetkovich, Ann. *Depression: A Public Feeling.* Durham, NC: Duke University Press, 2012.

———. "Public Feelings." *SAQ: South Atlantic Quarterly* 106, no. 3 (2007): 459–68.

Darwin, Charles. *The Descent of Man.* 1871. London: Penguin, 2004.

———. *The Origin of Species.* 1859. London: Penguin, 2009.

Davidson, Cathy, and Jessamyn Hatcher, eds. *No More Separate Spheres! A Next Wave American Studies Reader.* Durham, NC: Duke University Press, 2002.

Davis, Jeanie Lerche. "Family Dinners Are Important." *WebMD,* 2006, accessed July 5, 2017. http://www.webmd.com/a-to-z-guides/features/family-dinners-are-important.

Davis, Paul. *The Lives and Times of Ebenezer Scrooge.* New Haven, CT: Yale University Press, 1990.

Derrida, Jacques. *The Gift of Death.* Translated by David Wills. Chicago: University of Chicago Press, 1995.

Devi, Dayamayi. *Patibrata Dharma* (Religion of the Patibrata). Calcutta: Girish Vidyartana, 1870.

Dickens, Charles. *Bleak House.* 1853. London: Penguin, 1996.

———. *David Copperfield.* 1850. London: Penguin, 1996.

———. *Great Expectations.*1861. London: Penguin, 1996.

———. *Nicholas Nickleby.* 1839. London: Penguin, 1999.

———. *Our Mutual Friend.* 1865. Edited by Michael Cotsell. New York: Oxford University Press, 1989.

———. *Our Mutual Friend.* 1865. New York: Penguin Classics, 1997.

Dickensataleoftwocities. https://dickensataleoftwocities.wordpress.com. Reading group blog, a partnership between the Victorian Studies Centre at the University of Leicester and Dickens Journals Online.

"Dinner: 30 Minutes to a More Connected Family." *Aha!Parenting.com,* n.d., accessed June 25, 2017. http://www.ahaparenting.com/parenting-tools/family-life/dinner-connected-family.

Disraeli, Benjamin. *Coningsby, or, The New Generation.* 1844. Edited by Thom Braun. London: Penguin, 1983.

Doody, Margaret Anne. *The True Story of the Novel.* New Brunswick, NJ: Rutgers University Press, 1996.

Duff, David. *Romanticism and the Uses of Genre.* Oxford: Oxford University Press, 2009.

Duncan, Ian. *Modern Romance and Transformations of the Novel: The Gothic, Scott, Dickens.* Cambridge: Cambridge University Press, 1992.

Dyhouse, Carol. *Students: A Gendered History.* New York: Routledge, 2006.

Dzelzainis, Ella. "Radicalism and Reform." In *Oxford History of the Novel in English.* Vol. 3, *The Nineteenth Century Novel, 1820–1880,* edited by John Kucich and Jenny Bourne Taylor, 427–43. Oxford: Oxford University Press, 2012.

Edwards, Kim. "Unnameable Desire: Inter-female Intimacy in the Writings of Charles Dickens." PhD diss., University of Liverpool, 2013.

Eliot, George. *Daniel Deronda.* 1876. Edited by Terence Cave. London: Penguin, 1995.

———. *Essays and Leaves from a Note-book.* Vol. 21 of *The Writings of George Eliot.* Boston: Houghton Mifflin, 1908.

———. *Felix Holt, the Radical.* 1866. Edited by Lynda Mugglestone. London: Penguin, 1995.

———. *Middlemarch: A Study of Provincial Life.* 1871–72. Edited by Gregory Maertz. Ontario: Broadview Press, 2004.

———. *The Mill on the Floss.* 1860. Edited by Gordon S. Haight. Oxford: Oxford University Press, 1981.

———. *Romola.* 1862–62. Edited by Dorothea Barrett. London: Penguin, 2005.

Eller, Cynthia. *Gentlemen and Amazons: The Myth of Matriarchal Prehistory, 1861–1900.* Berkeley: University of California Press, 2011.

England, Maureen. "The Curious Case of Dolly Varden." Paper given at the 2015 British Association for Victorian Studies (BAVS) conference, Leeds, UK.

Esterhammer, Angela. *Romanticism and Improvisation, 1750–1850.* Cambridge: Cambridge University Press, 2008.

Esty, Jed. *Unseasonable Youth: Modernism, Colonialism and the Fiction of Development.* Oxford: Oxford University Press, 2011.

"Execution of Catherine Foster." *The Bury and Norwich Post, and East Anglian,* April 21, 1847, accessed June 4, 2013. *19th Century British Library Newspapers: Part II.*

"Execution of Elizabeth Martha Brown." *The Lancaster Gazette, and General Advertiser for Lancashire, Westmorland, Yorkshire, &c.,* August 16, 1856, accessed June 15, 2015. *19th Century British Library Newspapers: Part II.*

Fahnestock, Jeanne. "Bigamy: The Rise and Fall of a Convention." *Nineteenth-Century Fiction* 36 (1981): 47–71.

FanFiction. https://www.fanfiction.net. Discussion forum.

Fanlore. http://fanlore.org. Wiki.

Fasick, Laura. "Angels and Ingénues in Tennyson's *The Princess* and Gilbert and Sullivan's *Princess Ida.*" *Romanticism on the Net* 34–35 (2004), https://www.erudit.org/en/journals/ron/2004-n34-35-ron824/009437ar/.

———. "The Reform of Women's Education in Tennyson's *The Princess* and Gilbert and Sullivan's *Princess Ida.*" In *Gender and Victorian Reform,* edited by Anita Rose, 26–43. Newcastle upon Tyne: Cambridge Scholars, 2008.

Ferrall, Charles. "From Wells to John Berger: The Social Democratic Era of the Novel." In *The Cambridge History of the English Novel,* edited by Robert L. Caserio and Clement Hawes, 807–22. Cambridge: Cambridge University Press, 2011.

Festa, Lynn. *Sentimental Figures of Empire in Eighteenth-Century Britain and France.* Baltimore: Johns Hopkins University Press, 2006.

Flaubert, Gustave. *Madame Bovary.* 1857. Edited by Margaret Cohen. Translated by Eleanor Marx Aveling and Paul de Man. 2nd ed. New York: Norton, 2004.

Forster, E. M. *Aspects of the Novel.* New York: Rosetta Books, 2002.

Foucault, Michel. *The History of Sexuality.* Vol. 1, *An Introduction.* New York: Vintage Books, 1978.

Fowler, Alastair. *Kinds of Literature: An Introduction to the Theory of Genres and Modes.* Cambridge, MA: Harvard University Press, 1982.

Franklin, Caroline. *Female Romantics: Nineteenth-Century Women Novelists and Byronism.* London: Routledge, 2012.

Fraser, Derek. *The Evolution of the British Welfare State: A History of Social Policy since the Industrial Revolution.* 2nd ed. London: Macmillan, 1984.

Fraser, Robert. *The Making of "The Golden Bough": The Origins and Growth of an Argument.* New York: St. Martin's, 1990.

Frawley, Maria. *Invalidism and Identity in Nineteenth-Century Britain.* Chicago: University of Chicago Press, 2004.

Frazer, James G. *The Golden Bough: A Study in Comparative Religion.* 2 vols. London: Macmillan, 1890.

Frederickson, Kathleen. *The Ploy of Instinct: Victorian Sciences of Nature and Sexuality in Liberal Governance.* New York: Fordham University Press, 2014.

Freeden, Michael. *The New Liberalism: An Ideology of Social Reform.* Oxford: Clarendon, 1978.

Freedgood, Elaine. *The Ideas in Things: Fugitive Meaning in the Victorian Novel.* Chicago: University of Chicago Press, 2006.

Frost, Ginger. "Bigamy and Cohabitation in Victorian England." *Journal of Family History* 22, no. 3 (1997): 286–306.

Frow, John. "'Reproducibles, Rubrics, and Everything You Need': Genre Theory Today." *PMLA* 122, no. 5 (2007): 1626–34.

Frye, Northrop. *Anatomy of Criticism: Four Essays.* Princeton, NJ: Princeton University Press, 1957.

Fuller, Catherine M. *Across the Campus: A Story of College Life.* 1897. New York: Scribner, 1899. N. pag. Kindle file.

Furneaux, Holly. *Queer Dickens: Erotics, Families, Masculinities.* New York: Oxford University Press, 2009.

Gallagher, Catherine. *The Body Economic: Life, Death, and Sensation in Political Economy and the Victorian Novel.* Princeton, NJ: Princeton University Press, 2006.

———. *The Industrial Reformation of English Fiction: Social Discourse and Narrative Form, 1832–1867.* Chicago: University of Chicago Press, 1985.

———. "*Tess of the d'Urbervilles*: Hardy's Anthropology of the Novel." In *Tess of the d'Urbervilles,* edited by John Paul Riquelme, 422–40. Boston: Bedford/St. Martin's, 1998.

Garrett, Peter K. *The Victorian Multiplot Novel: Studies in a Dialogical Form.* New Haven, CT: Yale University Press, 1980.

Gates, Barbara T., and Ann B. Shteir, eds. *Natural Eloquence: Women Reinscribe Science.* Madison: University of Wisconsin Press, 1997.

Gert, Bernard. "Loyalty and Morality." In *Loyalty,* edited by Sanford Levinson, Joel Parker, and Paul Woodruff, 3–21. New York: New York University Press, 2013.

Gilbert, Pamela, ed. *Companion to Sensation Fiction.* Malden, MA: Wiley-Blackwell, 2011.

Gilbert, Sandra, and Susan Gubar. *No Man's Land: The Place of the Woman Writer in the Twentieth Century.* Vol. 2, *Sexchanges.* New Haven, CT: Yale University Press, 1989.

Gilligan, Carol. *In a Different Voice.* Cambridge, MA: Harvard University Press, 1982.

Glatt, Carra. "When Found, Make a Note Of: Tracing the Source of a Dickensian Legend." Forthcoming, *Nineteenth-Century Studies,* 28.

Goethe, Johann Wolfgang von. *Wilhelm Meister's Apprenticeship.* 1796. Translated by E. Blackall. Princeton, NJ: Princeton University Press, 1995.

Goodlad, Lauren M. E. "Afterword." In *Television for Victorianists,* edited by Caroline Levine. Special issue of *RaVon: Romanticism and Victorianism on the Net* 63 (2013), http://www.erudit.org/en/journals/ravon/2013-n63-n63/1025621ar/.

———. *The Victorian Geopolitical Aesthetic: Realism, Sovereignty and Transnational Experience.* Oxford: Oxford University Press, 2015.

———. *Victorian Literature and the Victorian State: Character and Governance in a Liberal Society.* Baltimore: Johns Hopkins University Press, 2003.

Green, Shoshanna, Cynthia Jenkins, and Henry Jenkins. "'Normal Female Interest in Men Bonking': Selections from *The Terra Nostra Underground* and *Strange Bedfellows.*" In *Theorising Fandom: Fans, Subculture and Identity,* edited by Cheryl Harris and Alison Alexander, 9–38. Cresskill, NJ: Hampton, 1998.

Green, T. H. *Lectures on the Principles of Political Obligation and Other Writings.* Edited by Paul Harris and John Morrow. Cambridge: Cambridge University Press, 1986.

Greiner, Rae. *Sympathetic Realism in Nineteenth-Century British Fiction.* Baltimore: Johns Hopkins University Press, 2012.

Grosz, Elizabeth. *Becoming Undone: Darwinian Reflections on Life, Politics, and Art.* Durham, NC: Duke University Press, 2011.

Guerlac, Suzanne. "Writing the Nation (Mme. de Staël)." *French Forum* 30, no. 3 (2005): 43–56.

The Habits of Good Society: A Handbook of Etiquette for Ladies and Gentlemen. London: James Hogg and Sons, 1859.

Hager, Kelly. *Dickens and the Rise of Divorce: The Failed-Marriage Plot and the Novel Tradition.* Burlington: Ashgate, 2010.

Haggard, H. Rider. "About Fiction." *Contemporary Review* 51 (1887): 172–80.

———. *She.* 1886. Edited by Daniel Karlin. Oxford: Oxford University Press, 1991.

Hall, Catherine. *Civilising Subjects: Metropole and Colony in the English Imagination, 1830–1867.* Chicago: University of Chicago Press, 2002.

Hammerich, Camilla. *The "Borgen" Experience: Creating TV Drama the Danish Way.* London: Arrow Films, 2015.

Han, Carrie. "Pickwick's Other Papers: Continually Reading Dickens." *Victorian Literature and Culture* 44, no. 1 (2016): 19–41.

Hardy, Barbara Nathan. *The Novels of George Eliot: A Study in Form.* 1959. Reprint edition. London: University of London Press, 1973.

Hardy, Thomas. "Candour in English Fiction." *New Review* 2 (January 1890): 15–21.

———. *Jude the Obscure.* 1895. Edited by Dennis Taylor and Patricia Ingham. London: Penguin, 2007.

———. *Tess of the d'Urbervilles.* 1891. Edited by John Paul Riquelme. Boston: Bedford/St. Martin's, 1998.

———. *Thomas Hardy's Public Voice: The Essays, Speeches, and Miscellaneous Prose.* Edited by Michael Millgate. Oxford: Clarendon, 2001.

Harrison, Mary-Catherine. "The Paradox of Fiction and the Ethics of Empathy: Reconceiving Dickens's Realism." *Narrative* 16, no. 3 (2008): 256–78.

Harvie, Christopher. *The Centre of Things: Political Fiction in Britain from Disraeli to the Present.* London: Unwin Hyman, 1991.

Hayward, Jennifer. *Consuming Pleasures: Active Audiences and Serial Fictions from Dickens to Soap Opera.* Lexington: University Press of Kentucky, 1997.

Hegel, G. W. F. *Aesthetics: Lectures on Fine Art.* 1835. Translated by T. M. Knox. 2 vols. Oxford: Oxford University Press, 1975.

———. *Greek Philosophy*. Vol. 2 of *Lectures on the History of Philosophy 1825–6*. Translated and edited by Robert F. Brown. Oxford: Oxford University Press, 2006.

Heilman, Ann. *New Woman Strategies: Sarah Grand, Olive Schreiner, and Mona Caird*. Manchester: Manchester University Press, 2004.

Held, Virginia. *The Ethics of Care: Personal, Political, and Global*. New York: Oxford University Press, 2006.

———. *Feminist Morality: Transforming Culture, Society, and Politics*. Chicago: University Chicago Press, 1993.

Hellekson, Karen, and Kristina Busse, eds. *The Fan Fiction Studies Reader*. Iowa City: University of Iowa Press, 2014.

Heller, Deborah. *Literary Sisterhoods: Imagining Women Artists*. Montreal: McGill-Queen's University Press, 2005.

Helsinger, Elizabeth K., Robin Lauterbach Sheets, and William Veeder. *The Woman Question: Social Issues, 1837–1883*. 3 vols. Chicago: University of Chicago Press, 1989.

Henry, Nancy. *The Life of George Eliot: A Critical Biography*. Malden, MA: Wiley-Blackwell, 2012.

Herbert, Christopher. *Victorian Relativity: Radical Thought and Scientific Discovery*. Chicago: University of Chicago Press, 2001.

———. *War of No Pity: The Indian Mutiny and Victorian Trauma*. Princeton, NJ: Princeton University Press, 2008.

Herder, Johann Gottfried. *Outlines of a Philosophy of the History of Man*. Translated by T. O. Churchill. London: Johnson, 1800.

———. *Philosophical Writings*. Edited by Michael N. Forster. Cambridge: Cambridge University Press, 2002.

Hillman, Susanne. "Men with Muskets, Women with Lyres: Nationality, Citizenship, and Gender in the Writings of Germaine de Staël." *Journal of the History of Ideas* 72, no. 2 (2011): 231–54.

Hills, Matt. *Fan Cultures*. New York: Routledge, 2002.

Hilton, J. L. "Andrew Lang, Comparative Anthropology and the Classics in the African Romances of Rider Haggard." *Akroterion* 56 (2011): n. pag. Accessed July 30, 2015.

Hinz, Evelyn J. "Rider Haggard's *She*: An Archetypal 'History of Adventure.'" *Studies in the Novel: A Forum on Fiction* 4, no. 3 (Fall 1972): 416–31.

Hirsch, Pam. "Barbara Leigh Smith Bodichon: Feminist Leader and Founder of the First University College for Women." In *Practical Visionaries: Women, Education, and Social Progress, 1790–1830*, edited by Pam Hirsch and Mary Hilton, 84–100. New York: Routledge, 2000.

Hirshman, Linda. "A 'Very Hostile' Response to Anne-Marie Slaughter." *The Atlantic Monthly*, July 5, 2012, https://www.theatlantic.com/business/archive/2012/07/a-very-hostile-response-to-anne-marie-slaughter/259425/.

Hobhouse, L. T. *Liberalism*. 1911. Oxford: Oxford University Press, 1964.

———. *The World in Conflict*. London: Unwin, 1915.

Holmes, John. "Darwinism, Feminism, and the Sonnet Sequence: Meredith's 'Modern Love.'" *Victorian Poetry* 48, no. 4 (2010): 523–38.

Hughes, Linda, and Michael Lund. *The Victorian Serial*. Charlottesville: University Press of Virginia, 1991.

Hughes, Winifred. *The Maniac in the Cellar: Sensation Novels of the 1860s*. Princeton, NJ: Princeton University Press, 1980.

Hühn, Peter. "Functions and Forms of Eventfulness in Narrative Fiction." In *Theorizing Narrativity*, edited by John Pier and José Ángel García Landa, 141–64. Berlin: Walter de Gruyter, 2008.

"Imperial Parliament." *The Morning Post*, April 20, 1847, accessed June 4, 2013. *19th Century British Library Newspapers: Part II.*

Innes, Sherrie. *Intimate Communities: Representation and Social Transformation in Women's College Fiction, 1895–1910*. Madison: University of Wisconsin Press, 1995

Jacobus, Mary. "Tess: The Making of a Pure Woman." In *Tearing the Veil: Essays on Femininity*, edited by Susan Lipshitz, 77–92. Boston: Routledge, 1978.

Jameson, Fredric. *Antinomies of Realism*. London: Verso, 2013.

Jamison, Anne. *Fic: Why Fanfiction Is Taking Over the World*. Dallas: BenBella Books, 2013.

Jann, Rosemary. "Darwin and the Anthropologists: Sexual Selection and Its Discontents." *Victorian Studies* 37, no. 2 (1994): 287–306.

———. "Revising the Descent of Woman: Eliza Burt Gamble." In *Natural Eloquence: Women Reinscribe Science*, edited by Barbara T. Gates and Ann B. Shteir, 147–63. Madison: University of Wisconsin Press, 1997.

Jenkins, Henry. *Fans, Bloggers, and Gamers: Exploring Participatory Culture*. New York: New York University Press, 2006.

———. *Textual Poachers: TV Fans and Participatory Culture*. New York: Routledge, 1992.

John, Juliet. *Dickens and Mass Culture*. Oxford: Oxford University Press, 2010.

Kames (Henry Home, Lord Kames). *Sketches of the History of Man Considerably enlarged by the last additions and corrections of the author.* 1774. Edited by James A. Harris. 3 vols. Indianapolis, IN: Liberty Fund, 2007.

Kaplan, Cora. "*Aurora Leigh*." In *Feminist Criticism and Social Change: Sex, Class and Race in Literature and Culture*, edited by D. Rosenfelt and J. Newton, 146–51. London: Routledge, 2013.

Kaplan, Fred. *Sacred Tears: Sentimentality in Victorian Literature*. Princeton, NJ: Princeton University Press, 1987.

Kaye, Richard A. *The Flirt's Tragedy: Desire without End in Victorian and Edwardian Fiction*. Charlottesville: University Press of Virginia, 2002.

Keen, Suzanne. *Empathy and the Novel*. New York: Oxford University Press, 2007.

Kettle, Arnold. *An Introduction to the English Novel*. Vol. 2, *Henry James to the Present Day*. London: Hutchinson University Library, 1953.

Kidd, David, Martino Ongis, and Emanuele Castano. "On Literary Fiction and Its Effects on Theory of Mind." *Scientific Study of Literature* 6, no. 1 (2016): 42–58.

Kilham, John. *Tennyson and "The Princess": Reflections of an Age*. London: Athlone, 1958.

Kincaid, James. *Tennyson's Major Poems: The Comic and Ironic Patterns*. New Haven, CT: Yale University Press, 1975.

Kittay, Eva Feder. "When Caring Is Just and Justice Is Caring." In *The Subject of Care: Feminist Perspectives on Dependency*, edited by Eva Feder Kittay and Ellen K. Feder, 257–76. Lanham, MD: Rowman & Littlefield, 2002.

Klettke, Cornelia. "Germaine De Staël: *Corinne Ou L'Italie:* Grenzüberschreitung und Verschmelzung der Künste im Sinne der frühromantischen Universalpoesie." *Romanische Forschungen* 115, no. 2 (2003): 171–93.

Knelman, Judith. *Twisting in the Wind: The Murderess and the English Press*. Toronto: University of Toronto Press, 1998.

Kontje, Todd. *The German Bildungsroman: History of a National Genre.* Columbia, SC: Camden House, 1993.

Kornfield, Sarah. "Re-Solving Crimes: A Cycle of TV Detective Partnerships." In *Cycles, Sequels, Spin-Offs, Remakes, and Reboots: Multiplicities in Film and Television,* edited by Amanda Ann Klein and E. Barton Palmer, 202–21. Austin: University of Texas University Press, 2016.

Kucich, John. "Appealing vs. Arguing in *Felix Holt*: From Paternalism to the Welfare State in Social Problem Fiction." Draft manuscript. May 23, 2016.

———. *Imperial Masochism: British Fiction, Fantasy, and Social Class.* Princeton, NJ: Princeton University Press, 2007.

Kurnick, David. "*Felix Holt*: Love in the Time of Politics." In *A Companion to George Eliot,* edited by Amanda Anderson and Harry Shaw, 141–52. West Sussex: Wiley-Blackwell, 2013.

———. "Unspeakable George Eliot." *Victorian Literature and Culture* 38, no. 2 (2010): 489–509.

Lacoue-Labarthe, Philippe, and Jean-Luc Nancy. *The Literary Absolute: The Theory of Literature in German Romanticism.* Translated by P. Barnard and C. Lester. Albany: State University of New York Press, 1988.

Laird, J. T. *The Shaping of "Tess of the d'Urbervilles."* Oxford: Clarendon, 1975.

"Lancaster Assizes." *The Preston Guardian etc,* March 9, 1867, accessed May 5, 2014. *19th Century British Library Newspapers: Part II.*

Lang, Andrew. *Custom and Myth.* London: Longmans, Green, 1884.

———. "Realism and Romance." *The Contemporary Review* 52 (1887): 683–93.

"The Late Murder of a Husband by His Wife Three Weeks after Marriage." *The Morning Post,* April 12, 1847, accessed August 16, 2014. *19th Century British Library Newspapers: Part II.*

"The Late Poisoning Case in Suffolk." *The Morning Post,* April 5, 1847, accessed August 16, 2014. *19th Century British Library Newspapers: Part II.*

Lavelle, Ashley. *The Death of Social Democracy: Political Consequences in the 21st Century.* London: Routledge, 2008.

"Law and Assize Intelligence." *The Northern Star and National Trades' Journal,* April 3, 1847, accessed August 16, 2014. *19th Century British Library Newspapers: Part II.*

Lawrence, D. H. "Study of Thomas Hardy." In *Phoenix: The Posthumous Papers of D. H. Lawrence,* edited by Edward D. McDonald, 398–516. 1936. New York: Viking, 1968.

Leckie, Barbara. *Culture and Adultery: The Novel, the Newspaper, and the Law, 1857–1914.* Philadelphia: University of Pennsylvania Press, 1999.

Ledger, Sally. *The New Woman: Fiction and Feminism at the Fin de Siècle.* Manchester: Manchester University Press, 1997.

Lesjak, Carolyn. *Working Fictions: A Genealogy of the Victorian Novel.* Durham, NC: Duke University Press, 2006.

Levine, Caroline. *Forms: Whole, Rhythm, Hierarchy, Network.* Princeton, NJ: Princeton University Press, 2015.

Levine, Caroline, and Mario Ortiz-Robles, eds. *Narrative Middles: Navigating the Nineteenth-Century British Novel.* Columbus: The Ohio State University Press, 2011.

Levine, George. *Darwin and the Novelists.* Chicago: University of Chicago Press, 1987.

Lewis, Lina M. *Germaine de Staël, George Sand, and the Victorian Woman Artist.* Columbia: University of Missouri Press, 2003.

Lindgren, Gunilla. *Higher Education for Girls in North American College Fiction 1886–1912*. Lund Studies in English 110. Lund, Sweden: Department of English, Lund University, 2005.

Litvack, Leon. "Dickens's Dream and the Conception of Character." *The Dickensian* 103, no. 1 (2007): 5–36.

Livesey, Ruth. *Writing the Stage Coach Nation: Locality on the Move in Nineteenth-Century British Literature*. Oxford: Oxford University Press, 2017.

"Lloyd's Weekly Newspaper." *Lloyd's Weekly London Newspaper*, April 4, 1847, accessed August 16, 2014. *19th Century British Library Newspapers: Part II*.

"Local News." *The Blackburn Standard*, March 13, 1867, accessed May 5, 2014. *19th Century British Library Newspapers: Part II*.

Loesberg, Jonathan. "The Ideology of Form in Sensation Fiction." *Representations* 13, no. 1 (1986): 115–38.

Lokke, Kari. *Tracing Women's Romanticism: Gender, History, and Transcendence*. London: Routledge, 2004.

Lowe, Brigid. *Victorian Fiction and the Insights of Sympathy: An Alternative to the Hermeneutics of Suspicion*. London: Anthem, 2007.

Lukács, Georg. *The Historical Novel*. Translated by Hannah Mitchell and Stephen Mitchell. Lincoln: University of Nebraska Press, 1983.

———. *The Theory of the Novel: A Historico-Philosophical Essay on the Forms of Great Epic Literature*. Translated by Anna Bostock. Cambridge, MA: MIT Press, 1971.

Lukes, Steven. "The Meanings of Individualism." *Journal of the History of Ideas* 32, no. 1 (1971): 45–66.

Luy, Marc. "A Matter of Lifestyle." *Project M*. July 3, 2012, accessed November 30, 2015. http://projectm-online.com.

Maine, Henry. *Ancient Law: Its Connection with the Early History of Society and Its Relation to Modern Ideas*. 1861. New York: Dorset, 1986.

Majumdar, Rochona. *Marriage and Modernity: Family Values in Colonial Bengal*. Durham, NC: Duke University Press, 2009.

Malan, S. C., Vicar of Broadwindsor. "The Late Execution at Dorchester." *The Times*, August 23, 1856, accessed August 16, 2014. *19th Century British Library Newspapers: Part II*.

Mallett, Frederick. "The Late Execution at Dorchester." *The Times*, August 16, 1856, accessed August 16, 2014. *19th Century British Library Newspapers: Part II*.

"A Man Murdered by His Wife." *The Times*, October 30, 1866, accessed May 5, 2014. *19th Century British Library Newspapers: Part II*.

Mangham, Andrew, ed. *The Cambridge Companion to Sensation Fiction*. Cambridge: Cambridge University Press, 2013.

Mann, Abigail. "Of 'Ologies and 'Isms: Mona Caird Rewriting Authority." In *New Woman Writers, Authority and the Body*, edited by Melissa Purdue and Stacey Floyd, 43–62. Newcastle upon Tyne, England: Cambridge Scholars, 2009.

Mansel, Henry. "Sensation Novels." *Quarterly Review* (April 1863): 483–91.

Marchalonis, Shirley. *College Girls: A Century in Fiction*. New Brunswick, NJ: Rutgers University Press, 1995.

Marcus, Sharon. *Between Women: Friendship, Desire, and Marriage in Victorian England*. Princeton, NJ: Princeton University Press, 2007.

Martell, Jessica. "The Dorset Dairy, the Pastoral and Thomas Hardy's *Tess of the d'Urbervilles.*" *Nineteenth Century Literature* 68 (2013): 64–89.

Mason, Emma. "Feeling Dickensian Feeling." *19: Interdisciplinary Studies in the Long Nineteenth Century* 4 (2007), https://doi.org/10.16995/ntn.454.

Matus, Jill. "The 'Eastern-Woman Question': Martineau and Nightingale Visit the Harem." *Nineteenth-Century Contexts* 21, no. 1 (1999): 63–87.

Maurer, Sara L. *The Dispossessed State: Narratives of Ownership in Nineteenth-Century Britain and Ireland.* Baltimore: Johns Hopkins University Press, 2012.

Maurice, F. D. *Queen's College, London: Its Objects and Methods.* London: Francis and John Rivington, 1848.

McAleavey, Maia. *The Bigamy Plot: Sensation and Convention in the Victorian Novel.* Cambridge: Cambridge University Press, 2015.

———. "The Plot of Bigamous Return." *Representations* 123, no. 1 (2013): 87–116.

McClintock, Anne. *Imperial Leather: Race, Gender and Sexuality in the Colonial Context.* New York: Routledge, 1995.

McCormack, Matthew. "Rethinking 'Loyalty' in Eighteenth-Century Britain." *Journal for Eighteenth Century Studies* 35, no. 3 (2012): 407–21.

McLennan, John F. *Primitive Marriage: An Inquiry into the Origin of the Form of Capture in Marriage Ceremonies.* 1865. Edited by Peter Rivière. Chicago: University of Chicago Press, 1970.

Meade, L. T. *A Sweet Girl Graduate.* 1891. New York: New York Book Company, 1910.

Meadowsong, Zena. "Thomas Hardy and the Machine: The Mechanical Deformation of Narrative Realism in *Tess of the d'Urbervilles.*" *Nineteenth Century Literature* 64 (2009): 225–48.

Menke, Richard. *Telegraphic Realism: Victorian Fiction and Other Information Systems.* Stanford, CA: Stanford University Press, 2008.

Michie, Elsie B. *The Vulgar Question of Money: Heiresses, Materialism, and the Novel of Manners from Jane Austen to Henry James.* Baltimore: Johns Hopkins University Press, 2011.

Michie, Helena. "Who Is This in Pain? Scarring, Disfigurement, and Female Identity in *Bleak House* and *Our Mutual Friend.*" *Novel: A Forum on Fiction* 22, no. 2 (1989): 199–212.

Michie, Helena, and Robyn Warhol. *Love among the Archives: Writing the Lives of Sir George Scharf, Victorian Bachelor.* Edinburgh: Edinburgh University Press, 2015.

Mill, John Stuart. "Essay on Marriage and Divorce." 1832. In *John Stuart Mill and Harriet Taylor Mill: Essays on Sex Equality*, edited by Alice M. Rossi, 67–84. Chicago: University of Chicago Press, 1970.

———. *On Liberty and The Subjection of Women.* Edited by Alan Ryan. London: Penguin, 2007.

———. "The Subjection of Women." 1869. In *On Liberty and Other Writings*, edited by Stefan Collini. Cambridge: Cambridge University Press, 1989.

Millar, John. *The Origin of the Distinction of Ranks; or, An Inquiry into the Circumstances which give rise to Influence and Authority in the Different Members of Society.* 1779. Edited by Aaron Garrett. Indianapolis, IN: Liberty Fund, 2006.

Miller, Andrew. "'A Case of Metaphysics': Counterfactuals, Realism, *Great Expectations.*" *ELH* 79, no. 3 (2012): 773–96.

Miller, D. A. *Bringing Out Roland Barthes.* Berkeley: University of California Press, 1992.

Millgate, Jane. *Walter Scott: The Making of the Novelist.* Edinburgh: Edinburgh University Press, 1984.

Mitchell, Sally. *The New Girl: Girls' Culture in England, 1880–1915.* New York: Columbia University Press, 1995.

Mittell, Jason. *Complex TV: The Poetics of Contemporary Television Storytelling.* New York: New York University Press, 2015.

Moers, Ellen. *Literary Women.* New York: Doubleday, 1976.

Moi, Toril. "A Woman's Desire to Be Known: Expressivity and Silence in *Corinne.*" In *Untrodden Regions of the Mind: Romanticism and Psychoanalysis,* edited by Ghislaine McDayter, 143–75. Lewisburg, PA: Bucknell University Press, 2002.

Monsman, Gerald. "Of Diamonds and Deities: Social Anthropology in H. Rider Haggard's *King Solomon's Mines.*" *English Literature in Transition 1880–1920* 43, no. 3 (2000): 280–97.

Montgomery, L. M. "A Girl's Place at Dalhousie College, 1896." *Atlantis: A Women's Studies Journal* 5, no. 1 (1979): 146–53.

Montiglio, Silvia. *Wandering in Ancient Greek Culture.* Chicago: University of Chicago Press, 2005.

Moody, Chris. "Bernie Sanders's American Dream Is in Denmark." *CNN Politics,* February 17, 2016, http://www.cnn.com/2016/02/17/politics/bernie-sanders-2016-denmark-democratic-socialism/.

Moretti, Franco. *Distant Reading.* London: Verso, 2013.

———. *The Way of the World: The Bildungsroman in European Culture.* Translated by Albert Sbragia. New York: Verso, 1987.

[Morley, John]. "*Felix Holt: The Radical.*" *Saturday Review* 21 (June 16, 1866): 722–24.

Morgenstern, Karl. "On the Nature of the Bildungsroman." Translated by Tobias Boes. *PMLA* 124, no. 2 (2009): 647–59.

Müller, F. Max. *The Science of Language.* London: Longmans, Green, 1899.

"The Murder by Poisoning.-Sudbury, Dec. 1." *The Times,* December 3, 1846, accessed June 26, 2015. *The Times Digital Archive.*

Nelson, Claudia. *Precocious Children and Childish Adults: Age Inversion in Victorian Literature.* Baltimore: Johns Hopkins University Press, 2012.

Nightingale, Florence. *Notes on Nursing: What It Is, and What It Is Not.* London: Harrison, 1860.

Noddings, Nel. *Caring: A Feminine Approach to Ethics and Moral Education.* Berkeley: University of California Press, 1984.

———. *Starting at Home: Caring and Social Policy.* Berkeley: University of California Press, 2002.

Norcia, Megan A. "Performing Victorian Womanhood: Elsie Fogerty Stages Tennyson's *Princess* in Girls' Schools." *Victorian Literature and Culture* 41, no. 1 (2013): 1–20.

Norton, Robert E. "The Aesthetic Education of Humanity: George Eliot's *Romola* and Schiller's Theory of Tragedy." *Journal of Aesthetic Education* 25, no. 4 (1991): 3–20.

Owenson, Sydney. *The Wild Irish Girl: A National Tale.* 1806. Edited by Claire Connolly and Stephen Copley. London: Routledge, 2000.

Pacini, Giulia. "Hidden Politics in Germaine de Staël's *Corinne ou l'Italie.*" *French Forum* 24, no. 2 (1999): 163–77.

Pandey, Gyan. "Can a Muslim Be an Indian?" *Comparative Studies in History and Society* 41, no. 4 (1999): 608–29.

Pateman, Carole. *The Problem of Political Obligation: A Critique of Liberal Theory.* Oxford: Polity, 1985.

Paxton, Nancy. "Mobilizing Chivalry: Rape in the British Novels about the Indian Uprising of 1857." *Victorian Studies* 36, no. 1 (1992): 5–30.

Percival, Alicia C. *The English Miss To-Day & Yesterday: Ideas, Methods, and Personalities in the Education and Upbringing of Girls during the Last Hundred Years.* London: Harrap, 1939.

Perry, Ruth. *Novel Relations: The Transformation of Kinship in English Literature and Culture 1748–1814.* Cambridge: Cambridge University Press, 2004.

Pfau, Thomas. "*Bildungsspiele*: Vicissitudes of Socialization in *Wilhelm Meister's Apprenticeship.*" *European Romantic Review* 21, no. 5 (2010): 567–87.

Phalèse, Hubert de, ed. *Corinne à la page.* Paris: Nizet, 1999.

Philp, Robert Kemp. *The Domestic World: A Guide to Social Economy.* London: Spottiswoode, 1872.

Plotz, John. *Portable Property: Victorian Culture on the Move.* Princeton, NJ: Princeton University Press, 2008.

Poulet, Georges. "The Role of Improvisation in *Corinne.*" Translated by Kevin Clark and Richard Macksey. *ELH* 41, no. 4 (1974): 602–12.

Psomiades, Kathy Alexis. "*He Knew He Was Right*: The Sensational Tyranny of the Sexual Contract and the Problem of Liberal Progress." In *The Politics of Gender in Anthony Trollope's Novels: New Readings for the Twenty-First Century,* edited by Margaret Markwick, Deborah Denenholz Morse, and Regenia Gagnier, 31–44. Burlington, VT: Ashgate, 2009.

———. "Heterosexual Exchange and Other Victorian Fictions: *The Eustace Diamonds* and Victorian Anthropology." *Novel: A Forum on Fiction* 33, no. 1 (1999): 93–118.

———. "Hidden Meaning: Andrew Lang, H. Rider Haggard, Sigmund Freud, and Interpretation." *RaVon: Romanticism and Victorianism on the Net* 64 (2013): n. pag. Accessed August 23, 2015.

———. "The Marriage Plot in Theory." *Novel: A Forum on Fiction* 43, no. 1 (2010): 53–59.

Pykett, Lyn. "The Cause of Women and the Course of Fiction: The Case of Mona Caird." In *Gender Roles and Sexuality in Victorian Literature,* edited by Christopher Parker, 128–42. Aldershot: Scolar, 1995.

Radford, Andrew. *Thomas Hardy and the Survivals of Time.* Hampshire: Ashgate, 2003.

Rajan, Supritha. *A Tale of Two Capitalisms: Sacred Economics in Nineteenth-Century Britain.* Ann Arbor: University of Michigan Press, 2015.

Redfield, Marc. *Phantom Formations: Aesthetic Ideology and the Bildungsroman.* Ithaca, NY: Cornell University Press, 1996.

Redvall, Eva Novrup. *Writing and Producing Television Drama in Demark: From "The Kingdom" to "The Killing."* Houndsmill: Palgrave, 2013.

Reid, Julia. "'She-who-must-be-obeyed': Anthropology and Matriarchy in H. Rider Haggard's *She.*" *Journal of Victorian Culture* 20, no. 3 (2015): 357–74.

Reimer, Mavis. "Traditions of the School Story." In *The Cambridge Companion to Children's Literature,* edited by M. O. Grenby and Andrea Immel, 209–25. New York: Cambridge University Press, 2009.

Richardson, Angelique. "Against Finality: Darwin, Mill and the End of Essentialism." *Critical Quarterly* 53, no. 4 (2011): 21–44.

———. "'People Talk a Lot of Nonsense about Heredity': Mona Caird and Anti-Eugenic Feminism." In *The New Woman in Fiction and in Fact: Fin-de-Siècle Feminisms,* edited by Richardson and Chris Willis, 183–211. Wiltshire: Palgrave, 2001.

Ricks, Christopher, ed. "*The Princess*, 1847." In *The Poems of Tennyson in Three Volumes.* Harlow: Longman, 1987, 2:180–95.

Rignall, John. *George Eliot, European Novelist.* Farnham: Ashgate, 2011.

Roof, Judith. *Come as You Are: Sexuality and Narrative.* New York: Columbia University Press, 1996.

———. "Out of the Bind: From Structure to System in Popular Narratives." In *Narrative Theory Unbound: Queer and Feminist Interventions,* edited by Robyn Warhol and Susan Lanser, 43–58. Columbus: The Ohio State University Press, 2015.

Rooney, Ellen. "Tess and the Subject of Sexual Violence: Reading, Rape, Seduction." In *Tess of the d'Urbervilles,* by Thomas Hardy, edited by John Paul Riquelme, 462–83. Boston: Bedford/St. Martin's, 1998.

Rosenberg, Aaron. "Romancing the Anthropocene: H. G. Wells and the Genre of the Future." *Novel: A Forum on Fiction.* Forthcoming.

Rossi-Wilcox, Susan M. *Dinner for Dickens: The Culinary History of Mrs. Charles Dickens' Menu Books.* London: Prospect Books, 2005.

Ruddick, Sara. *Maternal Thinking: Towards a Politics of Peace.* London: Women's Press, 1990.

Russell, Bertrand. *The Problems of Philosophy.* New York: Oxford University Press, 1997.

Ryan, Marie-Laure. *Possible Worlds, Artificial Intelligence, and Narrative Theory.* Bloomington: University of Indiana Press, 1991.

Sanders, Bernie. "What Can We Learn from Denmark?" *Huffington Post,* July 26, 2013, http://www.huffingtonpost.com/rep-bernie-sanders/what-can-we-learn-from-de_b_3339736.html.

Sarkar, Tanika. *Hindu Wife, Hindu Nation: Community, Religion, and Cultural Nationalism.* Delhi: Permanent Black, 2001.

Scaggs, John. *Crime Fiction.* London: Routledge, 2005.

Schaffer, Talia. *Romance's Rival: Familiar Marriage in Victorian Fiction.* New York: Oxford University Press, 2016.

Scharf, George. Personal diaries of Sir George Scharf 1845–1895. National Portrait Gallery, London. Manuscript NPG/7/3/1.

Scheick, William J. "Adolescent Pornography and Imperialism in Haggard's *King Solomon's Mines.*" *English Literature in Transition, 1880–1920* 34, no. 1 (1991): 19–30.

Schillace, Brandy L. "Curing 'Moral Disability': Brain Trauma and Self-Control in Victorian Science and Fiction." *Culture, Medicine, and Psychiatry* 37 (2013): 587–600.

Schiller, Friedrich. *On the Aesthetic Education of Man in a Series of Letters.* 1794. Edited and translated by E. M. Wilkinson and L. A. Willoughby. Oxford: Clarendon, 1982.

Schor, Hilary M. *Dickens and the Daughter of the House.* Cambridge: Cambridge University Press, 2000.

Schotland, Sara D. "Who's That in Charge? It's Jenny Wren, 'the Person of the House.'" *Disability Studies Quarterly* 29, no. 3 (2009): n. pag., accessed July 5, 2017, http://dsq-sds.org/article/view/933/1109.

Schreiner, Olive. *The Story of an African Farm.* 1883. Edited by Joseph Bristow. Oxford: Oxford University Press, 1992.

———. *Women and Labour.* Leipzig: Bernard Tauschnitz, 1911.

Scott, Gertrude Fisher. *Jean Cabot in Cap and Gown.* Boston: Lothrop, Lee & Shepard, 1914.

Scott, Walter. *Waverley.* 1814. Edited by P. D. Garside. London: Penguin, 2011.

Sedgwick, Eve Kosofsky. *Between Men: English Literature and Male Homosocial Desire.* New York: Columbia University Press, 1985.

———. *Touching Feeling: Affect, Pedagogy, Performativity.* Durham, NC: Duke University Press, 2003.

Seshagiri, Urmila. "Orienting Virginia Woolf: Race, Aesthetics, and Politics in *To the Lighthouse.*" *Modern Fiction Studies* 50, no. 1 (2004): 58–84.

Sevenhuijsen, Selma. *Citizenship and the Ethics of Care: Feminist Considerations on Justice, Morality, and Politics.* Translated by Liz Savage. New York: Routledge, 1998.

Shanley, Mary Lyndon. *Feminism, Marriage, and the Law in Victorian England, 1850–1905.* Princeton, NJ: Princeton University Press, 1989.

Sharpe, Jenny. *Allegories of Empire: The Figure of the Woman in the Colonial Text,* Minneapolis, MN: University of Minnesota Press, 1993.

Shaw, Harry E. *Narrating Reality: Austen, Scott, Eliot.* Ithaca, NY: Cornell University Press, 1999.

Shaw, Marion. *Tennyson.* Feminist Readings Series. Atlantic Highlands, NJ: Humanities Press International, 1988.

Showalter, Elaine. *Sexual Anarchy: Gender and Culture at the Fin de Siècle.* New York: Viking Penguin, 1990.

Shuttleworth, Sally, Gavin Dawson, and Richard Noakes. "Women, Science and Culture: Science in the Nineteenth-Century Periodical." *Women: A Cultural Review* 12, no. 1 (2001): 57–70.

Siegel, Jonah. *Haunted Museum: Longing, Travel, and the Art-Romance Tradition.* Princeton, NJ: Princeton University Press, 2005.

Silverman, Kaja. "History, Figuration and Female Subjectivity in *Tess of the d'Urbervilles.*" *Novel* 18 (1984): 5–28.

Simpson, Erik. *Literary Minstrelsy, 1770–1830: Minstrels and Improvisers in British, Irish, and American Literature.* London: Palgrave Macmillan, 2008.

Slater, Michael. *Charles Dickens.* New Haven, CT: Yale University Press, 2009.

Slaughter, Ann-Marie. *Unfinished Business: Women, Men, Work, Family.* New York: Random House, 2015.

———. "Why Women Still Can't Have It All." *The Atlantic Monthly,* July/August 2011, http://www.theatlantic.com/magazine/archive/2012/07/why-women-still-cant-have-it-all/309020/.

Slaughter, Joseph. *Human Rights, Inc.: The World Novel, Narrative Form, and International Law.* New York: Fordham University Press, 2007.

Sluga, Glenda. "Gender and the Nation: Madame de Staël or Italy." *Women's Writing* 10, no. 2 (2003): 241–51.

Smalley, Donald, ed. *Anthony Trollope: The Critical Heritage.* London: Routledge, 1995.

Snyder, Katherine V. *Bachelors, Manhood, and the Novel 1850–1925.* Cambridge: Cambridge University Press, 2004.

Soare, Monica. "The Female Gothic Connoisseur: Reading, Subjectivity, and the Feminist Uses of Gothic Fiction." PhD diss., University of California, Berkeley, 2013.

Solnit, Rebecca. "Woolf's Darkness: Embracing the Inexplicable." *New Yorker,* April 24, 2014, http://www.newyorker.com/books/page-turner/woolfs-darkness-embracing-the-inexplicable.

Sommer, Doris. *Foundational Fictions: The National Romances of Latin America.* Berkeley: University of California Press, 1991.

Sørensen, Asger. "Visiting the Neo-Liberal University: New Public Management and Conflicting Normative Ideas. A Danish Case." *Journal of Educational Controversy* 10, no. 1 (2015): 1–49.

Soyer, Alexis. *The Modern Housewife: Or, Ménagère.* London: Simpkin, Marshall, 1851.

Speare, Morris Edmund. *The Political Novel: Its Development in England and America.* 1924. 2nd ed. Oxford: Oxford University Press, 1966.

Spencer, Herbert. *The Principles of Sociology.* 1876. 3 vols. New York: D. Appleton, 1897.

Spilka, Mark. "Henry James and Walter Besant: 'The Art of Fiction' Controversy." *Novel: A Forum on Fiction* 6, no. 2 (Winter 1973): 101–19.

Spivak, Gayatri Chakravorty. "Three Women's Texts and a Critique of Imperialism." *Critical Inquiry* 12, no. 1 (1985): 243–61.

Sreenivas, Mytheli. *Wives, Widows, Concubines: The Conjugal Family Ideal in Colonial India.* Bloomington: Indiana University Press, 2008.

Staël, Germaine de. *Corinne ou l'Italie.* 1807. Edited by Simone Balayé. Paris: Gallimard, 1985.

———. *Corinne, or Italy.* Translated and edited by Sylvia Raphael. Oxford: Oxford University Press, 1998.

———. *Germany.* Translated by O. W. Wright. 2 vols. Cambridge: Riverside, 1871.

———. *Politics, Literature, and National Character.* Edited by Morroe Berger. New Brunswick: Transaction, 2000.

Starr, Elizabeth. "'A Great Engine for the Good': The Industry of Fiction in Elizabeth Gaskell's *Mary Barton* and *North and South.*" *Studies in the Novel* 34, no. 4 (2002): 385–402.

———. "'Influencing the Moral Taste': Literary Work, Aesthetics, and Social Change in *Felix Holt, the Radical.*" *Nineteenth-Century Literature* 56, no. 1 (June 2001): 52–75.

Stocking, George W., Jr. *Victorian Anthropology.* London: Free Press, 1987.

Stoddard Holmes, Martha. *Fictions of Affliction: Physical Disability in Victorian Culture.* Ann Arbor: University of Michigan Press, 2009.

———. "Victorian Fictions of Interdependency: Gaskell, Craik, and Yonge." *Journal of Literary Disability* 1, no. 2 (2007): 29–41.

Surridge, Lisa. *Bleak Houses: Marital Violence in Victorian Fiction.* Athens: Ohio University Press, 2005.

Swales, Martin. *The German Bildungsroman from Wieland to Hesse.* Princeton, NJ: Princeton University Press, 1978.

Sweat, Becky. "Whatever Happened to the Family Meal? Here's Why and How to Save it." *Virtual Christian Magazine,* 1997, accessed July 5, 2017, http://www.kubik.org/vcm/fam-meal.htm.

Tallie, T. J. "Queering Natal: Settler Logics and the Disruptive Challenge of Zulu Polygamy." *GLQ: A Journal of Lesbian and Gay Studies* 19, no. 2 (2013): 167–89.

Tanner, Tony. *Adultery and the Novel: Contract and Transgression.* Baltimore: Johns Hopkins University Press, 1979.

Tenenbaum, Susan. "*Corinne*: Political Polemics and the Theory of the Novel." In *The Novel's Seductions: Staël's* Corinne *in Critical Inquiry*, edited by Karyna Szmurlo, 154–62. Lewisburg, PA: Bucknell University Press, 1999.

Thomson, Fred C. "The Genesis of *Felix Holt*." *PMLA* 74, no. 5 (1959): 576–84.

Todorov, Tzvetan. *Genres in Discourse*. Translated by Catherine Porter. Cambridge: Cambridge University Press, 1990.

Tomaiuolo, Savario. "Sensation Fiction, Empire and the Indian Mutiny." In *The Cambridge Companion to Sensation Fiction*, edited by Andrew Mangham, 113–26. Cambridge: Cambridge University Press, 2013.

Tromp, Marlene. *The Private Rod: Marital Violence, Sensation, and the Law in Victorian Britain*. Charlottesville: University Press of Virginia, 2000.

———. "Throwing the Wedding Shoe: Foundational Violence, Unhappy Couples, and Murderous Women." *Victorian Review* 39, no. 2 (2013): 39–43.

Trumpener, Katie. *Bardic Nationalism: The Romantic Novel and the British Empire*. Princeton, NJ: Princeton University Press, 1997.

Tylor, Edward Burnett. *Primitive Culture: Researches into the Development of Mythology, Philosophy, Religion, Art and Custom*. 2 vols. 1871. Cambridge: Cambridge University Press, 2010.

Vallois, Marie-Claire. "Voice as Fossil: Madame de Staël's *Corinne or Italy*: An Archaeology of Feminine Discourse." Translated by Betsy Wing. *Tulsa Studies in Women's Literature* 6, no. 1 (1987): 47–60.

Vickery, John B. *The Literary Impact of "The Golden Bough."* Princeton, NJ: Princeton University Press, 1973.

Vincent, Patrick. *The Romantic Poetess: European Culture, Politics and Gender, 1820–1840*. Hanover: University of New Hampshire Press, 2004.

Vinson, Steve. "They-Who-Must-Be-Obeyed: Arsake, Rhadopis, and Tabubue, Ihweret and Charikleia." *Comparative Literature Studies* 45, no. 3 (2008): 289–315.

Visweswaran, Kamala. *Un/Common Cultures: Racism and the Rearticulation of Cultural Difference*. Durham, NC: Duke University Press, 2010.

Von Hendy, Andrew. *The Modern Construction of Myth*. Bloomington: Indiana University Press, 2002.

Wallsten, Peter, Lori Montgomery, and Scott Wilson. "Obama's Evolution: Behind the Failed 'Grand Bargain' on the Debt." *Washington Post*, March 17, 2012, https://www.washingtonpost.com/politics/obamas-evolution-behind-the-failed-grand-bargain-on-the-debt/2012/03/15/gIQAHyyfJS_story.html?utm_term=.f1876f141799.

Warhol, Robyn. "Introduction: Genre Regenerated." In Warhol, ed., *The Work of Genre*, http://quod.lib.umich.edu/cgi/t/text/text-idx?c=acls;idno=heb90055.0001.001;rgn=div3;view=text;cc=acls;node=heb90055.0001.001%3A5.1.1

———,ed. *The Work of Genre: Selected Essays from the English Institute*. ACLS Humanities E-Book, 2011. http://quod.lib.umich.edu/cgi/t/text/text-idx?c=acls;idno=heb90055.0001.001;rgn=div1;view=text;cc=acls;node=heb90055.0001.001%3A1.

Warhol, Robyn and Susan Lanser, eds. *Narrative Theory Unbound: Queer and Feminist Interventions*. Columbus: The Ohio State University Press, 2015.

Watt, Ian. *The Rise of the Novel: Studies in Defoe, Richardson and Fielding*. Berkeley and Los Angeles: University of California Press, 1957.

Weliver, Phyllis. "George Eliot and the Prima Donna's 'Script.'" *Yearbook of English Studies* 40, no. 1–2 (2010): 103–20.

Wempe, Ben. *T. H. Green's Theory of Positive Freedom: From Metaphysics to Political Theory.* Exeter: Imprint Academic, 2004.

Whorton, James. *The Arsenic Century: How Victorian Britain Was Poisoned at Home, Work, and Play.* Oxford: Oxford University Press, 2011.

Wiener, Martin J. "Alice Arden to Bill Sikes: Changing Nightmares of Intimate Violence in England, 1558–1869." *Journal of British Studies* 40, no. 2 (2001): 184–212.

Williams, Carolyn. *Gilbert and Sullivan: Gender, Genre, Parody.* New York: Columbia University Press, 2011.

Williams, Raymond. *The Country and the City.* Oxford: Oxford University Press, 1973.

———. *Culture and Society, 1780–1950.* New York: Columbia University Press, 1983.

———. *The English Novel: From Dickens to Lawrence.* New York: Oxford University Press, 1970.

Winnett, Susan. "Coming Unstrung: Women, Men, Narrative, and Principles of Pleasure." *PMLA* 103, no. 3 (1990): 505–18.

Winter, Sarah. *The Pleasures of Memory: Learning to Read with Charles Dickens.* New York: Fordham University Press, 2011.

Winyard, Ben. "'May We Meet Again': Rereading the Dickensian Serial in the Digital Age." *19: Interdisciplinary Studies in the Long Nineteenth Century* 21 (2015), https://doi.org/10.16995/ntn.737.

Wolff, Michael. *The Sensational Victorian: The Life and Fiction of Mary Elizabeth Braddon.* New York: Garland, 1979.

Woloch, Alex. *The One vs. the Many: Minor Characters and the Space of the Protagonist in the Novel.* Princeton, NJ: Princeton University Press, 2003.

Woolf, Virginia. *Orlando: A Biography.* 1928. Orlando, FL: Harcourt, 2006.

———. *A Room of One's Own.* 1929. Orlando, FL: Harcourt, 2005.

———. *To the Lighthouse.* 1927. Orlando, FL: Harcourt, 2005.

———. *The Years.* 1937. Edited by Anna Snaith. Cambridge: Cambridge University Press, 2012.

"World Happiness Report 2015 Ranks Happiest Countries." *Sustainable Development Solutions Network: A Global Initiative for the United Nation.* April 23, 2015. http://unsdsn.org/news/2015/04/23/world-happiness-report-2015-ranks-happiest-countries/.

Wynne, Deborah. *The Sensation Novel and the Victorian Family Magazine.* Basingstoke: Palgrave, 2001.

Yeazell, Ruth Bernard. *Fictions of Modesty: Women and Courtship in the English Novel.* Chicago: University of Chicago Press, 1991.

———. "Why Political Novels Have Heroines: *Sybil, Mary Barton,* and *Felix Holt.*" *Novel: A Forum on Fiction* 18, no. 2 (1985): 126–44.

Zanone, Damien. "L'esthétique du 'tableau philosophique' dans *Corinne ou l'Italie.*" In *"Une mélodie intellectuelle": Corinne ou l'Italie de Germaine de Staël,* edited by C. Planté, C. Pouzoulet, and A. Vaillant, 9–29. Montpellier: Université Paul-Valéry, 2000.

Zeitler, Michael A. *Representations of Culture: Thomas Hardy's Wessex and Victorian Anthropology.* New York: Peter Lang, 2007.

Zimmerman, Virginia. *Excavating Victorians.* Albany: State University of New York Press, 2008.

LIST OF CONTRIBUTORS

SUKANYA BANERJEE is Associate Professor of English at the University of Wisconsin, Milwaukee. She works at the intersection of Victorian studies and postcolonial studies, with a focus on nineteenth- and early-twentieth-century Britain and its empire. She has co-edited *New Routes for Diaspora Studies* (Indiana University Press, 2012) and is the author of *Becoming Imperial Citizens: Indians in the Late-Victorian Empire* (Duke University Press, 2010), which was awarded the Sonya Rudikoff Prize for best first book in Victorian studies. She is currently working on a book, *Loyalty and the Making of the Modern*, which examines how and why formulations of loyalty became critical to the understanding of modernity in nineteenth-century Britain and its empire.

ELISHA COHN is Associate Professor of English at Cornell University. She is author of *Still Life: Suspended Development in the Victorian Novel* (Oxford University Press, 2016) as well as essays in journals including *Victorian Studies, Nineteenth-Century Literature*, and *Contemporary Literature*. Her interests include the history of neuroscience, animal studies, affect theory, and ecocriticism. She is currently writing a book entitled *Animal Lives, Novel Forms*.

MARY JEAN CORBETT is University Distinguished Professor of English and Affiliate of the Women's, Gender, and Sexuality Studies Program and the Department of Global and Intercultural Studies at Miami University. She is the author of *Representing Femininity: Middle-Class Subjectivity in Victorian and Edwardian Women's Autobiographies* (Oxford University Press, 1992); *Allegories of Union in Irish and English Writing, 1790–1870: Politics, History, and the Family from Edgeworth to Arnold* (Cambridge University Press, 2000); and *Family Likeness: Sex, Marriage, and Incest from Jane Austen to Virginia Woolf* (Cornell University Press, 2008). She is completing a study entitled *Behind the Times: Virginia Woolf in Late-Victorian Contexts*.

IAN DUNCAN is Florence Green Bixby Professor of English at the University of California, Berkeley, where he works on the novel, Scottish literature, Romanticism, and Victorian literature and culture. He is the author of *Scott's Shadow: The Novel in Romantic Edinburgh* (Princeton University Press, 2007) and *Modern Romance and Transformations of the Novel* (Cambridge University Press, 1992); a co-editor of *Scotland and the Borders of Romanticism* (Cambridge University Press, 2004) and *The Edinburgh Companion to James Hogg* (Edinburgh University Press, 2012); and a general editor of the *Collected Works of James Hogg* and a new monograph series, *Edinburgh Critical Studies in Romanticism.* He is completing a book on the novel and the science of man in Europe, from Buffon and Goethe to George Eliot and Charles Darwin.

HOLLY FURNEAUX is Professor of English at Cardiff University. Her most recent book is *Military Men of Feeling: Emotion, Touch and Masculinity in the Crimean War* (Oxford University Press, 2016). She is also author of *Queer Dickens: Erotics, Families, Masculinities* (Oxford University Press, 2009). She is co-editor, with Sally Ledger, of *Dickens in Context* (Cambridge University Press, 2011) and editor of John Forster's *Life of Dickens* (Sterling, 2011).

JILL GALVAN is Associate Professor of English at The Ohio State University and the author of *The Sympathetic Medium: Feminine Channeling, the Occult, and Communication Technologies, 1859–1919* (Cornell University Press, 2010). Her past research has focused on long-nineteenth-century British media technologies, spiritualism, mesmerism, and psychical research and on both Victorian and contemporary ideas of the posthuman. Her current book project, which argues that fictions of marriage coevolved with literary ideas of interiority, is entitled *After Romance: Alienated Marriage and Modern Character Realism.*

LAUREN M. E. GOODLAD is Professor of English at Rutgers University. Her publications include *The Victorian Geopolitical Aesthetic: Realism, Sovereignty, and Transnational Experience* (Oxford University Press, 2015); *Victorian Literature and the Victorian State: Character and Governance in a Liberal Society* (Johns Hopkins University Press, 2003); *Worlding Realisms* (a special issue of *Novel* published in 2016); and the co-edited *Mad Men, Mad World: Sex, Politics, Style and the 1960s* (Duke University Press, 2007).

KELLY HAGER is Associate Professor of English and Women's & Gender Studies and Chair of Women's & Gender Studies at Simmons College, where she teaches Victorian Literature, Children's Literature, and the History of Feminism. She is the author of *Dickens and the Rise of Divorce: The Failed-Marriage Plot and the Novel Tradition* (Ashgate, 2010) and co-edited, with Talia Schaffer, a special issue of *Victorian Review*: "Extending Families." A contributor to *The Blackwell Encyclopedia of Victorian Literature, BRANCH: Britain, Representation and Nineteenth-Century History, Keywords for Children's Literature,* and *The Oxford Handbook of Children's Literature,* she has also published essays in *Victorian Literature and Culture, Children's Literature Association Quarterly,* and *ELH.*

ELSIE B. MICHIE is Associate Dean in the College of Humanities and Social Sciences and Professor in the Department of English at Louisiana State University. She has published on the Brontës, Mary Shelley, Elizabeth Gaskell, Jane Austen, Anthony and Frances Trollope, George Eliot, Henry James, Walter Scott, Charles Dickens, and Margaret Oliphant. Her most recent book is *The Vulgar Question of Money: Heiresses, Materialism and the Novel of Manners from Jane Austen to Henry James* (Johns Hopkins University Press, 2011). She is currently working on a monograph entitled *Trollopizing the Canon* about Frances Trollope's impact on Charles Dickens, Charlotte Brontë, George Eliot, and Harriet Beecher Stowe.

HELENA MICHIE is the Agnes C. Arnold Professor in Humanities and a Professor of English at Rice University. She is the author of five books in Victorian studies and the study of gender and sexuality. Her most recent, *Love Among the Archives: Writing the Lives of Sir George Scharf, Victorian Bachelor* (Edinburgh University Press, 2015), with Robyn Warhol, won the North American Victorian Studies Association's 2015 Best Book of the Year prize. Some of her other works are *Victorian Honeymoons: Journeys to the Conjugal* (Cambridge University Press, 2006); *Sororophobia: Differences among Women in Literature and Culture* (Oxford University Press, 1991); and *The Flesh Made Word: Female Figures and Women's Bodies* (Oxford University Press, 1987). Professor Michie teaches courses in feminist theory, Victorian literature and culture, and professional writing. Her current project, *Homing*, is about the historical emergence of the concept of home and comes out of her interest in the long and wide nineteenth century.

KATHY ALEXIS PSOMIADES is Associate Professor of English at Duke University. She is the author of *Beauty's Body: Gender and Representation in British Aestheticism* (Stanford University Press, 1997), and co-editor, with Talia Schaffer, of *Women and British Aestheticism* (University Press of Virginia, 1999). She is currently finishing a book entitled *Primitive Marriage: Victorian Anthropology and the Novel.*

TALIA SCHAFFER is a professor of English at Queens College CUNY and the Graduate Center CUNY. Schaffer is the author of *Romance's Rival: Familiar Marriage in Victorian Fiction* (Oxford University Press, 2016); *Novel Craft: Victorian Domestic Handicraft and Nineteenth-Century Fiction* (Oxford University Press, 2011); and *The Forgotten Female Aesthetes: Literary Culture in Late-Victorian England* (University of Virginia Press, 2001). She has co-edited a special issue of *Victorian Review*, "Extending Families," with Kelly Hager (2013); published a collection called *Literature and Culture at the Fin de Siècle* (Pearson, 2006); produced a scholarly edition of Lucas Malet's 1901 novel, *The History of Sir Richard Calmady* (Bloomsbury, 2003); and co-edited *Women and British Aestheticism* with Kathy A. Psomiades (University Press of Virginia, 1999). Schaffer has published widely on Victorian familial and marital norms, disability studies, women writers, material culture, popular fiction, and aestheticism. She is currently working on a project that adapts the feminist philosophy of "ethics of care" into a method for reading social relations in Victorian fiction.

MARLENE TROMP is Professor of Literature and the Campus Provost and Executive Vice Chancellor at the University of California, Santa Cruz. She is the author of *Altered States: Sex, Nation, Drugs, and Self-Transformation in Victorian Spiritualism* (State University of New York Press, 2006) and *The Private Rod: Sexual Violence, Marriage, and the Law in Victorian England* (University Press of Virginia, 2000), as well as of several articles on nineteenth-century literature and culture. She has also edited or co-edited and contributed to *Fear and Loathing: Victorian Xenophobia* (The Ohio State University Press, 2016); *Victorian Freaks: The Social Context of Freakery in the Nineteenth Century* (The Ohio State University Press, 2007); and *Mary Elizabeth Braddon: Beyond Sensation* (State University of New York Press, 2000). She has another book under review, *Force of Habit: Life and Death on the Titanic*, and is working on a new project on murder between sexually intimate people in the nineteenth century, *Intimate Murder: Sex and Death in the Nineteenth Century.*

INDEX

www.ingramcontent.com/pod-product-compliance
Lightning Source LLC
Chambersburg PA
CBHW031943110726
47902CB00001B/286

* 9 7 8 0 8 1 4 2 5 4 7 4 5 *